"[...] we set sail, after hearing mass, on 8 April 1518. In ten days we doubled Guaniguanico or St. Anton's Point, and after another ten days sailing discovered the island of Cozumel, which we had not sighted before, for with the current that was running we were driven much farther to the leeward than when we sailed with Francisco Hernández de Córdoba. We followed the southern shore of this island, and sighted a village with a few houses and a good anchorage beside it, which was free from reefs. The Captain and a number of us soldiers went ashore. But the inhabitants of the village had fled when they saw our ships under sail, for they had never seen such a thing before..."[...]".

Bernal Díaz del Castillo,
The Conquest of New Spain,
chapter VIII.

LEX

Welcome to Quintana Roo, a state that is one of Mexico's natural and cultural treasures, a window on the Caribbean with the unique flavor of the Yucatán Peninsula, in ancient times one of the principal strongholds of the Maya civilization.

We hope that the seductive embrace of the Caribbean, the caress of the sun, jungle and the memory of the Maya, in addition to traditional Mexican hospitality and a collection of cosmopolitan resorts offering every activity and service imaginable, will make your stay in this land truly unforgettable.

Quintana Roo is the only Mexican state with a coastline on the Caribbean, one of the world's most beautiful seas. A few fathoms from its dreamlike beaches, a line of breaking waves marks the entrance to an immense natural aquarium, a gift from Mother Nature and the corals, tiny organisms that took thousands of years to build the reefs. This is an invitation to explore for all who are fascinated by the underwater world.

The jungles and mangrove forests of Quintana Roo cast their own spell. They harbor a wealth of flora and fauna, enough wildlife to satisfy even the most demanding ecotourists and which is protected in reserves such as Contoy and Sian Ka'an.

Wherever you look you'll see the legacy of time, not only the awe-inspiring cities of the ancient Maya: Tulum, Cobá, Muyil, Kohunlich, Dzibanché and San Gervasio, but also legends of the Conquest and Colonial period, pirate raids and the spirit of independence of today's Maya.

This is the setting and we have the infrastructure for a multitude of vacation activities, sports, shopping and even investment, something to suit every interest so that your stay exceeds your expectations.

The people of Quintana Roo welcome you with open arms. Have a wonderful stay.

Lic. Félix González Canto
Governor of the State
of Quintana Roo

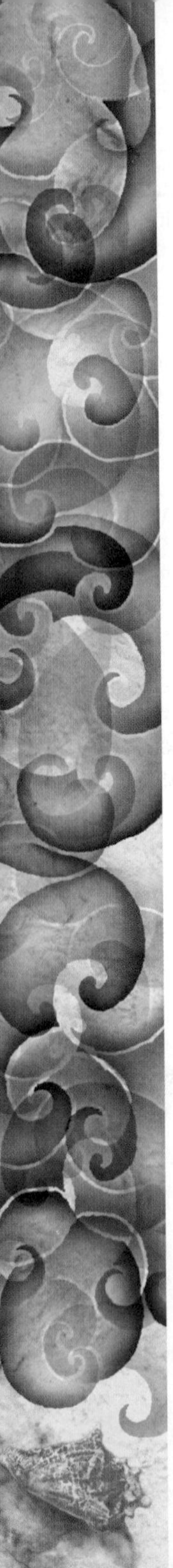

ear Friends,

Thanks to 30 years of hard work and the vision of the developers, the state of Quintana Roo is now world-famous as the Mexican Caribbean, a multi-destination with international appeal. In order to orientate travelers with different interests and help them get the most out of their stay, we have identified a number of themes or tourist circuits in the state.

Dynamic, modern and cosmopolitan, Cancún has every tourist service imaginable, packed into the length and breadth of its elegant Hotel Zone, a stretch of shoreline bathed by the irresistible turquoise waters of the Caribbean. This is your base for planning a variety of sightseeing itineraries.

Three islands off the Quintana Roo coast merit special attention and a place on any vacation schedule: visit Holbox, the island of fishermen; Isla Mujeres has all the ambiance of the Caribbean of yesteryear; and Cozumel's magnificent coral reefs have made it a favorite with the international dive community.

The Riviera Maya is a harmonious blend of grand hotels and low-impact accommodation and offers something for everyone, even those who want to leave their cares behind without abandoning their creature comforts and the non-stop partying offered by the state's other resorts. In contrast, Costa Maya, now an international port of call for cruise ships, is sparsely populated, the perfect spot for a retreat, for fishing, diving and exploring little known nature reserves and archeological sites.

A journey into the Provincia Maya offers you a glimpse of timeless villages deep in the Mayan heartland, and the chance to enjoy a cooling dip in *cenotes* and lagoons. Finally, state capital Chetumal, is the gateway to the south, a natural paradise peppered with archaeological sites.

So choose your destinations and combine different itineraries, we hope you enjoy your vacation in our state.

Quintana Roo State
Tourism Board

LEARN MORE ABOUT THE MEXICAN CARIBBEAN

QUINTANA ROO STATE TOURISM BOARD
E-mail: sedetur@qroo.gob.mx
Tel.: (998) 881 9000, Fax: (998) 881 9020
www.qroo.gob.mx

Subsecretary of Tourism Promotion
E-mail: qrooturi@prodigy.net.mx • turismo@qroo.gob.mx
Tel.: (983) 835 0860; Fax: (983) 835 0880

Cancún Convention & Visitors Bureau (OVC)
E-mail: info@cancun.info
Tels.: (998) 884 6531, 881 0400, Fax: (998) 881 0402
www.cancun.info

FIDEICOMISO DE PROMOCIÓN TURÍSTICA DE LA RIVIERA MAYA
E-mail: info@rivieramaya.com
Tels.: (984) 873 1260, 859 2173, 873 2850, 873 0003
www.rivieramaya.com

FIDEICOMISO DE PROMOCIÓN TURÍSTICA GRAND COSTA MAYA
E-mail: info@grandcostamaya.com
Tel.: (983) 832 6647; Fax: (983) 832 5130
www.grancostamaya.com

FIDEICOMISO DE PROMOCIÓN TURÍSTICA DE ISLA MUJERES
E-mail: infoisla@qroo1.telmex.net.mx
Tels.: (998) 877 0307, 877 0767
www.isla-mujeres.com.mx

FIDEICOMISO DE PROMOCIÓN TURÍSTICA DE COZUMEL
E-mail: info@islacozumel.com.mx
Tels.: (987) 872 3132, 872 7563; Fax: (987) 872 2809
www.islacozumel.com.mx

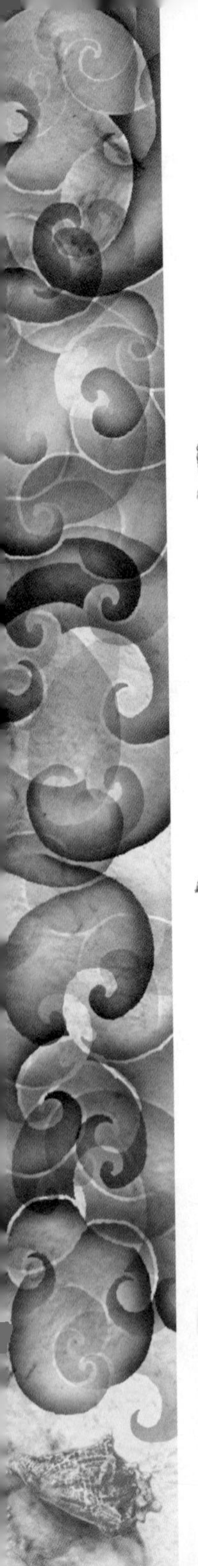

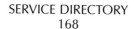

Lists of hotels, restaurants, travel agencies, consulates, car rentals, marinas, museums, bars and nightclubs in the different areas of Quintana Roo. Emergency numbers, lists of events, festivals and area codes are also included. For quick reference the directory has been divided into the following areas: Cancún, Isla Mujeres, Holbox, Cozumel, Riviera Maya, Chetumal and Southern Quintana Roo.

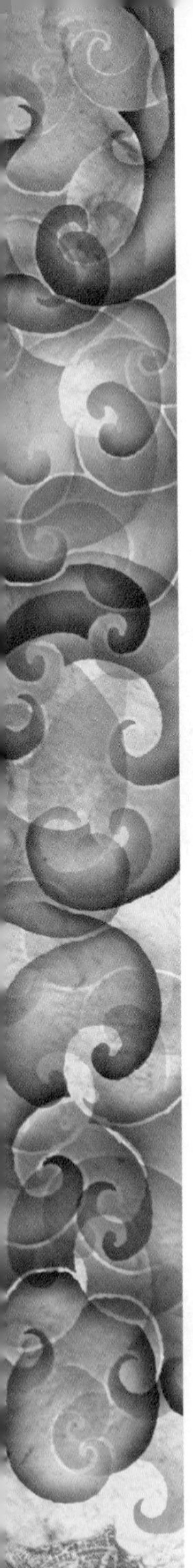

EDITORIAL VERÁS

Corporate President
Víctor Vera Castillo
director@caribemexico.com

Director Cire Vera Jufresa

Editor Joanna Green

Design
Luis Fernando Paredes, Tania Vera, Mario Sánchez
grafico@caribemexico.com

Collaborators
Texts: David Arrevillaga, Pilar Jufresa, Juan José Morales, Karen LeBlanc, Susanna Trejo, Claudia Meller. Translation: Sharon Van Bramer. Cartography: Leonardo Berges. Art: Roberto Franco, Mariana Romero. Coordinator: Guadalupe Belmont. Website: Flavio Reyes

Distribution Luis Ríos Vergara, Jesús Fraga

Photography
Gonzalo I. Arcila, Fulvio Eccardi, Adalberto Ríos, Editorial Raíces, Gonzalo Infante, José Antonio Granados, Alejandro Catalá, Luis Leyva, Antonio Díaz, Parques y Museos de Cozumel, Dr. Michel Antochiw, Banco de imágenes de la Oficina de Visitantes y Convenciones de Cancún, OVC.

Representatives

Mexico City
Alejandro Cisneros Méndez
Av. Revolución No. 1527 - 101, Col. Tlacopac, México D.F. 01040
Tel./Fax: (55) 5662-7330, 5662-5440

New York
P.O. Box 6178, New York N.Y. 10128 USA

Editorial Verás
Av. Náder No. 27, interior 1033, Sm. 2, Cancún, Q. Roo, Mexico, C.P. 77500
Tels.: +52 (998) 887 4684, 887 4564, 887 6666
E-mail: everas@cancun.com.mx
www.editorialveras.com • www.caribbeanmex.com

Editorial Verás would like to thank the following people and institutions for their help: Secretaría de Turismo del Estado de Quintana Roo, Centro Regional del Instituto Nacional de Antropología e Historia, Chetumal, Arqueóloga Adriana Velázquez, Directora Centro Regional del INAH, Fidecaribe, Colegio de la Frontera Sur, Semarnap, Amigos de Sian Ka'an, Sra. Nuria Jufresa, Dr. Michel Antochiw, Sr. Juan Xacur, Profesor Fermín Sosa, Universidad de Quintana Roo.

Printed by Pixel Press
Carretera Cancún-Aeropuerto km 15. Edificio Miami Herald, Planta Baja, Cancún, Quintana Roo, Mexico. Tels.: (998) 886-2232, 33 & 35
E-mail: atnclientes@pixelpress.com.mx

A word from the Editor:

Our region is growing in popularity and is visited by more and more people captivated by its natural beauty and cultural heritage. It is often the case, however, that our guests do not have a full panorama of area attractions and travel services.

Based in Cancún, Quintana Roo, Mexico, Editorial Verás has the solution. The company gathered together cartographers, editors, designers, computer programmers and photographers, each of whom contributed their talent, professionalism and knowledge of the area to produce a travel kit that celebrates the beauty of our land and provides the visitor with a wealth of reliable information on sites of interest and infrastructure.

Editorial Verás publications provide visitors with an in-depth look at a specific area, its tourist attractions, history and traditions. They include guides, maps and multimedia tools such as Cds and websites. The scope of individual publications varies - they may focus on a group of countries, a country or state, an area, city or even an archaeological site.

The goal of our publications is to familiarize visitors with the area, help them plan their excursions and have a wonderful vacation. We welcome suggestions that will help us enrich the guide and we would like to hear from you. Drop us a line and tell us about your experiences and discoveries during your stay in the Mexican Caribbean.

Yours sincerely,

Víctor Vera Castillo
Corporate President
Editorial Verás

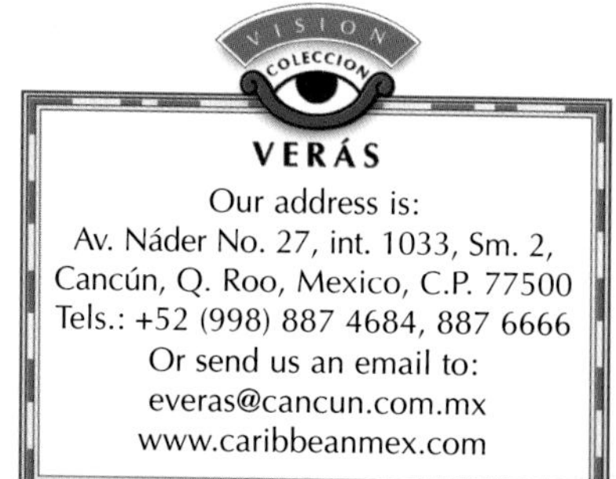

VERÁS
Our address is:
Av. Náder No. 27, int. 1033, Sm. 2,
Cancún, Q. Roo, Mexico, C.P. 77500
Tels.: +52 (998) 887 4684, 887 6666
Or send us an email to:
everas@cancun.com.mx
www.caribbeanmex.com

We hope that this guide to the Mexican Caribbean will prove useful during your stay. The publication features introductory sections on the geography, vegetation and wildlife of the state of Quintana Roo, its history and the traditions of its modern-day Mayan inhabitants. There is a complete description of the state and the services available in its cities and resorts.

Quintana Roo

Each section of the guide includes full descriptions of the countless sites of interest in a specific area, with distances and instructions on how to get there. Furthermore, a quick-reference list of symbols will tell you at a glance about the services and activities available at each site. Quintana Roo is also the gateway to the Maya World and this guide will give you an introduction to the ancient cities elsewhere in Southeast Mexico and Central America, not to mention the natural wonders, national parks, colonial cities and modern Mayan communities that are accessible from Cancún, Cozumel or Chetumal.

Traveler's Notebook

This section is full of tips on traveling in the Mexican Caribbean. You'll find information on accommodation and dining, transport and road tips, health, safety, money exchange, climate, trips and shopping. The final pages of the guide are taken up by the Service Directory which features up-to-date lists of hotels, restaurants, travel agencies, cruise boats, airlines, marinas and more.

Mayan numbers

Colección Verás guides on destinations in the Maya World also feature Mayan numbers. You'll find the numbers displayed at the top of the right hand page. The symbol "•" equals "1" and "▬" is "5." In the Mayan numerical system values increase by multiples of 20, so at 20 "•" equals 20, and "▬" would correspond to 100. From the number 20 and on, the symbols appear at the top, following the order down: twenty, hundreds and units. If we take the number 191 as an example, it would be represented as follows:

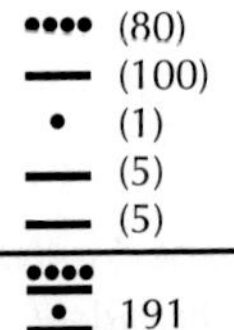

Map of the Mexican Caribbean

We hope that you find our map useful when traveling in Quintana Roo. It shows the state's most important cities, villages and archaeological sites, in addition to the network of primary and secondary roads. Parts of the neighboring states of Yucatán and Campeche, Belize and Guatemala are also featured. Symbols denoting the services (hotels, museums, airports, etc.) and activities available in each city or site of interest are also included in the map. Colección Verás maps feature illustrations of native birds and animals, ancient temples and colonial monuments, vignettes of indigenous life and scenes alluding to area history.

City maps and more

We have included maps of Holbox, Isla Mujeres, Puerto Morelos and the Hotel Zone and Downtown areas of Cancún, all in northern Quintana Roo. The Riviera Maya communities of Playa del Carmen, Puerto Aventuras, Akumal, Tulum, the island of Cozumel and the archaeological sites of Tulum and Cobá are also shown in greater detail. Places in the southern half of the state showcased with individual maps are Chetumal, Bacalar, Felipe Carrillo Puerto, Costa Maya and the ancient cities of Kohunlich, Dzibanché and Kinichná. A map of the Maya World is featured. Sites of interest and services are clearly marked with symbols and you'll find that companies listed in the Tourist Directory have a coordinate for easy reference on the maps.

Reliable information

The information in Colección Verás guides is as complete and up to date as possible. Nevertheless, please bear in mind that facts may change after the guide has gone to press.

Symbols used in the guide

- Nature reserve
- Archaeological site
- Church
- Beach
- Ethnic heritage
- Museum
- Historical monument
- Campsite
- Diving
- Fishing
- Snorkeling
- Cenote
- Windsurfing
- Sailing
- Boat trips
- Ferry
- Basketry
- Textiles
- Market
- Wood carving
- Pottery
- Information center
- Hotel
- Restaurant
- Airport
- Airstrip

NATURE

Quintana Roo is the easternmost state of the Yucatán Peninsula, and its territory (50,843 km^2) is a patchwork of ecosystems, rich in wildlife. From the air large parts of the state resemble a green carpet: this is the tropical forest about which so many tales have been spun. A land of great trees such as mahogany, cedar and chicozapote, it is the domain of the jaguar, monkeys still forage in the canopy and birds are abundant.

Towards the coast the jungle gives way to marsh, mangroves and a series of lagoons and bays where fresh water from underground rivers mixes with salt water. The reed beds and mangroves are home to birds such as herons and ibis; crocodiles and manatees can also be spotted.

The white beaches of the Mexican Caribbean are protected by a chain of coral reefs. Marine life is abundant, around 500 species of fish have been identified in the area. The islands of Holbox, Contoy, Isla Mujeres and Cozumel lie offshore.

The reserves in the state include Sian Ka'an and Cozumel Marine Park.

The Yucatán Peninsula, of which Quintana Roo forms part, is a relatively young landscape. A huge shelf of limestone, it emerged from the sea during the Pliocene and Pleistocene periods. It has thin soils, a tropical climate and is covered by jungle, marsh, mangroves and coastal scrub. The offshore reefs form part of the second longest barrier reef system in the world.

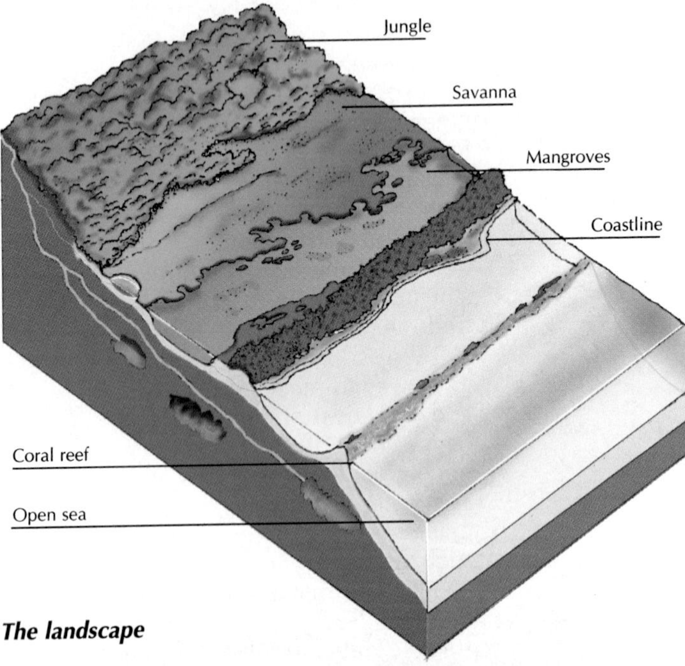

The landscape

Quintana Roo shares borders with Belize to the south, Guatemala to the southwest, Campeche to the west and Yucatán to the northwest. Its shoreline is bathed by the Gulf of Mexico to the north and the Caribbean to the east. The Quintana Roo landscape is flat, with a scattering of low hills (reaching a height of 310 m) along the Campeche border. Depressions known as *bajos* or *akalches* pit the surface of the plain. Lined with a layer of impermeable soil, they are prone to seasonal flooding and some even have lagoons. Along the coast depressions occur in a marshy area known as savanna.

High temperatures and rainfall have over time led to the formation of rendzina soils (*tsekel*) which are thin, (20 cm), stony and infertile. Variants appear in Southern Quintana Roo: *solonchak* soil is sandy and has a high saline content and deposits of *kankab* occur on hillsides, this is a well-drained, acidic red soil.

Quintana Roo's only surface river is the Hondo which is also the natural frontier between Mexico and Belize. During the rainy season, throughout the state, water accumulates in holes and cavities in the rock called *sartenejas* and in *aguadas* (dolines), natural or man-made trenches. The water stored in these ponds tides farmers over the dry season.

The coast

The shoreline is peppered with headlands and inlets and a series of bays, three of which are very large: Ascensión, Espíritu Santo and Chetumal. There are also long stretches of white beach whose march along the coast is broken by the occasional rocky wave platform and some low cliffs in the Tulum area.

Reefs and Caribbean islands

From Contoy Island to the Belizean border, the coast is shadowed by a series of barrier and fringing reefs which form part of the Mesoamerican Reef System, the second longest reef in the world. Off the coast of Southern Quintana Roo lies Chinchorro Bank, Mexico's largest coral atoll. All the state's reefs harbor a wealth of marine life and are protected by law. Several islands lie off the coast of Quintana Roo. Their sizes may vary but they all share a similar origin, coralline limestone rock and sandy soils. Cozumel is the nation's largest inhabited island and is famous for its reefs, Isla Mujeres has a laid-back Caribbean ambiance, Contoy is an important bird sanctuary and little-known Holbox lies near rich fishing grounds.

Lagoons

The coast is dotted with lagoons, bays and inlets, some of which lie in depressions along fault lines or are the product of tectonic movements. The water table is not far below the surface in the coastal strip and shallow lagoons are common. Northwest of Chetumal, Bacalar is a long, narrow lake fed by numerous underground rivers. It has an outlet to the Hondo River via the Chac stream, and several channels through the mangroves link it to Chetumal Bay. The Guerrero lagoon system, also in the Chetumal area, comprises 15 km^2 of interconnected lagoons and channels of turbid, brackish water with occasional patches of clearer, colder fresh water. Known as *ojos de agua* (literally 'eye of water'), these areas are underground streams welling up through the rock

Cenotes and underground rivers

Limestone is porous and water seeps through fissures and crevices in the rock until it reaches the water table. This means that there are virtually no surface rivers on the Yucatán Peninsula as water circulates underground through a labyrinth of channels or rivers.

Over time erosion weakens the walls and roofs of underground caves and channels and they collapse forming cenotes (from the Maya word *dznot*) or sinkholes, for thousands of years the only source of fresh water on the Peninsula.

Formation of a cenote

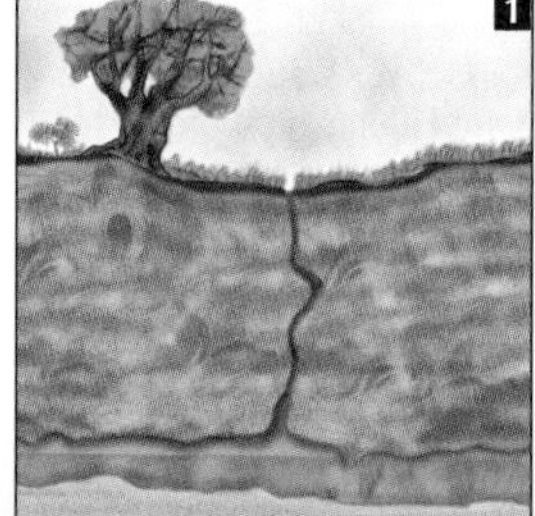

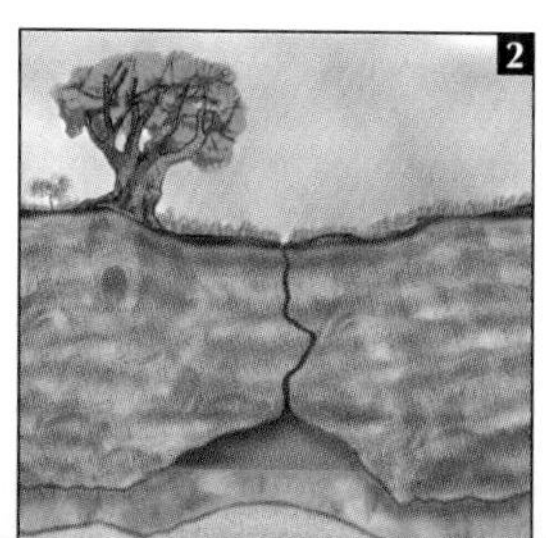

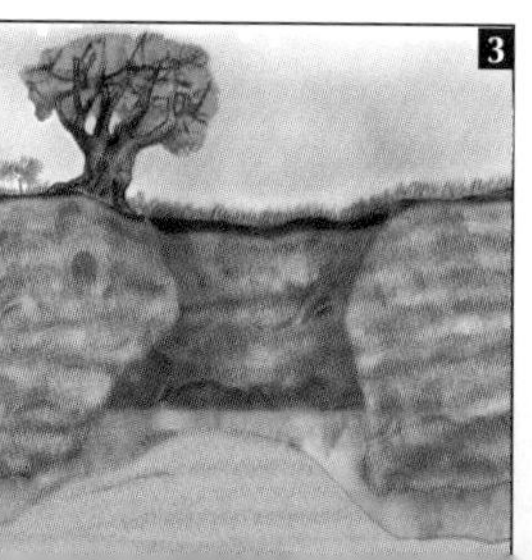

Quintana Roo's geography, tropical climate and soil conditions give rise to a number of ecosystems. Jungle, savanna, mangrove and marsh, coastal and reef ecosystems exist in different areas of the state and each one has its own distinctive vegetation and wildlife.

Jungle

Forests in southern Quintana Roo

View of the coast

The jungle

Several kinds of tropical forest occur in the state, depending on the amount of rainfall the area receives and the soil regime.

Referred to as *selva alta,* high growth jungle is semi-evergreen forest which grows in the south where rainfall is more abundant and soils are more fertile. Trees can exceed 30 meters in height and in the dry season they shed between 25 and 50% of their leaves. Common species are zapote, ramón (breadnut) and mahogany.

The jungle classed as *selva mediana* (medium growth semi-evergreen forest) is found in Central and Northern Quintana Roo. Although the earth is infertile it does have a high level of humidity due to the presence of cenotes in the area. Trees reach heights of between 15 and 30 meters and lose 50 - 75% of their leaves at some time during the year. Climbing plants and epiphytes are abundant and there are many bushes and palms. Chicozapote and chaca are common trees.

Medium deciduous forest grows along the border with the Yucatán. The ceiba or silk cotton tree, ziricote and dyewood (palo de tinte, found in marshy areas), are abundant. A thin strip of low growth deciduous forest is found along parts of the coast. Guayacán, guaje (a member of the acacia family) and several species of palm, particularly the kuka, abound here.

Coastal ecosystems

Quintana Roo has an 860-km-coastline bathed by the Caribbean Sea and the Gulf of Mexico (from Cabo Catoche to Holbox). Soils are sandy and a ribbon of dunes runs down the littoral between the beach and the wetlands. Aloes, succulents, sea grape, salt-loving shrubs, stunted trees and palms are found along the shore and they provide a habitat for 130 species of land bird in addition to countless seabirds. The beaches are composed of fine white sand , the result of reef erosion. They are Quintana Roo's greatest asset and are an important nesting area for the endangered sea turtle. The inhabitants of Quintana Roo's coastal villages earn their livelihood from the sea.

Savanna

Limited in extension but ecologically important, the savanna is a strip of seasonally flooded marshland adjoining the mangroves. It consists of thorn forest, grasslands peppered with acacia or palm trees, stands of dyewood and reed beds. Small islands of jungle, rich in wildlife, are scattered across the landscape. Located on slightly higher ground, usually around a cenote, *petének* or hummocks are found only on the Yucatán Peninsula, in Cuba and Florida. The largest area of savanna is in the Sian Ka'an Biosphere Reserve.

Underwater world

The reefs that hug the Quintana Roo coast are the foundation for an ecosystem as complex as it is fragile. This world of beauty is inhabited by around 500 species of fish of all shapes, sizes and a kaleidoscope of colors, sponges, molluscs, crustaceans such as the spiny lobster, starfish, sea urchins and algae. Stretches of the reef are popular with divers, either because they are particularly beautiful or are easy to reach, for example the reefs in the Cancún-Isla Mujeres area, Cozumel, along parts of the Riviera Maya and Sian Ka'an shoreline or the Chinchorro Bank which is also a ships' graveyard.

Mangroves and marshes

One of the most important ecosystems in the state, mangroves and marshes are found along the coast and on the banks of the Hondo River. Mangroves are rich in flora and fauna and their immense value to coastal ecology is only just being understood. They harbor a variety of insects, crustaceans, small reptiles and amphibians which are a food source for wetland birds. The shallow, nutrient-rich waters are also important fish spawning areas. Moreover, the buttress roots of the mangrove anchor sediments thus preventing coastal erosion. Many birds make their home in area mangroves, including 15 members of the heron and egret family, ibis and roseate spoonbill. Pelicans, osprey and frigate birds can also be seen. Crocodiles, crabs and frogs dwell in the channels that meander through the mangroves and in lagoons.

Depending on where they are found, the jungle trees of Quintana Roo reach heights of between 15 and 30 meters. Important forestry species include mahogany, cedar and rosewood as well as lesser known varieties such as pucté, chacah, zapote, ziricote, chechen and coralillo.

Zapote

Dyewood

Mahogany

Rosewood

Zapote

Also known as sapodilla, the zapote or *Manilkara achras* is a jungle-dwelling tree which reaches heights of between 10 and 15 meters and is abundant in eastern Yucatán, southern and western Campeche and Quintana Roo. It bears a sweet, fragrant fruit known as chicozapote yet it is best known as the source of the milky white sap used in the manufacture of chicle or chewing gum.

The ancient Maya were familiar with the sap of the zapote, they called it *sicté* and used it as a gum. Yet it wasn't until 1860, during the presidential term of Antonio López de Santa Anna, that chicle was produced on a commercial scale. James Adams, an American entrepreneur saw the potential of the gum, he added sugar and artificial flavorings to the elastic but insipid chicle and created the chewing gum we know today.

Chicle production took off during World War One when American soldiers chewed it to calm their nerves and assuage their thirst. Mexico's first gum companies were founded in 1923 and by the end of the decade factories had also sprung up in Germany, Japan and Egypt.

Dyewood

Also known as Campeche or logwood, *Haematoxylon campechianum* grows in marshy areas and reaches heights of between 8 and 15 meters. Its bark and wood yields a rich reddish-brown dye once used in the European textile industry. During the 16th, 17th and 18th centuries, galleons laden with the wood set sail from the Yucatán bound for Spain. Pirates got wind of the rich cargos and attacked the ships repeatedly. Then some of them decided to strike out and engage in the lucrative business themselves.

Logwood camps were founded on the island of Tris in the Laguna de Términos in Campeche, in Southern Quintana Roo and in Belize.

Orchids

The jungle floor is covered with rotting leaves which decompose to form a layer of organic material (humus). Bushes, palms, smaller trees, ground dwelling orchids and vines all start their lives here. Humus also accumulates along tree branches and provides nutrients for epiphytes, plants that grow on the tree but obtain their food from the air. Epiphytic plants include philodendron, many varieties of orchid, often with colorful and fragrant flowers, and bromeliads. Orchids and bromeliads also grow in the mangroves.

Ceiba

The sacred ceiba

Also called *yaxché* or *pochote*, the ceiba (*Ceiba pentandra*) is the sacred tree of the Maya. The ancients believed that it sustained the universe: its roots plunged into the Underworld, its trunk grew up through the world of men while its branches and spreading crown reached the heavens. Centuries later, the Mayan inhabitants of central Quintana Roo still revere the noble tree.

The ceiba can reach heights of 18 meters, it has a straight trunk and its branches radiate from the bole in an umbrella-like crown. The bark is greyish-brown and the wood is cream-colored. The flowering season is from August to November. Green pods subsequently form and when ripe burst open to reveal seeds covered by a white cotton, hence the name silk cotton or kapok.

Other flowering plants

A deep pink variety of the flor de mayo (*Plumeria rubra*) or the frangipani of the tropics is native to the Yucatán Peninsula. The kitamche (*Caesalpina gaumeri*) is a member of the acacia family which bears lovely yellow or red flowers with orange spots. Other plants with striking flowers are the ziricote or cordia (deep orange) and the coastal spider lilies. Many flowering trees have insignificant blooms that exude a strong perfume making them attractive to bees. Trees and shrubs from other tropical regions of the world such as hibiscus, flamboyant, cassia, allamanda, oleander, ixora, bougainvillea and beaumontia also abound in the parks and gardens of the state.

Flamboyant

Home to myriad marine creatures, the coral reef is one of the world's richest ecosystems and perhaps its most fragile. The reefs of the Mexican Caribbean are some of the finest in the hemisphere.

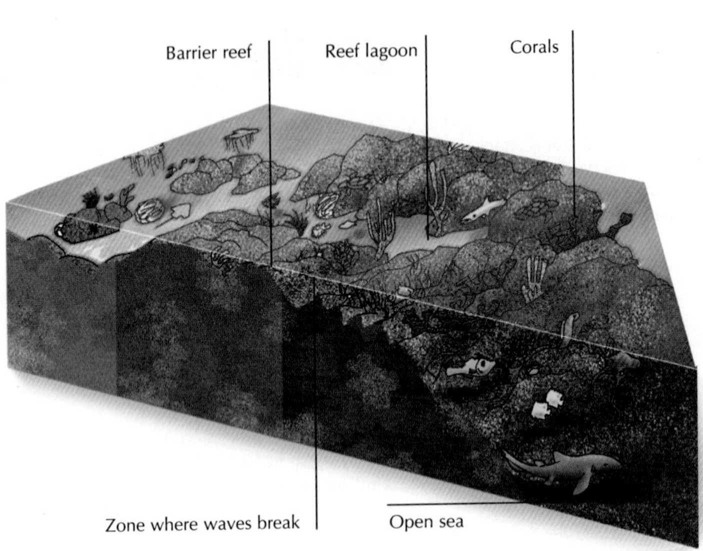

What is a coral?

Corals are simple multicelled creatures called polyps which have an external skeleton of calcium carbonate. Polyps form colonies and it is this, in addition to their limestone shells, that allows them to build hard structures that can withstand wave action, provide a habitat for other plants and animals and shape the seascape of tropical latitudes.

Corals are divided into two categories: hard, such as elkhorn and brain which resemble stone, and the soft species, known as gorgonians which include sea fans and feathers. Over 70 varieties of coral have been recorded on reefs in the Mexican Caribbean.

In order for corals to flourish, certain environmental conditions must exist: warm temperatures, low levels of sediment, clear waters so that sunlight can reach the zooxanthellae, microscopic plants which live inside the polyps producing sugars and waste products used to form the chalk skeleton. Soft corals lack zooxanthellae and therefore water clarity is not such an important factor, in fact they can be found at depths of 100 meters. When the optimum conditions are met for coral growth, these tiny organisms are capable of forming chains of reefs and coralline islands.

How does a reef form?

As the polyps grow they divide and form colonies. A reef is the gradual accumulation of coral colonies which grow on top of one another and it takes thousands of years to build. Coral growth varies from one species to another but it is painfully slow, some varieties grow between two and three millimeters a year.

In 1842 Charles Darwin identified three kinds of reef: fringing reefs which grow in shallow water, close to shore, barrier reefs which are much longer and continuous, and coral atolls which are circular or oval in shape and occur further out to sea. Atolls have a deep, central lagoon and in some areas of the tropics are associated with the peaks of extinct submarine volcanoes. Darwin's classification was later modified to include patch reefs.

Sunlight, water depth and temperature, sedimentation, wave action and ocean currents influence the growth of a reef, its shape, size and the varieties of coral and other marine creatures present.

Shoal of porkfish

Underwater gardens

The reef is a silent and strange world of incredible beauty. Coral buttresses, walls and pillars are festooned with algae, sponges, sea fans, anemones, star fish and sea urchins. Shells, crabs, lobsters and ghost shrimp lurk in crevices and there are fish everywhere: silvery shoals of jacks darting above the reef, stately angel fish, porkfish, parrot fish, damsels, surgeons – a whirlwind of iridescent fins and scales. Then the larger inhabitants make their appearance: snappers, groupers, moray eels, rays and sea turtles.

If the reef is spectacular during the day, by night it is dazzling. Colors are brighter, even more fish venture out to feed and the coral is a sea of waving tentacles as the polyps filter nutrients from the water.

The jungles and wetlands of the state are rich in wildlife. Quintana Roo's location between the neoarctic and neotropical biological zones means that it has species from both. The state also has several endemic (found only in the area) species of bird and rodent.

Ocelot

Mammals

The jungle is a complex ecosystem and home to a bewildering array of wildlife. The state's burgeoning population and other factors such as deforestation have had a detrimental effect on the landscape, and have pushed some species of animals to the brink of extinction.

However, despite the gloomy scenario, area jungles still harbor a range of mammals from mice, shrew and bats to the five members of the feline family: jaguar, ocelot, margay, puma and jaguarundi. Other jungle dwellers include deer, anteater, agouti, armadillo, coatimundi, tapir, peccary, kinkajou, spider and howler monkeys. Chetumal Bay and the Hondo River are a refuge for otters and the state's largest mammal, the manatee.

Water birds

A variety of sea and water birds congregate in the dunes and wetlands along the Quintana Roo coast. The great blue, boat-billed and green heron, ibis and spoonbill are among the waders found in the mangroves while the coast is patrolled ceaselessly by pelicans, frigate birds, gulls and terns. A few pairs of the extremely rare jabiru stork, the largest bird in the Americas, can occasionally be spotted in remote areas of southern Quintana Roo.

In the north of the state, the island of Contoy is an important bird sanctuary and the coastal lagoons of Yalahau and Chacmochchuc attract flocks of flamingos that filter the sediments in the shallows for the tiny crustaceans that are their staple food.

Reptiles and amphibians

Snakes and other reptiles flourish in the heat and humidity of the forest, boas, rattlesnakes, coral snakes and the fer de lance are some of the species found here. The prehistoric iguana and the crocodile are the state's largest lizards and there are a host of amphibians. Tree frogs are particularly colorful, their bright hues a warning to predators.

Coralillo

Hummingbird

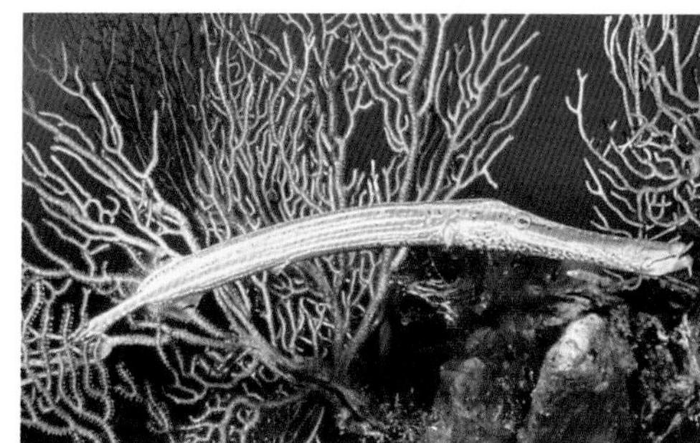

Trumpet fish

Jungle-dwelling birds

At dawn the state's forests echo to the sound of bird calls. In fact, the Yucatán Peninsula is one of the world's most important bird areas, there are more species in the region than in the United States and Canada combined and their number is swelled every winter by the arrival of countless migrants. Furthermore, scientists have recorded more species in southern Quintana Roo than in the whole of Europe and a number of endemic varieties. Jungle dwellers include the toucan, parrot, ocellated turkey, great curassow, chachalaca and the striking motmot.

Fish & crustaceans

The coastal waters of Quintana Roo are rich in marine life. The reefs fringing the Caribbean shoreline are home to innumerable fish, crustaceans and molluscs. Reef-dwelling fish include the colorful angel, tang and sergeant major as well as red snapper, hogfish, grouper, bass and dogfish, all exploited by local fishermen. Other species of commercial value are crustaceans such as the spiny lobster and shrimp, and molluscs like the octopus and pink conch.

The mangroves, lagoons and cenotes are inhabited by countless fresh water species, some of which are endemic like the cave-dwelling blind fish.

Insects

High temperatures and plentiful rainfall accelerate leaf rotting and the formation of humus. This warm, humid environment is perfect for insects and they are everywhere. There is a host of colorful butterflies, wasps, bees, flies, ants and beetles of all shapes and sizes.

VERÁS

Reserves in Quintana Roo

Almost 21% of Quintana Roo's territory is protected as a reserve or national park. Of note are the Sian Ka'an Biosphere Reserve, Chinchorro, Uaymil and Yum Balam reserves, Contoy Island Special Biosphere Reserve, Cozumel Reef National Park, the Manatee Sanctuary in Chetumal Bay, the Isla Mujeres, Punta Cancún and Punta Nizuc National Marine Park, Puerto Morelos Reef Park, Tulum National Park (all archaeological sites are protected areas) and the San Felipe Bacalar Research Station.

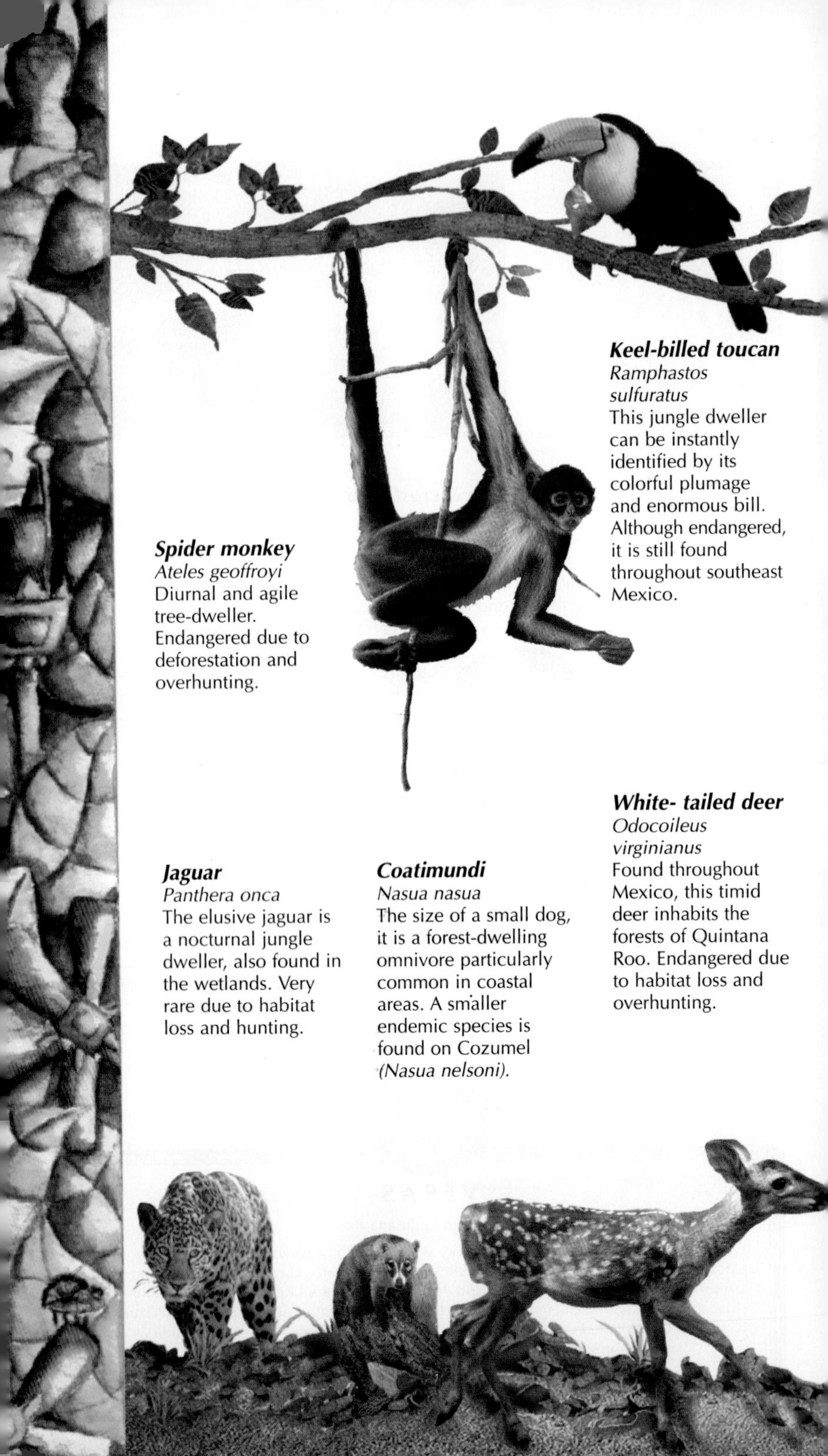

Keel-billed toucan
Ramphastos sulfuratus
This jungle dweller can be instantly identified by its colorful plumage and enormous bill. Although endangered, it is still found throughout southeast Mexico.

Spider monkey
Ateles geoffroyi
Diurnal and agile tree-dweller. Endangered due to deforestation and overhunting.

Jaguar
Panthera onca
The elusive jaguar is a nocturnal jungle dweller, also found in the wetlands. Very rare due to habitat loss and hunting.

Coatimundi
Nasua nasua
The size of a small dog, it is a forest-dwelling omnivore particularly common in coastal areas. A smaller endemic species is found on Cozumel *(Nasua nelsoni).*

White- tailed deer
Odocoileus virginianus
Found throughout Mexico, this timid deer inhabits the forests of Quintana Roo. Endangered due to habitat loss and overhunting.

Yellow-lored parrot
Amazona xantholora
Noisy, small green bird with a distinctive red patch on the wings. Found in tropical forest and scrub. Endangered.

West Indian Manatee
Trichechus manatus
Huge aquatic mammal found in coastal lagoons and mangroves where it grazes on sea grass. Rare.

Frigate bird
Fregata magnifiscens
Seabird known for its aerial acrobatics, it can reach speeds of 190 km per hour. It nests in large colonies in the mangroves and on islands.

Boat-billed Heron
Cochlearius cochlearius
Shy, nocturnal heron with attractive brown plumage which lives in the mangroves and marshes. Its name refers to its broad, flattened beak.

Great White Egret
Ardea occidentalis
The largest member of the heron family, it can be recognized by its yellow bill and legs. It inhabits the mangroves and lagoons along the Quintana Roo coast. Several smaller varieties of heron also inhabit the wetlands.

White-lipped Peccary
Tayassu pecari
The peccary is larger than its cousin, the collared peccary and forms herds of up to 300. Endangered and found only in the jungles of southern Mexico.

Green turtle and Loggerhead turtle
(Chelonia mydas) (Caretta caretta)
Found in the waters of the Mexican Caribbean. Rare due to poaching, pollution and loss of habitat.

HISTORY

Experts believe that the first villages on the Yucatán Peninsula were founded between 500 and 300 B.C., although the exact date is unclear.

During the Classic period the Mayan cities of Cobá, Dzibanché and Kohunlich flourished. Tulum (see left), the inland port of Muyil and Cobá prospered during the Post-Classic period and Cobá's importance as a regional trade center waxed. Muyil was linked to the coast via canals that wind through the wetlands.

The Post-Classic Yucatán was divided into chiefdoms or *cacicazgos*. After the fall of Mayapán ca 1450, there were no less than 19 chiefdoms. Ekab, Cochuah and Chetumal were fiefs located in what is now Quintana Roo.

When the Spaniards first set foot on Mexican soil, the Yucatecan Maya were beset by hardships. Nevertheless, the Europeans found subjugation of the Indians no easy task. It wasn't until 1546 that they controlled large parts of the Peninsula and were able to divide the land into *encomiendas* or landholdings. The estates soon foundered and the region was abandoned. The area's isolation attracted pirates who sought refuge along the coast between Bahía de la Ascención and Honduras.

Independence brought little change to the Peninsula and in 1847, the Caste War ignited the entire region. The greatest in a long line of Mayan rebellions, it continued for more than 50 years.

In 1902, Quintana Roo became a territory and was declared a state in 1974.

Archaeological zones, many of them unexplored, pepper the Quintana Roo landscape. Sites along the coast are testimony to the importance of the north-south Caribbean trade route still in use at the time of the Conquest, while the ancient cities of the south date from the Classic period and had links with city states in the Petén. Artificial reservoirs, irrigation and raised fields improved crop yields and evidence suggests that up to one million people inhabited pre-Conquest Southern Quintana Roo, more than the state's present-day population.

Early inhabitants

The first permanent settlements on the Yucatán Peninsula date from 500 - 300 B.C. although evidence of an earlier human presence has been found in Loltún Caves. Little is known about the first wave of settlers but experts believe they may have been hunter-gatherers moving northwards from the Petén and other areas where Mayan civilization had already begun to evolve. Such bands founded villages throughout the Peninsula and turned to corn cultivation. Over time some communities grew more important and became cities or ceremonial centers such as Cobá, Kohunlich and Dzibanché. The area's earliest date inscriptions were found on Stela 1 at Tulum for A.D. 564, Ichpaatun A.D. 593, on a wooden lintel at Dzibanché for A.D. 618.

Petén architectural style

The Classic period

Cities such as Cobá, Kohunlich, Dzibanché and Muyil flourished during the Classic period (A.D. 250 - 1000). Cobá and Muyil, and Tulum, Xel-Há and Tankah on the coast, became important trading centers with links to cities in the Yucatán and beyond. In the South, Kohunlich and Dzibanché had trade and political relations with city states in Campeche (Calakmul) and Guatemala (Tikal). Links were so strong that they transformed the area's architectural style which is clearly influenced by that of the Petén.

Post-Classic period

Cities throughout the Yucatán continued to trade during the Post-Classic when the area was dominated first by Chichén Itzá and Uxmal and then by Mayapán (1263 - 1461). Many cities in Quintana Roo, particularly those along the coast, reached their peak during this period and commerce was their driving force. The canoes of Chontal traders from Tabasco and Campeche skirted the Quintana Roo shoreline on their way south.

After the fall of Mayapán, the political landscape of the Peninsula changed with the formation of 19 cacicazgos or city states, three of which were in Quintana Roo: Ekab to the north; Cochuah along the modern-day frontier between the state and Yucatán, and Chetemal in the south.

The Maya of Quintana Roo

Mayan cities were inhabited by the ruling class. At the heart of the city lay the sacred precinct of temples where ceremonies were staged and great lords issued the edicts that regulated daily life. While the nobility resided in palaces, commoners lived in huts in the hinterland, tending their fields and rarely venturing into the city.

To surmount the difficult environmental conditions – infertile soils and torrential summer rains, yet paradoxically no rivers – the Maya utilized a number of techniques which enabled them to increase crop yields. These included raised seed beds, called *kaanche,* use of household refuse as a fertilizer, terraces, irrigation and floating plots in marshy areas.

They grew corn, chiles, beans, squash and tomatoes and tended fruit trees. Cotton and cacao were cultivated for trade. The Maya supplemented their diet with game, fish and plants they gathered in the forest. They also traded *copal* or incense. Bee keeping was important and the Maya exchanged honey and beeswax for other trade goods.

The home of a Mayan peasant

Social classes

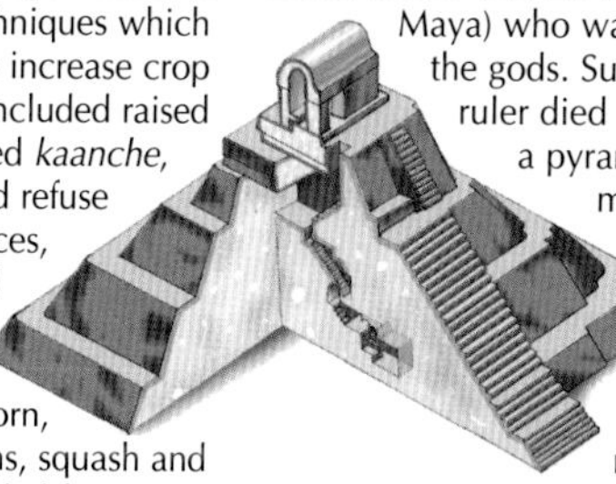

Mayan society was deeply divided. At the top of the social ladder was the ruler, (*ahau or halach uinic* in Maya) who was the earthly representative of the gods. Such was his holiness that when a ruler died he was buried in a tomb deep in a pyramid (see below), built as a lasting memorial to his life. An offering of jade, pottery and even food was arranged around his bier. The priests occupied the second rung of the ladder and were followed by lords who maintained the peace and imparted justice. Nobles, warriors, artists and merchants came next and on the bottom rung were the peasants who supplied the food and cash crops, as well as labor for building temples, pyramids and palaces.

Mayan gods

a. Itzamná
b. Ixchel

Religion dominated all aspects of Mayan life. Natural and supernatural planes were as one; good and malignant spirits inhabited the world and the gods ruled supreme.

The exact number of Mayan deities is uncertain but the following were particularly important in the area. The chief god Itzamná had many manifestations and his wife, Ixchel, was the goddess of childbirth, fertility and weaving. According to Mayan legend she taught women how to weave on the backstrap loom and from far and wide they traveled to Cozumel to worship at her shrine. The sun god Kinich Ahau (Lord of the Solar Face) is associated with the enormous stucco masks at Kohunlich which probably deify the ancient rulers of the city. Ah Mucen Cab is the descending god who appears in carvings at Cobá and Tulum in Quintana Roo and Sayil and Chichén Itzá in neighboring Yucatán. The deity is also associated with the god of the bees, "he who watches over the honey" and is said to be one of the sky bearers.

Tulum

Art

The Maya were accomplished artists, painting their pottery with brightly colored scenes featuring gods, sacred animals and even rulers. Temples and other buildings were decorated with murals, bas-reliefs, and masks or figures molded from stucco plaster. Standing stones known as stelae depict rulers and are covered with glyph inscriptions which record major events during their reigns. They are a historical record which epigraphers have utilized to piece together the fortunes of cities throughout the Maya World.

Mayan carvers mastered the mediums of stone, jade, bone, shell and wood to perfection to create figurines, jewelry and masks, among other things. The lintels recovered at Dzibanché are among the few wooden objects which have survived the ravages of time.

Architecture

A number of different architectural styles are evident in Quintana Roo's Mayan sites, some show foreign influences which are the result of cultural contacts with city states in the Petén (Tikal) and Southern Campeche (Calakmul). Buildings at Kohunlich and Dzibanché are a blend of Petén and Río Bec building styles and Cobá is also Petén in inspiration. Coastal centers such as Tulum, Xel-Há, Muyil, Tankah and El Rey exhibit the East Coast architectural style which is characterized by low buildings with smooth friezes, columns, flat or vaulted roofs and walls that have a slight outward tilt.

Mask at Kohunlich

The coming of the Spaniards

When the Spaniards first set foot on the Yucatán Peninsula they found a land at war with itself. However, when the Maya perceived the threat to their world they put up a fierce resistance. Despite their efforts, superior weaponry and horses gave the Europeans victory in battle, and cruel repression and epidemics soon brought the Indians to their knees.

Ancient prophecies

Mayan priests were the mouthpieces of the gods and when they spoke people listened to their prophecies. According to the Books of Chilam Balam (chronicles), in the 8th year of 13 Ahau the *ah kines* or priests of the sun god predicted that a strange people would visit the area. Friar Diego de Landa related that Aztecs and Mayans had prophesied that a pale-skinned race from the east would visit them bringing catastrophe and the end of their world, many years before they were subjugated by Francisco Montejo. In Maní, a priest or *chilán* called Ah Cambal (" he who answers the demons") foretold that the Maya would be conquered by an alien people who worshipped only one god and overcame demons with a piece of wood the Indians called *vahom-che* (risen tree), obviously a reference to the Cross.

Gonzalo Guerrero, father of a new race

In 1511, a Spanish galleon foundered on Alacranes reef, near Cabo Catoche. Twenty people were washed ashore, and after several years only two were still alive: Friar Gerónimo de Aguilar and Gonzalo Guerrero, a sailor. Aguilar was eventually rescued by Hernán Cortés but Guerrero decided to stay with the Maya. His bravery and military prowess won him the trust of the chief of Chetemal who made him a *nakóm* or captain. Turning native, he married a noblewoman and assimilated Mayan dress and customs (see below). He and his wife had three children, the first *mestizos* (mixed race, European-native) in Mexico.

The first Spanish expeditions

In 1517, an expedition led by Francisco Hernández de Córdoba set sail from Cuba in search of slaves and new lands. The Spaniards landed on Isla Mujeres and claimed it for Spain. Then they set their course westwards for Cabo Catoche where they were attacked by the Indians. Back on board, the Spaniards continued their voyage. On returning to Cuba, they reported to Governor Diego Velázquez that the land was rich and that there was gold. A year later, Juan de Grijalva reconnoitered the coast and made landfall on Cozumel. They sailed on and espied from afar Mayan cities such as Tulum and Xel-Há.

In 1519, Hernán Cortés headed a third expedition. At Cozumel he picked up Jerónimo de Aguilar before setting sail for the west, the start of a journey that would culminate in the conquest of Tenochtitlan, glorious capital of the Aztecs (now Mexico City).

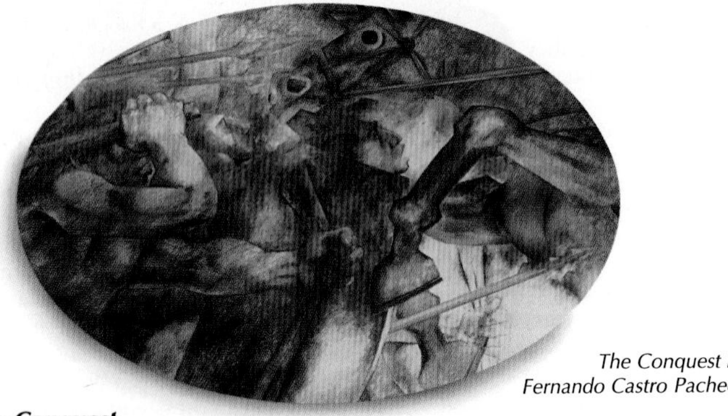

The Conquest by Fernando Castro Pacheco

The Conquest

In 1526, Francisco de Montejo was charged with the conquest of the Yucatán Peninsula and Cozumel. In October, 1527 he landed on the coast of Ekab in an area where the Maya proved friendly, even helping the Spaniards build some palm-thatched huts. The settlement they founded was called Salamanca de Xel-Há and it proved shortlived; the Spaniards were decimated by the tropical diseases prevalent in the area.

Montejo was soon back on the Peninsula, this time making a foray from the port of Campeche towards the north while his son Francisco de Montejo alias 'El Mozo' stayed in Campeche and Alonso Davila took an overland route through Quintana Roo in search of gold. Davila's 1531 journey took him to Tulmó and then on to southern Quintana Roo. The gold proved elusive, the area dangerous, and when he reached Chetemal all he found were ruins. The Maya had torched the city before fleeing into the jungle. In this desolate spot he founded a settlement called Villa Real. The Indians were dauntless and, after a year and a half of raids, Davila and his men had to retreat.

Several years passed and when the Spaniards returned to the Yucatán they found an Indian population debilitated by disease and droughts and split into two rival camps. This made things easier for Gaspar and Melchor Pacheco who were ordered to conquer Quintana Roo. In 1544, they left Mérida and savagely fought their way to Bacalar where they founded Salamanca de Bacalar. However, the desolation and dire poverty of the site was a deterrent to potential colonists and many returned to Mérida.

Colonial life

Victory theirs, the Spaniards divided the Yucatán Peninsula into encomiendas or land grants which they seized as spoils of war. Mayan inhabitants of the land grants had to work for the owner and pay him tribute. Estates (*haciendas*) and plantations sprang up in many parts of the Peninsula, however, the poor soils and unswerving hostility of the Maya meant that most encomiendas failed, especially in Quintana Roo. Mayan rebellions were commonplace and conditions along the eastern seaboard were so unfavorable for the foundation of Spanish communities, that the few colonists gradually abandoned the area.

San Felipe Fort, Bacalar

The scourge of pirates

Although it only had 30 inhabitants, Bacalar was the most important settlement in Quintana Roo in 1630. As it was a supply station on the merchant shipping route to the provinces of Guatemala and Honduras, it was a magnet for pirates and there were raids throughout the century.

In 1640 one such pirate, Peter Wallace, settled on the shores of the Hondo River, the southern limit of Spanish influence, and began to cut logwood. The colony he founded was the forerunner of British Honduras, now known as Belize, a derivation of "Wallace."

In 1652 Cuban buccaneer Diego el Mulatto, sacked Bacalar, and the attacks persisted well into the 18th century until the authorities decided to build a fort in 1729. The threat from pirates over, Bacalar prospered from the export of mahogany, logwood, sugar, goats, pigs and some fruit.

Other pirates associated with Quintana Roo are Captain Henry Morgan (later British Governor of Jamaica) and Miguel Molas who had hiding places on Cozumel. Pirate and slaver Fermín Mundaca retired to Isla Mujeres and built a splendid hacienda (see Isla Mujeres Section p. 76).

Economic activities

Despite the sparse population of the territory there was some economic activity. Cacao, honey, beeswax, cotton, salt, tropical hardwoods such as mahogany, cedar and pucté, and logwood were harvested in the area and shipped out.

Mayan uprisings

Dispossessed, enslaved and harshly treated, it's not surprising that the Maya tried to throw off their shackles. The first Indian rebellion flared up in 1546, in Valladolid and Bacalar. There were others between 1639 and 1655 and in 1761, Jacinto Canek challenged the Spaniards by leading an uprising with religious overtones that historians now consider the forerunner of the Caste War.

The 19th century & Caste War

Mexican Independence from Spain in 1821 did nothing to alleviate Mayan suffering and their quiet hatred of the Yucatecan ruling class (*blancos* or whites) exploded with a fury in the Caste War, a conflict which would last for more than 50 years and decimate the area population. In 1847, a rebellion began in Tepich and spread to other villages such as Tihosuco, Ichmul and Sacalaca along the Yucatán-Quintana Roo border. The rebels showed no mercy to the whites, they were outsiders and had to be swept from the Peninsula so that the Maya could be free once more. By May 1848, all seemed lost for the Yucatecans. The Maya were poised to drive their oppressors into the sea when instead, they laid down their arms and returned home to tend their fields in time for the rains.

The Yucatecans regrouped and with the aid of Mexican troops were able to win back control of many areas. The rebels fled to the remote jungles of central Quintana Roo where they fought a prolonged guerrilla war against the army with arms smuggled in by gunrunners from British Honduras.

The Caste War

The Talking Cross

Tired and demoralized, the Maya were on the brink of defeat when a miracle, albeit contrived, gave them back their self esteem. In the form of a talking cross they received a sign that God was on their side and this gave them the heart to continue fighting. In 1850, José María Barrera, a mestizo from Peto, traced three crosses into the bark of trees. These symbols transmitted a message from God which was imparted to the faithful on October 15, 1850 as a sermon written by Juan de la Cruz. A community called Chan Santa Cruz ("Little Holy Cross") had sprung up around the crosses months before the sermon was read and its inhabitants were called *cruzoob* ("followers of the cross"). José María Barrera utilized a ventriloquist called Manuel Nahuat to be the mouthpiece of the crosses and tell the Maya what God wanted them to do. A temple with two rooms was built to house the crosses. The congregation gathered in the hall and the Talking Cross was kept in the inner sanctum or "La Gloria."

19th & 20th centuries

In 1893, the frontier between Mexico and Belize was drawn up and the eastern region of the Peninsula belonged to the state of Yucatán. In 1896, military commander Othón P. Blanco founded the city of Payo Obispo (now Chetumal) on the banks of the Hondo River. Created in 1902, the territory of Quintana Roo was named in honor of Andrés Quintana Roo, hero of the Mexican struggle for Independence.

The sacred Mayan city and rebel stronghold of Chan Santa Cruz was taken by General Ignacio Bravo in 1901; he subsequently renamed it Santa Cruz de Bravo. The military campaign against the rebels drew to a close, their ranks were diminished by epidemics, famine and they were demoralized by the death of their leaders. The Caste War officially ended on July 1, 1904 but the cruzoob continued their struggle, albeit covertly.

As agricultural and forestry development began in the region, the territory of Quintana Roo was also used as a penal colony, receiving the opponents of the regime of President Porfirio Díaz

Payo Obispo, scale model

until 1911. In 1910, Santa Cruz de Bravo (now Felipe Carrillo Puerto) and Vigía Chico were the most important settlements in the territory, the former as the capital and the latter as its port. Santa Cruz de Bravo was returned to the Maya in 1915 and Payo Obispo became the capital. By 1918, Francisco May, the supreme leader of the Maya held Quintana Roo in an iron grip, both politically and militarily and had a monopoly on chicle production as the middle man between Mexican and foreign concessionaires and international companies.

New settlements

The construction of Payo Obispo had scarcely begun when settlers began to arrive from Belize, Guatemala and Campeche, despite a shortage of drinking water; poor sanitation and rampant malaria. To the north, the territory was virtually unexplored and its communities – Isla Mujeres, Cozumel, Puerto Morelos and Santa María (now Leona Vicario) – survived in isolation, no roads to link them. From 1920 to 1929, Payo Obispo suffered from political instability and its growth was slow. Four groups inhabited the territory: the Maya (the original inhabitants), chicleros, colonists involved in commerce and government officials and Chinese, Koreans and Afro-Caribbeans who had crossed the border from Belize. Chicle production plummeted during the global economic slump of 1929.

Chicleros

20th & 21st centuries

In 1939, Lázaro Cárdenas declared Quintana Roo a federal territory. The large estates in the north were broken up and the land redistributed, those belonging to foreign companies were expropriated and forest reserves were created. Chetumal grew and migrants from other parts of Mexico settled in the territory. From 1940 -58, cooperatives and unions emerged, the chicle industry revived and a literacy campaign was launched in the Zona Maya.

Progress

From 1958 - 1974, federal government investment, colonization and the formation of ejidos (communal landholdings), important socioeconomic and political changes and an integral development plan (1972 - 1976) triggered the modernization of Quintana Roo. These factors, and even more importantly, the start of construction in Cancún in 1970, paved the way for the transformation of the territory into a fully fledged state on October 8, 1974.

Isla Mujeres & Cozumel

In the 1930's, the tiny island of Isla Mujeres became one of President Lázaro Cárdenas' favorite holiday getaways. Its inhabitants, mostly fishermen, benefitted from presidential attention in terms of social and economic development.

Cozumel captured world attention in the 1950's when word of its magnificent coral reefs spread. Hotels were built and the tourism that began as a trickle became a steady flow.

A star is born: Cancún

At the end of the 1960's, the Cancún area was earmarked for tourism development. It had all the attractions. Investment poured in, the airport, roads and public services were installed and hotel building began. What started life as a dream became a huge success and, today Cancún is the country's most important resort and one of the most popular destinations in the world. An economic powerhouse, it generates a large percentage of the state's income (Quintana Roo itself accounts for 36 percent of Mexico's tourism revenue). In terms of demographic growth it is also one of the most dynamic cities in the country and is the Yucatán Peninsula's most prosperous urban center.

Cancún has the second most important airport in the country. It is linked to the rest of the country by a network of good roads.

Its success has converted Quintana Roo into the Mexican tourist state par excellence, paving the way for more projects which will contribute to the economy and diversify traditional activities.

Puerto Morelos

The Mexican Caribbean

One such project is the Riviera Maya, a 160-kilometer coastal strip (from Cancún to Tulum) which plays host to resorts and hotels lining its seemingly endless beaches. Caves, cenotes, several inlets, archaeological sites, jungle, lagoons and mangrove forests are other area attractions. Playa del Carmen and Puerto Aventuras are the principal resorts, complemented by smaller developments at Akumal, Punta Bete, Puerto Morelos, Paamul, Xpu-Há, Xel-Há, Xcacel, Tankah and Tulum. Planners hope that the recently inaugurated Costa Maya project will repeat the success of resorts in northern Quintana Roo without competing for the same market. Stretching from Punta Herrero to Xcalak in the south, it is limited to low impact resorts geared towards eco- and adventure tourism. The program also includes plans for the restoration of ancient cities such as Bacalar (with the 18th-century San Felipe Fort and the 55-kilometer-long lagoon) and the consolidation of Chetumal as the economic center of southern Quintana Roo and the gateway to some of the Maya World's most important archaeological sites: Kohunlich, Dzibanché, Oxtankah, Chacchoben and Chakanbakán.

Xcalak

PEOPLE

Poor soils and a shortage of fresh water may have done little to foster the growth of large cities in ancient times. Nevertheless, when the Spaniards first set foot in the area they found a considerable population arrayed against them. European diseases and the effects of war and slavery decimated the Maya and the territory was abandoned for 300 years, with the exception of Bacalar.

The boom in forestry and chicle harvesting in the early 20th century gave a boost to the economy, particularly in the south. The last 30 years have seen a population explosion in Quintana Roo as migrants from other parts of Mexico and abroad travel here in search of work and a better life. The resorts of Cancún, Cozumel and Playa del Carmen, Chetumal and villages along the shores of the Hondo River are the communities recording the fastest growth rates.

Central Quintana Roo, also known as the Zona Maya is an area of scattered rural communities where the Maya still cling to ancient beliefs and customs. In other parts of the state, however, the population is a mix of Mexicans, Maya and foreigners. Along the coast and around Chetumal, there is a strong Caribbean influence, and it gives the state its unique atmosphere.

Quintana Roo is one of Mexico's youngest states and it has the fastest growth rate. In 2000, the population was just over 870,000, of which 45% were born here and the rest are from other parts of Mexico or are foreigners. The state is divided into eight municipal districts (*municipios*): Benito Juárez, Isla Mujeres, Solidaridad (Riviera Maya), Cozumel, Felipe Carrillo Puerto, Othón P. Blanco (Chetumal), José María Morelos and Lázaro Cárdenas.

Town and country

The majority of the state's inhabitants live in cities such as Cancún, Chetumal, Cozumel and Playa del Carmen. District capitals and rural communities account for the rest.

A melting pot

Quintana Roo is an interesting mix of people from all over Mexico and the world, not to mention the Maya whose ancestral home it is. Foreigners who have settled in the state include groups from the Lebanon and other countries along the Levant that arrived at the turn of the century, Guatemalans, Belizeans, Canadians, Americans, Europeans and even Asians. Caribbean influence permeates Chetumal and other communities along the border with Belize, notably in the cuisine, architecture and music.

Economic activities

Poor soils hinder agricultural development and commercial farming is restricted to the south, on the shores of the Hondo River, where sugar cane, rice and citrus fruit are cultivated. Tourism is the most important economic activity and the state's leading source of income and commerce ranks second. Other activities are fishing, ranching, beekeeping and forestry.

The Maya family

With its well defined roles, the family is the single unit that binds Mayan communities together. Women keep house, preparing meals, raising children and tending livestock and the orchard while the man cultivates the *milpa* or cornfield, which is the mainstay of the household. Corn, beans, squash and chiles are grown in the milpa and the woman tends beds of coriander, radish, tomato, jicama, cucumber and chile and a variety of fruit trees. Many familes also obtain some of their income from beekeeping and chicle harvesting. Although cattle ranching is a secondary activity, most families keep pigs and poultry.

The Maya of Quintana Roo produce wicker and straw baskets, *hipiles* (traditional cotton dresses) and wood carvings.

Mayan house and land

The *Na*, a 2000-year-old tradition

Although modern architectural styles and materials have invaded Maya communities, the traditional house or *na* still dominates the rural landscape as it has for thousands of years. The classic Mayan house is oval or rectangular and has a sloping thatched roof fashioned from plaited palm leaves. It is surrounded by a plot of land called a *solar* where the pig pen (*chiquero*), chicken coop and vegetable garden are located. Some Mayan women grow their vegetables in the ancient *kanche* or raised bed.

Mayan communities

Although many people of Mayan origin live in Cancún, Chetumal, Playa del Carmen and other cities, the majority still dwell in the Zona Maya where they are the largest demographic group. The Zona Maya extends across the district of Felipe Carrillo Puerto, José María Morelos and parts of Solidaridad (Riviera Maya) and Lázaro Cárdenas. In this remote area of jungle and scattered villages, the inhabitants still honor the customs of their forefathers.

Social organization

The political framework of Mayan communities is twofold: national, in accordance with the laws of the state which are enforced by a subdelegate who is elected by a village assembly. The subdelegate's responsibilities include public order, calling meetings, community work or *fajinas* and registering births and deaths.

The other body, the military company, dates from the days of the Caste War. Although Mayan chiefs still lead the companies, their influence only covers moral issues. This form of organization extends to the *cruzoob* (followers of the cross) and *macehuales* (the common people) and is inextricably linked to their religious beliefs.

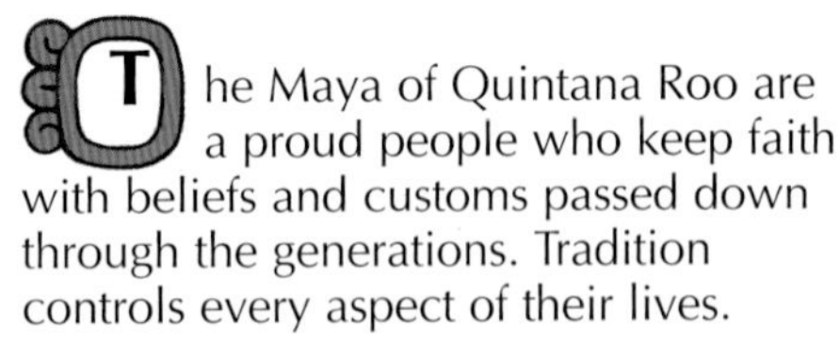

The Maya of Quintana Roo are a proud people who keep faith with beliefs and customs passed down through the generations. Tradition controls every aspect of their lives.

Religious syncretism

Mayan religious beliefs are a mixture of ancient ceremonies and the Christian rituals introduced by 16th-century missionaries. Isolation and the effects of the Caste War also played a part in the transformation of religious customs. In the Zona Maya, the inhabitants go to church and also attend ceremonies conducted by the *H-men* or Mayan priest.

The Cross

A belief in the Cross unites the Maya. During the Caste War it was a symbol of their armed struggle but its history goes back further. The ancient Maya were familiar with the concept of the cross long before the arrival of the Spaniards. For them it symbolized the four cosmic ways indicated by the cardinal directions. The modern Maya believe that the cross is the most sacred symbol of the Almighty and the medium he uses to communicate with mankind. For the cruzoob, not all crosses are of equal importance as hierarchies exist within the area, nevertheless, all are ruled by the Holiest Cross which stands guard in a sanctuary in the village of Tixkakal Guardia. Macehual communities have patron crosses which originally belonged to certain local families and rank second. Passed down from generation to generation, family crosses are kept in a tiny temple and follow in the hierarchy.

The spirit world of the H-men

The H-men or Mayan priest conducts ancient ceremonies, cures ailments and predicts the future. The Maya believe that illnesses are caused by evil spirits and to alleviate the suffering they turn to the H-men who uses ceremonies, offerings and plants with medicinal properties to help them. To make predictions the H-men uses a crystal disc called *zaztún* (luminous stone) or *xunan* (wife) because it is his inseparable companion. Every two years, the H-men undergoes an exorcism called *U-Lohol-Ah-Kin* to purify himself after contacts with inhabitants of the supernatural world and to be at peace with them.

Mayan ceremonies

One of the most important Mayan rituals is the *Cha chaac,* which is a plea to the rain god to send water to the corn fields. With the *Wahikol* or "food in the corn field," the Maya thank God, the guardians of the earth (earth lords) and their ancient deities for the harvest, while the *Hets'Lum'um* or "calming the earth," appeases the earth lords. The *Hóoche* is the offering of the first fruit of the harvest to God and the guardians. Before the beehives can be opened and the honey removed, offerings are made to the Virgin Mary and the Lord's Prayer is recited. The Day of the Dead (Nov. 1-2) is honored with the *Hanal-pixan* or "feast of the dead." Other ceremonies unite the community and mark events in their lives, for example betrothal, marriage and the *hetzmek* or baptism.

Mayan ceremony

The other world

The supernatural plays an important role in the lives of the Maya. There are good and evil spirits who can bring prosperity, health and love or cause economic hardship, illness, family problems and even death. Offerings are made to appease them.

Aluxes

These are tiny spirits (different sources describe them as children or old men) who wander through the corn fields and forests waylaying men and asking them for food. If farmers ignore their requests the *alux* will wreak havoc on his corn and may also spread sickness, steal or break things. However if the farmer makes offerings of food, the alux will become the guardian spirit of his field and protect it from thieves. Some people believe that the aluxes were originally clay idols placed in ancient temples throughout the area and that they came to life.

Snake woman of the forest

The female being called the *Xtabay* is shrouded in mystery and there are several versions of the myth. According to one story she is an evil spirit who dwells in the trunk of an ancient ceiba. She preys on men who venture into the jungle alone, suddenly appearing in the form of a lovely but snake-like woman and luring them off the path. She bewitches them so that they forget everything, makes them mad and sends them to hell. Another version relates that the Xtabay controls moral behavior in the community, punishing those who commit crimes or violent acts by stealing them away and killing them. The *cizin* or devil can be conjured up by just calling his name and is called *kakazbaal* (a very bad thing). He is a shape shifter and his disguise varies with his purpose at the time.

Cancún

As recently as the late 60s, Cancún was a fishing village with a handful of inhabitants and the island was a 17-km-long sandbar, only 50 m wide in some places, covered with coconut groves. A group of bankers, visionaries every one, saw the area's potential and convinced the Mexican government to invest. Construction began and a few years later Cancún became the nation's most important resort.

Today, 26,194 rooms and 28 years later, Cancún is a world-class vacation spot, welcoming three million visitors a year drawn by its peerless white-sand beaches, turquoise seas, the longest reef in the hemisphere and a perfect climate. Now add the presence of three offshore islands two of which were destinations in their own right–and the most famous city of the ancient Maya (Chichén Itzá), Mérida, the colonial capital of the Yucatán, and the Riviera Maya just down the road, not to mention the wealth of attractions in Southern Quintana Roo and you've a combination of assets no other resort in the world even comes close to duplicating. The residential area, or Downtown Cancún has also grown at a phenomenal rate. Like the Hotel Zone it has its hotels, restaurants, bars, stores, markets and malls, in addition to banks and public services.

The Hotel Zone, though technically an island. is rarely referred to as one. If you discount the 20 meters that would be the beach (and was federal property anyway), there wasn't even space for a dirt track, much less five-star hotels. Rendering this narrow spit of land suitable for high-rise construction was a challenge. In the end 300 meters of lagoon were 'reclaimed' using *sascab* (limestone) as infill to create the future home of over 80 upscale hotels, shoppng centers, restaurants, golf courses, discos, various embarcaderos, a four-lane highway and all the rest. Downtown Cancún and the international airport are located on the mainland.

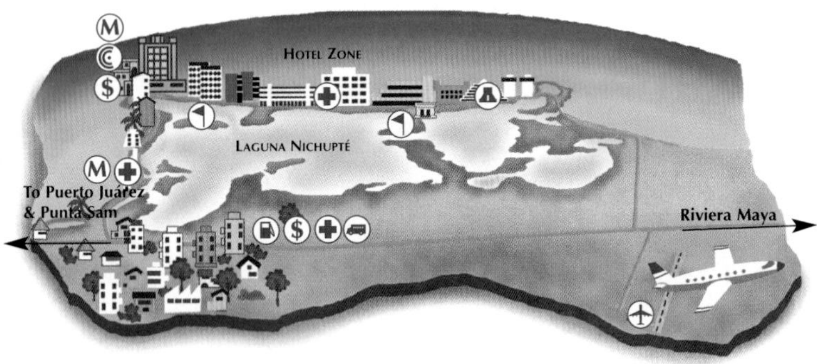

Key

Airport	Bus station	Museum
Bank	Convention Center	Hospital
Golf course	Gas station	Archaeological site

Downtown Cancún

Cancún is growing, the population has jumped to more than 500,000 in less than 30 years and most people live Downtown. All city government offices are located downtown, together with the banks, post office, police and fire stations, schools, hospitals and supermarkets. The ethnic profile of the city is mixed, and Mayan women from the rural areas can be seen in the streets, speaking their own language and sporting the *hipil* (dress). A walking tour of Avenida Tulum, the main street is recommended.

Kukulcán Boulevard

Kukulcán Boulevard is the four-lane highway linking the Hotel Zone with Downtown. It is beautifully landscaped, on one side lie the hotels and the Caribbean and on the other, the Nichupté Lagoon. A bike path runs along the first section of the boulevard which is enhanced by reproductions of sculptures from Mexico's early cultures, Mexica, Toltec, Olmec and Maya.

Puerto Juárez & Punta Sam

The fishing villages of Puerto Juárez (4 km) and Punta Sam (6 km) are located about 10 and 15 minutes north of downtown Cancún. Passenger ferries to Isla Mujeres embark from Puerto Juárez every 30 minutes or so; and there are water taxis. Car ferries embark from Punta Sam.

Getting around

The taxi fare in the city center is currently $12 pesos. Rides to destinations outside the city limits are more. Taxis hired from taxi ranks or *sitios* charge more than the basic rate. Fares within the Hotel Zone are higher and should be posted in the taxis and at your hotel. If not, ask the bellboy the going rate to your destination, and agree on the price before getting in the vehicle. Many taxis offer private tours. Buses are cheap, the fare is currently $6 pesos. Two companies operate routes linking different areas of the city. Routes 1 and 2 serve the Hotel Zone, look for the word "*Hoteles*" on the windscreen. Buses also make the run from Tulum Ave. to Puerto Júarez and Punta Sam. During rush hour and on Sundays the Hotel Zone buses are crowded.

The Hotel Zone: paradise surrounded by water

The Hotel Zone is shaped like the number 'seven'. To the north is Mujeres Bay, and about 8 km offshore, Isla Mujeres. To the east is the Caribbean and to the west is Nichupté Lagoon, all 28.8 sq. km of it. The island is connected to the mainland by bridges at either end; one spans the Nichupté Canal just four kilometers from town, the other, the Nizuc Canal. At this end, the road continues west for several kilometers to meet Highway 307.

Travel from Cancún

Getting to neighboring Yucatán is easy by road. Sites of interest include Chichén Itzá (200 km), Izamal (268 km), Valladolid (160 km), Mérida, the Puuc Route sites and Río Lagartos reserve (263 km). Traveling south from Cancún, visitors can explore the Riviera Maya, Southern Quintana Roo and Campeche and even cross the border into northern Belize and Guatemala, obviously a trip of longer duration.

Environment

Cancún has a tropical climate and sub-tropical vegetation: low-canopy jungle and coastal wetlands with stretches of mangrove forest. It is an environment conducive to plants and trees of great color and beauty: acacia, tamarind and flamboyan; hibiscus and bougainvillea in all of its riotous shades. Some species loose their leaves in the dry season, most do not.

Local wildlife

A variety of wildlife lives in the mangroves and jungle of the Hotel Zone. Birds are abundant, herons, ibis, brown pelicans, magnificent frigate birds, gulls, ospreys, terns and cormorants can be spotted in the lagoon or patrolling the beaches.

Iguanas, some up to a meter long, can be observed sunning themselves on walls and rocks in the Hotel Zone.

City parks and the jungles that surround the urban area are home to flycatchers, orioles, warblers, doves, swallows, woodpeckers, hawks, buzzards, hummingbirds, parrots and the occasional toucan. Mammals include raccoons, squirrels, fruit bats, coatimundis and possums.

History

Evidence of human occupation in the Hotel Zone spans the Late Preclassic (300 B.C. to A.D. 100) to the Post-Classic (A.D. 1200-1550) periods of Mayan history. Inhabitants of the Hotel Zone's only restored site – El Rey – lived off both the land and sea: fishing, collecting salt, growing corn and cotton, bee keeping and harvesting trees for copal. The Post-Classic period corresponds to the culture's maritime trading heyday, and Cancún was one of the many ports of call which linked the Gulf of Mexico to the Gulf of Honduras.

The right conditions for development

The choice of this corner of the Mexican Caribbean for a resort was not arbitrary. Factors such as climate, beaches, the Caribbean, reefs, nearby archaeological sites, a plentiful labor force, and the proximity of major U.S. population centers were given priority and Cancún was 'go' on all counts.

A resort springs up

Work on Project Cancún began in 1970. The first order of business was to clear the jungle and fill in enough of the lagoon to have room to build on (the Pok-ta-Pok Golf Course is built entirely on landfill!). Nothing like Cancún had ever been attempted; engineers, architects and advertising executives faced tremendous obstacles which they overcame by thinking creatively. Some of the big names are Javier Solórzano, who is credited with planning downtown Cancún; José María de la Torre and Carlos Náder, both of whom contributed to the final 'look' of the Hotel Zone. Náder died in an airplane crash and Avenida Náder was named for him.

Cancún's early days

Cosmopolitan Cancún

Since the beginning, Cancún has attracted major social, cultural and political events, many of them world-class. In 1981, just 11 years after its founding, 23 heads of state met here for the historic North-South Reunion, and in 1983, the Latin American presidents who were members of the Contadora group congregated for another groundbreaking meeting. The Miss Universe Pageant was broadcast from Cancún in 1989 and the resort currently stages a Jazz Festival and events celebrating Mexican and Caribbean culture, a marathon and the annual Triathlon World Cup, in addition to other international sporting competitions.

Cancún and the world

Stunning scenery, water sports, nightlife, dining and shopping opportunities, an extensive portfolio of side trip options and state-of-the-art tourist infrastructure have made Cancún one of the most popular resorts in the world. It is visited by travelers from every walk of life and every corner of the globe: Canada, the United States, Brazil, Argentina, Germany, Spain, France, Britain, Italy, Finland, the Netherlands, Ireland, Japan, Russia and many other nations. And the city's fame continues to grow, reaching into new markets every year.

Cancún today

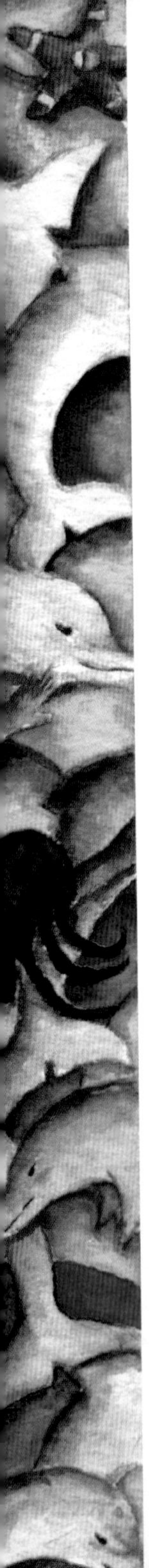

Beaches

The white sands of the Mexican Caribbean are composed of tiny fragments of shell and coral and are always cool to the touch, quite a relief in the hot midday sun. The side of the Hotel Zone that gives out to the Caribbean is fringed with powder-white beaches. The stretch from town to Punta Cancún faces Mujeres Bay and the water, being sheltered, is shallow and calm.

The water on the open-ocean side of the Hotel Zone, from Punta Cancún to Punta Nizuc is just the opposite, characterized by pounding surf and currents. Care should be exercised on these beaches as the undertow can be quite strong. Always check the warning flags on the beach in front of the hotels: red or black mean dangerous conditions, yellow that precaution is needed and green or blue that conditions are ideal for swimming. Bayside playas or beaches include Las Perlas, Juventud, Linda, Langosta, Tortugas and Caracol, while on the Caribbean shoreline there's Gaviota Azul, Chac Mool, Marlín, Ballenas and Delfines.

Some bayside beaches have embarcaderos or docks from which the different tourist boats come and go, for example Playa Langosta, Playa Caracol, Playa Tortugas and Embarcadero Isla Mujeres/Playa Linda.

Signs mark the access to the public beaches, which can become quite crowded on Sundays and holidays when local families enjoy a day out. Trash cans are few and far between and fill up quickly so if you can't find one please take your garbage with you when you leave.

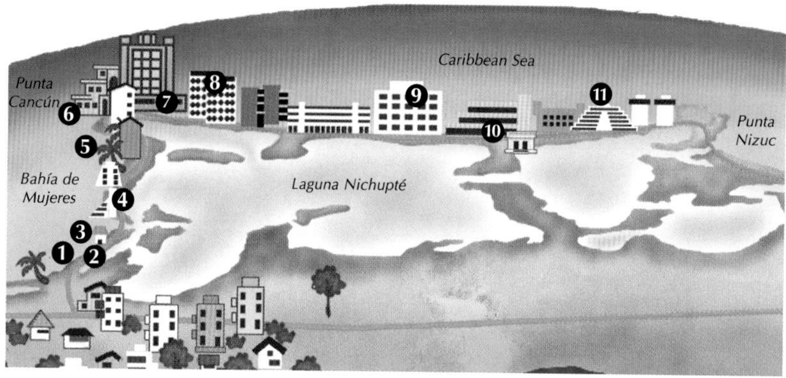

Location of public beaches

- Playa Las Perlas 1
- Playa Juventud 2
- Playa Linda 3
- Playa Langosta 4
- Playa Tortugas 5
- Playa Caracol 6
- Playa Gaviota Azul 7
- Playa Chac-Mool 8
- Playa Ballenas 9
- Playa Marlín 10
- Playa Delfines 11

Thatched palapas or shade umbrellas, bars and restaurants dot the shoreline and there's always something going on, impromptu games of beach volleyball or football or sometimes even concerts. Not all the beaches are so crowded, however, just a short stroll away are near-deserted stretches of sand.

The hotels line the shore between the public beaches and have their own access points. Palapas, chairs and sun beds are available for their guests and there are plenty of beach bars and restaurants open to anyone. Activity directors organize beach games and aerobics, there's also parasailing for those who want a bird's eye view of Cancún and hotel marinas offer jet ski, wave runner and other water sports.

Strong winds blowing in from the Caribbean or the south can occasionally change the coastline. Waves breaking on a beach at a certain angle and with greater power can erode the sand and deposit it further north on the coast. Hence some beaches may become smaller for a season while others grow. Hawkers selling silver sometimes approach tourists on the beach. Apart from the annoyance factor, we recommend that you don't buy their wares as the jewelry they offer is not silver but an alloy called *alpaca*. Visit one of the jewelers in the Hotel Zone malls or Downtown for the real thing.

Diving and Snorkeling

The best and most accessible reefs off the coast of Cancún lie in the bay between the Hotel Zone and Isla Mujeres. Cancún's reefs lie in relatively shallow water which means they get a lot of sunlight, hence the fantastic colors and formations. Apart from the sea fans corals and sponges, divers regularly spot barracuda, rays, millions of bright tropical fish and sometimes even a sea turtle or two. Water clarity can reach up to 200 feet, and is routinely 80 to 90. Resort courses and certification available. Marinas are located throughout the resort, on both the ocean and the lagoon.

The different reefs

Cancún's reefs are part of a system, a collection of formations at varying distances from shore and from each other. Water depth, reef profile and resident sea life are the variables that characterize the different reefs and the diving experience each offers. Chitales, depth 18-20 ft., has a lot of elkhorn coral, sea fans, sponges, surgeonfishes, snappers, and tangs. Lavandera and Cuevones, at 15-25 ft, are small chains of coral covered with sponges, anemones, crustaceans, molluscs and impressive sea fans; Cuevones is also riddled with nooks and crannies and small caves, home to sharks and moray eels plus dozens of species of tropical fish. Other reefs go by such names as Manchones, Grampín, Herradura, San Toribio, El Túnel and San Miguel.

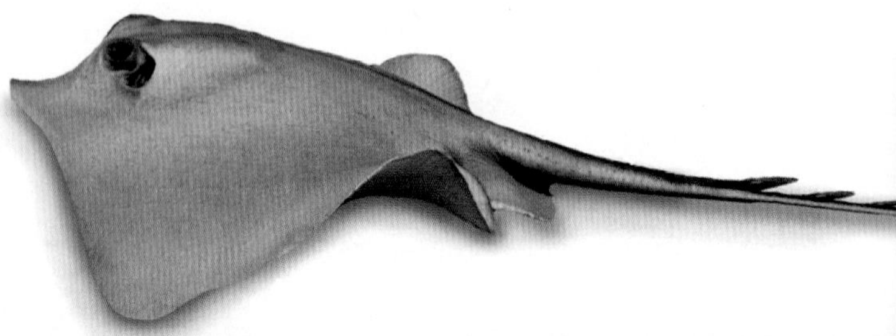

Submarines and glass-bottom boats

Those wishing for an underwater experience without having to get their feet wet, can try a glass-bottom boat or even a submarine. These are especially good options for senior citizens or families with small children. The marine world of the Caribbean is thus accessible, without risk or discomfort, in an adventure designed to be shared. A marine biologist guide will act as a guide, pointing out different species of fish and other coral dwellers and describing the complex reef ecosystem. Lunch and soft drinks are usually included. Consult any travel agent for details and departure times.

Daytime cruises

Day cruises let you explore Cancún's offshore islands. Isla Mujeres is the most popular choice, though tours to Cozumel and to non-inhabited Contoy, the bird sanctuary, are also available (see a travel agent) Cruises are meant to be entertaining and in addition to open bar and lunch, may include a lot of shipboard fun and games, even live music. Ferry services to both Isla Mujeres and Cozumel also exist: those to Isla Mujeres leave every 20 minutes from Puerto Juárez located 10 minutes north of downtown Cancún; the crossing takes 15 to 30 minutes. Ferries to Cozumel leave hourly starting at 6am from Playa del Carmen, located 45 min. south of Cancún; the crossing takes 50 min. Isla Mujeres is very low-key and laid back, Cozumel is more developed and considered the diving mecca of the region. Both are great getaways and very different from Cancún. Flights to Cozumel available from Playa del Carmen and Cancún. For more information on Cancún's sister islands turn to the relevant section of this guide.

VERÁS

Corals are very fragile, the slightest disturbance of their environment can kill them. Furthermore, coral has a painfully slow growth rate; a 2-inch 'souvenir' can take years to grow back. Divers are urged to respect the reefs and avoid touching or standing on them. They should keep their distance, several feet from the coral, and avoid stirring up sand with their flippers. Keeping the body free of oils and lotions when in the water also helps prevent water pollution. Boats should approach the reef area slowly and anchor well away from the corals. Abide by the rules and help Cancún preserve the reefs so that future generations may also enjoy them.

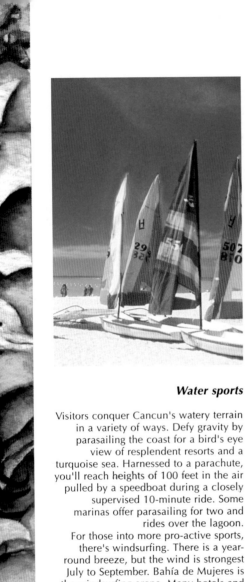

Water sports

Visitors conquer Cancun's watery terrain in a variety of ways. Defy gravity by parasailing the coast for a bird's eye view of resplendent resorts and a turquoise sea. Harnessed to a parachute, you'll reach heights of 100 feet in the air pulled by a speedboat during a closely supervised 10-minute ride. Some marinas offer parasailing for two and rides over the lagoon.

For those into more pro-active sports, there's windsurfing. There is a year-round breeze, but the wind is strongest July to September. Bahía de Mujeres is the windsurfing arena. Many hotels and marinas rent gear and give lessons.

Boogie boards and water tricycles are fun for all ages, waterskiing is practiced on the lagoon, lessons available. Hobie cats, sunfish and kayaks are rented on the lagoon; the latter also on the bayside of the Hotel Zone.

Nature lovers will enjoy the Jungle Tours run by Cancún's marinas. Participants drive their own speedboat or waverunner in a guided tour of Nichupté Lagoon and its mangroves on their way to the ocean and a bit of reef snorkeling. Jungle Tours are a great way to see the local flora and fauna. Common residents are osprey, herons and kingfishers.

Activities for landlubbers

Cancún is a golfers' paradise and the Hotel Zone has four golf courses. The Pok-ta-Pok is an 18-hole, par 72 course with vistas of both ocean and lagoon, restaurant, bar and rentals. Designed by Robert Trent Jones Jr., the course has its own Mayan ruins. The 18-hole par 72 Hilton Cancún Beach and Golf Resort is located on the shores of the lagoon and has the El Rey archaeological site as a backdrop. The others are the 18-hole par 3 at the Meliá Cancún Hotel, and the 9-hole, par 3 at the Gran Oasis Hotel.

Green fees are reasonable and equipment available at every course. Most of the 5-star and Grand Tourism hotels have tennis courts, some floodlit for night play, resident pros and equipment. The larger hotels also have an on-site spa/gym/health club.

Daytime activities

Real bullfights are performed every Wednesday at 3:30 pm, in the Plaza de Toros in downtown Cancún Bullfighting was introduced to Mexico by Spain in the 16th century and is one of this country's oldest traditions. A bullfight is a ritual with several movements. At half-time visitors are entertained with regional dances, games and Mexican rodeo feats. Cancún's Plaza de Toros is listed in the Guinness Book of World Records because of its unique year-round season. The bullfighting season traditionally runs for three months beginning in December.

For non-spectator sports, there are rollerblades and bicycles for rent and the Hotel Zone's, 10-mile bike path, lit for nighttime cruising, and alive with walkers, joggers, cyclists, and skaters during the day. The path runs on the bayside of Kukulcán Blvd., from downtown to the Viva Hotel. Mopeds and buggies are also available along Kukulcán Boulevard.

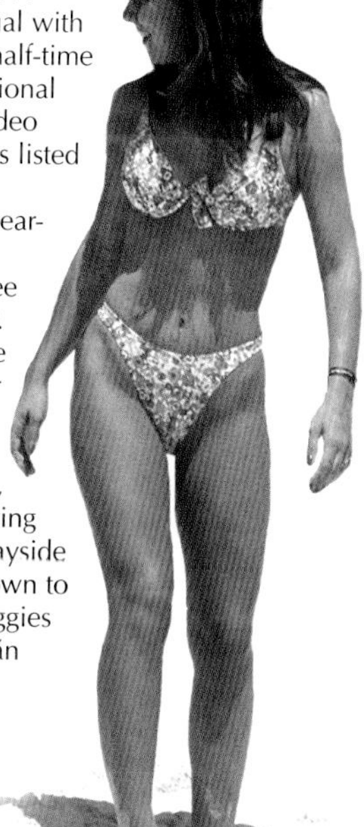

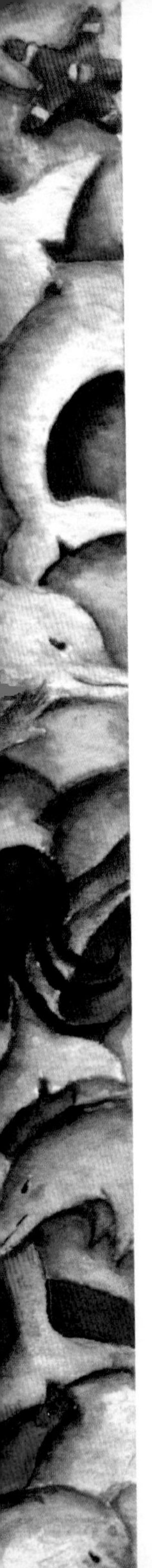

Family fun

Cancún is definitely kid-friendly. Restaurants offer special kid menus and prices; the bigger hotels usually sponsor activity programs for kids that include surpervised beach and pool time, sports, indoor games, craft classes – even miniature golf. Other 'fun for the family activities include bowling and fun arcades (at Kukulcán and Las Américas malls, Wol-Ha children's center) and movie-going. Cancún has several cinemas showing English language films with Spanish subtitles (children's films are often dubbed into Spanish). There are the Nautilus and the Subsea Explorer submarines, the Aquarium, the Nizuc Water Park with slides, rides and fun for the whole family and several dolphin swims. At the Embarcadero, the rotating Scenic Tower offers the best views of Cancún.

Ecotourism

In contrast to ultramodern, high-density Cancún, the surrounding area is wild and undeveloped, perfect for eco-adventures. Worthy examples include birding trips to Isla Contoy and tours of the Sian Kaán Biosphere Reserve, a 1.3 million acre coastal ecosystem of tropical forests, lagoons and wetlands. The reserve is habitat for more than 350 species of birds and the domain of pumas, jaguars, monkeys and crocodiles. For tours, contact the non-profit, Amigos de Sian Ka'an.

For nature buffs and birders, the Río Lagartos National Park, a four-hour drive north of Cancún is also a must. This salt marsh and estuary nesting ground for some 30,000 flamingos is also the habitat for another 270 native and migratory species. In the Riviera Maya nature parks such as Xcaret, Xel-Há and Tres Ríos provide encounters with nature and a range of activities such as horseback riding, watersports (snorkeling, diving, kayaks, fishing), swimming, trail biking, jungle walks, even swimming-with-dolphins.

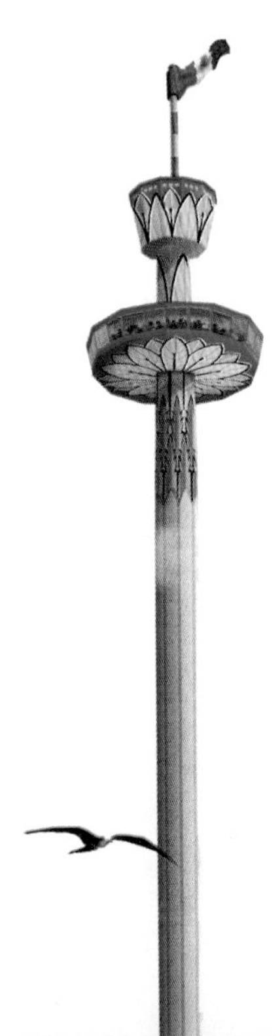

Sport fishing

Cancún is an angler's paradise. Bass, dorado, barracuda, bonito, tuna and grouper bite year round, while from April to August the billfish (white and blue marlin sailfish) are running and Cancún becomes the headquarters of the international fishing tournaments that are staged in the resort, Isla Mujeres, Cozumel and the Riviera Maya at different times during the season. There are two major fishing grounds and trolling is the name of the game: the Grieta, an underwater valley of tremendous proportions and depth that runs along the eastern coast of Isla Mujeres; and the Corrientada, the fast-moving shipping lanes located east of Contoy. International rules of catch and release apply for marlin and other game fish. Sport cruisers with chairs, outriggers and up to six lines are available for 4, 6 and 8-hour charters; boats can also be shared. All charters include captain, first mate, bait, beer, soft drinks and lunch.

Important species of game fish

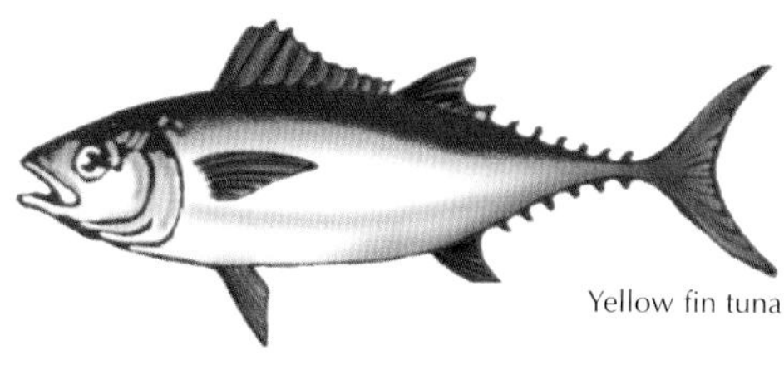

Yellow fin tuna

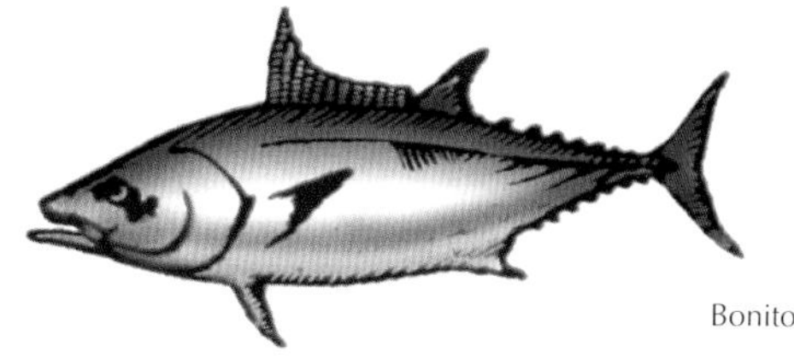

Bonito

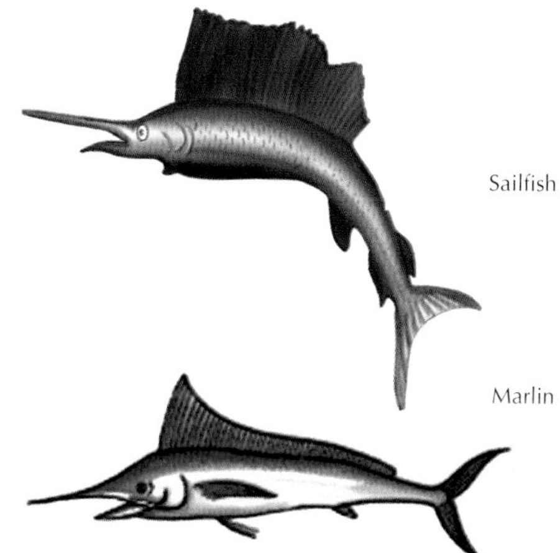

Sailfish

Marlin

Barracuda

Dorado

Shopping malls

Avid shoppers come in all sizes, shapes and nationalities and Cancún's malls are a fit destination. In the Hotel Zone alone there are a number of ultramodern malls.

Forum by the Sea

Striking architecture and a beachfront terrace with a wonderful view of the Caribbean. Houses several theme restaurants and bars, a disco, cinemas, jewelers, casual and designer ware stores.

Plaza Caracol

At the heart of the Hotel Zone, this is one of Cancún's largest malls with more than 200 stores (boutiques, art galleries, jewelers, perfumeries and designer wear stores) and some of the resort's finest eateries.

Kukulcán Plaza

Ultramodern mall with sports, fashion and beachwear, leather goods, a range of Mexican crafts, perfumes and fine jewelry, pharmacies, art exhibitions, bowling alley, games center, food court, bars and first-class restaurants; subterranean parking for 1,000.

La Isla Shopping Village

Located on the shores of the lagoon, La Isla is one of Cancún's latest malls and offers fine restaurants, stores with everything from crafts and clothes to jewelry and perfumes, bars, a waterfront food court and entertainment options for the whole family such as the Passage of Terror, the Interactive Aquarium and Mayaventuras.

Plaza Flamingo

Overlooking the lagoon with a design reminiscent of ancient Mayan architecture; a range of unique shops and restaurants, including a good food court.

El Embarcadero

This waterfront emporium is worth a visit for the range of activities on offer: craft shops, a Mexican restaurant, the Museum of Popular Mexican Art, the Mexican Fair and the Rotating Scenic Tower. Boats bound for Isla Mujeres depart from the quay and the Teatro de Cancún (theater) regularly brings plays, concerts and other events to Cancún from Mexico City and elsewhere.

Markets

Ki Huic and Plaza Garibaldi are *mercados de artesanías* or craft markets located in the middle of Tulum Avenue in downtown Cancún. Vendors stock crafts from all over the country. Markets let visitors mix with the locals and practice their Spanish. In addition to greengrocers, butchers and herbalists, traditional mercados have such typically Mexican shops like *dulcerías* (candy stores) which also carry *piñatas*. For neighborhood mercados that also carry crafts try Mercado 28, behind the Post Office, or Mercado 23, at Tulum and Chichén Itzá avenues. Downtown malls include Plaza Las Américas, Chinatown, Plaza Bonita (next to Market 28), Plaza Las Avenidas, Las Palmas and Cancún 2000. The major supermarkets are Walmart, Comercial Mexicana, Chedraui, Gigante, Sam's Club and Costco.

Mexican handicrafts

Mexico is a country of artisans and her handicrafts are among the country's greatest assets. Every region produces something different and Cancún brings it all together. Silver from Taxco, rugs from Oaxaca, Talavera pottery from Puebla, textiles from Chiapas – it's all here, indeed the variety and selection is almost overwhelming. The wonderful thing about handicrafts is that every object is a singular work of art, an expression of traditional beliefs and a unique representative of the country in which it was made.

Other shopping centers

Apart from American-style megamalls, there are many strip malls and craft markets in the Hotel Zone filled with everything from textiles to Talavera. Most will be a short walk or taxi ride from your hotel. The most popular of these are: El Parián, a cluster of shops, banks, nightclubs and restaurants next door to the Convention Center; Coral Negro Market, adjacent to the Party Center, more than sixty shops showcasing handicrafts; El Zócalo, just across the road, a craft 'market'; La Mansión-Costa Blanca, upscale shops and restaurants; Plaza La Fiesta, a department store of folk art, gold and silver jewelry; and Plaza Lagunas, Plaza Mayafair, Plaza Las Velas, Plaza Nautilus and Plaza Terramar are combination shopping mall and office complexes. Most stores are open 9am.-10pm. Most plazas usually have exchange houses, many have automatic tellers.

Colorful creations

Mexico's craftsmen and women have created a world inhabited by fantastic creatures of every imaginable color, shape and form. Watch for objects in jade, bronze, tin, copper and onyx; sterling silver and gold filigree jewelry, household ornaments and tableware (a real bargain); handcarved hardwoods (furnishings and adornments); furniture; papier mâché and handmade figures in clay; trees of life, glass,

piñatas, musical instruments, ceremonial masks, Panama hats, cowboy sombreros, baskets, rugs, sarapes or blankets, shawls, ethnic clothing (huipils and guayabera shirts), hammocks, amate or bark paper paintings, wooden toys, *alebrijes* (strange, brightly colored creatures carved from wood), leather (shoes, boots, bags and jackets) and objects of woven palm.

Luxury merchandise

Cancún is a free port and merchandise from around the world is sold here, especially perfumes, cosmetics, watches, crystal, clothing, sporting and leather goods. Precious and semiprecious stones are available at fabulous savings.

The selection of diamonds, sapphires, rubies, amethysts, topazes, emeralds and pearls is, again, amazing and the sales people, if not professional gemologists, know what they're talking about. All pieces /stones come with written guarantees of quality.

Cigars

Cancún is smokin' when it comes to an international selection of premium cigars. Many cigar aficionados, particularly visitors from the United States, are thrilled to find commercial humidors stocked with habanos and fine Mexican cigars such as Cruz Real and Te Amo. Mexico controls but does not prohibit the importation of cigars from Cuba and from the other cigar-rolling nations of the Caribbean. Watch for Cohiba, Montecristo, Bolívar, Romeo y Julieta and others. To avoid bogus habanos check for green splotches on the box and wrappers, the green and white Cuban Government seal and factory code and the Hecho en Cuba legend. Premium Cuban cigars usually sell for $14 to $30 dollars apiece while Mexican cigars range from $4 to $10 dollars each.

Mexican silver

Mexico outshines other countries when it comes to silver. What began as an ancient art is now a modern-day symbol of national pride. After the Conquest, Mexico was one of the first New World nations to mine and ship quantities of silver overseas, and it is still a leader in silver production today. Talented silversmiths produce fabulous jewelry, original creations and reproductions of pre-Hispanic designs, encrusted with semi-precious stones, everything from rings, necklaces and earrings to unusual decorative items. Wide selections in engraved and filigree pieces including flasks, boxes and cases can be found in most markets and malls. To be sterling silver, the piece must bear the stamp "925", meaning 925 parts pure silver and 25 parts alloy (for strength).

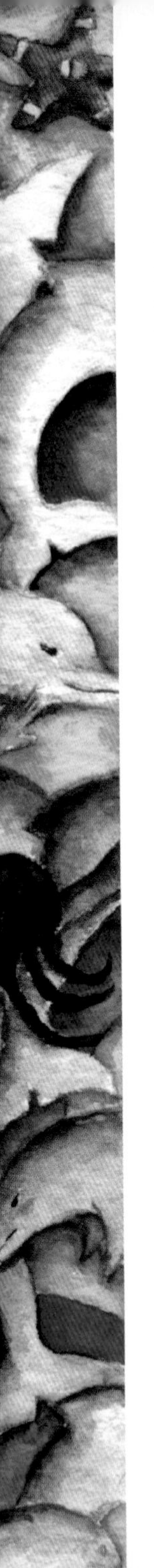

Eating out

There are well over 300 restaurants in Cancún, among them gourmet establishments and the world's most popular fast food. Every eatery has something special and just about every dining experience is available. Dinners can choose from Mexican, specialities from the four corners of the nation to boot, and a variety of international cuisines. The choice of eatery and ambiance is no less important, there are romantic, candelit bistros, tropical-style waterfront terrace restaurants and stylish cafés. Some feature live music and even floor shows. For those who cannot live without a hamburger or pizza, there are plenty of fast food outlets both in the Hotel Zone and Downtown.

Variety of cuisine

The cuisines of the world are well represented, in atmospheres that range from formal to food-court familiar, with prices to suit all wallets. Chinese, Japanese, American, Spanish, Argentinian, German, French, Italian, Arabian, Caribbean, Mexican, Yucatecan and so forth, and the seafood is great everywhere. Health food and vegetarian options are also available. Dinner theater and restaurants with truly sophisticated floor shows (Caribbean, Flamenco, Mexican themes) are yours for the asking. Consult a travel agent or any concierge for tips—and don't limit yourself; sample widely both downtown and in the Hotel Zone.

Variety matters

Visitors can embark on a worldwide culinary tour in Cancún's resort and urban areas. To kick off, there's Mexico's traditional and its haute cuisine which continue to attract tourists with tacos, enchiladas and the classic, *chiles en nogada*. There is Caribbean and Gulf seafood, beef from Sonora, Puebla's spicy *mole* and *chile poblano* dishes, plus Yucatecan mainstays such as *panuchos*, chicken or pork *pibil* and *sopa de lima*. There's a restaurant or eatery for every taste, budget, and agenda.

Most hotels and many independent restaurants serve sumptuous breakfast buffets and brunches which are a great way to sample Mexican dishes such as *molletes* (bread rolls or baguette spread with refried beans, cheese, and hot sauce), *chilaquiles* (a tortilla, chicken, cheese and tomato/chile casserole), *rajas con queso* (strips of poblano chile pepper in melted cheese and cream), and *huevos rancheros* (fried eggs on a tortilla bathed in hot sauce). Dinner is a stunning array of choices from home-style eateries to theme restaurants. Most close between 11 p.m. and midnight although fast-food chains and downtown, sidewalk cafes stay open until the early hours of the morning. Mexico's own version of fast food can be found in downtown stands and street-corner vendors selling *tortas* (sandwiches) *tacos, tamales* and *licuados* (fruit drinks). The clientele of downtown sidewalk cafes and taco stands are the locals, so menus may only be in Spanish and the waiters probably won't speak English.

Service

Cancún's high hospitality standards mean nothing less than first-class service. Accomplished chefs and food industry professionals from around the world are employed in Cancún's restaurants and hotels.

In Mexico it is considered an insult for waiters to submit a bill before it's requested so visitors must ask "La cuenta por favor", the bill please. Visitors who wish to pay in US dollars should note that change will be given in pesos. Expect the establishment's exchange rate to be lower than the bank's; this is only logical. And check operating hours carefully as many restaurants don't open for breakfast and lunch starts later in Mexico.

Nightlife

When the sun goes down, the city lights up. The Hotel Zone (and downtown, but to a lesser degree) is peppered with nightclubs, discos and restaurants that roll up the rug when the kitchen closes. There are salsa bars and reggae clubs, a variety of live music in lobby bars and rock 'n roll everywhere else. The discos are late-night affairs, the action starting around midnight.

Ballets folklóricos

During your stay, you might see Mexican folk dances performed as part of a dinner show or a Fiesta Mexicana theme night in a hotel. They are part of the nation's heritage; every region has its own dance, some date from the pre-Hispanic period or show clear Spanish influence, and others are lively renditions of later European dances such as the polka. Mexico does indeed cross the stage in a spectacle of song, music and dance. The most famous dances are the Jarabe Tapatio (Jalisco), the Yaqui Deer Dance (Sonora), the Dance of the Viejitos (Michoacán) and La Bamba from Veracruz, which is performed by graceful women in lacy white dresses. Xcaret Park stages a nightly Mexican theme show featuring a variety of colorful dances from all over the country and more than 250 performers.

Mexican aperitifs

Mexico's national drink, tequila, is a vacation must.The liquor is distilled from the fermented juice of the blue agave plant. Tequila ages anywhere from seven months to seven years. Younger tequilas are colorless and labeled *blanco*. The expensive aged tequilas called *añejado*, are golden. Mexicans drink tequila in two ways, either by licking salt from the hand, knocking back the shot, then sucking a lime, or by drinking it straight, with a chaser of *sangrita*, a chile and tomato preparation. *Mezcal* is also made from an agave, look for the worm in the bottle. Mexican beers are international favorites and wines are also coming into their own, gaining recognition in foreign markets.

Fiestas Mexicanas

Fiestas Mexicanas are staged by the bigger hotels. Shows usually feature a cockfight and rope tricks by cowboy showmen called *charros*, mariachi music, folk dancing, a Mexican cuisine buffet and handicraft exhibits. Consult any travel agent or the concierge.

Bars

Cancún's bar scene offers an earlier start to the evening, less crowds, and generally no cover charge. Big, TV screen sports bars, happy hour at hotel lobby bars, spectacular ocean or lagoon-front bars, rock or movie memorabilia bars, plus theme restaurant-bars serve up cocktails for any mood or occasion. The party hearty set prefer bars with live music, dancing waiters, hip disc jockeys, crazy drinking contests and shots of tequila provided by roving waitresses. In downtown Cancún, visitors can experience real Mexican *cantinas* (bars) with complimentary *botanas* (snacks) as well as a variety of less touristy restaurant bars. Your choice of music ranges from rock to reggae, mellow jazz, guitar, string quartets and solo pianists.

Discos

The club scene in Cancún rivals that of any big city. Glamorous, high-tech discos and nightclubs feature the latest light and sound systems. Discos aren't 'happening' until midnight and don't close before dawn. Most charge a cover ranging from $10 to $20 USD. Watch for special events like Ladies Night, Latin Music Night, 80's Retro, hard body contests etc. Everybody dresses for the disco and you've lots of latitude. Expect lines during the high season. Live-music alternatives are the Salsa or Caribbean music clubs which import top Cuban talent for a taste of the real thing.

Mexican music

Mexico's true language is music. Mariachis, Yucatecan trios and marimba are standard for the region, though Mariachi is the quintessential Mexican sound. Hire them on the spot along Yaxchilán Ave, Downtown, where they congregate nightly. The cost of a serenade is agreed after a session of bargaining which takes place when the musicians state their initial fee. When the singers approach your table ask them how much they charge per song, you may think that the serenade is free.

Night Cruises

Dinner cruises are popular in Cancún. Some focus on romance, others on the party. The romance and lobster set sail on the Nichupté Lagoon, while the booze cruises pop over to Isla Mujeres for a buffet dinner, a variety show and lots of fun and games on the beach. Vessels range from Spanish galleons to motor cruisers to Mississippi paddle boats. Check departure times for ships leaving at sunset for some breathtaking views.

The city of Cancún

The city of Cancún was planned with the same creativity as the Hotel Zone using a design that called for huge residential blocks, called *supermanzanas* with interconnecting walkways and gardens. Major thoroughfares and avenues were named after great Mayan cities; the cross streets after the region's animal and plant life, geographical features and places throughout Mexico.

Tulum Avenue

Running north to south, Tulum is the 'main drag' downtown. This broad, tree-lined boulevard is covered from one end to the other with flea markets (handicrafts!) shops, boutiques, pharmacies, money exchange houses, perfumeries, banks, cinemas, bowling alleys, restaurants, bars, malls, and supermarkets. City Hall, the Police, Tourism and Fire departments, as well as the bus terminal abut Avenida Tulum.

Other avenues

Yaxchilán Avenue, further 'inland' from Tulum, is another important thoroughfare located at the very hub of the community. It is lined with small hotels, shops, bars, restaurants, pharmacies, hospitals and vets.

Avenida Cobá is the extension of Kukulcán Blvd (the Hotel Zone highway). Running west to east, it moves traffic from one part of town to the other. For several blocks after crossing Tulum, Cobá is host to a supermarket, hospital, and a plethora of small businesses – florists, video centers, travel agencies and a few restaurants.

Avenida Bonampak is the first light you hit coming out of the Hotel Zone. It's hard to miss, since one corner is occupied by a gas station and the intersection itself by a huge fountain. Running north-south, it parallels Avenida Tulum, and like Tulum runs into López Portillo at its northern end. The bullring or Plaza de Toros is located at its southern end. Other important avenues are Uxmal, Chichén Itzá, Kabah, Náder, Sunyaxchén, Xel-Há (location of the post office), Tankah and José López Portillo.

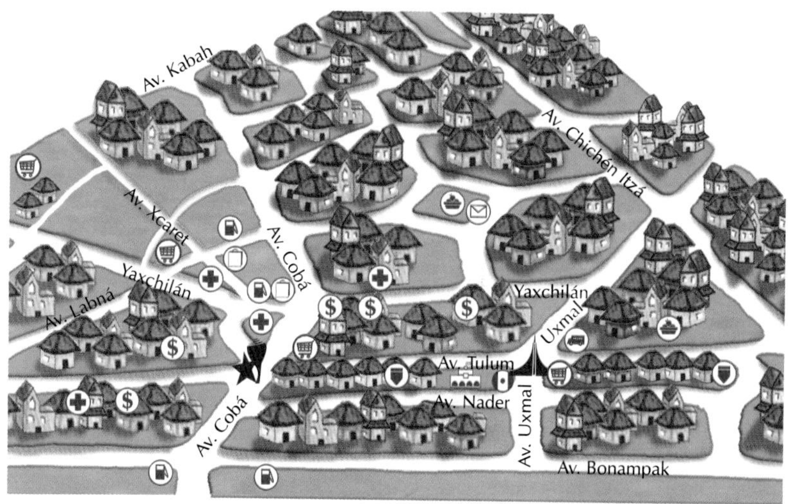

Cancún City

Bank	($)
Bus Station	
Mail	
Police station	
Gas station	
Market	
Immigration	
Hospital	

Future growth

Mexico's fastest growing resort is even now engaged in several projects, a continuation of the Mexican Government's, Cancún Master Plan, a program for growth that is ecologically sensitive. An undeveloped area southwest of the Hotel Zone, towards the airport, is poised for more hotels, housing, golf courses and a modern hospital. North of the Hotel Zone, Puerto Cancún is slated for construction; a luxury marina with low-rise hotels and waterfront properties.

Cancún & the business world

The business world has been captivated by Cancún's world-class convention infrastructure. The state-of-the-art Convention Center, largest in the Caribbean, has made Cancún an international hub for meetings, incentive travel and trade shows. The facility has 54,000 feet of meeting space, 22 salons including a press room, a ballroom and a modern sound and communications system. Some of the larger hotels also have their own convention centers. Trained in-house staff at the hotels and Convention Center offer a full range of services and technical support.

Local destination management firms and other companies provide a range of services: audiovisual support and equipment, display/exhibition gear, booth rentals, translation and intrepretation services, theme parties, customized merchandise, transportation and tours for conventioneers and their guests. Many restaurants specialize in groups, and are pleased to design special menus or cater an event, banquet or a theme party.

Convention Center

CONSULT THE TOURIST DIRECTORY

El Rey

Although Cancún was inhabited during the Late pre-Classic (300 B.C. - A.D. 100), the ancient temples in the area are much later. El Rey is the most accessible ancient Mayan site in or near the city. It is located in the Hotel Zone at km 17.5 (opposite Delfines Beach). The structures at El Rey are Late Postclassic period (1250-1550) and include 16 buildings, two plazas and two ceremonial walkways on a stretch of land overlooking the Nichupté Lagoon. The architectural style is in keeping with other contemporary sites such as Tulum, Xel-Há and El Meco. This supports the theory that the inhabitants of El Rey had trade and cultural ties with other coastal communities. Structure 3B is the best preserved building in the group. You can visit the site during the day and return at night (from 5 p.m.) for a show that includes a walk through the ruins, a visit to a Mayan village to see what life was like before the Conquest, dinner featuring regional specialties and the reenactment of an ancient legend.

El Meco

The most important mainland site in the Cancún area is El Meco, located north of downtown Cancún in the Isla Mujeres municipio or district.

Access to the site is off the Puerto Juárez-Punta Sam highway, right before the ferry dock at Punta Sam (the northernmost of the two docks in the area.)

El Meco is a post-Classic site that may have been one of the more important communities in northern Quintana Roo.

The site's civic-religious center has 14 structures still standing, among them, the tallest in this part of Quintana Roo from whose top there is an excellent view of Chacmochchuc Lagoon and the Caribbean. El Meco is protected by marshlands and mangroves and looks out over the Caribbean.

Take insect repellent if you decide to visit the site.

Clay figure, Cancún Museum

Other sites in the Hotel Zone

The few ancient remnants of the Pok-ta-Pok Golf Course (Pok-ta-Pok means ball game in Maya) were preserved in situ; a structure called Yamil Lu'um is located on the grounds of the Sheraton Hotel, and San Miguelito, another spot, is located across the street from Royal Mayan.

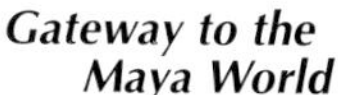

Gateway to the Maya World

Cancún certainly lives up to its name. Travel agencies offer a range of day trips to the archaeological sites in the area such as Tulum, Cobá and Chichén Itzá (Yucatán). Longer excursions will take you to Uxmal and the Puuc Route (Kabah, Sayil, Xlapak and Labná) in the Yucatán, to the ancient cities of Kohunlich and Dzibanché in southern Quintana Roo, to Palenque in Chiapas, and further afield to Tikal in Guatemala and Copán in Honduras.

Cancún Museum

Located next to the Convention Center in the Hotel Zone, the museum operates under the auspices of the Instituto Nacional de Antropología e Historia. It boasts a good collection of exhibits pertaining to the Mayan presence in Quintana Roo. Artifacts on display include the stone and stucco head from El Rey, clay figurines of men, women and animals from the island of Jaina in Campeche, stelae unearthed at Cobá and San Gervasio on Cozumel and incense burners from Dzibanché, carved jade, stone carvings, rings, bracelets and necklaces made from carved shells and pot shards.

The museum frequently stages exhibitions and art shows by local and nationally acclaimed artists.

Museum of Mexican Popular Art

Located in El Embarcadero, this museum gathers the finest handicrafts from all over Mexico under one roof. The collection is organized by theme: religion, music, dance, toys, the kitchen, traditional dress, among others, and divided into sections. Visitors who want to learn more about Mexican life and history will love this museum. Some of the items on display are also available for purchase in the on-site shop.

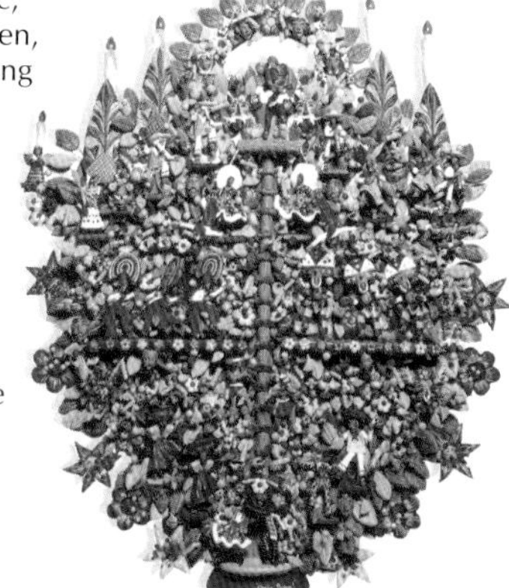

CONSULT THE TOURIST DIRECTORY

Cancún hotels

Whether it's business or pleasure, visitors can count on around 140 hotels with over 26,200 rooms to suit every taste and budget. Cancún hosts around three million tourists a year with more hotels planned for future development. Twenty percent of properties are Gran Turismo or deluxe, Mexico's highest category, exceeding even five-star standards. Luxurious beachfront properties, all-inclusive resorts, family oriented hotels, conference and golf resorts, and private condominiums fill the 14-mile long Hotel Zone, overlooking both the open Caribbean and the Nichupté Lagoon. In addition to famous-name Mexican hotels, prestigious European, North American and Japanese chains have properties in Cancún. Beachfront hotels have the highest rates and cheaper accommodation is available in the vicinity of the Cancún Golf Course and in downtown Cancún. Room services in downtown hotels range from the bare minimum (hot water and ceiling fans) to full amenities such as air-conditioning, pools, gyms, restaurants and bars. An easy-to-use bus system provides affordable transportation to and from the beach area.

Services

Sterling service, world-class chefs and multilingual staff personify Cancún's hotels and resorts. Services for luxury hotels include giant pools with swim-up bars, tennis courts, spas, gyms, beauty parlors, boutiques, restaurants, kids' clubs, nightclubs and mini markets. They also have tour and car rental desks and water sports centers. Room amenities include mini bars, safes, cable or satellite TV and balconies with ocean views.

While most hotels offer meeting rooms, a few specialize in conventions and have the installations, equipment and staff necessary to cater large events.

Dozens of hotels now operate all-inclusive packages covering accommodation, unlimited food, drink, evening entertainment, water sports and use of the gym.

The larger hotels often have nurses or doctors on call for emergencies.

Other accommodation options include timeshares or fully furnished condos and villas that rent by the day, week or month.

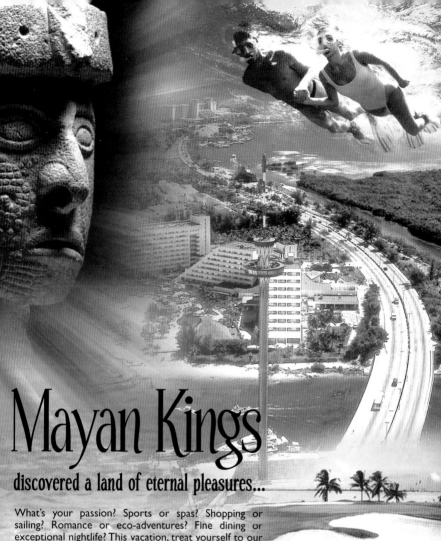

The Islands

In addition to Cozumel – Mexico's largest inhabited island and a tourist destination in itself – Cancún is flanked by the smaller islands of Isla Mujeres, Contoy and Holbox. All of them are lovely bits of coral-based terra firma, covered with sand and basking in the sun.

Holbox is 10 km off the northern tip of the Yucatán Peninsula. It spreads for 40 km, east to west, linking the Gulf of Mexico with the Caribbean Sea. It is riddled with wetlands and only two kilometers across at its widest point. The locals are fishermen and birding is spectacular.

Contoy is a federally-protected bird sanctuary located north of Cancún, east of Cabo Catoche [the tip of the peninsula]. The island is 7.3 km long, 800 m wide, and home to both resident and migratory species.

Isla Mujeres is the most popular of the northern islands, and certainly the easiest to reach. There are day trips and a regular ferry service from Cancún. Only seven km long, a kilometer wide, Isla is a destination in itself. Playa Norte has the best beaches and most of the action. Isla is provincial Mexico and very different from its younger, flashier sister across the bay. People come for a weekend and stay the month.

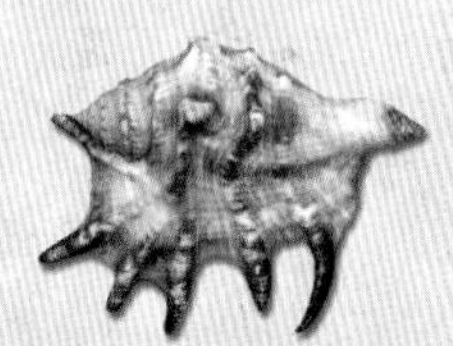

The chain of islands off the coast of northern Quintana Roo are the treasures of the Mexican Caribbean: Isla Mujeres, Contoy, habitat of countless sea birds, and Holbox, a remote and little-visited island of fishermen.

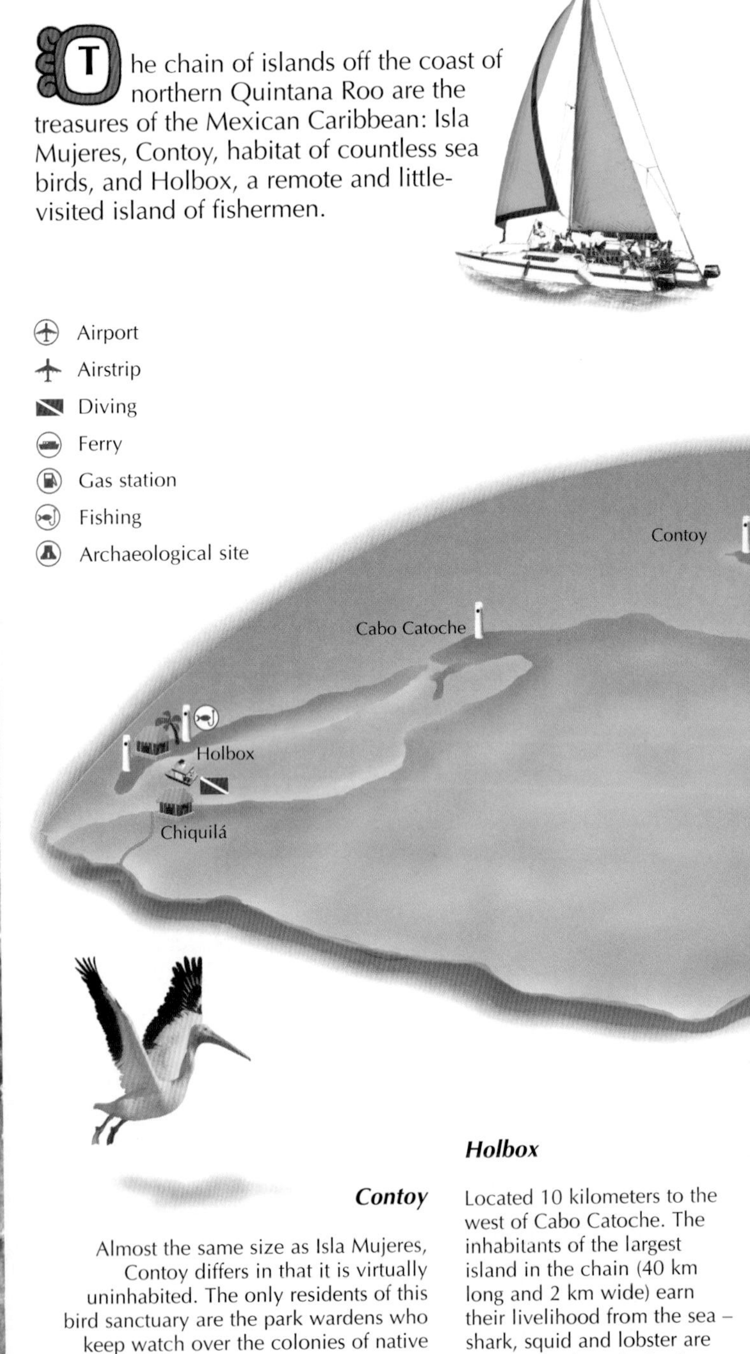

Contoy

Almost the same size as Isla Mujeres, Contoy differs in that it is virtually uninhabited. The only residents of this bird sanctuary are the park wardens who keep watch over the colonies of native and migrant sea birds and waders. Trips to Contoy are available in Cancún.

Holbox

Located 10 kilometers to the west of Cabo Catoche. The inhabitants of the largest island in the chain (40 km long and 2 km wide) earn their livelihood from the sea – shark, squid and lobster are the principal catch. Ferries depart from the mainland port of Chiquilá.

Isla Mujeres

A short boat ride from Cancún, this tiny island is the laid-back Caribbean of yesteryear, something which makes it a very popular day trip destination. Passenger boats depart from Puerto Juárez, Punta Sam and several docks in the Hotel Zone.

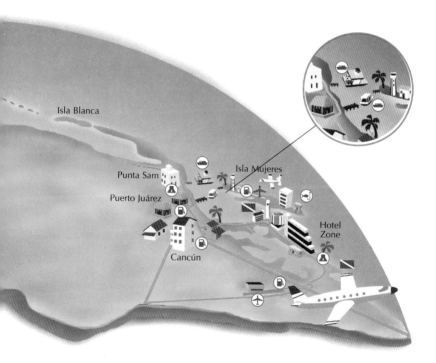

Isla Blanca
Punta Sam
Puerto Juárez
Isla Mujeres
Hotel Zone
Cancún

CONSULT THE TOURIST DIRECTORY

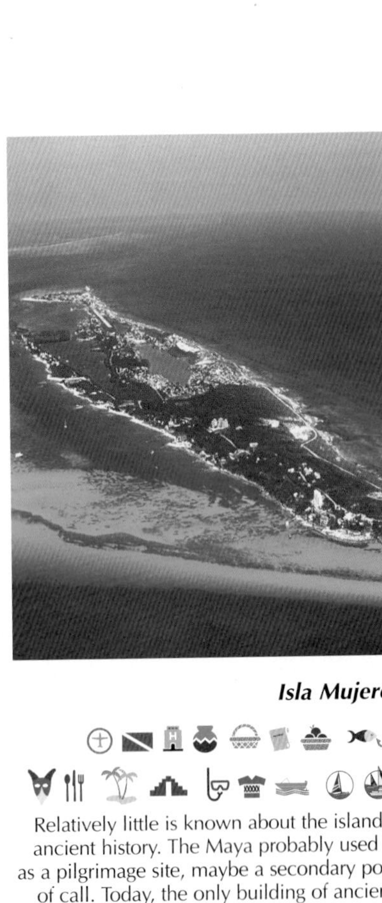

Isla Mujeres

Relatively little is known about the island's ancient history. The Maya probably used it as a pilgrimage site, maybe a secondary port of call. Today, the only building of ancient Mayan construction is a small stone edifice (temple or lighthouse) standing alone on the island's southern tip.

How the island got its name

There are several versions of this tale. According to Francisco López de Gómara, when the Spanish explorer Francisco Hernández de Córdoba anchored off the island in 1517, he reported the existence of feminine idols at a shrine and called the place Punta or Isla Mujeres ('Point' or 'Isle of Women'); this version is the most widely accepted. Another version asserts that when the Spaniards first set foot on the isle, the local men were out fishing, leading the visitors to believe that the sole inhabitants were women. Another states that the Mayan name of the island was Ixchel (the Mayan goddess of fertility, who was apparently associated with the island in some capacity) and that young virgins were sent there before marriage so that the goddess would bless them with fertility and problem-free pregnancies.

Pirates

During the pirate heyday of the 17th and 18th centuries, ocean-going scalliwags and desperados of every stripe sailed the Caribbean, raiding mainland cities for gold, silver, dyewood and supplies, the various inhabited islands and each other. They sought refuge on Isla Mujeres and probably treated the island as a supplies station, picking up water and salt.

Isla's Macax Lagoon was a sheltered harbor for the likes of Henry Morgan and Jean Lafitte. The last pirate to visit Isla Mujeres was slave trader/pirate Fermín Mundaca, who fell in love with an island girl called "La Trigueña." Unhappily for him she scorned his suit and to win her heart, Mundaca built an elegant hacienda that he hoped to share with her. It was not to be, however, La Trigueña married another and Mundaca spent his final days in Mérida where he succumbed to drink and a broken heart. The ruins of the hacienda are located in the southern part of the island and are worth a visit. Mundaca's tomb lies in the island cemetery and is marked by a skull and crossbones.

Hacienda Mundaca

Island activities

In spite of its reduced size, the island is full of things to see and do. The northern tip of the island is known as Playa Norte or Cocos and it is the finest beach on the island. Powder white sand, shallow, calm and crystal-clear waters mean that it is ideal for swimming and windsurfing, sunbathing or even sunset watching.

Shopping

Isla's narrow streets are full of shops stocking beachware and handicrafts from all over Mexico. Look for pottery, wood carvings, Panama hats, weavings from Chiapas and Oaxaca, Yucatecan hipiles, textiles, hammocks, obsidian, onyx, local art and Mayan-style carved shells. The island is famous for the fine gold and silver jewelry created by local jewelers.

A trip round the island

Getting your bearings on Isla is easy. The village is on the northern tip of the island, just a short stroll from Playa Cocos, also known as Playa Norte, and right behind the harbour. Colorful wooden houses, shops, bars and restaurants line the bustling streets that lead on to the main square. Most island eateries specialize in seafood which is served in a variety of delicious ways.

To explore the island take a taxi or rent a moped, bike or golf cart from one of the rentals in the village. Visitors wishing to take their own car over to the island can do so from Punta Sam. Traveling south along the road from the village will take you to Hacienda Mundaca, several beaches, the Turtle Farm and the dolphin enclosure. El Garrafón Park and the lighthouse on the southern tip of the island. The rocky east coast of the island is picturesque but not recommended for swimming.

Lodging

Accommodation on Isla Mujeres runs from the sophisticated hideaways of the rich and famous: exclusive five-star hotels, elegant b&b's and luxury waterfront condos, to four, three and two-star inns. There's something for every taste and every budget. Reserve well in advance during international holidays: Christmas, New Year and Easter (March or April).

Diving and Snorkeling

Diving and snorkeling are such major draws, they deserve special mention. There are many reefs between Isla Mujeres and the mainland. Some are close enough to the surface you can enjoy them without diving, and so tours often include snorkelers. Of note are the reefs in the El Garrafón area, El Farito which lies in shallow waters and is ideal for free diving and Los Manchones, so named for the coral buttresses which reach heights of between three and five meters. Also of interest to divers are the Cruz, a bronze cross which as an alternative dive site relieves pressure on nearby reefs and the sunken statue of the Virgin. Both are located in the bay and islanders make an annual pilgrimage in honor of the Virgin. There are dive shops in the dock area and on the beaches.

Sportfishing

Everything that applies to Cancún by way of fishing, applies to Isla Mujeres, the same fishing grounds of La Grieta and La Corrientada, and a fishing tournament during billfish season (April to August). In addition, the island hosts an international sailing regatta, the object of which is a race from St. Petersburg, Florida to Isla Mujeres the last days in April.

Boat trips

In Puerto Juárez on the mainland or on Isla itself, the local fishermen offer day trips to and around the island. The round trip fare includes a seafood lunch (fresh fish caught and prepared during the voyage), a visit to one of the beaches on the west coast of Isla Mujeres and a spot of snorkeling.

"El Garrafón"

This pretty bay is one of the most popular spots for snorkeling and diving and exploring the underwater world. Visitors can also spend a day in a hammock or by the pool, enjoy the view from the Rotating Scenic Tower or take a stroll along the cliff path to Punta Sur, the site of a tiny Mayan temple dedicated to the goddess Ixchel.

The Sculpture Park

This park on Punta Sur was the brainchild of Mexican sculptor, Sebastián. He gathered Mexican and international artists to donate a sample of their work to be exhibited at the site. Manuel Felguérez, Eduardo Stein, José Luis Cuevas, Sebastián, Pedro Cervantes, Helen Escobedo are just some of the Mexican artists who participated in this creative encounter, along with 11 more from overseas. The view of the colorful and multiform sculptures, added to that of Punta Sur and the Caribbean, is spectacular.

The island today

Isla Mujeres is a laid-back provincial island, half Caribbean and half Mexican. Its people are fishermen, divers and shopkeepers by vocation and inclination. Nobody's in a rush, everybody knows everybody, and foreigners are welcome. Since the late 50s, the island has been a destination in its own right and visitors measure their stays in weeks, not days. The locals get around on mopeds and bikes. Downtown Isla is a cluster of shops, informal restaurants and cafés, and bars where the strains of reggae, salsa, rock, jazz and romantic ballads can be heard. Dinner or a drink at a waterfront restaurant or bar on Playa Norte or Cocos is an enjoyable way to spend the evening.

VERÁS

Ramón Bravo

Born in Piedras Negras in Coahuila, in 1926, Ramón Bravo was a underwater cameraman and a tireless conservationist who astonished the world with his wonderful photos of reefs, coral colonies and other marine life. He lived on Isla Mujeres for many years and knew every minute detail of the Quintana Roo coast from Holbox to Chetumal Bay. He broke the news of the Cave of Sleeping Sharks and made many documentaries on the Mexican Caribbean, some of which received awards in Mexico and abroad. He also published seven books and worked on several films on the underwater world, as a screenwriter and cameraman. He died on February 21, 1998 and the best way to honor his life is to continue with his conservation work.

CONSULT THE TOURIST DIRECTORY

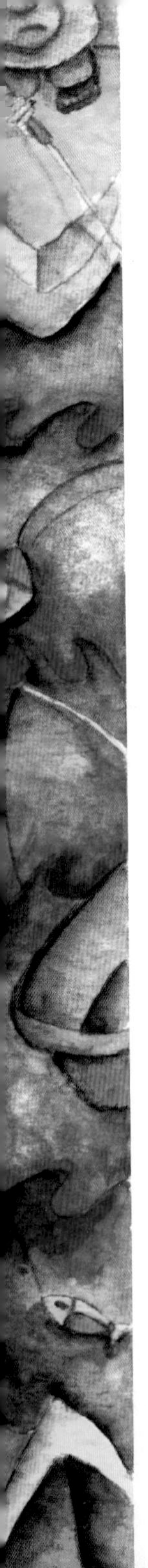

Contoy

Isla Contoy

This federally-protected bird sanctuary and special biosphere reserve is located about two hours by boat from Cancún, to the north of Isla Mujeres and Isla Blanca. With the exception of a science and research station, it is uninhabited and overnight stays are prohibited. Contoy is about seven kilometers long, less than a kilometer wide and covered with sand dunes, mangroves, shallow lagoons and lovely beaches. There is a well of fresh water in the southern part of the island used by the occasional fisherman. A chain of reefs lies at depths of between three and five meters to the south of the island, this is the beginning of the Great Mayan Reef. Contoy is the permanent or seasonal home of 100 resident and migratory bird species. Residents include brown pelican, roseate spoonbills, magnificent frigatebirds, cormorants, ibis, terns (see right) and herons. From May to October, hawksbill and loggerhead turtles come ashore to lay their eggs. A small museum located near the island's only dock acquaints visitors with island ecology. Two companies offer all-day excursions to Contoy.

Holbox

Quintana Roo's northernmost island, Holbox is home to a population of fishermen who work the rich fishing grounds off Cabo Catoche. It is one of Quintana Roo's best kept secrets, a tranquil refuge perfect for nature lovers.

The village

The village is rustic and the atmosphere is friendly: sandy streets lined with palm-thatched huts, wooden houses and a main square with a bandstand. Several small restaurants serve fresh seafood and there are comfortable, sometimes even luxurious, tropical-style thatched *cabañas* (bungalows) for rent along the waterfront. Holbox has been targeted for low-impact, low density tourist development and accommodation and dining options on the island are on the rise.

Where two seas meet

Cabo Catoche is the cape at the northern tip of the Yucatán Peninsula, and the place where the Caribbean meets the Gulf of Mexico in a mingling of turquoise, emerald and aquamarine waters. The combination of nutrient-laden ocean currents and the upwelling of cooler waters provide optimum conditions for marine life and the area is important for the fishermen of Holbox who bring in catches of shrimp, shark, octopus and a variety of fish. The island boasts a fine stretch of deserted shoreline ideal for beachcombing – a variety of shells of all shapes and sizes wash up on the sand. During the summer months the rare hawksbill turtle leaves the sea to lay its eggs on the island's shores. Prized for its carapace, used to make tortoiseshell, the hawksbill is now protected by international law.

A world of birds

Local fishermen will rent their boats for trips to the Yalahau lagoon (also known as Conil lagoon) where countless species of bird nest in the mangroves and marshes, the Isla de Pajaros (Bird Island), Isla Morada and the Ch'ich islet. Great blue and boat-billed herons, great white, snowy and reddish egrets, brown and white pelicans, ibis, roseate spoonbills, osprey and the occasional flock of flamingos, are just some of the species that can be spotted during the excursion. Dolphins sometimes play in the wakes of boats crossing the lagoon. Yalahau and the surrounding marshes are part of the Yum Balam Reserve.

Surrounding areas

Boat trips can also be arranged to Ojo de Agua Yalahau, a freshwater spring/cenote in the mangroves on the mainland and to the Río Lagartos Reserve in the Yucatán. True adventurers might be able to persuade a fisherman to take them to through the lagoon, mangroves and jungle to Boca Iglesia, the ruins of a 16th-century church. This colonial monument is all that remains of a shortlived Spanish garrison founded during the first expedition to conquer the Maya. Cabo Catoche and Boca Iglesia are in the area known as Ekab. An important chiefdom in ancient times, it was one of the first to be visited by the Spaniards in 1517. Unexplored Mayan ruins dot the area.

Getting to Holbox

Take Highway 180 to Nuevo Xcan. En route you'll pass through the villages of Leona Vicario, Valladolid Nuevo and Cristóbal Colón, among others. Look out for roadside stalls selling embroidered dresses and blouses, citrus fruit and plants. At Nuevo Xcan take the road north to Kantunilkín and the port of Chiquilá. It's a three-hour drive and there are many potholes. The ferry from Chiquilá takes 30 minutes to Holbox and the last boat is at 5 p.m. If you miss it one of the local fishermen will ferry you across in his water taxi.

Riviera Maya

The allure of Quintana Roo extends beyond Cancún; in fact, Cancún is just the beginning. From the resort to the ancient city of Tulum a series of destinations runs down the coast. This part of the state is called the Riviera Maya.

Carretera 307 covers the length of this 130-km strip, flanked by jungle and occasionally interrupted by roads shooting off at right angles. These lead to the Riviera Maya's towns and resort communities, as well as its stunning, white-sand beaches. The coast is set with cenotes, coves and ancient ruins, and the Great Maya Reef is just offshore.

During ancient times, the eastern coast of the Yucatán Peninsula was a thriving trade area. After the Conquest the region became a wilderness and stayed that way until the early 1900s when foreign companies began exploiting the area's chicle resin and its precious hardwoods.

Moving south from Cancún, the most interesting stops along the Riviera Maya are: Puerto Morelos, Playa del Carmen, Xcaret, Puerto Aventuras, the chain of beaches from Xpu-Há to Akumal, Xel-Há and Tulum. Cozumel lies off the coast from Playa del Carmen and the ancient city of Cobá is a short drive from Tulum.

The Riviera Maya spreads out along Highway 307, the road to state capital Chetumal. There are road works on some stretches of the route further south so please heed warning signs and reduce speed. The entrances to the various resorts and communities is clearly marked, look for signs on your left (north-south direction). Some of the access roads are paved, others are dirt roads and conditions vary. They cut through areas of jungle and mangrove before reaching the beach.

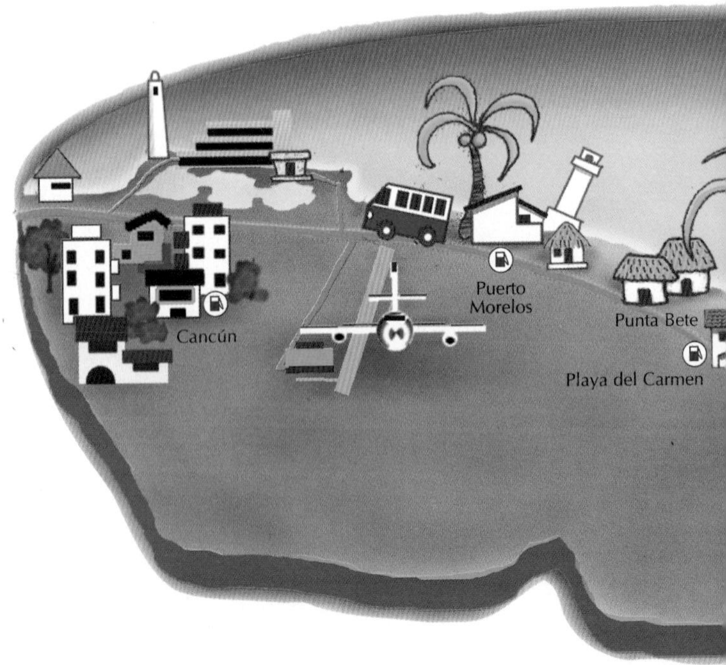

Cobá and Sian Ka'an

Cobá can be reached from the Riviera Maya; you'll see the signpost for the turnoff in Tulum. The Sian Ka'an Biosphere Reserve begins a few kilometers south of Tulum. To reach the fishing village of Punta Allen follow the coast road south from Tulum; after Boca Paila the pavement reverts to dirt track. For the archaeological site of Muyil (also in Sian Ka'an) continue on Highway 307 for about 20 minutes until you see the sign for Muyil.

Accommodation

Options range from deluxe to rustic; five star hotels with all the services, smaller inns and secluded tropical-style bungalows or *cabañas*. There are campsites in some parts of the Riviera, such as Paamul and Xpu-Há.

Trips to Cozumel

Getting to the island is easy. There are regular passenger ferry crossings from Playa del Carmen throughout the day, and a car ferry from Puerto Morelos.

Piers
Gas station
Cozumel
Paamul
Puerto Aventuras
Xcaret
Xpu-Há
Akumal
Xel-Há
Tulum
To Cobá

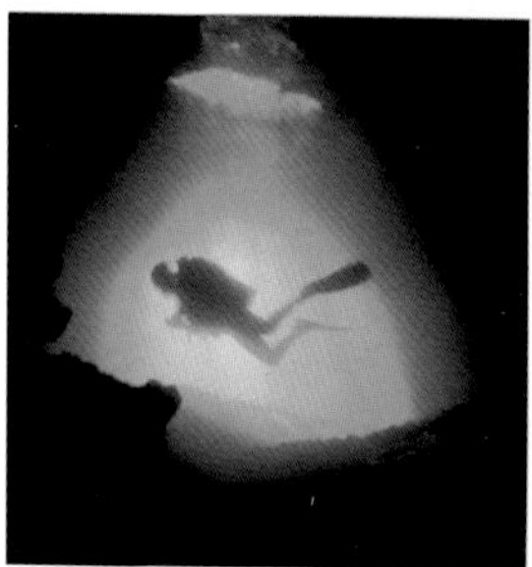

Development

The Riviera Maya has become an important destination in its own right and is growing all the time. Attractions are varied and there is something for everyone, from lovely beaches and nature parks to tourist resorts.

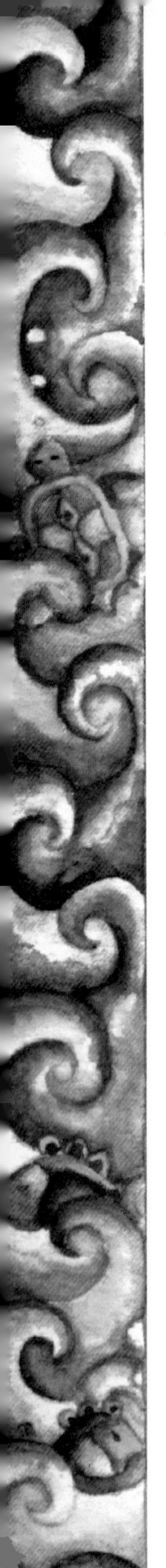

Puerto Morelos

Just 36 km south of Cancún is one of the oldest settlements on the coast, the quiet town of Puerto Morelos. The community has grown so much over the last ten years, that it had to spread west, across the highway and into the jungle. About 100 years ago it boomed as the region's hardwoods and chicle set sail for the U.S. and Europe through its port. Today the town is best known for its varied lodging: everything from large five-star hotels to budget inns and condominiums, and seafood restaurants. Its beaches are uncrowded and the section of the Great Maya Reef lying offshore has just been declared a national park.

The town square is lined with craft shops and restaurants, there's even a second-hand bookshop stocking a large selection of titles in English and Spanish. Sunday is a good day to visit for the square comes alive with the give and take of a small-scale fair.

Puerto Morelos is a fishing community and the seafood is understandably excellent. Accompanied by pelicans and flocks of gulls, you can watch the fishermen unload their catch on the quay and know that within a short time it will be on your plate in one of the waterfront restaurants.

A string of shops along the highway at the entrance of town hawks all manner of crafts; principal among them is the gentleman selling authentic Panama hats (which connoisseurs know come from Becal, Campeche and not Panama). He'll explain how the toppers are woven in the caves in his native Campeche where intense humidity keeps the fibers supple.

Car Ferries to Cozumel

Puerto Morelos is home of the car and freight ferries to Cozumel. The crossing takes about two and a half hours. People traveling to the island without freight or a car are encouraged to use the passenger ferries leaving from Playa del Carmen. Although there is a departure schedule, delays are frequent, up to several days at times.

CrocoCún

Back on the highway and just north of the turnoff to the town (32 km, 20 mins from Cancún) is the CrocoCún crocodile farm. CrocoCún breeds the Moreletti crocodile, the species most often found in the region. The jungle grounds are lovely and there are spacious enclosures housing other species native to the region such as spider monkeys, white-tailed deer and coatimundi. The entrance on the highway is well marked. Restaurant and gift shop on the premises.

Other sites of interest

Puerto Morelos has beaches just outside town, to reach them take the road south from the main square to Punta Estrella. Visitors can take a trip into the forest to learn about Mayan medicinal plants or travel inland along the Ruta de Cenotes, a route that will take them to several sinkholes and the chicle harvesters camp at Central Vallarta.

Dr. Alfredo Barrera Marín Botanical Garden

Located one kilometer south of Puerto Morelos, the Barrera Marín Botanical Garden protects over 60 acres of jungle and marshland vegetation. Sites of interest range from a post-Classic Mayan ruin to a replica of a chicle harvesters camp. There are areas devoted to wild orchids, bromeliads, cacti, agaves and medicinal plants and a nursery of native species, examples of traditional Mayan housing and a lookout tower for sweeping views of the area. Wildlife is plentiful, especially avifauna, and though the park doesn't open until 9 a.m., caretakers will let birders in at dawn. Spider monkeys, iguanas, foxes, agouti and great curassow are occasionally seen. Insect repellent is de rigeur.

En route to Playa del Carmen

This stretch of the corridor runs through jungle and grasslands past ranches big and small. Along the beach are several vacation housing and resort developments with names like Playa del Secreto and Playa Paraíso. Signposts indicate the access to beaches and resorts en route.

Rancho Grande

Horseback tours at Rancho Loma Bonita (east side of the highway) take riders through the jungle and along the beach for a look at cenotes and small lagoons.

Tres Ríos

Some 54 km to the south of Cancún is the Tres Ríos ecopark which gets its name from the crystal-clear "rivers" that flow through the mangroves. There are cenotes, areas of jungle, a salt marsh and a beach. Activities on offer include swimming, kayak, biking, horse riding, snorkeling and diving. Transport to the park is available from Cancún and Playa del Carmen.

Punta Bete

The turn-off for Punta Bete is 66 km south of Cancún (55 min.) and minutes before reaching Playa del Carmen. The beaches are lovely, the offshore reef is good for snorkeling and diving, and wildlife abounds in the jungle. There are bungalows, a campsite and a restaurant at Punta Bete and larger hotels at Posada Capitan Lafitte and Xcalacoco.

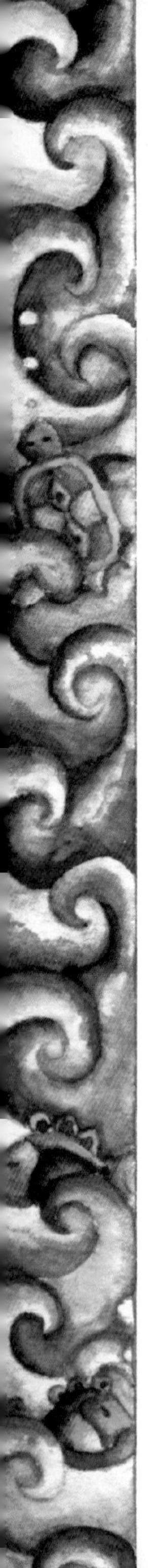

Playa del Carmen

Playa del Carmen (68 km) is the fishing village that has followed in the footsteps of Cancún and is now a boom town. Located halfway to Tulum, it is the ferry port for Cozumel and the nearest town to some of the state's biggest tourist attractions. Its cosmopolitan atmosphere has made it a favorite with Mexican and foreign tourists alike.

A brief history

Known as Xaman-Há in ancient times, Playa del Carmen was settled by fishermen from the pre-Classic period onwards, and was the embarkation point for the sacred island of Cozumel, site of a shrine dedicated to the goddess Ixchel. Women from all over the Yucatán made the perilous crossing to the island in open canoes. A few structures from the period are still visible in the town; the temple in Playacar is the most accessible.

Phenomenal growth

Playa is one of the fastest growing communities in Mexico, its thriving tourism sector a magnet for people from all over the country in search of employment and a new way of life. The town is also the home of a flourishing expat community, particularly Europeans, who fall in love with its laid-back Caribbean ambiance.

Mexican and foreign corporations and developers have also moved into the area, building deluxe hotels, restaurants, stores, bars and other tourism-related facilities, creating jobs, and transforming Playa into a truly international resort.

Despite the town's continued growth, a short walk from the bustling streets lie secluded beaches and small bays with few people in sight.

Accommodation options

Tourist services are on the increase in Playa del Carmen, on a par with the annual number of visitors to the popular beach destination. Finding a place to stay in Playa is never a problem, there are a variety of options in all price ranges and their number is growing all the time: 3,000 hotel rooms went up over the last two years. There are deluxe and five-star beachfront resorts with all the services, economical city hotels, inns, guest houses and waterfront cabañas or bungalows. Some of the larger hotels are all-inclusive and their rates include transport, room, meals, drinks and excursions; smaller hotels often offer European-style bed and breakfast plans. Located south of the pier, Playacar is the site of most of the largest hotels and there are several tropical-style bungalow and villa complexes to the north of town.

The town

Until a few years ago, Playa del Carmen was where you went to get to Cozumel. Only a few international visitors returned year after year to soak up the sun on its lovely beaches.
Today it's the second most important destination on the coast. Called Playa by initiates, the town is a lively community. The beaches are perfect, if slightly more populated than they were five years ago, there are reefs offshore and jungle nearby, and the ambience is unmistakably bohemian.

Caribbean ambiance

Quinta Avenida (fifth avenue) is the center of town and closed to all but foot traffic for half its length. A colorful enclave of restaurants, cafes, dive shops, one-of-a-kind boutiques, craft shops, smallish hotels and European-style B&Bs, La Quinta and its many cross streets is the grid of Playa's social and business life, the heart of its nightlife. Street musicians, artists, dancers and other impromptu-type performers such as mariachi bands and Yucatecan trios are a common sight, day and night.

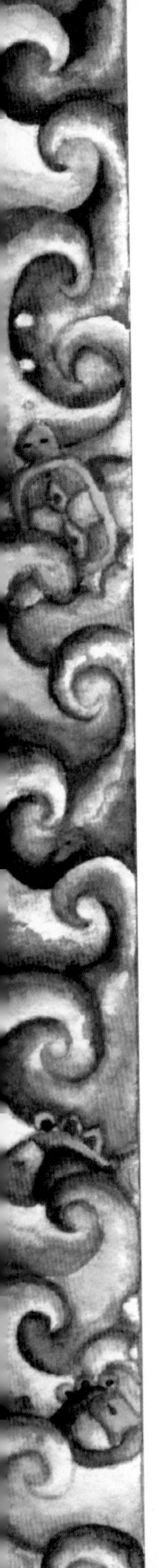

Exploring the area

Playa del Carmen is ideally located for exploring the area and local travel agencies and hotels offer a range of half-day and day trips to sites of interest in the Riviera Maya and further afield such as Chichén Itzá, Uxmal, Cozumel, Holbox, the archaeological sites in Southern Quintana Roo and Tikal in Guatemala.

Other trips on offer include jungle treks, cruises, horse riding and visits to Xcaret, Xel-Há, Tres Ríos, Xpu-Há and area cenotes.

What to do in Playa

The list of what to do in Playa is long and varied. You can sunbathe, windsurf, sail, kayak and skydive. Dive shops offer diving and snorkeling trips to the reefs in the Cozumel Marine Park and sites along the Riviera Maya. Sportfishing is excellent in the Cozumel Channel, and boats and equipment are available at local marinas. There's the nearby jungle and its cenotes to explore, an aviary at Playacar and the Tulum and Cobá ruins (post-Classic and Classic-post-Classic) just down the road.

Restaurant hopping is not such a bad idea either. The range of cuisine is almost overwhelming: Italian restaurants vie with Mexican, Yucatecan, seafood, Argentinian, Japanese and French. There's a plethora of natural eateries, salad and espresso bars, and so on ad infinitum. You could stay for three months and eat in a different place every day.

Nightlife

Local bars offer live music (reggae, rock, tropical, jazz, Mexican, Latin American, etc.) for listening and dancing. There are also a couple of discos.

Ferries to Cozumel

The ferry dock in Playa del Carmen is one of the town's busiest venues. Cozumel is the largest inhabited island in Mexico, the region's dive spot par excellence and a major destination in its own right since the 1950s. The island is visible from shore and the crossing takes from 40 to 50 minutes, depending on the wind. A boat leaves every 30 minutes, starting about 5 a.m. and the majority of these are modern, air-conditioned water jets. Dolphins can often be spotted during the crossing.

Playacar

Playacar is a fully-fledged community replete with a hotels, mall, restaurants, aviary, condos and villas. It spreads south from the ferry dock and can be accessed on foot at that point. The main entrance, is off the highway, about two kilometers south of the entrance to Playa del Carmen. The on-site 18-hole golf course is carved out of the jungle, includes cenotes and is considered one of the most challenging in the state.

Xaman-Há Aviary

Located on the grounds of Playacar, the aviary was created to protect, show and breed native birds, especially species in danger of extinction. Paved paths traverse 1.8 hectares of medium-growth tropical forest rich in birdlife. There are several small cenotes on the grounds.

The compound is presently home to over 200 birds belonging to 60 different species, among them macaws, parrots, great curassows, crested guans, motmots, toucans, ibis, herons, egrets, jacanas and flamingos. The most popular feature of the aviary is its walk-through cage, a huge space enclosed by nets that gives the impression of seeing these birds in the wild. In fact wild birds such as orioles, hummingbirds and turtle doves often venture into the cage.

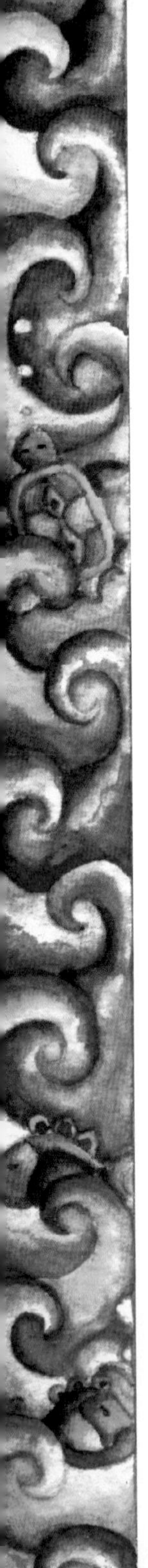

Xcaret

Xcaret is a nature-and-Mexican culture theme park located on the coast, at the site of an ancient settlement. It is 75 km south of Cancún, seven kilometers south of Playa del Carmen. The park encompasses an area of jungle, a natural inlet and a palm-fringed beach. There are so many activities going on that you really need a whole day here. Facilities include several sit-down restaurants and a number of snack bars and a shop. Round-trip transportation is available from Cancún for a reasonable fee. Departures at 9, 10 and 11 a.m. from the Xcaret Terminal at Playa Caracol in the Hotel Zone. Buses return to Cancún at 4:30 or 8 p.m.

History

Known as Polé during the post-Classic period, Xcaret was a major port of call for the seagoing Maya. Its cenotes may have been used for purification rituals enacted prior to a voyage, or to crossing the sea to visit the Ixchel sanctuary on Cozumel. The park is dotted with small archaeological sites from this era. In the main service area there is a small museum featuring scale reproductions of the Maya World's most important ancient cities.

In a remote area of the park lie the ruins of a chapel built by the Spaniards in the 16th century. By the time Cancún was under construction, the Polé acreage was in the hands of a local family who sold it to the creators of Xcaret in 1992. An example of ecologically compatible development, the park is one of the nation's showplaces.

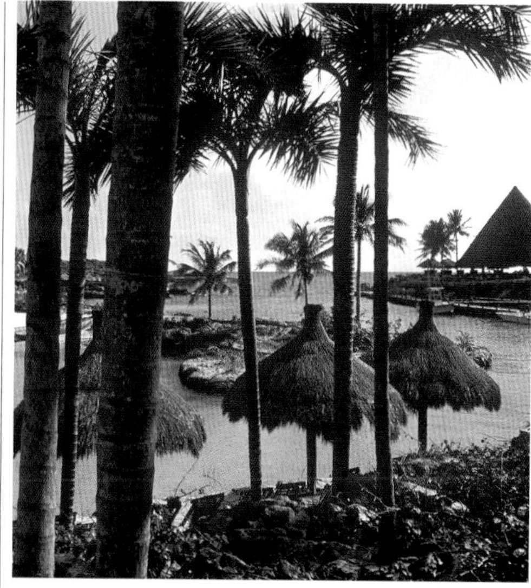

Underground rivers

The principal attractions are two underground rivers. They are part of the network of subterranean streams that honeycombs the Yucatán.

A world of attractions

Other features include an aquarium which showcases the different areas of a coral reef and its colorful inhabitants; a botanical garden with its collection of orchids and a mushroom farm; the butterfly farm; the island of jaguars and pumas and another one for monkeys; an aviary with a breeding program for endangered species; the bat cave, deer corner and a manatee pool; and the Mayan village. Activities range from horseback riding and swimming with dolphins to diving and snorkeling. The Rotating Scenic Tower offers panoramic views of the jungle and the Caribbean.

The Caleta area

The natural inlet or *caleta* is home to countless species of colorful fish which can be seen from the path. By the restaurant there is a sea turtle enclosure housing a number of these engaging reptiles, some hatchlings, others approaching adulthood. Xcaret collaborates with local authorities in the turtle conservation program. Eggs are collected from the nests and the young are kept in ponds until they are large enough to have a better chance of survival in the wild. On the other side of the rocks, the bay is perfect for sunbathing. This is also the site of one of the park's dolphin enclosures. Xcaret operates a popular dolphin program and has successfully bred a number of the animals, something which has won the park international acclaim.

Xcaret by night

"Xcaret de Noche" is the park's after dark program, and is well worth staying on for. It takes place in the Gran Tlachco, a thatched theater housing 6,000 people. The entertainment ranges from a Mayan ritual and the reenactment of the pre-Hispanic ball game, at one point with the rubber ball alight, to Mexican folk dances and the presentation of the Papantla flyers.

CONSULT THE TOURIST DIRECTORY

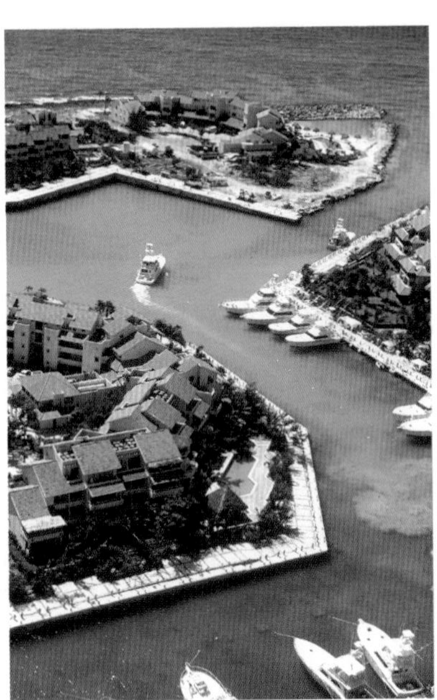

The beaches from Paamul to Xcacel offer some real delights: windswept shores, half moon bays and jungle-shrouded coves and inlets. Some of the beaches have hotels, others do not. There is an area of cenotes just south of Puerto Aventuras.

Paamul

The lovely inlet of Paamul is 15 km (10 mins) past Playa del Carmen, and 85 south of Cancún. A half moon of turquoise sea surrounded by jungle, one-time home of manatees and sea turtles, Paamul offers bungalows and campsites for backpackers and recreational vehicles, and is rumored to have the best seafood restaurant on the coast. Frightened off by all the activity the manatees are long gone, but the turtles return every summer to lay their eggs in the sand.

Puerto Aventuras

The megaproject known as Puerto Aventuras covers more than 240 hectares including three kilometers of white-sand beach. Located 89 km south of Cancún and 20 km (15 mins) past Playa del Carmen, Puerto Aventuras is an upscale resort community with private homes and condos, five-star hotels, some of them all-inclusive, beach clubs, dive and sportfishing shops, restaurants, stores, a dolphin enclosure and a 280-slip marina. Activity options are limitless, all services and most facilities open to the public.

Ancient and modern

Puerto Aventuras has its own golf course which is both beautifully landscaped and quite demanding, a tennis school, spa and gym. There's even a tiny Mayan temple located on the shores of the Chacalal inlet and a Nautical Museum run by CEDAM (a Mexican underwater archaeology association) which showcases objects recovered from Spanish galleons that foundered on area reefs during the Colonial period.

Cenotes in the Puerto Aventuras area

A couple of kilometers south of Puerto Aventuras lie several interesting cenotes. The Chacmool cenote is comprised of several interconnecting bodies of water which have only recently been explored. The expedition divers discovered tunnels, caves and the longest underwater stalactite in the world, 12 meters long. Other cenotes open to the public are Cenote Azul, the twin cenotes Cristal and El Escondido, Kan Tun Chi, Sask'alech-Há, Zazil-Há and Uchil-Há. All have crystalline waters, some an intense blue color, and a few are suitable for swimming. Rustic wooden signs beside the highway mark the entrances to the cenotes and there is an entry fee.

Cenote Aktun Chén

Aktun Chén

This 400-hectare nature park is located between Akumal and Xel-Há and the highlight is undoubtedly a walk through a cave full of stalactites and stalagmites. The jungle is pristine and rich in flora and fauna. Look out for the chicozapote tree, the source of chicle. The entrance fee includes a guided tour of the cave, entry to the herpetarium and the small regional wildlife zoo.

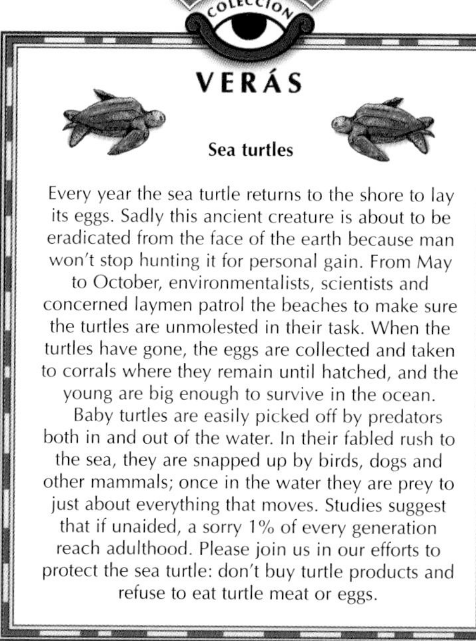

VERÁS

Sea turtles

Every year the sea turtle returns to the shore to lay its eggs. Sadly this ancient creature is about to be eradicated from the face of the earth because man won't stop hunting it for personal gain. From May to October, environmentalists, scientists and concerned laymen patrol the beaches to make sure the turtles are unmolested in their task. When the turtles have gone, the eggs are collected and taken to corrals where they remain until hatched, and the young are big enough to survive in the ocean.

Baby turtles are easily picked off by predators both in and out of the water. In their fabled rush to the sea, they are snapped up by birds, dogs and other mammals; once in the water they are prey to just about everything that moves. Studies suggest that if unaided, a sorry 1% of every generation reach adulthood. Please join us in our efforts to protect the sea turtle: don't buy turtle products and refuse to eat turtle meat or eggs.

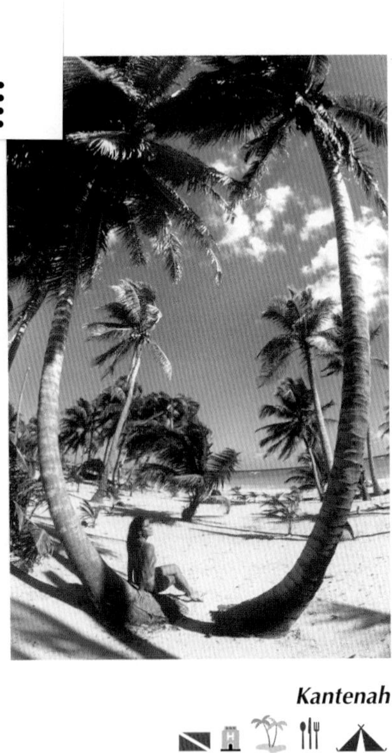

Kantenah

Just south of Xpu-Há, this palm-fringed bay is the perfect place to rock gently in a hammock and enjoy the breeze. The waters of the bay are calm and there are offshore coral formations ideal for snorkeling and diving. Kantenah is the site of the El Dorado Beach Resort, a tropical-style hotel with full services.

Akumal

A few kilometers down the road from Xpu-Há (36 km from Playa del Carmen) is the coastal development with most seniority. Akumal ("Place of the Turtle" in Maya) is located on a tranquil bay with the reef just offshore. Two species of rare sea turtle (loggerhead and green) return to the Akumal beaches every spring to lay their eggs which are then protected by local conservationists.

Akumal is a major dive site and the bay is a good spot for snorkeling. Just to the north is Half Moon Bay with its condos, and still further north is the Yalkú inlet.

Owned by local diver and photographer, Gonzalo Arcila, Akumal Dive Shop offers a variety of dive excursions, cave diving and a catamaran cruise to Xaac, a tiny bay only accessible by sea. A Mayan temple or lookout crowns a rocky promontory beside the bay.

Greater Akumal has several entrances, each leading to a different part of Akumal and slightly different services, though all lead to food, lodging and the beach.

Yalkú

To the south of Akumal

Driving south from Akumal, the next turnoff is to Club Oasis Akumal, an all-inclusive resort nestled in a bay protected by a reef. Dining and water sports, facilities are excellent. Immediately to the south is Playa Aventuras, a DIF-administered youth hostel (DIF is a Government department concerned with family welfare and social issues.). The beach slopes gently down to the calm waters which are protected by an offshore reef. For information on the hostel contact the DIF offices in Cancún or Chetumal.

Akumal

Xcacel

Windswept Xcacel, with its crescent-shaped bay is a romantic spot, a great place to watch the sun and moon rise over the Caribbean. Sea turtles nest here in the summer, and the beach was recently declared a sanctuary for this endangered animal.

The jungle-entrenched cenote just south of the bay is a favorite haunt on weekends. Camping facilities; seafood at a little palapa restaurant. Xcacel is 51 km (40 mins) south of Playa del Carmen. At the time of going to press the protected area status of this site was in doubt.

Xel-Há

Xel-Há is a fascinating network of coastal channels and lagoons that is easily one the most popular stops in the Riviera Maya.

History

"Xel-Há" is Maya for "where the water comes in." Although the site was occupied during the Classic period (A.D. 250 - 900), it reached its peak in the post-Classic (A.D. 900 - 1500) when Xel-Há functioned as a port and trading station, and probably as an embarkation point for crossings to Cozumel. The site extends 800 m along the ocean and a kilometer and a half inland. The architectural style of Xel-Há is the same as that of neighboring Tulum, a style referred to as 'east coast'. Structures include the Castillo, the Structure of the Columns, the Temple of the Birds and Lothrop Group. The Spanish arrived in 1528, re-christening the place, "Salamanca de Xel-Há". What remains of the archaeological site is located in the jungle, across the highway from the park (separate entrance).

CONSULT THE TOURIST DIRECTORY

Xel-Há today

The locals say Xel-Há is the greatest natural aquarium in the world, and they may be right. The chain of inlets, lagoons, cenotes and underground rivers is surrounded by jungle. The waters are calm and crystal-clear, a mix of freshwater springs and ocean. Swimmer-friendly fish make the place a delight, and in areas recently opened to the public, visitors float down the waterways in oversized inner-tubes. Swimming and snorkeling are permitted in certain areas and the use of suntan lotion is prohibited. Fishing is not allowed. Park services include changing rooms, shops, restaurants, snorkel rentals and a dolphin program. Xel-Há is 54 km (45 mins) from Playa del Carmen,115 km from Cancún. Pay at the gate, or purchase tickets beforehand in Cancún or Playa. The archaeological site is managed by INAH and is not part of the Xel-Há park; a separate entry fee is levied.

Tankah

The only sign marking this site is the temple on the left-hand side of the highway and the dirt track that runs next to it. Tankah was one of the most important ports on the eastern coast of the Yucatán Peninsula during the Late Classic and Post-Classic periods.

Another track with a sign reading "Casa del Cenote" leads to the beach, a seafood restaurant, some small hotels and houses. A cenote lies in the mangroves behind the beach and is connected to the ocean by subterranean tunnels which should only be explored by trained divers with a professional guide. You can swim and snorkel the cenote's surface and the reefs in the bay.

Bahía de Punta Solimán

A secluded bay perfect for sunbathing and snorkeling that is also the site of a seafood restaurant popular with locals and tourists alike.

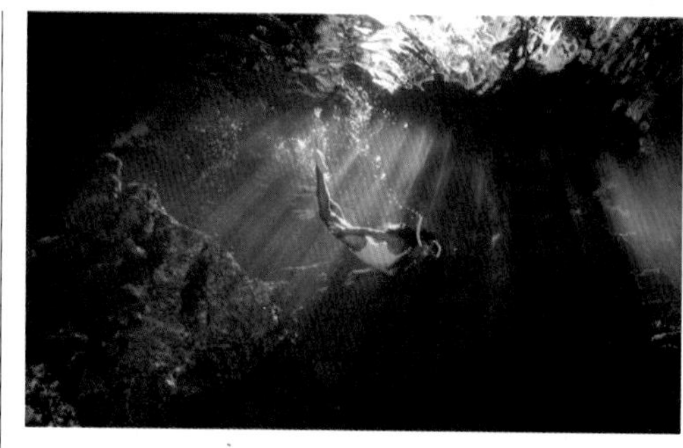

Cenotes

Cenotes and underground rivers flowing towards the sea are found throughout the Riviera Maya. Considered sacred sites by the ancient Maya, cenotes are now a major area attraction. Some local companies offer jungle tours which include a visit to a cenote and a spot of snorkeling. Cenote diving is dangerous and should only be done by qualified speleologists, and as a member of a tour led by a local dive master.

Cenote Nohoch Nah Chich

Located on San Felipe Ranch, Nohoch Nah Chich is one of the world's longest underground river systems. A team of intrepid cave divers led by Mike Madden explored 250,000 feet of the course. Over 1500 dives yielded a series of amazing finds including millions of stalactites and stalagmites, tunnels large enough to drive a bus through and the skeletons of prehistoric sea turtles and an elephant.

Cenote Dos Ojos/Hidden Worlds

The world's largest cave diving and snorkeling park, Hidden Worlds, is the site of Dos Ojos, a 64-km flooded cave system which is another of the longest underground rivers in the world. With a chain of cenotes to explore, the park is a haven for snorkelers and professional cave divers alike. The dive center offers trips.

El Taj Mahal

This cenote doesn't look that attractive from the surface but for divers who descend four to five meters and swim to the other side, the view is magnificent: an enormous cavity the size of a theater with two openings in the roof through which the light filters in. For good swimmers only.

Calavera

Three kilometers from Tulum, en route to Cobá, at the end of a tiny path into the jungle, this is one of the area's most challenging and dangerous cenotes for divers (take a long rope).

Gran Cenote

Located in the vicinity of Calavera cenote, this sinkhole is renowned for its caves which have stretches of sand and rock floors, blue and green waters and roofs festooned with stalactites.

Car Wash

Local people once washed their cars in this cenote, hence its name. It is located three kilometers to the north of Gran Cenote and ten meters from the Tulum-Cobá highway.

Cenote Cristal

There are two cenotes at this site: one is very accessible, resembles a pool and with no cave. The other is larger and more attractive and a kilometer from the first sinkhole.

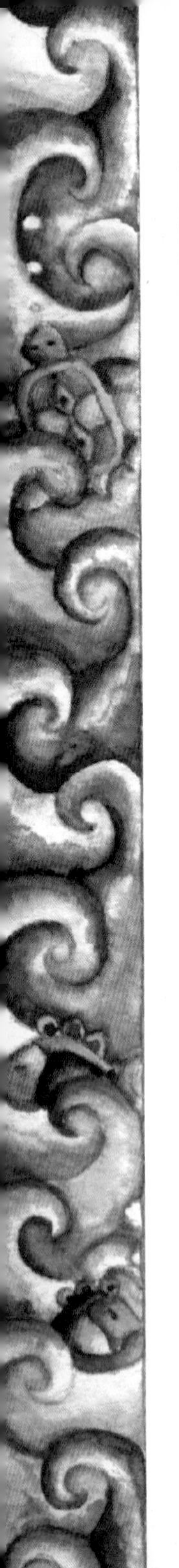

Tulum

The ancient Maya port of Tulum is a two-hour drive from Cancún (129 km) and the final stop on the Riviera Maya.

History

Tulum's greatest attraction is its location. It stands on a bluff facing the rising sun, commanding views of the Caribbean that are nothing less than spectacular. In Maya, Tulum means "wall," and the city was christened thus in the early 1900s because it is a walled city and one of the very few the ancients ever built. Research suggests it was called Zama or "to dawn" in its day, which is appropriate given the location.

The earliest date lifted from the site is A.D. 564 (the inscription on a stela). This places Tulum within the Classic period, though we know that its heyday was much later – A.D. 1200-1521 – during the late Post-Classic period.

Tulum was a major link in the Maya's extensive trade network, both maritime and land routes converged here. Artifacts found in or near the site testify to contacts that ranged from Central Mexico to Central America and every place in between: copper rattles and rings from the Mexican highlands; flint and ceramics from all over the Yucatán; jade and obsidian from Guatemala and more.

The first Europeans to see Tulum were probably Juan de Grijalva and his men as they sailed reconnaissance along the eastern coast of the Yucatán in 1518. The Spaniards later returned to conquer the Peninsula, unwittingly bringing Old World diseases which decimated the native population, and Tulum, like so many cities before it, was abandoned to the elements.

First modern explorers

The adventurers, John L. Stephens and Frederick Catherwood, already known for their journeys in Central America, arrived at Tulum in 1841. They cleared the vegetation, studied the city and what remained of its structures and published their findings a year later. Frederick Catherwood's drawings of El Castillo (see left) are famous.

Later, in the 20th century archaeological research continued under the consecutive directorships of Samuel Lothrop, William Sanders and Arthur Miller.

Artistic detail, Tulum

Aerial view, Tulum

The ceremonial center

Probably once used for rituals or ceremonies, the plaza at the center of the city is flanked by the so-called Castillo to the west. The Castillo, sometimes referred to as the lighthouse, is the tallest building at Tulum and the most famous. It stands on that above-mentioned bluff, commanding a view of the ocean and coast for miles in both directions. The structure underwent several stages of building and the lintels of its upper rooms are carved with the plumed serpent motif. The rooms themselves are vaulted in classic Mayan style.

The Temple of the Descending God is another interesting structure. On the façade is a figure sculpted head down, and the walls inside show traces of the original pigments applied by the Maya. The descending figure is thought to represent a deity and Tulum appears to have been the center of his cult. The Temple of the Initial Series façade bears several stucco figures and the earliest date found at Tulum came from a stela in the inner sanctum.

Other buildings

Also important is the Temple of the Frescos which is filled with murals, now mostly erased by time and the elements. The temple shows traces of several building styles. The House of the Columns is more complex than most structures at the site and worth examining. It's a palace-like structure with four rooms whose principal entrance faces south. Six columns support the roof of the main room and there's also a roofed sanctuary.

With the exception of its eastern flank, which is open to the sea, Tulum is completely encircled by a low wall. Watchtowers rise from the two corners of its western flank and within each tower is an altar.

A tiny cove nestles at the foot of the cliffs. With its apron of snow-white sand, this caleta was where the trading canoes would slip ashore.

The Descending God

Honey provided the ancient Maya with sustenance and an important trade item. The honey bee was revered as the god Ah Muzencab, the descending god, who always appears head first, as if in a sting position. Carved images of Ah Muzencab ("he who guards the honey") can also be seen at nearby Cobá, and Sayil and Chichén Itzá in the Yucatán. He seems to have been an important deity for the Maya and was one of the sky bearers in ancient mythology. Incense burners showing the god carrying honeycombs have been unearthed in the area.

Economically-priced lodging is available in the village of Tulum located almost next door to the ruins, and there are a slew of lodging options along the coast south of Tulum, en route to Sian Ka'an. These range in price and quality, and many are built exclusively with regional materials.

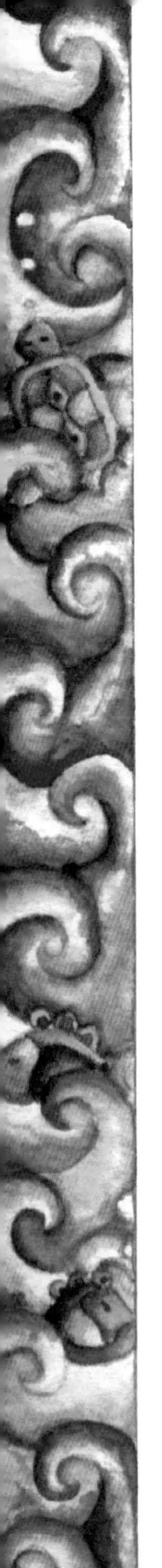

Cobá

Deep in the jungle and clustered around a series of shallow lakes, about 41 km from Tulum, lies the ancient city of Cobá. This ceremonial center flourished during the Classic and Post-Classic periods, at its peak its influence extended over 99 km^2. The park at Cobá covers 6 km^2 of the city.

Early Explorers

John L. Stephens was the first to mention Cobá. A local priest told him of its existence when Stephens was in the Yucatán in 1842. Yucatecans José Peón Contreras and D. Elizalde made cursory sketches of the major structures in 1886, and Theobert Maler took the first photograph of Nohoch Mul, the tallest pyramid in the peninsula, in 1891. The first official exploration of Cobá took place in 1926 when a group of Carnegie Institute archaeologists headed by J.S.E. Thompson, Harry Pollack and Jean Charlot toured the site.

History

Cobá was settled as early as A.D.100-250, the Late pre-Classic and Early Classic periods of Maya history. No structures from that time have survived, but we do have artifacts – buildings, stelae and ceramics – from the Classic period, which for Cobá ran from A.D. 400 to 1100. In the Middle Classic period, sometime between A.D. 600 and 800, Cobá's rulers built a network of formal roads or *sacbe* radiating from the Cobá Group; stelae were commissioned and the city expanded east, building the Nohoch Mul, the Chumuc Mul and the Macanxoc groups. Some Post-Classic buildings at Cobá show Petén architectural influences, while others are clearly East Coast and similar to those at Tulum. The extraordinary dimensions of Cobá's structures, however, are the result of superimposed layers of construction, one after the other over a long period of time – a process probably begun in the Classic period. Greater Cobá extends for some 70 sq. km. The land is arable and has adequate supplies of fresh water. The Maya were able to grow enough corn to feed themselves and still have a surplus to market. The network of roads suggests expansion and trade, and as a consequence political, economic and social control of the region. A.D. 400 to 900, Cobá was the area's major city. It stockpiled and controlled goods and services to northern Yucatán, and to the eastern seaboard.

Ball court

Las Pinturas group

The city and its architecture

The majority of the ruins at Cobá correspond to what would have been simple housing. Only the limestone foundations remain, and these are hard to see because of the vegetation. Each house/foundation is enclosed by a low, stone wall, or sometimes several are grouped together within a single wall.

The Cobá Group

Located between the Cobá and Macanxoc lakes. The oldest in the city, this group is composed of a plaza and numerous buildings. Sacbes 3, 14, and 15 originate in the plaza; the first running north, the other two, south.

The Iglesia, or Church is crowned with a temple and stands 24 m tall. In front of the Iglesia, Stela 11 is venerated by the local Maya who say it embodies the Virgin of Colebí. The Ballcourt is north of the Iglesia.

The Nohoch Mul Group

The Maya took advantage of natural elevations in the land to build their most imposing piece of architecture. Structure 1, or the Nohoch Mul pyramid for which the group is named, rises 42 m off the plain and is the tallest ancient building in northern Yucatán. Its southern face has two flights of stairs; both leading to rooms referred to as temples 1 and 2. The remains of boar, monkey and numerous birds were dug up in the temples. In Temple 2 is a fragment of Stela 29; an offering of conch shells and jade buried at its base.

About 70 m southeast of the pyramid is Stela 20, the best preserved piece of monumental sculpture found at the site. The stela shows five figures; the principal one stands on the back of a bound captive, the others, all males, are off to the side in a posture of reverence.

The Macanxoc Group

The pride of the group are its eight stelae and nine circular altars. Stela 1 is important for bearing four initial series dates, all of which correspond to the 8th century A.D.

The Maya used stelae to commemorate important events, such as births, deaths, accessions, alliances, marriages and great victories, and to mark the passing of *katuns* (a period of 20 years in the Mayan calendar). These free-standing, stone slabs were dated and etched with figures and hieroglyphics that described the incident being commemorated and are found at sites throughout the Maya World.

Art and Architecture

Cobá enjoyed close ties with the Maya of the Petén (Guatemala). Methods of construction appear similar: blocks of stone, reinforced with mortar and surfaces covered with stucco, then painted red. The lintels and figures found in niches were painted a variety of colors. Other elements found in Cobá include recessed lintels and niche figures pictured upside down, or 'descending'. Some of the smaller structures recall architecture found along Quintana Roo's Caribbean shore called 'east coast' or Costa Oriental. Cobá has been only superficially restored and little studied. Artifacts found to date include stelae and molded stucco fragments showing glyphs and the vestiges of murals in Las Pinturas group.

The roads of Cobá

The *sacbe* of Cobá were built to facilitate the city's political and economic control of its territory and were also used to advantage during religious events that called for processions. The *sacbeob* can be divided into regional, rural and local roads. Two regional roads radiate from the site: Cobá to Yaxuná, at 101 km is the longest sacbe in the Maya World and Cobá to Ixil is 19 km long. Archaeologists have numbered them 1 and 16 respectively. Access/exit ramps were sited at intervals along both routes.Eight rural roads have been discovered. These linked villages with the city. The 35 local roads connected the rural and the regional roads to each other. Connecting roads were from one to 20 m wide, and anywhere from six to 728 m in length. At the start of Sacbe 3 (in the Cobá Group) is a smooth stela on which items, notices etc. were presumably painted on a layer of stucco.

Getting there

From the Riviera Maya, take Highway 307 to Tulum and follow the turnoff marked "Cobá". It's a 40-minute drive to the site. An alternative route is to take Highway 180 east (the road to Chichén Itzá and Mérida) to Nuevo Xcan. The turn-off south to Cobá is identified with a sign; you can't miss it, and from there it's another 62 km to the site. From Chichén Itzá you can also take the road to Valladolid and on to the colonial village of Chemax and a back road to Cobá. There are a couple of hotels at Cobá and several restaurants.

Today's Maya

Cobá is surrounded by Mayan communities, whose artisans work in wood and stone, and whose women embroider the hipiles or dresses worn in the Yucatán. Most of the locals speak Maya and Spanish as a second language. The road runs through areas of jungle, cornfields and villages where thatched huts predominate.

Punta Laguna

Along the Nuevo Xcan - Cobá road is the small community of Punta Laguna. The lake for which the village is named is near the road and there are minor ruins in the area. One of the community leaders is a man called Don Serapio. Together with his sons and a few villagers, he offers boat trips on the lake and jungle walks. It's best to take the tour at either dawn or dusk, for your chances of spotting spider monkeys foraging in the trees and seeing some of the birds that inhabit the area increase considerably. The jungle harbors deer, peccary, and the smaller wild cats: margay, jaguarundi and ocelot. There are turtles and crocodiles in the lake. Tours provide income for these people, most of whom are farmers and beekeepers. A good time to visit is May 3, the festival of the rain god Chaac.

Mayan priest, San Juan

San Juan

The village of San Juan is located 16 km from Cobá. Its inhabitants are farmers who recently joined together in a grand adventure toward greater financial freedom. Working with a group called Fundación Maya Kuxkinal they've created a program called San Juan, Cultura Viva (San Juan, A Living Cultural Experience).

The concept is to turn San Juan into a living theater with scenes acted at different sites around the village. The tableaux reveal aspects of Mayan culture, traditions and legends.

The goal of Maya Kuxkinal is to involve more villages in the program and give them an opportunity to preserve their culture and benefit from doing so. The San Juan Cultural Experience is available as a day trip, for more information contact Maya Kuxkinal at (998) 887-6666.

Pac Chen

Visitors to this village not only experience Mayan culture first-hand, they also can explore the jungle accompanied by a local guide and find out about the flora and fauna. For adventure buffs there are activities as diverse as kayaking on the lagoon, rappelling down a cenote wall and swinging across the water on a cable. Traditional cuisine is prepared by the women of the village. Available only through travel agencies in the Riviera Maya and Cancún, the Pac Chen tour forms part of a sustainable development project designed to help the villagers. The community is located 25 kms north of Cobá on the road to Nuevo Xcan.

The Riviera Maya invites you to explore the Mexican Caribbean...

- Spectacular beaches, nature parks and tiny villages...
- Cenotes, caves, inlets and archaeological sites

The Riviera Maya is:

Adventure, diving and cave diving, kayak trips through the mangroves, rappel on cliffs and cave walls, jungle expeditions, fishing that's fun but respects the environment...

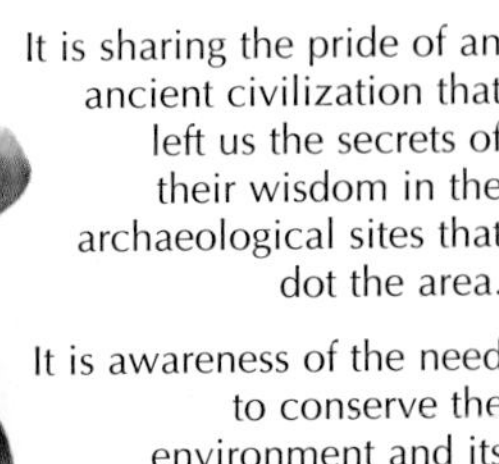

It is sharing the pride of an ancient civilization that left us the secrets of their wisdom in the archaeological sites that dot the area.

It is awareness of the need to conserve the environment and its riches...

It is meeting the modern Maya and learning about their traditions...

Cozumel

Located 20 km off the eastern coast of the Yucatán Peninsula, Cozumel is the largest inhabited island in Mexico.

The island has been settled since the beginning of the common era. It rose to prominence among the Maya as both a trading post and religious center, but was abandoned as a result of the Spanish Conquest. It remained uninhabited after that, visited only by fishermen or the occasional pirate. It was reborn in 1852 when Yucatecans fleeing the Caste War, migrated to the island in droves.

The refugees-cum-settlers dabbled in farming and ranching, but for years the island's main source of income derived from chicle. Harvested throughout the peninsula from the zapote tree, the world's first chewing gum was processed at the mainland camps then sent to Cozumel for exportation Fishing was a sideline. International tourism discovered Cozumel in the 60s, thanks to the oceanographer Jacques Cousteau whose documentaries showcased the island's spectacular reefs. Today, Cozumel is a world class dive destination and a major cruise ship port-of-call.

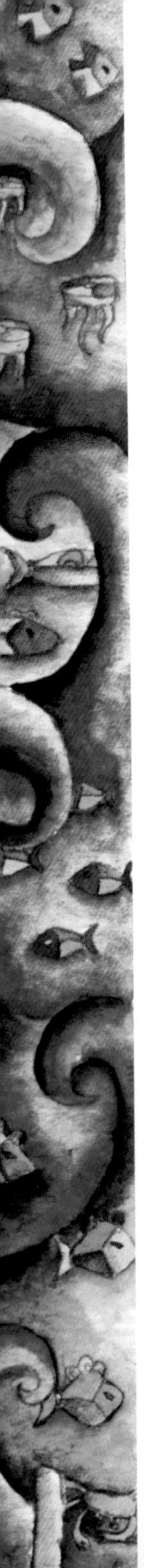

Land of the swallows

The island's original name was Cuzamil, Maya for 'place of the swallows', and the bird still visits in great numbers when migrating between North and South America.

Cozumel differs from the other offshore islands in the region in both origin and size. It began life as a coral reef and finished as a limestone shelf, same as the peninsula. It's carpeted with jungle and its waters are more than 600 meters deep.

Cozumel au natural

Cozumel is a flat plain 16 kilometers wide and 48 kilometers long. You can just about drive round the entire island on the coast road. The shoreline changes from sandy beach and relatively no surf on the leeward side of the island, to ironshore and strong currents on its windward side.

Flora and fauna

The island is a verdant plain of jungle with trees up to 20 meters high, and mangroves and dune vegetation on the coast.

Cozumel is home to most of the creatures found on the mainland and several endemic species, animals found only on the island. They include the dwarf raccoon (*Procyon pygmaeus*), the Cozumel coatimundi (*Nasua nelsoni*) and four species of bird which rarely, if ever leave the island despite the short distance to shore. The two most common of these are the Cozumel wren *(Troglodytes beani)* and the Cozumel Pinto (*Spindalis zena.*)

San Gervasio

Prehispanic growth

The earliest evidence of human occupation dates to the Late pre-Classic period, 300 B.C. to the Early Classic A.D. 300. The population continued to increase, peaking during the island's heyday in the post-Classic period, A.D.1200 to 1600. At that time its many communities were connected by a system of stone roads.

Trade and religious center

During the post-Classic period, Cozumel served as both a seaport and a religious retreat. It was the first port-of-call on a trade route that ran from Xicalango (Campeche) on the Gulf Coast of México to Nito, Guatemala and Naco, Honduras. The port of Cozumel handled a considerable volume of trade and its merchants were affluent and politically influential.

The island was furthermore sacred to the goddess Ixchel, and home to one of the most renowned oracles in ancient Mesoamerica: Ah Kin, or 'He of the Sun' named for the sun mask he wore.

The goddess Ixchel

Ixchel was a major deity in the Maya pantheon of gods and the center of her cult was in Cozumel. Her consort was Itzamná, god of wisdom and knowledge, and together they were the creator couple. Ixchel was associated with the moon, after the sun, the most important body in the heavens. She reigned over the forces of fertility in all its many manifestations, principally the harvest and childbirth. She was also the goddess of medicine and weaving. Women from all over the Maya World made the dangerous journey to her island shrine.

The Old World meets the New

The Spaniards saw Cozumel for the first time in 1518. Expedition leader Juan de Grijalva claimed Cozumel and the surrounding seas for the Spanish crown. The conquistadors then prudently left the island without attempting to subject or convert its inhabitants.

It was Cortés, on his successful bid to conquer Mexico, begun in 1519, who visited the island and destroyed its temples. The Maya of Cozumel never submitted to Spanish rule, however, simply because there weren't enough of them left to do so. The Spaniards carried diseases against which the Indians had no defenses, and in the case of Cozumel, the population was so decimated by measles that in 1570 only 300 people were alive, and by 1600 the place was deserted.

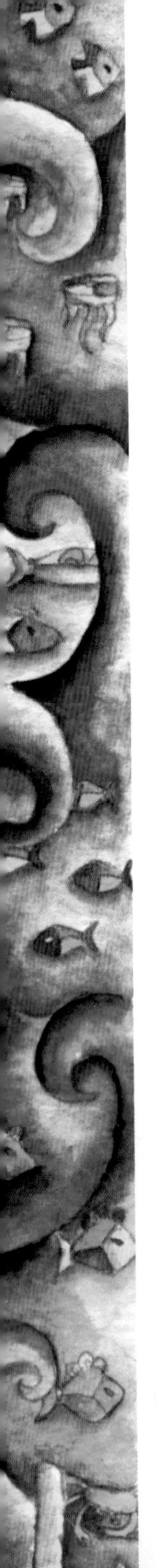

The age of pirates

From 1600 to about 1850 anarchy reigned, a Who's Who of ocean-going renegades converted the Caribbean into their own private sea. Lawlessness was rampant, the Spanish lost control of the region and Cozumel became a refuge for pirates such as Henry Morgan. The outlaws rested, repaired their ships and took on supplies in Cozumel. From here they raided ports in the Caribbean and the Gulf of Mexico. They never established a permanent town, however, as they did on Términos Island in Campeche or Belize. In fact, little is known of those 250 years, and the only pirate to leave his mark on the island was the Spaniard Miguel Molas. Molas was an adventurer, a smuggler, a businessman and a settler. The northern tip of Cozumel is called Punta Molas in his honor.

The island is resettled

During the early years of the Caste War, between 1848 and 1849 two different groups of refugees made for the island and settled. The first was a group of approximately 50 middle class, mestizo families (mostly merchants and craftsmen) and their servants. The second was a clutch of 350 Maya. The first and dominant group appropriated the best land and founded the town of San Miguel on the western coast. The Indians were forced inland, where they founded El Cedral, even today, the only other town in Cozumel.

For more than a century following its resettlement, business was good and the island's position as a seaport grew in importance. The fishing industry was negligible throughout the 19th century, while the island exported its sugar, cotton, beef, sisal and fruit to mainland Mexico and the United States. It was also responsible for warehousing and shipping abroad the chicle and copra (coconut) harvested on the peninsula–which was actually its main source of income during this time.

San Miguel de Cozumel

The Great Depression (1930s) seriously affected the island economically. It bounced back during WWII by supplying the Allies with raw materials and something more. The Mexican Government agreed to let the U.S. Air Force build a base on the island; from which planes patrolled the Caribbean for Nazi submarines. The Americans abandoned the base at the end of the war, but the runways were left intact and facilitated Cozumel's reincarnation as a tourist destination–its most successful role to date.

Tourism

The development of Cozumel as a vacation destination differs significantly from that of Cancún, which followed the dictates of a government-issued Master Plan. Cozumel's growth has been gradual and spontaneous, the work of individual entrepreneurs reacting to opportunity. For the longest time, the island offered only simple hospitality and small to medium-size hotels. Nevertheless, tourists of every stripe and nationality came, especially divers, for word of the island's spectacular reefs and crystal clear, waters had leaked with the airmen stationed on the island during WWII. Tourists began arriving in the late 50s and early 60s; but after Cancún captured the imagination of the travel industry worldwide, they came in droves.

San Miguel de Cozumel

Only one out of every three visitors to Cozumel goes diving; the other two come to visit the island and its only real town, San Miguel de Cozumel. In spite of the ever-increasing population and its ranking as an international destination, San Miguel has managed to accommodate growth without losing its essential Caribbean-Mexican island flavor. The Cozumeleños live very much as they always have. There is a good deal of community spirit, everybody knows everybody and the whole island participates in events such as carnival. There are many excellent shops, craft stores, restaurants, boutiques, bars and discos aimed at the tourists, and while most of the island lives off tourism, it hasn't allowed itself to be swallowed up by it – and there's the difference. The real, the native Cozumel is very much in evidence, and to see it, just stroll through the streets of San Miguel, sit in the square or walk along the waterfront boulevard.

Accommodation

The island boasts a variety of accommodation options. There are deluxe, five, four and three-star hotels with all the services in the Hotel Zones, north and south of San Miguel, and small inns in the city.

CONSULT THE TOURIST DIRECTORY

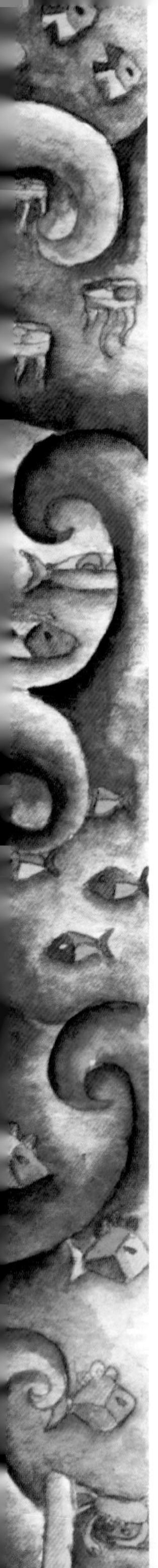

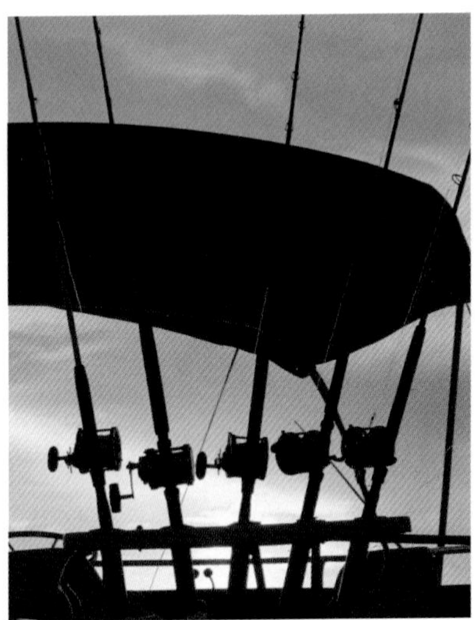

On the surface

You don't have to be a diver to see Cozumel's underwater world for yourself. The waters bathing the leeward coast are so calm and clear that snorkeling is safe along most of the shoreline.

Beaches & activities

Cozumel has some fine beaches, those on the leeward coast are sheltered and suitable for swimming. Windward beaches are beautiful but the currents and undertow are strong and swimming is not recommended. To reach each the windward shore take the cross-island highway. In addition to diving, snorkeling and sport fishing, island marinas offer windsurfing, water ski, jet ski, sailing and cruises on glass-bottomed boats.

Discover the magic of the Chankanaab Reef on board the Atlantis TS/XII, Latin America's only real submarine. During the voyage, the air-conditioned vessel will dive to 110 feet to give its passengers a panoramic view of the reef and its colorful inhabitants.

The Cozumel Country Club boasts an 18-hole par 72 golf course which was designed by the Nicklaus Corporation.

Travel agencies in San Miguel operate a variety of tours to sites of interest on the mainland such as Tulum.

Exploring the island

You can drive to the *faro* or lighthouse on Punta Celarain, the southernmost tip of the island, part of the Punta Sur Ecopark. En route to the lighthouse and a Navigation Museum, you'll pass El Caracol archaeological site, several beaches and secluded bays and the Colombia and Chanchacaab lagoons.

Traveling north from San Miguel, you'll pass through the Hotel Zone and can continue to Punta Molas, the northernmost point of the island and site of another lighthouse.

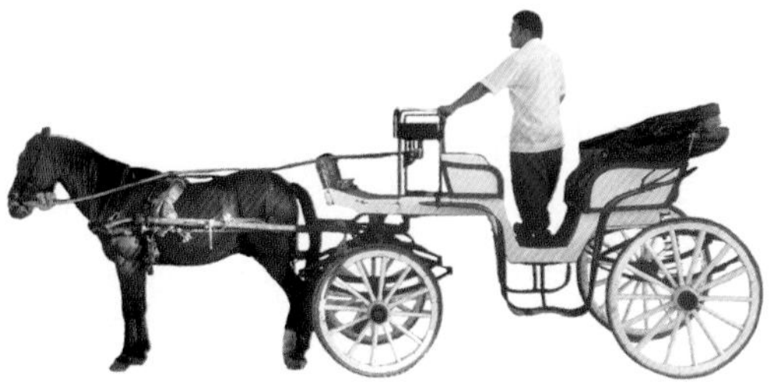

Chankanaab

The Island Museum

Located on the waterfront or *malecón* (Rafael Melgar Ave.), between Calles 4 and 6 norte. The museum showcases the origin, evolution and ecology of the island, as well as its human history from the Maya to the present day. Worth a visit.

Archaeological sites

Research indicates there are 25 ancient sites on the island, most of which are difficult to access and have not yet been restored; others were destroyed when the air base was built in the 40s. The most famous site is San Gervasio, with its six clusters of buildings spread over an area of three square kilometers. Some of the buildings are of considerable height, and set upon grand platforms. The site is located in the middle of the island and is accessible from the cross-island highway.

The other site worth mentioning is El Cedral, where the original stucco and color applied by the ancients are still visible.

Chankanaab Park

The park offers visitors a variety of attractions and never fails to please. A cenote, or natural sinkhole located in the park and near the beach is linked to the open ocean by an underwater passage. This tunnel, and the exchange of water it permits, is the reason for the extraordinary corals growing in the cenote (typically a fresh water phenomenon).

The park's beach is lovely and the ocean calm, perfect for snorkeling and free-style swimming. Dozens of species of tropical fish and small corals inhabit the area. The park's Botanical Garden has a section dedicated to indigenous island plants, and another harboring 350 species of tropical plants from over 20 different countries. There is a swim-with-dolphins program and an 'interactive' museum with reproductions of ancient Mayan landmark structures. The park has changing rooms, snorkel rentals, a dive shop, restaurant and other services.

Isla de la Pasión

This bit of terra firma is located off the beach, north of the city and easily reached by small, sightseeing boats. The beaches are lovely and there is a wealth of bird life. The mainland beach parallel to the island is also a good choice for sunning.

Sportfishing and horseback riding

Cozumel provides some of the best deep-sea fishing in world. Charters are available from many sources; check the agencies downtown, or go directly to the docks, located on the coast north of San Miguel.

You can also enjoy a horseback tour of the jungle. To get the most out of such an excursion, ask for a guide well-versed in island history and in the local flora and fauna.

Cozumel is rated among the top five dive destinations in the world, thanks to the condition, number and variety of its reefs, the range of its marine life and the warmth and clarity of its waters. Visibility rarely drops below 85 ft. and goes as high as 200, while the temperature hovers at a toasty 80º F (25-27º C).

Reefs

Along the western or leeward coast are about 25 reefs of diverse size and description. Some are in reasonably shallow, tranquil waters and appropriate for novice divers; others are a challenge for the experienced, and still others are suitable for folks of intermediate skills. The characteristics of each reef and its respective currents allow for different dive techniques and 'drift diving' – where you're pulled along by the current, viewing the walls of coral in passing – is one of them. Drift diving is the norm for the western side of the island where calm seas and strong currents are the prevailing conditions. The tourists of Cozumel support more than 100 different dive shops. Only certified, card-carrying divers can dive without on-site instruction. When choosing a dive shop, check that it has all its permits and meets the safety standards required by law.

Marine life

Hundreds of species of tropical fish and other marine life live on the reef – creatures of every size, shape and color. Local sea bass and groupers are huge and so used to visitors you can observe them up close.

Every species of coral is visible, including the gorgonians or sea fans, whose undulating forms add grace and beauty to an already magical terrain.

Highlights

Let's take a look at the different reefs and what they offer in terms of marine life. We've classified them according to the level of expertise required to dive them. Dive masters will give you more information. Some reefs such as Paraíso and Chankanaab are popular spots for night diving.

For Novice Divers

Paraíso North. Located near the cruise ship dock, Paraíso North consists of three long reefs running parallel to the shore. Inhabitants include huge coral heads, sponges two meters in diameter and large schools of brilliant, Blue Chromis (*Chromis cyaneus*). Maximum depth: 45 ft.

Paraíso South. Two reefs, each about 500 meters long are thick with candy bass, sea cucumbers, numerous varieties of angel fish and other exotic denizens of the not-so-deep. Maximum depth 45 ft.

Chankanaab. A good location for sunken objects – some deliberately scuttled. You'll see anchors, cannon, a fishing vessel and a bronze Christ. Chankanaab is the only reef where the current runs south. Maximum depth 55 ft.

Balones de Chankanaab. This reef is in slightly deeper water. Its name (balls of ...) comes from the quantity of coral heads growing here. There are pillars, or craggy mountains of coral four to 10 meters tall, riddled with tunnels inhabited by creatures such as lobster, moray eels and manta rays. Best at 60-70 ft.

Palancar Gardens A section of the larger Palancar Reef, with depths of 40-70 ft and an easy current. Coral grows profusely and fish are abundant.

La Herradura A particularly beautiful reef. It features a curve of coral buttresses, canyons, and terraces with dropoffs starting as shallow as 30 ft.

Villa Blanca Dropoff The wall's average depth is 70 ft, but the dropoff plunges for miles. Drift diving is the name of the game here. Highlights: shoals of fish, sponges and sea fans. Access: Villa Blanca Hotel beach. Depths of 50-100 ft.

For intermediate divers

San Francisco. A reef rich in marine life, with moderate to strong currents. The shallowest wall dive in Cozumel. Best dived at 30-50ft.

Punta Tunich. Fanciful coral formations rich in color at this site, but few fish. Strong current, fast drift diving.

Tormentos. Beautiful heads of coral, moray eels, bass, grouper, and colorful angelfish. Depth of 40-70 ft.

Paso el Cedral. Principal attractions here are the moray eels and the giant groupers. Maximum depth 60 ft.

Santa Rosa. One of the most popular reefs, it's an area of coral buttresses on the lip of the dropoff, with, caverns, mammoth-sized sea fans and spectacular giant sponges. Best dived at 50-80 ft. Current can be strong.

For advanced divers

Palancar. A favorite. Palancar is huge (5.6 km long) and you won't see it all in 20 dives. It is known for its coral columns. Shallower parts: depths of 20-40 ft.; deep Palancar: 100-120 ft and for advanced divers only

Palancar Caves. An area of caves within Palancar Reef. Entrance is at a depth of 45 feet, the exit, at 120 ft.

Colombia. Another awesome section of reef. The huge coral heads rise to the height of a two-story house. Huge anemones and sea fans, and a great quantity of fish. Shallower sections: 15-35 ft.; deeper sections: 60-80 ft.

Punta Sur. Beautiful underwater terrain, rich in marine life but limited to divers with the specialized training and experience required for especially deep diving. Average dive depths: 90-120 ft.

Provincia Maya

Central Quintana Roo, a section of Caribbean coast that includes the Sian Ka'an Biosphere Reserve and the area known as the Zona Maya, exists in stark contrast to the northern half of the state. The north contains over half a million full-time residents living in the various resorts of Cancún, Isla Mujeres, Playa del Carmen and Cozumel, while in the more than 6,000 sq. km of the reserve, the population is under 1,000. The north is urban and modern; the center of the state is rural and traditional, inhabited by indigenous Maya living in the small communities of their ancestors.

The Maya of central Quintana Roo are descendents of the *cruzoob*, the rebels of the Caste War who fled into the jungle, to a stronghold they called Chan Santa Cruz. They still speak Maya and keep many of the old ways: rituals, fiestas, religious beliefs and agricultural methods. There are few archaeological sites in the area and the colonial churches lie in ruins – most were torched by the Maya during the Caste War – it is the people of the Zona Maya that are interesting.

En route to the coast, some 60 km from Felipe Carrillo Puerto, lies Sian Ka'an. Around 35% of this huge reserve is still in pristine condition and most of the Yucatan's ecosystems are found here. Plant and animal life is extremely diverse and a visit to the reserve is worthwhile.

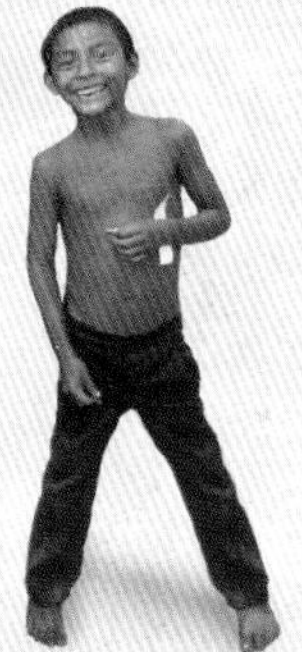

The central area of the state is little-known and rarely visited. Nevertheless, it is an interesting trip for history (vestiges of the Caste War and the opportunity to visit modern Mayan communities) and nature (the Sian Ka'an Reserve) buffs alike.

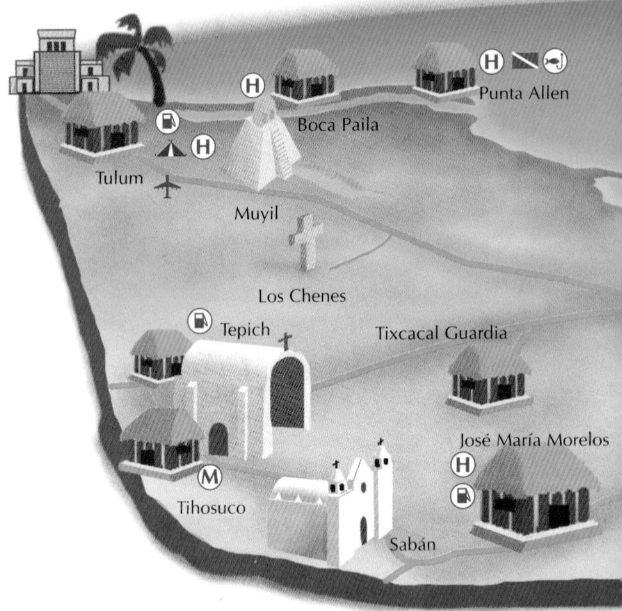

Zona Maya

This large area borders Sian Ka'an to the east and the neighboring state of Yucatan to the west. Its northern limit is the Tulum-Cobá area, and to the south, the village of Limones. It encompasses José María Morelos and Felipe Carrillo Puerto municipal districts. The latter is also the name of the capital of the Zona Maya. Roads spread out from this bustling town linking it to remote villages.

Sian Ka'an

The largest reserve in Quintana Roo, it protects areas of jungle, marsh, mangrove forest, coastal dunes, coral reefs, cenotes, lagoons and the two large bays of Ascencion and Espiritu Santo. Trips to the reserve consist of a boat ride through the wetlands.

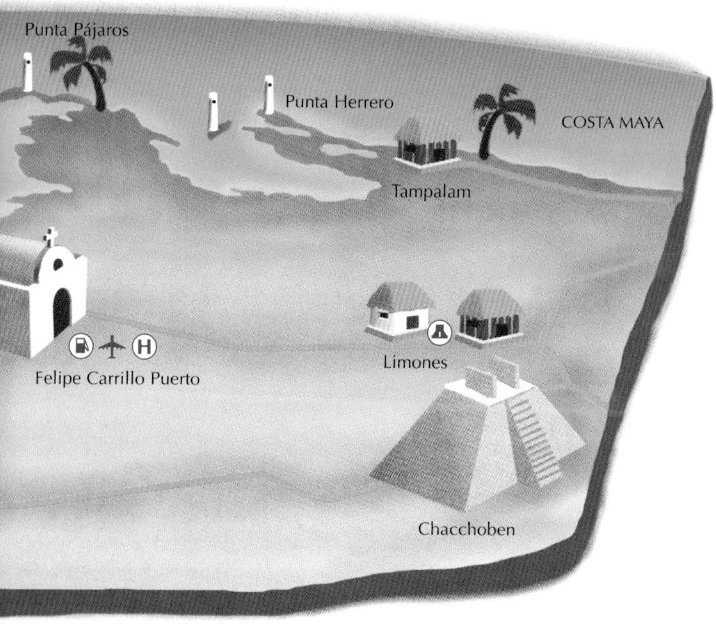

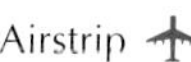
Airstrip

Diving

Gas station

Hotel

Museum

Fishing
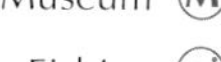
Campsite

Archaeological site

Respect for Mayan customs

Like their ancestors, today's Maya are extremely devout. Every aspect of their lives is influenced by religious beliefs and supernatural beings and they take the ancient rituals very seriously. Visitors who wish to witness a ritual must first ask the village authorities and ask for permission to take photos – this may not be granted in some cases. Entry to the sanctuaries where the Cross is kept is strictly prohibited.

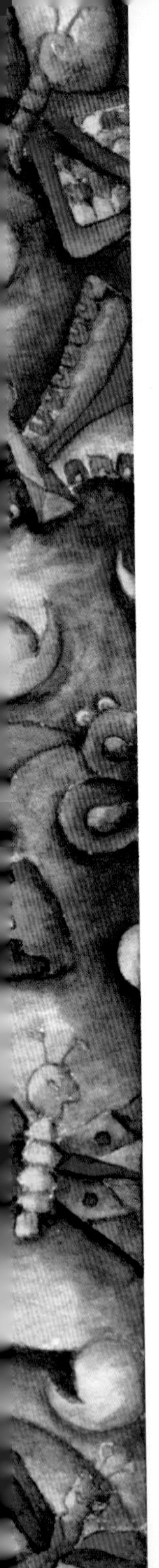

Tepich

Some 50 km from Valladolid is the village of Tepich, where on July 30, 1847, the infamous struggle known as the Caste War began. The village church is one of the few colonial structures in the state. It's a somber building, singularly free of ornamentation, even less so than most of the churches in the Yucatán. Historians believe that the reason for this is twofold: because the area is historically a poor one, and because the Maya, who never totally submitted to the Spanish, only did their bidding reluctantly, and then, only the minimum required. This meant they built the church but did not decorate its façade.

Tihosuco

"The place of the copal tree" in Maya, Tihosuco is 85 km from Felipe Carrillo Puerto on Highway 295. In 1686, the village was sacked by pirates Lorenzillo and Grammont, it recovered only to be razed again during the Caste War. Tihosuco is home to the Museo de la Guerra de Castas which is located in a restored 19th-century house. The museum reconstructs the history of Mayan rebellion from the 16th century through the 20th with maps, photographs, engravings and historical documents. There are also portraits by local painters, Marcelo Jiménez Santos and Elio Carmichael.

The town library is worth a visit, and also housed in an interesting building, this time one of colonial vintage; and the roof of the church is partly destroyed, a souvenir from the war. The rest of Tihosuco is a rare mix of European and native Maya. Its colonial architecture was partially restored in 1997 in honor of the 50th anniversary of the Caste War. Many of these buildings, however, are shells for the town was abandoned during the war and stayed empty for almost 75 years. When the natives re-inhabited the place, they used the inner patios of the mansions for their traditional thatched huts. On the outskirts of town is the hacienda of legendary Mayan leader, Jacinto Pat. Other villages in the area with colonial churches are Sabán and Sacalaca.

Chacchoben

Tixcacal Guardia

Further down Highway 295 is the turn-off for Tixcacal Guardia or Xcacal, religious and spiritual heart of the Zona Maya. It is home to the Maya who most fiercely defend their autonomy and are keepers of the Cruz Parlante or 'talking cross' that gave the rebel warriors heart to fight on during the Caste War. When Chan Santa Cruz ('little holy cross') – the crosses' original home and stronghold of the cult that grew round it – fell to government forces during the war, the cross was hidden in the jungle until sanctuary was found.

The church in which the cross now rests is open to the public only on feast days, and even then the relic is not on display – even to the Maya themselves. It stands on an altar covered with veils in a blocked-off section of the church called La Gloria, and no one enters this inner sanctum without express permission from the native authorities. The cross is guarded 24 hours a day by armed Maya who hail from all over the region, hence the different pronunciations or versions of the town's name.

Felipe Carrillo Puerto

Felipe Carrillo Puerto

Formerly, Chan Santa Cruz , Felipe Carrillo Puerto is the administrative, political and economic center of the Zona Maya of Quintana Roo. The town was founded in 1850 with the name Chan Santa Cruz, on the site where a cross allegedly began to speak to the Maya, and it quickly became a rebel stronghold, even capital of the Maya nation. Imbued with religious zeal, followers of the Cruz Parlante viewed the rebellion as a kind of holy war. The government was unable to take Chan Santa Cruz for half a century, though it tried repeatedly. Chan Santa Cruz grew during the war years, and when it finally fell in 1901, it had many large stone buildings, a network of well-kept streets and a spacious main square. The church (18 m by 30 m) is presumably the only European-style building in the Americas designed and constructed by indigenous peoples.In 1932, the town was re-christened Felipe Carrillo Puerto in honor of the assassinated Maya-speaking ex-governor with whom the Indians identified.

Chacchoben

Chacchoben ('red corn') is one of the more important settlements to the north of the Bacalar Lagoon. Temples I and II, and a third structure as yet unnamed were built during the Early Classic period in the Petén style characteristic of Southern Quintana Roo at that time. The latter structure harbors a mural with a ceremonial theme. Several different groupings – residential and ceremonial – are under excavation as we go to print.

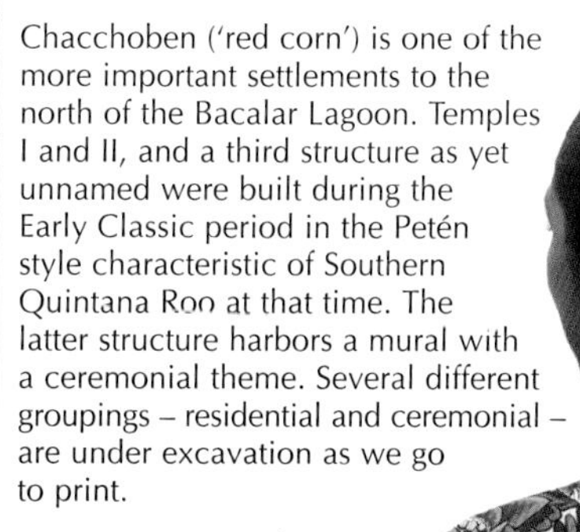

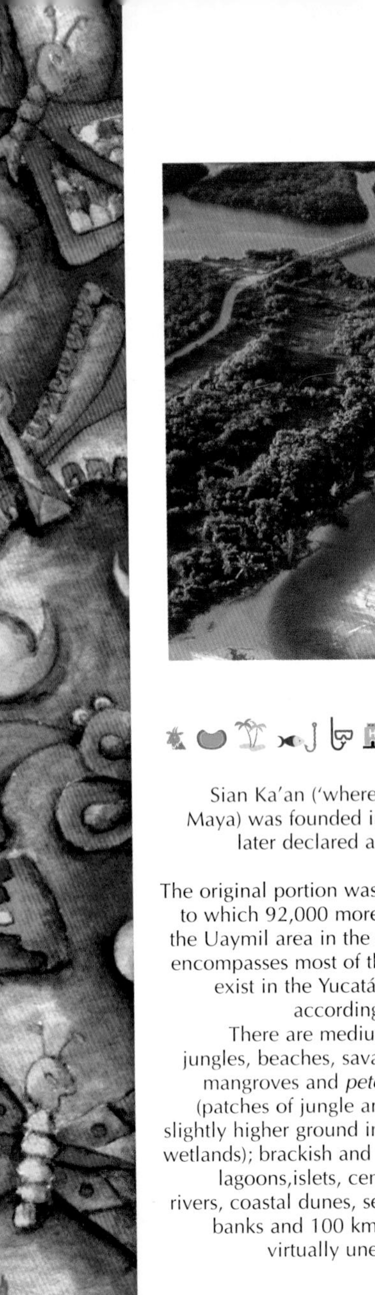

Sian Ka'an

Sian Ka'an ('where the sky begins' in Maya) was founded in 1986 and a year later declared an UNESCO World Heritage Site.

The original portion was 526,000 hectares to which 92,000 more were added from the Uaymil area in the south. The reserve encompasses most of the ecosystems that exist in the Yucatán Peninsula and is accordingly rich in wildlife.

There are medium and low-growth jungles, beaches, savannas, marshlands, mangroves and *petenes* or hummocks (patches of jungle around a cenote, on slightly higher ground in the middle of the wetlands); brackish and fresh water coastal lagoons,islets, cenotes, underground rivers, coastal dunes, sea grass beds, sand banks and 100 km of untouched and virtually unexplored coral reef.

Flora and Fauna

Sian Ka'an is a wonderland of plants and animals. Over 800 plant species have been identified to date, including the indigenous and threatened Kuíkab Palm *(Pseudophoenix sargentii)*. Over 350 species of bird call the reserve home (all of Europe only has 400). The majority of these are water birds, 70 species total including osprey (*Pandion halietus*) and 16 species of heron. During the breeding season, large colonies of frigate bird, pelican, egret and ibis congregate in the mangrove forest. There are even a few breeding pairs of jabiru, a rare stork that is the largest bird in the Americas. The reserve is alive with jaguar, tapir, peccary, temazate or brocket deer, grison, tayra, coatimundi, anteater and tropical porcupine, 100 species of mammal altogether, while offshore there's over 70 species of coral and a never-ending –if properly husbanded – supply of spiny lobster *(Panulirus argus)*, bedrock of the local economy.

Ancient Ruins

Ancient Mayan ruins are plentiful throughout the peninsula and the protected acreage of Sian Ka'an is no exception. More than 20 sites have been located, the most outstanding being Muyil on the shores of the Muyil Lagoon, 15 km inland from the coast. A channel (partly manmade, partly natural) running from the settlement to the coast gave the Maya access to the sea, making Muyil, for all intents and purposes a port city. The well-marked turn-off for Muyil is 25 km south of Tulum on Hwy. 307.

Getting There

Sian Ka'an is open to the public. The easiest way into the reserve is via the dirt road that runs south from the ruins at Tulum (accessed through the village of Tulum). As you head south on this road, the ocean is to your left, the jungle to your right. Watch for birds, especially in the winter; mammals and reptiles. You can wander about on your own, but by far the best way to see the reserve is with the people who know it best, Amigos de Sian Ka'an.

Muyil

They operate a trip through the wetlands, along the canal connecting Muyil to the sea; a jungle tour is also available for those with more time. Well into the reserve is the Boca Paila Lagoon (left) and its fishing camps; and still further south, on Ascension Bay is the town of Punta Allen. The fishermen of Punta Allen will take visitors to the ancient village of Vigía Chico, now deserted, and to Cayo Culebras, the mangrove islet populated by a colony of frigate birds.The residents also hire out as guides to fly fishermen as the area is known as one of the finest, saltwater fly fishing grounds in the world.

Amigos de Sian Ka'an/Friends of Sian Ka'an

Amigos de Sian Ka'an is a non-profit organization that together with governmental and other agencies generates funds to help maintain the reserve and finance research and educational projects. Amigos offers tours to the public and promotes the sale of handicrafts produced by reserve inhabitants.

Chechén

VISION COLECCION

VERÁS

Chechén

The trees that grow in the forests of Quintana Roo have different qualities, some yield fine woods, others fruit and still others are valued for their bark or sap. Found in the coastal woods, chechén is a paradox. There are two varieties: red chechén is harmful, a mere touch of its leaves causes a man's skin to blister, whereas its cousin, the black chechen has healing properties. Its leaves are applied as a poultice to the blisters caused by the red chechén.

CONSULT THE TOURIST DIRECTORY

Southern Quintana Roo

Nature has been generous to Southern Quintana Roo. It's a fascinating mix of jungles, wetlands, lagoons, white sand beaches and coral reefs, rich in wildlife. The ancient Maya populated the area, building cities that still astonish all who visit them. The Spaniards conquered the Maya and, although their settlement was intermittent, left buildings such as San Felipe Fort as testimony of their presence.

Historians also believe that the first Mexican mestizo (half European and half Mayan) was born in Southern Quintana Roo. Chetumal, capital of the state and border town par excellence, lies on the shores of the bay of the same name. Chetumal Bay is also the mouth of the Hondo River, the only river in Quintana Roo and the natural frontier between Mexico and Belize. Make Chetumal the base for exploring Southern Quintana Roo and the sites of interest in neighboring areas such as Southern Campeche, Belize and northern Guatemala.

The Costa Maya (Mayan Coast) is a remote stretch of untouched Caribbean shoreline which has been earmarked for low-impact ecodevelopment on account of its lovely beaches. A boat ride from Majahual or Xcalak is Chinchorro, the largest coral atoll in Mexico, home to myriad marine creatures.

The development that began in Cancún thirty years ago and continued along the Riviera Maya and on the islands of Cozumel and Isla Mujeres, has spread to Southern Quintana Roo in recent years. Infrastructure has been upgraded in the area and new roads, docks and airstrips have been installed. Tourism is being promoted by the government as an alternative to the traditional activities of farming and forestry. Planners hope that it will create jobs, boost living standards and revenue. The local tourism industry is growing, particularly along the Costa Maya, and hotels, restaurants and other related services are on the increase.

Chetumal and hinterland

State capital and gateway to the south and sites of interest in Southern Campeche, Belize and Guatemala, Chetumal overlooks the huge and shallow bay of the same name.
The portfolio of tourist services on offer in Chetumal has grown somewhat over the last few years. There are more hotels, travel agencies and a ferry link across the bay to the Costa Maya.
Chetumal has its own attractions, among them the Museum of Mayan Culture, the City Museum and the bayfront boulevard.

Costa Maya

The newly christened Costa Maya is a strip of white sand and turquoise sea far to the south, running from Punta Herrero to the fishing villages of Majahual and Xcalak. The offshore reefs are part of the Great Maya Reef and the huge coral atoll known as Chinchorro Bank is just a boat ride away.

The Costa Maya is becoming popular with divers, sport fishermen and birders. It is the Mexican Caribbean's newest destination and is targeted for low impact, low density development.

Water and jungle

In Southern Quintana Roo Nature's bounty takes the form of a network of lagoons, the greatest of which is Bacalar. Chetumal Bay and the Hondo River lie at the heart of an important agricultural area. Visitors can explore the sites of interest along the shores of Chetumal Bay or Bacalar for themselves or contact a local agency for a tour of the lagoons or a trek through the jungle.

Punta Pájaros
Punta Herrero
COSTA MAYA
Banco Chinchorro
Majahual
Xcalak
F. Carrillo Puerto
Limones
Bacalar
Chetumal
Chacchoben
Dzibanché
Kohunlich
La Unión
Tres Garantías
Chakanbakán
Xpuhil
Río Bec

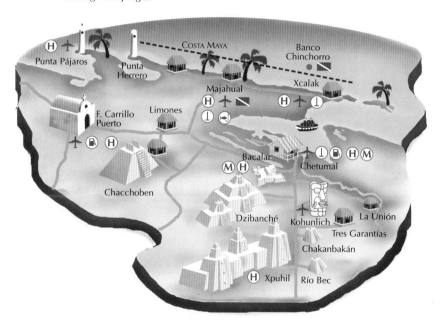

Mayan heritage

Evidence of the ancient Maya's interest in the area can be seen at the Classic period sites of Dzibanché-Kinichná and Kohunlich, Oxtankah and Chakanbakan. Chetumal is also conveniently located for side-trips to the archaeological sites in Campeche and the northern reaches of Belize and Guatemala.

Diving
Gas Station
Hotel
Pier
Museum
Fishing

CONSULT THE TOURIST DIRECTORY

When the Spaniards arrived Chetumal was known as Chetemal or Chactemal, "the place where the red cedar is plentiful" and was one of numerous principalities into which the Yucatán Peninsula was then divided. That of Chetemal ran from Bacalar to southern New River (Belize), a land of recurrent natural disasters, dense forest and fiercely independent natives the Spaniards found impossible to subjugate. After several attempts they abandoned the area, leaving the Maya to their own devices.

Chetumal

Chetumal is the capital of Quintana Roo, easternmost state of the three composing the Yucatán Peninsula. It was founded in 1898 and called Payo Obispo by Lt. Othón P. Blanco who'd been sent to subdue the rebels of the Caste War and stop the arms trade the latter had going with Belize. In 1936, the prosperous bayside city was renamed Chetumal, a clear allusion to its Mayan roots.

Chetumal is your classic Mexican Caribbean town; quiet, tropical and prey to the occasional hurricane. Clapboard housing, louvered windows made from wood, thatched palapas and cement-blocks create the look so typical of provincial Yucatán.

The city has hotels and restaurants to suit all tastes and wallets as well as other tourist services. Its importance has grown over the last few years; not only is it the logical base of operations for visits to the many reserves, beaches and archaeological sites of the south, it is the gateway to Belize and Central America.

Ambience & attractions

Nestled on the shores of Chetumal Bay and surrounded by mangroves, marshes and jungle rich in

mahogany and zapote, the city has its own attractions. The Museo de la Cultura Maya (Museum of Mayan Culture) offers a thorough exposé of the civilization that put Quintana Roo on the map. Exhibits cover Mayan history and the culture's ceramic and apicultural traditions. The Museo de la Maqueta features a scale model of Payo Obispo, created by Luis Rehinard Macliberty, as it appeared in the 1930s when the streets were lined with colorful wooden houses built in the style of the British colonies in the Caribbean. Chetumal also has a City Museum.

Cultural activities

Annual festivals are a serious affair, especially Carnival, with its floats and contests. The city's ethnic profile is an interesting one, thanks to the arrival of foreigners who began migrating into the area at the turn of the century: Indians, Lebanese, Chinese, western Europeans, etc. And finally, the emergence of Cancún as the gateway to the Maya World has brought Chetumal, another gateway, into focus. Chetumal is the natural jumping off point for excursions to a wide variety of destinations within the area.

Monuments

Monuments of note include the Mestizaje, which glorifies the origins of the mestizo race; Bandera ('flag') with its obelisk and three figures; Pescador ('fisherman'), a structural ode to the occupation of many of the region's inhabitants; and the city's working lighthouse or *faro*.

The Club de Yates (yacht club) is a center of activity for this city-on-the-bay. There's a lot of coming and going on the water and along the Hondo River, the natural border between Mexico and Belize.

Chetumal has recently come alive. Both energy and imagination is being spent on the look and life of the city. The waterfront boulevard is a popular meeting place and there are plenty of parks and gardens. The locals are also encouraged to build in the traditional style, and preserve any example of original Caribbean architecture that is still standing.

VERÁS

The monument known as the Homenaje al Mestizaje is the first thing you see driving into Chetumal. It shows three figures, a white man who has obviously gone native, his Indian wife and their offspring. This is Gonzálo Guerrero, the shipwrecked Spaniard who started over in the Yucatán, taking up the cause of the Maya and fathering the first individuals of mixed Indian and Spanish blood. The culture of mestizo-ism permeates every aspect of Mexican society, it is its most basic element and integral to national identity. Mexico is almost 90% mestizo and the only Latin American country that is.

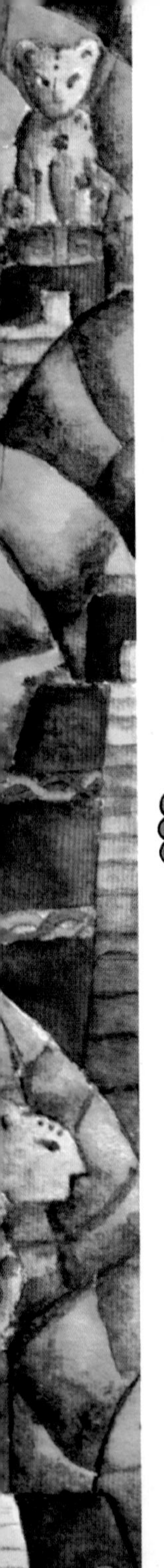

The bay is the city's landmark feature and the focus of its recreation. Boating and swimming are the favorite pastimes. An isolated section of the bay was recently named a Manatee Sanctuary. Most of the city's more idiosyncratic features are visible from the water: the El Pescador monument, the faro/lighthouse, the Palacio del Gobierno/state administration building and the Congreso del Estado/state congress building. The city looks best seen from the water in the evening.

Sites of Interest

Chetumal Bay gives out to the ocean and to the Hondo River, the waterway that divides Mexico from Belize. The area overflows with popular beaches and bay islands and is rife with day-trip possibilities.

Isla Tamalcab

Tamalcab is an island of white sands and calm waters sitting in the middle of Chetumal Bay (two kilometers off shore). Its tropical vegetation is forever rustling in answer to a permanent, if gentle sea breeze. Folks go here to fish, swim, snorkel, dive and relax. The surrounding waters are peppered with *ojos de agua* or fresh water underground springs which well up through cracks and crevices in the rock.

There are no services on Tamalcab so you must pack in everything you'll want, including food and water. The island has unrestored Mayan ruins (platforms, plazas and columns) and is home to species such as agouti, a rodent the size of a small dog, spider monkeys, coatimundi and a variety of birds including blue heron, snowy egret, great white egret and osprey.

Boat transportation to tiny Tamalcab is available from Calderitas.

Oxtankah

Calderitas

The sloping shoreline and shallow water of Calderitas make it a great recreational beach for visitors and locals alike. There are thatched palapas and shade umbrellas along the shoreline and local fishermen offer boat trips around the bay.

Just eight kilometers north of Chetumal, the site's rustic, tropical-style restaurants are famous for their fresh seafood and sweeping views of the bay and Isla Tamalcab.

To get to Calderitas, head north on Ave. Heroes, then take a right at the fork (km 6.5) and the beach is 1.5 km later.

Oxtankah

The name means 'three neighborhoods' although it has also been translated as 'place of the ramón (the ramón or breadnut tree bears a nut gathered by the ancient Maya and ground into flour). Intermittent building went on at Oxtankah for centuries: its first structures date from A.D. 200 - 600 and remnants from the period have survived at Plaza Abejas and Plaza de las Columnas. Oxtankah was then abandoned for 800 to 900 years until the Maya built a humbler settlement with stones from the first. Remains have also survived. Colonial sources state that Gonzalo Guerrero lived at Oxtankah. By 1531, the Spaniards had arrived, and Alonso de Ávila christened the settlement, Villa Real de Chetumal. The Indians' hostility forced the foreigners to flee within two years. During that time they built a church, and the presence of both Mayan and European architecture is what makes Oxtankah so interesting. To reach the site head north on Ave. Heroes until it becomes a dirt track (the Calderitas-Tampalán road). At km 11.5, go left and follow the signs.

VISION COLECCION

VERÁS

Convention says that when European sailors first saw manatees they took them for women. The manatee is a marine mammal that has breasts for suckling its young; it also loves to stand upright in the water, hence (presumably) the confusion. Manatees (*Trichechus manatus*) belong to the order of *sirenidae* (sirens), however, which suggests the 'full figured' mammal has been deceiving man for a long time. Hunting, habitat destruction and pollution have decimated the manatee, worldwide. The manatee of Quintana Roo have also been blighted by ever-increasing tourism and its propensity for motorized water toys. Speed boats frighten the animals and propellers often mutilate them. A portion of Chetumal Bay and of the Hondo River (100,000 hectares) has been set aside as a manatee refuge to protect the 100-120 animals left in the region.

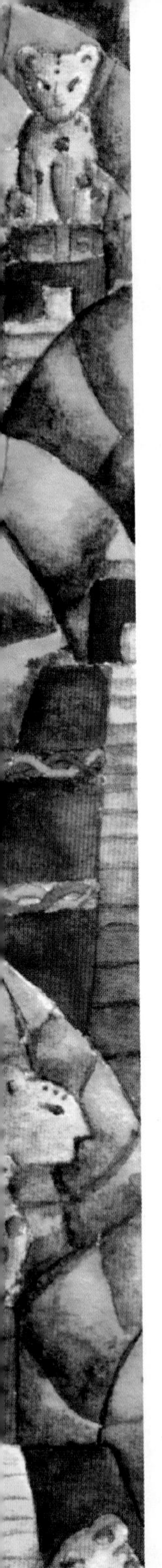

Bacalar

Bacalar figures prominently in the history of the area. Known to the Maya as Bak´Halal or 'place of the reeds', it was the most important community in the ancient principality of Uaymil, and the region most warred against by the Spanish during the Conquest.

The Maya put up terrific resistance, but conquistador Gaspar Pacheco was cruel and determined enough to win a victory of sorts, and the respite to found Villa de Salamanca de Bacalar in 1545.

The settlement was never a success nor at all productive during the Colonial period. The Indians were hostile and refused to work, and the colonists feared them. However, while it survived it operated as a port for goods bound for Europe (its lagoonside location giving it access to the sea via Chetumal Bay). Merchandise from all over the region, and as far away as Honduras and Guatemala filled its warehouses. Exports included palo de tinte or dyewood, and rumor of the city's wealth soon made it the target of every pirate in the Caribbean.

Cenote Azul

Bacalar Lagoon

Also known as the 'lagoon of seven colors' for its multiple shades of blue, Bacalar Lagoon is 38 km northwest of Chetumal and stretches along the Chetumal-Cancún highway. It is 50 km long and an average of 2 km wide. It runs into the Hondo River from a stream called the Chac, and into Chetumal Bay via a network of shallow channels.

Bacalar is filled with great little places to spend an afternoon or even a few days. Restaurants are plentiful and the local seafood and regional cuisine is excellent. Watersports, particularly waterskiing, windsurfing, sailing and fishing are easily arranged.

The town of Bacalar hosts an annual fishing tournament in August. Other lagoons worth visiting in Southern Quintana Roo are Milagros, Xul-Ha and Guerrero, respectively.

Fort of San Felipe

The community was attacked so often during the Colonial period that Governor Antonio de Figueroa y Silva ordered the construction of a fort. Juan Podio was drafted for the job and began work in 1729 on what is today a stellar example of 18th-century military architecture. San Felipe is a square plaza surrounded by thick stone walls, a deep moat and four rhomboid-shaped ramparts mounted with cannon. The compound included a place to store food, a weapons room, a watchtower and sleeping quarters for the men. The common areas were distributed between the fort's two buildings: a rectangular structure at the center of the enclosed plaza, and a smaller, two-storied building that housed the watchtower. The fort originally had a drawbridge, and the moat was planted with sharpened stakes instead of water for defense. San Felipe was restored conserving all its original elements and today houses the Museo de Historia Regional (Regional History Museum).

San Felipe Fort

Cenote Azul

Just south of the town of Bacalar, and a stone's throw from the lagoon, is possibly the deepest sinkhole in the world, the Cenote Azul. Surrounded by dense forest, the cenote is filled with cold, clear water over 90 meters deep. Swimming and diving are allowed, but keep children away from the water's edge. The site has a restaurant serving regional cuisine and there are changing rooms and parking. Parrots, toucans, agoutis, deer, spider monkeys and other native wildlife are kept in cages beside the steps leading down to the cenote.

To reach Cenote Azul, leave Chetumal and head north following the signs to Cancún, keeping to Highway 307. The cenote is located 15 km after the Escárcega turn-off. The entrance is well marked.

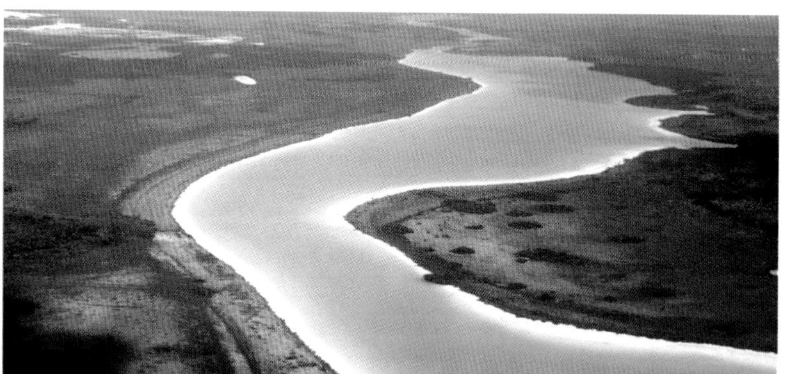

Bacalar Lagoon

CONSULT THE TOURIST DIRECTORY

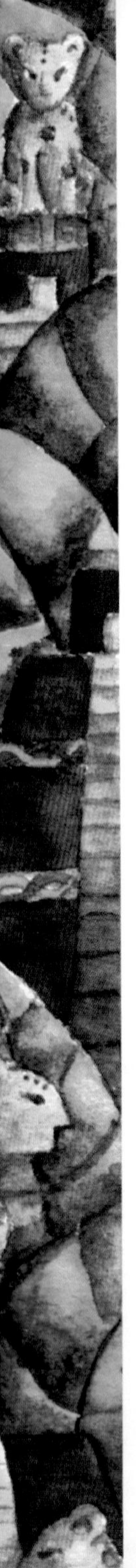

Kohunlich

The name kohunlich comes from two English words: 'cohune' (a palm tree native to Belize) and 'ridge' for, 'cohune ridge' or 'the ridge where the cohune palm grows'. The site was first reported in 1912 by American archaeologist Raymond Merwin who dubbed it Clarksville. Kohunlich is surrounded by smaller sites that were each occupied for a few years. The area may have been inhabited throughout the entire Classic period, A.D. 250-900.

Kohunlich was excavated in the 60s by Víctor Segovia who concluded that the colossal stucco masks, carved moldings and recessed corners evident in the Temple of the Masks, which was built during its initial period of construction, linked it to the Petén region (Tikal). A second phase belonged to an architectural style dubbed Río Bec (the Acropolis' substructure), and a third and final phase was characterized by indifferent construction and the use of perishable materials.

The masks of Kohunlich are the focus of attention and the reason for the site's fame. They reflect the complexity of ancient Maya society and are superb works of art. The masks recall Kinich Ahau, the sun god, but weren't intended as straight representations of the deity as originally thought. Scientists now believe the masks are actually portraits of the city's rulers, men who chose to identify themselves with the god in order to legitimize their rule. The masks are framed with anthropomorphic figures associated with the jaguar god of the underworld.

The Palacio Norte or North Palace is a majestic structure, the one-time residence of a great lord or ruler. The Elevated Patio of the great foundation is itself built on an older building. This earlier structure is accessed via stairs that lead to a courtyard around which various rooms are located. Archaeological research indicates this, the Complex of the 27 Stairs, was used as housing for the nobility.

To reach Kohunlich head north out of Chetumal to the Escárcega-Campeche highway 186). Take this turn-off and head west, the exit for Kohunlich is at km 60 and well-marked. Once off the highway you'll come to the community of Francisco Villa, and the ruins are about 9 km further (follow the signs).

Chakanbakán

Chakanbakán ('in the middle of the savanna' or 'surrounded by the savanna') is located very near the town of Caoba (93 km from Chetumal) en route to Escárcega. The site is currently under excavation.

Chakanbakán is important for its antiquity, and for having one of the greatest collections of giant masks in the Maya World. The structure called Nohoch Balam was built between 300 and 50 B.C. and shows Olmec influence. Its rubble foundation is skillfully plastered with stucco, a technique associated with Peten-style architecture. Experts believe the masks represent deities with close links to the jaguar, an animal the Maya greatly revered.

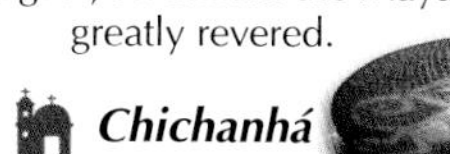

Chichanhá

Founded by the Spaniards in 1687 as Santa Rosa de Chichanhá, the settlement had the largest indigenous population of any town in what is today Southern Quintana Roo. Chichanhá was also the headquarters or district seat of the (church) missions established for the area which was known as the "pimienta (pepper) region."

Chichanhá had a violent history. It was the site of bloody confrontations during the Caste War and finally abandoned due to continued hostility from the Maya. After that it fell into obscurity until 'discovered' early in this century by researchers such as Maurice de Perigny and Eric Thompson.

In a jungle clearing lie the remains of a late-17th-century Franciscan church.

Dzibanché

Dzibanché

Dzibanché was an important city that flourished from A.D. 300 to 1200. The site was discovered in 1927 by Thomas Gann who christened it Dzibanché, or 'carved in wood'. It was named after Temple VI whose zapote wood lintels are set with dates. The site's outstanding structures are labeled Temple I and II. In the first, a well-constructed tomb with quality offerings was found. The nature of the grave goods and the fine construction suggest it was built for someone important. Among the items found within it was a vessel whose lid bears a sculpted owl leading, inevitably, to the temple being named Temple of the Owl.

Also located at Dzibanché are the Temple of the Cormorants; the Patio of Xibalbá and its North and South plazas; and the Gann Plaza, location of Structure XIII. Also called Building of the Captives, Str. XIII is embellished with artwork showing persons in submissive positions.

Kinichná ('house of the sun') is just 2 km north of Dzibanché and was part of the larger site. Kinichná is small, but its structures are beautifully embellished. The site consists of small buildings and a modest plaza where the long, symmetrical structure called the Acropolis is located. The Acropolis appears to glorify the power of Dzibanché, and the Petén architectural style in which it was built dates it to sometime between A.D. 200 and 600.

To reach Dzibanché, take Highway 186 to the Morocoy turn-off (about km 58). The turnoff for Dzibanché is 3 km beyond Morocoy.

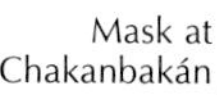

Mask at Chakanbakán

Southern Quintana Roo is blessed by nature. Its many 'eco-niches' and their relatively pristine condition make the south the perfect eco-tour destination. Birdlife is abundant, with over 300 colorful species in the jungles and wetlands, and the area is home to endangered mammals such as the jaguar, howler monkey, tapir, peccary, otter and manatee. Visitors can trek deep into the forest; glide through the mangroves in search of birds and crocodiles, rent a cabin or camp on the beach.

Great curassow

Jaguar

Tres Garantías

This forest reserve is located between Chetumal and La Unión. The villagers of Tres Garantías are farmers and woodsmen who live off the land, exploiting the resources of their tropical forest habitat, specifically its precious hardwoods (mahogany, cedar, pucté and ramón). A few families have turned portions of their acreage into a reserve designed to protect the land and its resources and to generate additional income for the farmers who are in the process of creating ecotourism projects.

The La Pirámide camp is located within the reserve. It offers the hospitality of rustic cabins with basic services.

Guided tours of the forest provide visitors with the chance to learn about the jungle, its towering trees, its giant ferns and varied wildlife; its jaguar, deer, tapir, peccary, fox and its hundreds of species of bird, such as the toucan and chachalaca. You may even hear the eerie call of the howler monkey as it echoes through the forest with tremendous force.

Visits to Tres Garantías are booked through travel agencies in Chetumal; a minimum of eight days advance notice is required.

Boat travel on the Hondo

Cenote Cocodrilo Dorado

The Cocodrilo Dorado Cenote (sinkhole of the golden crocodile) is a gem of a site located along the Hondo River, in the hills en route to La Unión. According to a local legend, a golden crocodile inhabits the depths of the cenote and occasionally makes an appearance. Tours are booked through agencies in Chetumal and usually include river travel, a spot of kayaking along a stream that flows into the Hondo River (Estero Franco), meals, lodging and transportation to the embarkation point. The Cocodrilo Dorado camp is rustic but adequate, with tents. This is a great getaway for nature lovers. Birders will be in their element, there are plenty of jungle trails, best explored at dawn when the birds are at their most active. A 75-meter limestone bluff with a good rock face for climbing and absailing overlooks the cenote.

Hondo River

The Maya called the Hondo, Nohoch Ucum, or 'great river' because of its impressive size. The river is a natural border between Mexico and Belize. It is navigable its entire 156-kilometer length and was used extensively by the ancients, especially for the transportation of goods. Long ago the river was a Venice of giant, open canoes piled high with men and merchandise from the four corners of the Maya World. Legend has it that 17th-century Scots buccaneer Peter Wallace gave up piracy to grow dyewood, the stuff was that valuable to the European clothing industry. He was not alone, and the illegal logging camps which flourished in southern Quintana Roo along the shores of the Hondo River, and in Campeche, were a thorn in the side of the Spanish authorities. The pirates/loggers sometimes reverted to their lawless trade and Bacalar was raided on several occasions. Wallace's camp and others like it in Belize became part of the British colony that sprang up there.

The Hondo is a jungle river enhanced with mangrove islets and the perfume of wild orchids. Its banks are alive with deer, tapir, agouti and a variety of birds. Cruising the river is an unforgettable experience, one that may include a glimpse of a manatee, one of nature's rare and now seriously endangered creatures, herons, ospreys, iguanas, monkeys and peccary. If the Hondo River divides Mexico from Belize it also brings the two nations together, for both countries have equal right to the Hondo, its past and its future.

Howler monkey

Majahual

The section of coast running from Majahual to Xcalak has been christened the Costa Maya – a veritable idyll of white sand and turquoise sea. Rustic accommodations are gradually being improved upon, but the setting is perfect just as it is. The turnoff to Majahual is located on Highway 307, at the southern exit of a village called Limones, north of Bacalar. The Costa Maya is currently being promoted as a cruise ship destination and a port of call for yachtsmen doing the Caribbean circuit.

Majahual

For years, Southern Quintana Roo was ignored by investors in love with Cancún, the state's megaresort to the north. But times change and while Cancún is still growing, the Costa Maya is drawing eyes south, specifically to Majahual as a logical 'base of operations'. Majahual is a traditional fishing village with a few rustic seafood restaurants, about to become your best bet for a Caribbean getaway – au natural.

There's a landing strip, some small hotel and bungalow developments on the beach and a cruise ship terminal. The access roads in and around Majahual have been finished and will link the village to other beaches or sites targeted for development such as Río Indio, Placer, Uvero, Punta Pulticub and Río Huach.

The Costa Maya highway will stretch north to Punta Herrero, a fishing village on the shores of Espíritu Santo Bay, in the Sian Ka'an Biosphere Reserve.

Majahual's perfect, palm-lined beaches and crystal-clear waters were made for sunning, bathing and snorkeling. Fishermen will be happy too, coastal lagoons are rich in tarpon and snook, and many of the hotels offer sport fishing for marlin and sailfish.

In addition, Majahual has long been the place from which divers and sightseers embark for Chinchorro Bank, the world-famous atoll located 30 km offshore.

The turnoff to Majahual is 145 km north of Chetumal on Carretera/Highway 307 and well marked.

Banco Chinchorro

Xcalak

The Costa Maya in its pristine state has two settlements large enough to be called villages, Majahual and Xcalak; but Xcalak has always had something Majahual doesn't, the distinction of being the southernmost community not only in the state of Quintana Roo, but in the nation (on Mexico's eastern flank). For a long time the town's only visitors were divers on the way to Chinchorro, but with the Costa Maya project in the wings, Xcalak has begun to put time and energy into the creation of low impact services designed for the ecotourist market. Beach-front lodging runs from no-frills bungalows to small hotels, and facilities for boating, birdwatching, diving and sport fishing are in place. Area beaches are attractive and there are several lagoons nearby. Xcalak has a landing strip, and can be reached via Majahual, or by water via the new ferry service operating out of Chetumal, which is the faster route if you're in Chetumal to begin with.

Banco Chinchorro

Chinchorro is the largest atoll in Mexico and part of the second longest coral reef system in the world. It covers an area of approximately 500 sq. miles, most of it taken up by the lagoon of crystal-clear water at its center (created by the atoll's characteristic ring shape). The water is from one to eight meters deep in the lagoon, dropping to 200 meters and more outside the atoll.

The reef and its lagoon provide sport for both divers and snorkelers and just about every variety of coral is present: elkhorn, staghorn, brain, star, fire and the soft corals, or gorgonians, popularly known as sea fans. Sponges come in all sizes, and along with tropical fish such as the angel, parrot, damsel, squirrel and pork fish, tangs, wrasses to name but a few, are the reef's most colorful inhabitants. Sea turtles feed on beds of sea grass, and barracuda, snapper, bass and grouper are in constant attendance.

For many, the biggest draw is Chinchorro's catalogue of sunken ships, the reason it's known as 'the ships graveyard'. Galleons, 19th-century merchantmen and modern cargo boats have all foundered on local reefs.

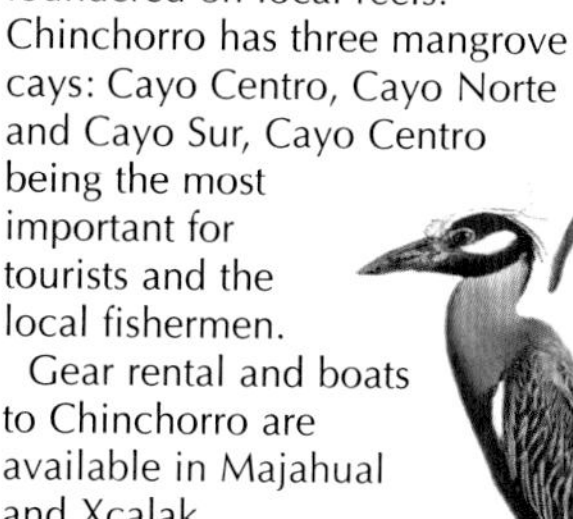

Chinchorro has three mangrove cays: Cayo Centro, Cayo Norte and Cayo Sur, Cayo Centro being the most important for tourists and the local fishermen.

Gear rental and boats to Chinchorro are available in Majahual and Xcalak.

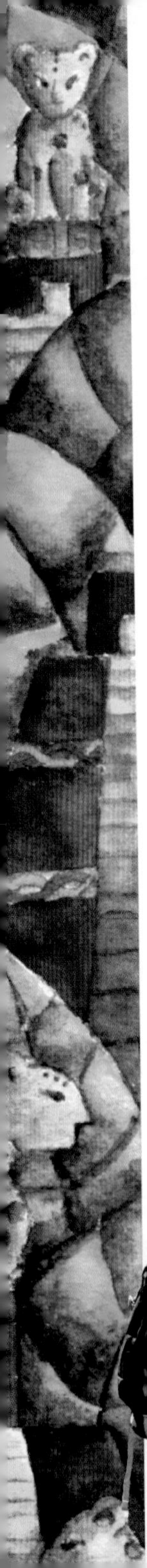

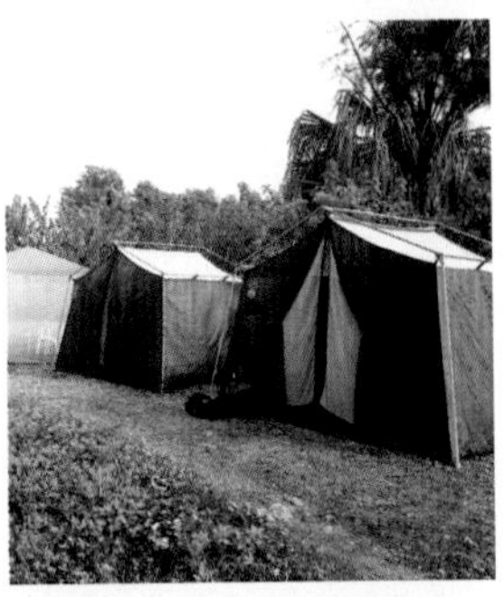

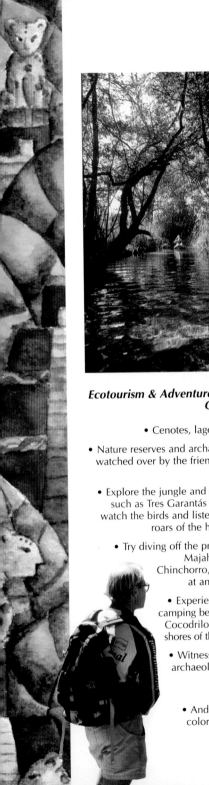

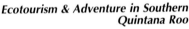

Ecotourism & Adventure in Southern Quintana Roo

- Cenotes, lagoons and rivers
- Nature reserves and archaeological sites watched over by the friendly inhabitants of the area.
- Explore the jungle and nature reserves such as Tres Garantás where you can watch the birds and listen to the distant roars of the howler monkey.
- Try diving off the pristine shores of Majahual and Banco Chinchorro, or cave diving at an inland cenote.
- Experience the thrill of camping beside Cenote del Cocodrilo Dorado on the shores of the Hondo River.
- Witness the majesty of archaeological sites like Kohunlich and Dzibanché
- And the enchanting colors of the Bacalar lagoon.

MEXICO & THE MAYA WORLD

Once home to some of the most important cultures in ancient America, Mexico is steeped in history and colorful traditions. Its landscapes are equally diverse and the vast territory is a biological treasure house.

From north to south, east to west, Mexico offers something for every visitor. The country is divided into six tourist regions: The Pacific (Baja California Norte and Sur, Sonora, Sinaloa and Nayarit); The North (Chihuahua, Durango, Coahuila, Nuevo León and Tamaulipas); Colonial Mexico (Michoacán, Jalisco, Zacatecas, Aguascalientes, Colima, San Luis Potosí, Guanajuato and Querétaro); The Heart of Mexico (Mexico City and the state of Mexico, Morelos, Guerrero, Hidalgo and Tlaxcala); The Route of the Gods (Veracruz, Puebla and Oaxaca) and the Maya World (Chiapas, Tabasco, Campeche, Yucatán and Quintana Roo).

The Mexican Maya World welcomes the Caribbean in the state of Quintana Roo and crosses the border into Central America and the nations of Guatemala, Belize, Honduras and El Salvador.

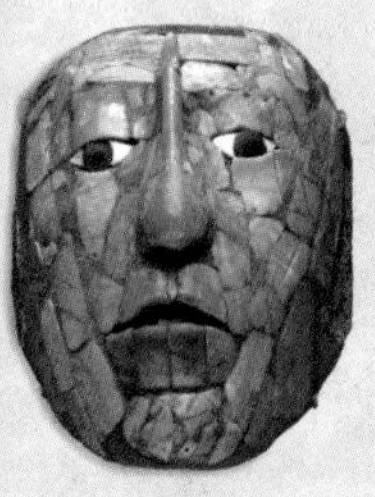

In the Maya World there are mountains, jungles, wetlands, savannas, beaches and islands– with the wildlife to match. Spanish colonial cities rose from the ashes of ancient temples and today's prevailing Mestizo culture is the result of the two races, white and Indian, having merged so long ago. Modern services and transport make traveling the Maya World a pleasure. Hotels, restaurants and other facilities exist everywhere.

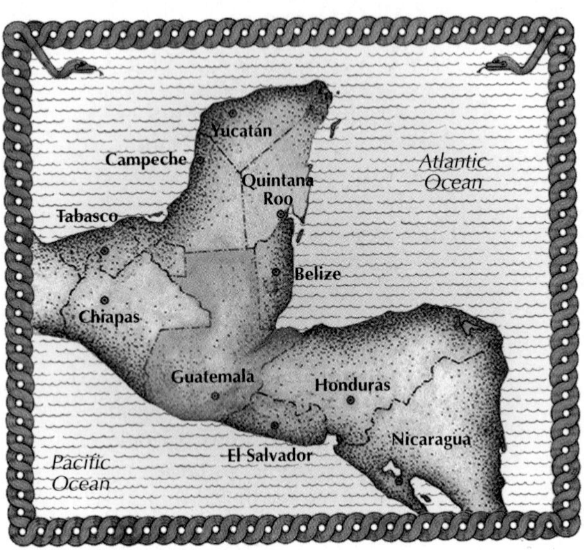

Traveling through the Maya World

Regional airlines operate flights to area archaeological sites. From Cancún you can fly to Chichén Itzá and Palenque; Tikal in Guatemala via Flores and Copán in Honduras. From Cancún, Chetumal and Cozumel you can fly to cities in southeast Mexico and to destinations in Central America with connections to the United States, South America and Europe. Bus service is good throughout the region and renting a car is a viable option.

Quintana Roo

From Cancún, in the north of the state, connections are available to just about anywhere in the Maya World. Cancún International Airport, second busiest in the nation after Mexico City, services the carriers of the world and offers regular connections to major cities in the area. The roads linking the state to Yucatán, Campeche, Tabasco and beyond are in good condition and easy to follow.

Yucatán

Yucatán is the location of Chichén Itzá, Uxmal and the Puuc Route sites. The state has nature reserves, ancient ruins and colonial churches and convents, some of the latter dating from the 16th century. Henequen haciendas from the 19th century still stand on the outskirts of Mérida, the state capital, and the countryside is rife with native Maya communities.

Mérida

Mérida is filled with architecture from the Colonial period exemplified by the Cathedral, Casa Montejo and the Tercera Orden, La Mejorada and Las Monjas churches. Government buildings such as the Palacio Municipal and Palacio de Gobierno, and Cantón Palace date from the late 19th, early 20th centuries. Paseo Montejo boulevard is flanked by mansions dating from the same period.

Uxmal

Uxmal is a Late Classic, Puuc-style city (A.D. 600-900) with superb architecture. Principal structures include the Sorcerer's Pyramid, the Nun's Quadrangle and the Governor's Palace. A World Heritage Site, Uxmal is located 78 km south of Mérida, along Highway 261.

Ruta Puuc

A chain of lesser sites located 25 km south of Uxmal. Kabah, is connected to Uxmal via a sacbe that ends under an arch and its principal structure is the Codz-Pop. Sayil has a three-tiered palace, Labná a magnificent korbel arch, and Xlapak a fine palace.

Uxmal

Chichén Itzá

Chichén Itzá was already a center of note during the Classic period. A group of warriors and merchants called the Itzá Maya moved into Chichén in the 10th century, making it the center of a unified Yucatán.

The city's Maya-Mexican period ran from A.D. 850-1250, though it was in decline by 1150 and abandoned by 1250, for reasons unknown.

The earliest architecture, such as Las Monjas in Old Chichén, is built in the Puuc style and belongs to the Late Classic period (A.D. 600-900), as does El Caracol or Observatory.

The Castillo or Kukulcán Pyramid, the Ballcourt, Warrior's Temple, Temple of 1000 Columns, and the Tzompantli platform are sited around the Great Plaza in New Chichén, also known as Toltec Chichén. The Sacred Cenote, connected to the Great Plaza by a ceremonial road called a sacbe, is considered part of the Great Plaza grouping. Chichén Itzá is located about 200 km west of Cancún, via Highway 180.

Valladolid and Izamal

During the Colonial period, several cities were founded in the Yucatán, of note are Valladolid and Izamal. Founded in 1543, Valladolid would become the colonial capital of eastern Yucatán. Buildings of note include the San Bernadino Church, the Convent of Sisal (16th century) and the Cathedral (17th century).

Izamal is a city with a past. Its architecture, even today is a mix of Maya and Spanish Colonial. The bright yellow convent and church, constructed by the notorious Friar Diego de Landa in 1552, is the center of worship for Our Lady of Izamal, patron saint of Yucatán, one of the two most venerated icons in the region. Valladolid is 160, and Izamal 268 kilometers from Cancún via the toll road (autopista) or federal Highway 180 to Mérida.

Other attractions

Also worth a visit are the Balancanché and Loltún Caves, the Dzitnup Cenote and the Ría Lagartos and the Celestún national parks.

Campeche

Campeche City was the first Spanish settlement on the peninsula. Fortified to stave off pirates, it is the only walled city in Central and North America today. The ramparts enclose the historic center of Campeche, recently declared a World Heritage Site. The *baluartes* (wall towers) are called Soledad, Santiago, San Pedro and San Pablo. City sights include the Regional Museum, the Cathedral and the San Francisco and San Román churches.

Sites of interest

Worth a visit are the Calakmul Biosphere Reserve and the Calakmul archaeological zone; ancient sites elsewhere in the state are Becán, Chicanná, Xpujil, Edzná, and the island of Jaina (famous for its clay figurines). The state also boasts craft villages and colonial monuments. Travel services are good throughout the state.

Chiapas

The gateway to Central America, Chiapas has some of the most spectacular scenery, in Mexico: Agua Azul Falls, Misol-Ha Falls, Montes Azules, Montebello Lakes and the Sumidero Canyon are nature reserves and harbor a variety of wildlife. Ancient Mayan sites include Palenque, Bonampak, Yaxchilán and Toniná. Many communities boast colonial churches and San Cristóbal de Las Casas, Chiapa de Corzo and Comitán are worth a visit. Tuxtla is the state capital. Places of interest include the San Marcos Cathedral, Casa de las Artesanías, Regional Museum, Teatro de Ciudad (theater) and the Miguel Álvarez del Toro Zoo.

Tabasco

The Olmec, a Mesoamerican mother culture, flourished in Tabasco. The Pantanos de Centla Biosphere Reserve is the state's most important protected area.

Edzná, Campeche

Palenque, Chiapas

La Venta, Tabasco

The capital, Villahermosa is the home of La Venta Park Museum, which features the colossal stone heads associated with the Olmec. Mayan sites include Comalcalco and Pomoná and Oxolotán reflects the state's colonial period.

Belize

Copán, Honduras

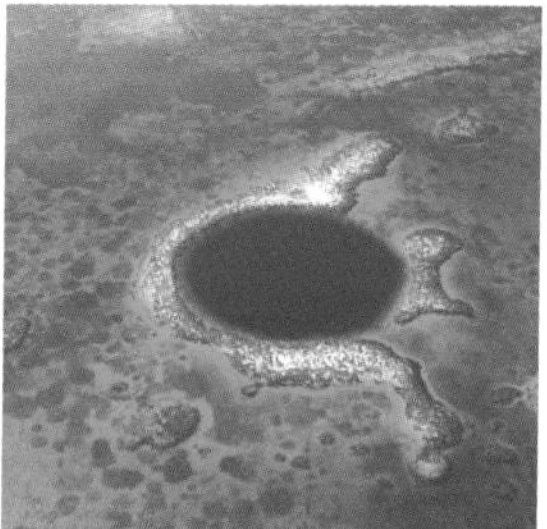
Blue Hole, Belize

Copán, Honduras

Santa Ana, El Salvador

Belize

The only English-speaking nation in Central America, Belize offers a glimpse of the Caribbean with its wooden houses, cuisine and music. Ancient Maya centers of note are Caracol, Cuello, Altun Ha, Xunantunich, Lubaantun and Lamanai. The country is also filled with nature reserves: the Cockscomb Basin Jaguar Sanctuary, Mountain Pine Ridge, Columbia Forest Reserve and others. Good beaches include those at Dangriga, Placencia and San Pedro, with the longest reef in the hemisphere and 200 cays right off shore.

There are flights to Belize City from Cancún or travelers can drive or take the bus across the border from Chetumal. The capital is Belmopán but Belize City is still the most important city.

Honduras

Honduras is located at the heart of Central America and its vast biodiversity is protected in 107 reserves. Copán, a major city of the ancient Maya, is located in the west, near the Guatemalan border. Colonial Honduras is present in the cities of Tegucigalpa (capital), Trujillo and Comayagua. The country is home to several ethnic groups, in addition to the mestizo, all of which live together comfortably.

El Salvador

El Salvador may be the Maya World's smallest country, but it too has many sites of interest including Mayan ruins, colonial architecture, beaches, volcanoes and nature reserves. The capital, San Salvador, is a blend of old and new, traditional and modern.

Tikal, Guatemala

Guatemala

Guatemala is another country rich in attractions. Areas of interest are the Altiplano or highlands, Guatemala City and Antigua Guatemala; the Petén, the tropical forest setting of Tikal; Alta and Baja Verapaz; and the Caribbean coast. Considered the cradle of Classic period civilization, Tikal was occupied from 800 B.C. to A.D. 900. Landmark structures include Temples I and II, the North Acropolis, Central Acropolis, the Pre-Classic Plaza of the Great Pyramid and Temple IV, which at 74 m is the tallest pyramid in the Maya World.

Guatemala City is the nation's modern capital and a good base of operations for visiting the country. It was founded in 1776 and much of its late, baroque-style colonial architecture is still standing.

La Antigua Guatemala is perhaps the loveliest, if the most tragic city in Guatemala. It was capital of Central America for some 200 years and almost completely destroyed by earthquakes on more than one occasion. The ruins of 16th and 17th-century palaces, churches and convents give the place a mysterious, otherworldly air.

Lake Atitlán, Guatemala

Many of the nation's indigenous groups inhabit the highlands. Worth a visit are the villages of Panajachel, on the shores of Lake Atitlán, Santiago Atitlán, Sololá, Todos Santos Cuchumatán and Totonicapán. In Chichicastenango, visitors discover the traditions and mystic beliefs of the Quiché Maya.

Quetzaltenango is the capital of the western highlands. The Espíritu Santo Cathedral, City Hall and Teatro de la Ciudad (theater) date from the colonial period and 19th century.

Guatemala is easily reached from Quintana Roo. There are flights from Cancún to Guatemala City and to Flores in the Petén (Tikal). You can also drive to Flores from Chetumal (via Belize).

Through whose eyes should I look at you?

M e
once seen...

xico

always cherished

Traveler's Notebook

The Traveler's Notebook gives you an overview of Quintana Roo and the areas through which you'll be traveling. We list available services and point out sites of interest. We advise you on where to stay, where to eat, what to buy and how and where to exchange money. We discuss the different modes of travel and what's best for each area. At the end of the section you'll find lists of airlines, hotels, restaurants, travel agencies, car rentals and more.

We hope you find the Notebook useful, but do ask that you keep in mind that information may change after we've gone to press.

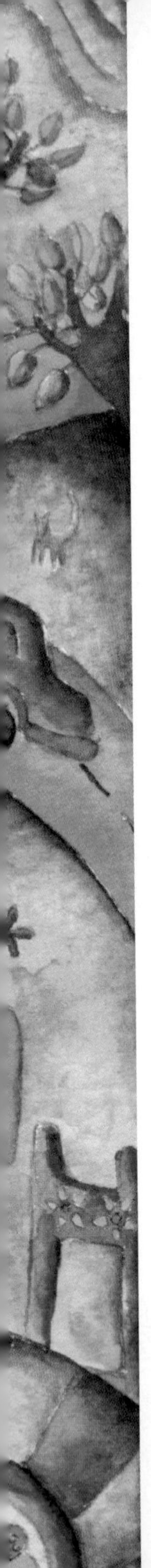

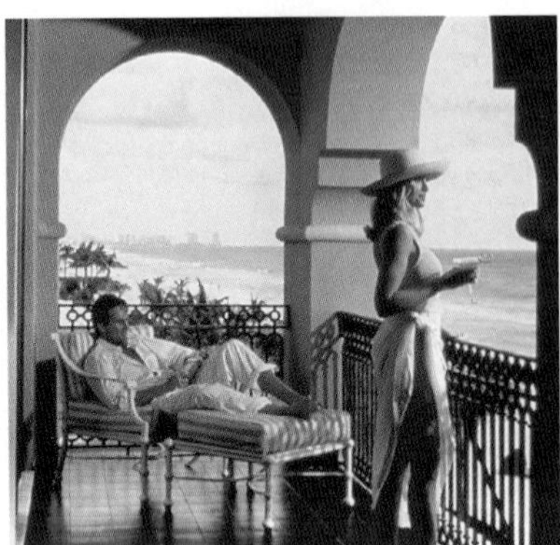

Accommodation & Cuisine

Quintana Roo has accommodation to suit every taste and wallet. There are modern hotels of all sizes and design, with every service imaginable, along the beaches in Cancún, Cozumel, Playa del Carmen and at some spots in the Riviera Maya. On Isla Mujeres, to the north of the ferry terminal in Playa del Carmen, along most of the Riviera Maya and the Costa Maya in Southern Quintana Roo, there are a variety of smaller hotels, many of which are actually cabaña or bungalow-style resorts with a tropical flavor and lots of atmosphere.

Hotel services

The larger hotels in Cancún, Cozumel and other major tourist spots have an extensive portfolio of services ranging from restaurants, bars, pools, shops, travel agencies and car hire to business centers, convention salons, gyms, spas and marinas. Services do vary from hotel to hotel, however, even though prices may be similar.

Reservations

If possible, you should make a reservation beforehand and always arrive at your next hotel early. Hotels in popular destinations sometimes have a check-in limit and may not respect reservations after this time.

Currency

In Mexico the peso is the currency and it is available in the following denominations: 500, 200, 100, 50 and 20 peso notes and 20, 10, 5, 2 and 1-peso coins. There are also 50 and 20 and 10-centavo coins.

Money exchange

Transactions can be conducted in the airport, hotels, banks, bureau de change and even some shops. Visitors should bring U.S. dollars and/or travelers cheques, other currencies can be difficult to change outside the resorts. Make sure that your money is not defaced, stamped or torn as banks will not accept marked notes.

Most banks open at 9 a.m and close between 5 and 7 p.m. Some are open for Saturday morning banking.

Change

Always carry plenty of change, it may be difficult to change large denominations in villages. This applies to dollars and pesos.

Credit cards

All the major credit cards are accepted in the area. There are ATM's for Visa and Mastercard in larger towns.

Shopping

Shopping in Quintana Roo's resorts is an enjoyable activity, whether you bargain for crafts in a market, examine delicate silver in a shop or look for imported perfumes and luxury goods in a modern mall.

What to buy

Mexican handicrafts make excellent souvenirs and area shops and markets are full of them. Veritable works of art, they reflect the creativity of the nation's artisans; the variety is breathtaking and each state has its own specialty. Items to look for include weavings from Chiapas and Oaxaca; rugs and blankets; pottery; wooden masks, figures and furniture; reproductions of Mayan bas-reliefs; basketry and straw hats; rag dolls; hammocks; leather; glassware; amber; amate bark paintings; onyx and copper.

Mexico is a leading producer of silver and its silversmiths are some of the most talented in the world. Visitors will find fine jewelry and sculptures on display in stores in Cancún, Cozumel, Isla Mujeres and Playa del Carmen.

Markets

Area markets offer everything from crafts, fruit, vegetables, flowers, meat and poultry to crockery and hardware. Cities and towns have permanent markets. There are even special craft enclaves for visitors in Cancún and Cozumel.

Supermarkets

Supermarkets in the state's resorts stock a wide range of domestic and imported goods. Many of the brands you are familiar with will be more expensive here than in your own country because they are imported.

Shopping malls

There are shopping malls in Cancún, Cozumel and Playa del Carmen where visitors can find art, sculptures, jewelry, fine crafts and everything from perfumes and designer labels to watches and clothing.

VERÁS

Bargaining

Regateo or bargaining is an art and visitors are expected to try their hand in markets and craft villages. Bear in mind that the first price quoted is always higher than the actual value of the item. The idea is to reach a satisfactory price for both seller and buyer, something that may take several minutes of negotiations.

Whether they decide to sample the local cuisine or stick to international favorites, visitors will find eating out a pleasure in Quintana Roo's many resorts. Mexicans are hospitable people and service is given with a smile as you dine in surroundings that range from a elegant restaurant to a rustic beachfront palapa.

The taste of Mexico

The country boasts one of the most varied cuisines in the world and to understand its diversity you have to look at its history.

Pre-Hispanic Mexicans cultivated corn, tomatoes, squash, beans and chiles. Corn was used in a number of ways: roast, ground, toasted or in *tortillas* and *tamales.* A drink called *atole* was also made from water and corn flour, when cacao was added, it was called chocolate.

When the Spaniards first set foot in Mexico they encountered new cultures, animals, birds, plants and even cuisines. Over time, they introduced livestock, vegetables, fruit, herbs and spices and the resultant blend of native and Old World ingredients is something that sets Mexican cuisine apart from all the rest.

Every region has its own specialties. Northern, Central (the Bajío), Southeast Mexico and both coasts all offer distinctive dishes made with local ingredients. Mexican cuisine is a cornucopia of flavors, colors and delicious smells. Beef, pork, lamb, seafood, vegetables, fruits and seeds are mixed with herbs and spices in a variety of ways.

Although the nation may be famous for the taco, a tortilla stuffed with meat or other fillings and rolled up, there's much more to it than that. Why not try some *salsas* (sauces), *sopas* (soups), *recados* and *adobos* (spice mixes) and *moles* (savory-sweet sauces made with chocolate, chile and spices, served on chicken or turkey), *chiles rellenos, enchiladas...,* you'll not be disappointed.

Yucatecan - worth trying

Specialties to look out for are *panuchos* and *salbutes* (fried tortillas topped with turkey, lettuce and pickled onion); *papadzules* (hard-boiled egg tacos in a pumpkin and tomato sauce); *sopa de lima* (chicken and lime soup); *tikinxic* (grilled fish); *relleno negro* or *chilmole* (turkey and pork in a sauce made with a black recado); *queso relleno* (a Dutch cheese stuffed with minced pork, olives, nuts, herbs and spices and topped with two sauces); *poc chuc* (grilled pork) and *cochinita pibil* (marinated pork, wrapped in banana leaves and cooked in an oven or pit).

Hottest chile in the world

Chile salsas of varying degrees of hotness are always served with a Mexican meal. Go easy on chile if you are not used to its fiery taste. This applies nowhere more so than in Yucatán, home of the world's hottest chile, the habanero. This heart-shaped scorcher is served raw, in a *salsa mexicana* with chopped tomato, onion and coriander or in a sauce called *xnipec* which contains pickled onion and lime juice.

If you overdo it and *enchilarse* – a burning sensation in the mouth, throat and on the lips, lick some salt grains.

History of Yucatecan cuisine

A blend of native ingredients used by the ancient Maya, European and Oriental flavorings introduced by the Spaniards during the Colonial period, and later additions from the Caribbean and the Middle East, Yucatecan cuisine is one of the most interesting regional dining experiences in Mexico. Ingredients first used by the Maya include corn, beans, tomatoes, chiles, squash, chaya (a spinach-like plant), avocado and achiote (annatto). The Spaniards introduced citrus fruit – limes and Seville oranges feature in many dishes, chicken, beef, dairy products, coriander, garlic, olives, oregano and rice. Pork, chicken and turkey are widely used in Yucatecan recipes, usually in conjunction with recados, which may contain achiote, Seville orange juice, pepper and chiles.

From other countries

In Cancún, Cozumel, Playa del Carmen, Chetumal and other resort areas, visitors can sample a different cuisine each night. Chinese, Italian, Spanish, French, Argentinian, Brazilian, Japanese, Thai and Lebanese restaurants exist and there are steak houses, international eateries and vegetarian cafes. Seafood is abundant and tasty – lobster and shrimp are served in a variety of imaginative ways – and there are many fast food outlets for those who cannot live without a hamburger, pizza or fried chicken.

Beverages

Mexican cerveza or beer is excellent – try Dos XX, Corona, Superior, Sol, Tecate , Montejo and León Negra. There are some good domestic brands of wine and tequila is the national drink. Non-alcoholic beverages range from the traditional *horchata* (sweetened rice water), *jamaica* (dried flower petals steeped in water) and *aguas frescas* (fruit juices diluted with water) to *refrescos* or soft drinks in a variety of flavors.

Water

The largest hotels often have their own purification systems and the rest provide bottled, purified water.

When to eat

Breakfast (*desayuno*) is served from 7 and 10 a.m. Lunch (*comida*) is the main meal, served from 1 - 3 p.m. and most people eat dinner (*cena*) between 6 and 10 p.m.

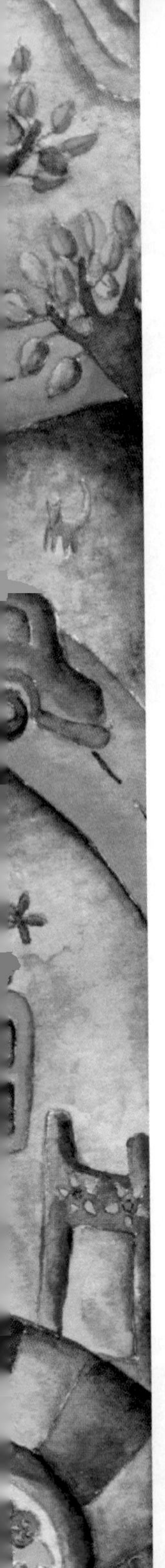

Here are a few pointers on traveling in the region.

Tours in the area

Quintana Roo's location means that it is in all ways the gateway to Mexico and particularly to the countless natural and historical attractions scattered throughout the Maya World. Travel agencies in Cancún, Cozumel and Playa del Carmen offer a variety of excursions to sites of interest in the area, for example Chichén Itzá, Río Lagartos, Mérida and Uxmal in the neighboring state of Yucatán. The archaeological sites of Palenque in Chiapas and Tikal in northern Guatemala are now only a short plane ride away and day trips are also available.

Using Chetumal as their base visitors can explore the archaeological sites and reserves of Southern Quintana Roo, the state of Campeche, Belize and northern Guatemala.

By air

Cancún's airport receives flights from all over the world and regular connections are available to destinations in Mexico, the United States, Europe and South America. A regional air network links cities throughout Southeast Mexico and Central America making travel in the Maya World simple and convenient. Aerocaribe, Aviacsa and Grupo Taca have their own routes linking sites such as Chichén Itzá, Palenque, Tikal and the cities of Cozumel, Chetumal, Mérida, Villahermosa, Tuxtla Gutiérrez, San Cristóbal de Las Casas, Tapachula, Guatemala City and Belize City. Flights are also available to Oaxaca, Huatulco, Veracruz and Acapulco from Cancún. The Central American airlines, Grupo Taca fly to San Pedro Sula in Honduras (for Copán, Tegucigalpa and the Bay Islands) and to San José in Costa Rica.

By car

Traveling by car gives you the freedom to explore Quintana Roo and the Yucatán Peninsula at your own pace. Major routes are Highway 307 from Cancún to Chetumal, the Mérida-Cancún toll road, Highway 180 which also connects Mérida and Cancún, Highway 186 from Chetumal to Escárcega in Campeche and 261 from Mérida to Uxmal.

Avoid night driving, some stretches of highway between villages are poorly lit and people and animals stray on to the roads. Be prepared for *baches* or potholes which may develop on highways after torrential rain.

Topes or speed bumps are located at the entrances and exits to villages and on many city streets. They are marked with a sign which is often just before the speed bump.

In order to avoid a nasty jolt, your best bet is to slow down when approaching a community. Speed limits are 90 k.p.h. on highways (110 k p.h. on toll roads) and 40 k.p.h. in built up areas. Familiarize yourself with road signs before setting out and note the location of gas stations along the route you are going to travel. Gasoline is sold by the liter (one liter is around 1/4 gallon). Newer cars take lead-free gas called Magna Sin or Premier, Nova is for older vehicles. In the event of a breakdown, place a branch in the road a few meters behind the car. This will indicate to drivers that

Stop

No parking

Keep to the right

Speed limit

No overtaking

Archaeological site

Colonial site

Mechanic

Public beach

there is a parked car ahead. Police patrol the highways and the Ángeles Verdes corp also provides assistance.

By bus

First and second-class buses are cheap in Mexico. Second-class buses are crowded and slower. Deluxe, non-stop buses also ply the Cancún - Chetumal and Cancún - Mérida routes. Always get to bus terminals early as tickets and seats go fast. It may be possible to reserve a seat on a first-class bus.

Renting a car

The major international rental agencies have offices in Cancún and Cozumel airports and desks at the most important hotels. To rent a car you need a valid driver's license, passport and a credit card. You must also be over the age of 21. Check the vehicle before leaving the agency.

Safety

Safety is an important issue when visiting an new city, whether abroad or in your own country. Follow a few simple guidelines for a problem-free vacation.

Driving

Never leave valuables in a parked car; if you break down leave someone watching the vehicle. Always respect the speed limits indicated on signs.

Walking

Be attentive and keep a firm grip on your bag or wallet. Money and passports should be kept in a hidden pocket or money belt. Take a copy of your passport and tourist card and keep them in a separate place, just in case you lose the original. Store money, airline tickets and other valuables in a hotel safety deposit box.

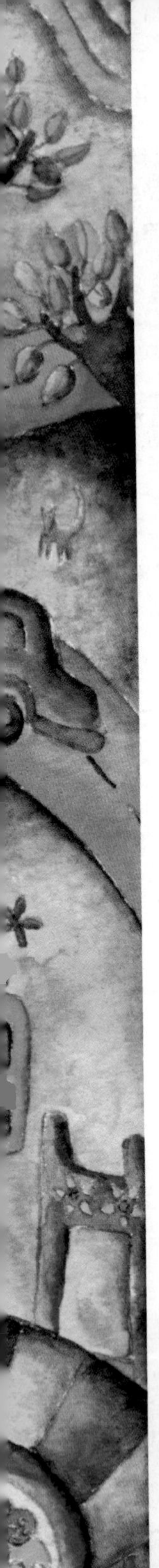

Breaking the law

In Mexico, the possession of drugs is an offense punishable by heavy jail sentences and fines. The possession, sale and purchase of pre-Hispanic artifacts and endangered animal and bird species (skins or products such as turtle oil cream, tortoiseshell and black coral are also illegal.

Health

With a few simple precautions, visitors to Quintana Roo should have a problem-free vacation.

Insurance

Before traveling to Quintana Roo call your insurance company to check on medical coverage in the region. Wherever you travel in the world, it is always wise to take out a policy if you do not have insurance.

Vaccinations

Consult your doctor beforehand about the vaccinations you may need for a trip to the area.

Stomach upsets

Whenever you travel to a different country, your body takes a while to adjust to local conditions, food and microbes, and stomach upsets are common. A few precautions may help prevent problems: Drink purified bottled water. Tap water may not always have been purified outside the resorts. Be wary of ice – check to see if it is made from purified water– and the fruit drinks sold on the streets. Watch what and where you eat. Meat, poultry and seafood that is partially cooked should be sent back, likewise avoid raw seafood. Make sure that fruit and vegetables have been sterilized. If you are sick, drink lots of bottled water, try peptobismol, kaopectate or the soothing local remedy of *te de manzanilla* (chamomile tea). Call a doctor if your symptoms last more than 48 hours.

Medical services

If all else fails, consult a local doctor, many of whom speak English. There are Social Security hospitals (Seguro Social) and private clinics in Quintana Roo's towns and cities. The Red Cross also operates in the area.

What to wear and what to read are just some of the questions first-time visitors to Quintana Roo ask. Here are some tips on traveling in the region.

Climate and rainfall

The Yucatán Peninsula lies in the tropics and temperatures may reach 29 - 40 °C (85 °F - 100+°F) during the day in the summer months. Night temperatures are between 21°C and 23°C. The winter months are somewhat cooler. There are two seasons in the Yucatán Peninsula: the dry season or *invierno* (winter), from November to April and the rainy season or *verano* (summer), from April to November. Temperatures do not vary a great deal but the amount of rainfall does. The climate is less humid in the winter although storms characterized by strong winds, cooler temperatures and heavy rain may blow in from the Gulf of Mexico. Called *nortes*, they last two or three days. Rainfall during the summer months normally takes the form of afternoon downpours, accompanied by thunder and lightning. Even when it is not raining humidity levels are extremely high. Sea breezes provide some relief from the heat along the coasts.

What to wear

Cool, cotton clothing is recommended for the Yucatán Peninsula. The sun is strong so always wear a hat and sunglasses; use a sun block to avoid burning and limit your sunbathing time. Make sure you drink plenty of bottled water as dehydration can be a problem in the hot, humid climate.

Sturdy leather shoes are required for walking in the archaeological sites. Trousers, long-sleeved shirts, socks and boots are a must if you are going into the jungle. You need this extra protection against mosquitoes, ticks and spiny plants. Use repellent to ward off the attacks of biting insects.

Water safety

Take care on the beaches along the open ocean side of the Hotel Zone in Cancún and the windward side of Cozumel. Offshore currents and the undertow can be strong. Always swim with someone else and do not venture out of your depth. If you feel that you are being swept away do not fight the current, let it take you parallel to the coast and then swim to shore.

If you feel very tired, overheated or have just eaten wait a while before swimming. Do not venture into the water if you have been drinking. Always check the depth of a pool before diving in and make sure that there is no one in that area of the pool when you jump. Children should always be watched even when they are wearing armbands or life jackets.

Flags fly on the beaches of the Hotel Zone in Cancún indicating ocean conditions.

Red or Black: Danger
Yellow: Precaution needed
Green/blue: Calm

Sun sense

Quintana Roo has a tropical climate and the sun's rays are fierce. Use a good sun block and limit your exposure, starting with 15 minutes on the first day and gradually increasing it by five or 10 minutes. Take care between noon and 4 p.m. when the sun is at its strongest and sunburn is most likely to occur. Visitors with pale or sensitive skins should always wear a strong sun block. Protect your eyes with sun glasses, a visor or hat. Aloe Vera aftersun remedies are soothing if you do overdo it but visitors with a serious case of sunburn should seek medical advice.

Siestas

People still take the traditional *siesta* or after-lunch nap in many parts of the Yucatán Peninsula and it makes good sense as it can be sweltering. Shops and offices close during the hottest part of the day (usually from 2 or 3 - 5 p.m., although this varies from town to town). Although this practice is less common in Cancún and other resorts, some smaller stores still close for lunch.

Communications

Mexico's national telecommunications company is called Telmex and MCI and AT & T also operate in the country. Card or coin-operated phones are located in public places. You can purchase a phone card in tobacco stores, pharmacies and some shops. There are also *casetas de larga distancia* or long distance phone and fax offices in many towns and cities; some are even beginning to offer access to the Internet. You can also call or send faxes from your hotel but service charges are high.

Telephone System

To call Mexico from outside her borders one must use the international direct dialing code required by one's country, followed by Mexico's country code, 52, plus the area code of the city in Mexico being called, plus the local number. For example, to call Cancún from the United States dial: 011 [international direct dialing code] + 52

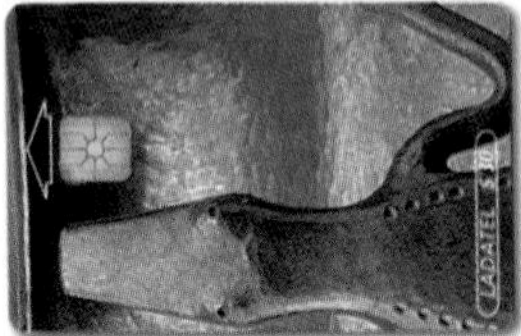

[Mexico's country code] + 998 [area code for Cancún, Quintana Roo] + local number.

Post Offices

Mark your envelope with the words *por avión*, or airmail. Post office hours vary from place to place.

Newspapers, magazines & books

National daily newspapers published in Spanish include *La Jornada, Reforma* and *El Universal.* Cancún has its own Spanish and English language newspapers.

The larger hotels in Cancún, Cozumel and Playa del Carmen stock foreign newspapers such as the *New York Times, Wall Street Journal, Miami Herald, USA Today* and *Le Monde*. Area bookstores stock publications in Spanish and English on the nation's geography, history and culture and some may also carry a limited line of English language bestsellers.

Taxes

Value Added Tax (IVA) on goods and services in Quintana Roo is 10% (15% elsewhere in Mexico). To that, hotels add an additional 5% which is factored into their rates.

Tips

Tipping is expected and to the usual set of people: waiters, maids, bellhops, airport luggage carriers, tour guides and so forth. Taxi drivers are not tipped, except in special cases. Ten to 15% is the norm, more at your discretion if the service warrants it. When the tip is included in a bar or restaurant bill, the check will clearly say so; otherwise, you're expected to tip.

Immigration and Customs

Visitors to Mexico pass through immigration and customs at the first port of entry. The airlines provide forms (for immigration and customs) that must be filled out and presented to the respective agents. Items such as animals, agricultural products and cash in excess of $10,000 US must be declared on the Customs

Chichén Itzá

Declaration form. It behooves travelers to read carefully and declare truthfully. The first stop after leaving the plane is Immigration where officials check passports/I.D. and stamp visas. Note the visa's expiration date; you must leave the country on or before that date or seek a renewal through the agency's offices. Travelers then retrieve their luggage and move to customs. At customs, agents collect the forms and ask travelers to press a button connected to what looks very like a stop light. If the traveler gets a green light, he passes through with no check; if, on the other hand he gets the red light, all bags and carry-ons are subject to a check.

Language

Spanish is the first language in Mexico. English is spoken widely in tourist resorts and major cities. If you do not speak Spanish carry a dictionary and phrase book with you. In villages throughout Quintana Roo you will hear Maya being spoken.

Archaeological Sites

Archaeological sites are national parks and as such free on Sundays and national holidays. An admission fee is charged on all other days. All sites are open daily 8 a.m. to 5 p.m. The use of video requires special permits (purchased at ticket counter) and flash cameras are prohibited wherever pigments are visible on ancient surfaces. Bilingual guides can be hired at the site entrance.

Museums

The National Institute of Anthropology and History (INAH) operates museums throughout the Yucatán Peninsula, at the archaeological sites of Chichén Itzá, Uxmal and Dzibilchaltún and in Mérida and Cancún. Also worth a visit are the museums in Cozumel, Chetumal and Bacalar. Visitors traveling on to Mexico City should not miss the National Anthropology Museum.

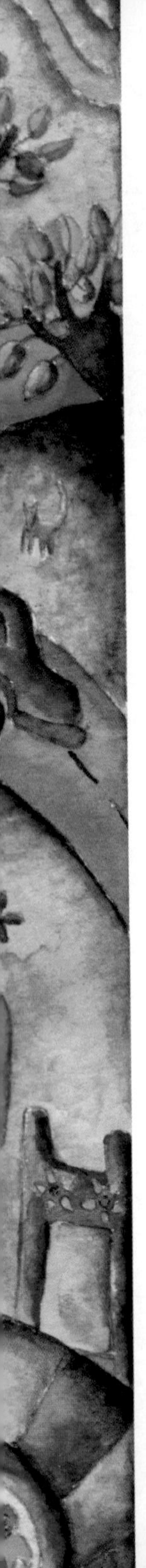

Weddings

The Mexican Caribbean is an increasingly popular destination for weddings; indeed the Riviera Maya was recently voted the world's most popular honeymoon destination by Modern Bride magazine. If you would like to tie the knot in Quintana Roo, we suggest that you contact a local wedding coordinator. In the meantime, here is some general information on civil and religious ceremonies.

In Mexico, as in many other countries around the world, the civil marriage is the legally binding ceremony that changes your marital status from single to married. The judge who performs the ceremony may do it in the Registry Office (Registro Civil) or outside the office in the place of your choice, for example, your hotel, for a higher fee. The documents needed to apply for the wedding license are as follows: full blood tests, an interview with a medical professional, valid passport, a birth certificate which must be translated in Mexico by an authorized legal translator, the Mexican tourist visa, divorce decree or death certificate of spouse if applicable (copies). You also need four witnesses; if they are foreigners

they must present valid passports and visas.

For religious or spiritual ceremonies the minister requires two witnesses. If you decide you want a religious ceremony, please bear in mind that you must conduct the civil ceremony to legalize your marriage. You can either do it here in Mexico or back home in accordance with the laws of your own country.

Wedding consultants will do all the paperwork for you so that you can enjoy your stay. They will take you through the legal process step by step, ensuring that it is done as quickly as possible and will help you plan every aspect of your event from the setting and the catering to flowers, photographers and transport. Many of the larger hotels in the state have their own wedding coordinators and offer services ranging from a simple ceremony on the beach to a full-blown event with a reception, musicians and dancing, and honeymoon packages.

Information sources: The Cancun Visitors & Convention Bureau (OVC) and the State Tourism Board keep lists of reputable wedding consultants.

Conventions

With its convention center, hotels, infrastructure, communication and transport facilities, Cancun used to be the only convention destination in the Mexican Caribbean, hosting national, regional and global events ranging from multinational company conventions and pharmaceutical industry seminars to World Trade Organization ministerial meetings. This is no longer the case, Isla Mujeres, Riviera Maya and Cozumel can now cater to the convention market with their portfolio of hotels offering state of the art meeting facilities and staff to organize events and catering. For top-level, small group meetings, there are also plenty of exclusive retreats to choose from. Finally, as conventions are never all work and no play, examples of activities on offer for free days include day trips to archaeological sites and nature parks, island cruises, shopping, diving, golf and sport fishing.

Real Estate

Mexico is a land of opportunity for investors and owning land or property and running a business is easier than ever. Foreigners may buy and develop land for residential property (non residential property must be registered with the Mexican Foreign Office, the Secretaría de Relaciones Exteriores) in the Mexican Caribbean by means of a fideicomiso or trust.

A fideicomiso is a trust established with the Mexican bank of your choice by which the bank holds title of the property in trust for you the purchaser. You are the sole beneficiary of the trust, holding all rights and you can live in your property, rent it, make improvements and even sell it. Fideicomisos run for 50 years and may be renewed or bequeathed. You pay a minimal annual fee to the bank and the only time it intervenes is if you sell your property to another foreigner.

Local real estate agents will advise you on investment opportunities, where land is for sale, the legal, environmental and building permits required and the property options available, for example timeshares, beachfront condos and villas. Another source of information for potential investors is Fidecaribe, the Chetumal-based government body in charge of commercializing land in Quintana Roo.

www.caribbeanmex.com

With our Virtual Guide you will be able to tour and enjoy the Mexican Caribbean, explore every corner of the peninsula using our maps, learn more about the destinations, look for information about the State, see fabulous pictures and take a virtual tour in our multimedia gallery and much more. In our Virtual Guide, you will find everything you can imagine about the Mexican Caribbean, so be curious and explore our portal!

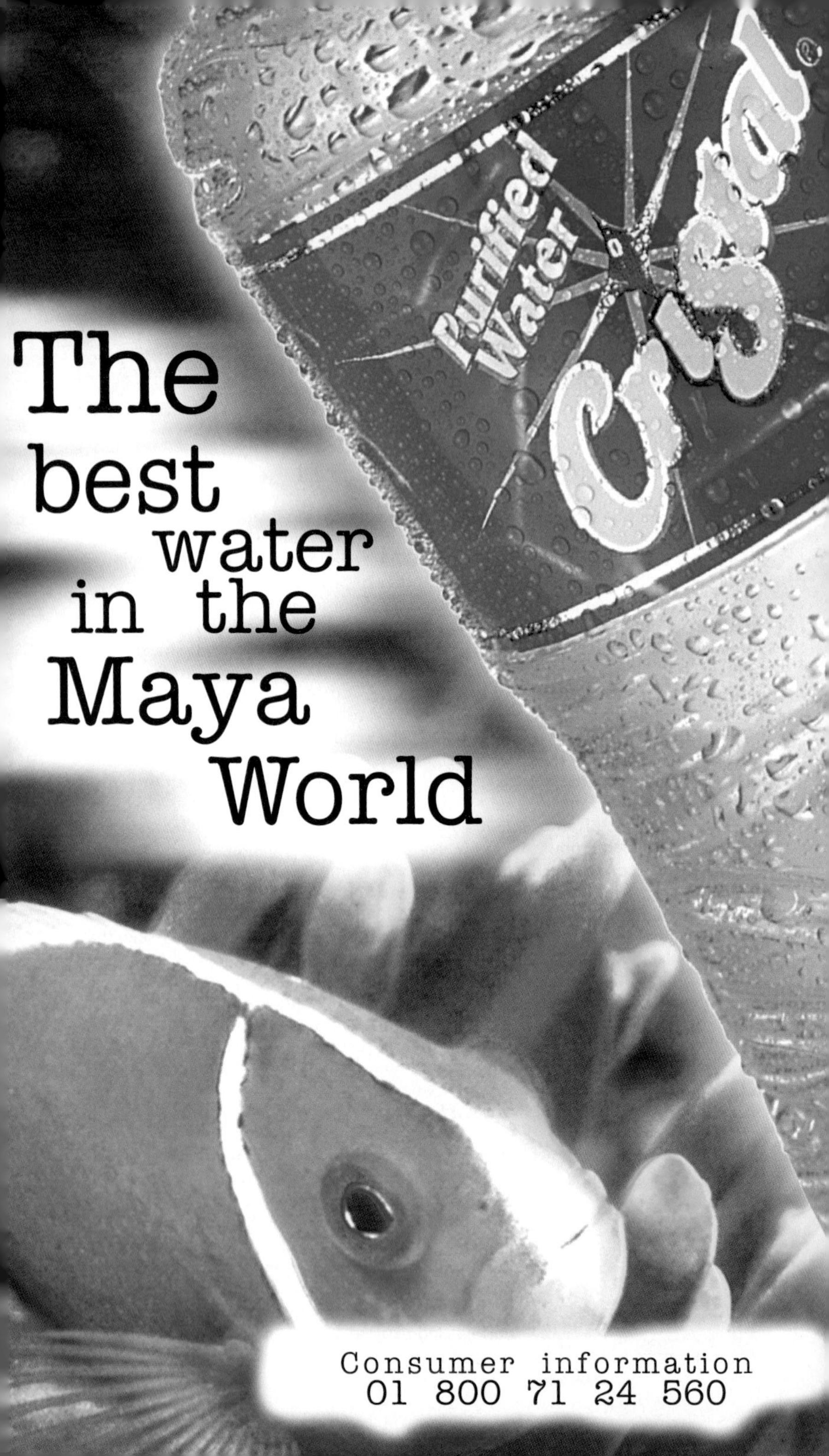

Cristal®
Purified Water
The best water in the Maya World
Consumer information
01 800 71 24 560

TRAVEL DIRECTORY

Cancún

175

Isla Mujeres

230

Holbox 239

Cozumel

242

Felipe Carrillo Puerto 255

Riviera Maya

256

Chetumal & The South

299

The following is a list of the symbols used in the descriptions of services and a reference to map locations. In addition to tourist services, we have included information on sites of interest, travel tips and useful tables to help you during your stay. Please bear in mind that information may change after this guide has gone to press. Some hotels and restaurants requested that price or category information be omitted from their listing.

GLOSSARY OF STREET TERMS: *Calle*: Street; *Esq.* /On the corner of ; *Por*: Close to or on the corner of; *Piso*: Floor; *Mz. /Manzana*: Block; *L. /Lote*: Number; *Andador*: Walkway; *Fracc.*: Development; *Dpto.*: Apartment; *Edif. Edificio:* Building; *Reg. Región*: Region; *Zona*: Zone; *Centro Comercial*: Commercial Center; *Carr. /Carretera*: Highway; *Int. /Interior*: Inside number; *Ret. /Retorno*: Turnoff; *Col. /Colonia*: District; *Conjunto*: Complex; *Mercado*: Market; *Prol.*: Extension; *Puerto de Abrigo*: Natural harbour; *Priv. /Privada*: Private street; *Carretera Costera:* Coast road.

REFERENCE TO SERVICES DISPLAYED ON MAPS.

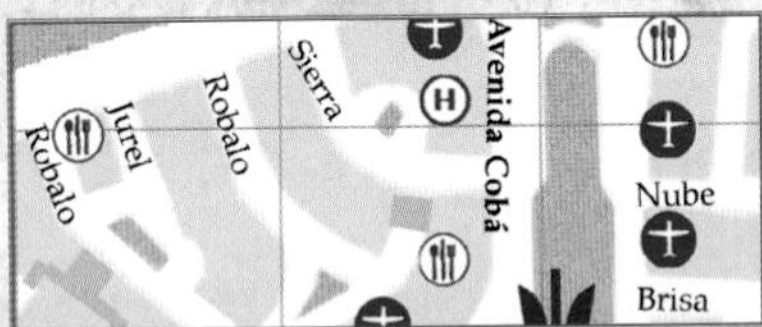

Look for the map coordinate beside the name of each company, this refers you to the map of the city in question, for example, : **C-09** ***Aerocozumel.***

Cancún has two maps: services in Downtown Cancún are shown in blue.

The majority of the hotels have a reference number with which you can identify them on the corresponding map.

In general, the services without a reference are outside the map area.

TRAVEL AGENCIES. In addition to the languages spoken by staff and the services offered by the company, we also indicate whether they offer:

- Plane tickets
- Circuits
- Groups
- Individual tourism
- Adventure Tours
- Cultural trips
- Ecotourism
- Archaeological trips
- Boat trips
- Buses
- Representation services
- Transfers

MARINAS. In addition to the languages spoken by staff and the services offered by the company, we also indicate whether they offer:

- Diving
- Boat trips
- Jungle tour
- Kayak
- Jet Ski /wave runner
- Sport fishing
- Snorkeling
- Water ski
- Windsurf
- Yachts
- Guides
- Cave diving

RESTAURANTS. The price range is given in dollars and is given per person for a meal that includes one drink, a starter, main course and dessert or coffee. Some restaurants may change their prices and opening hours according to the season; "off" season is generally considered to run from April 15 to December 15 while high season encompasses Christmas, New Year, January, February, March, Easter week and breaks for national holidays.

- UP TO $8
- BETWEEN $8 & $15
- BETWEEN $15 & $25
- BETWEEN $25 & $35
- MORE THAN $35
- Air-conditioning
- Bar
- Groups
- Live music
- Dance floor
- Reservations
- Show
- Formal dress

Credit cards

VI VISA MC MASTER CARD AE AMERICAN EXPRESS

- House specialty
- Opening hours

LOCATION. In the case of hotels and restaurants we specify whether they are beachfront or lagoon-side, or if they are in the city.

- Beachfront
- Lagoon
- Downtown/City

HOTELS. Rates (subject to change) will give you a rough idea of the daily cost of a standard double room. Rates vary according to the season. "Off" season is generally considered to run from April 15 to December 15 while high season encompasses Christmas, New Year, January, February, March, Easter week and breaks for national holidays. Some hotels offer special group rates and packages. Rates are given in dollars.

LOW SEASON	HIGH SEASON
Up to $50	Up to $50
Between $50 & $100	Between $50 & $100
Between $100 & $180	Between $100 & $180
Between $180 & $250	Between $180 & $250
Between $250 & $350	Between $250 & $350
More than $350	More than $350

CATEGORY. The classification system used in Mexico by most hotels has categories that run from one to six stars (Deluxe). We have also included a special category, which would cover small and exclusive hotels or eco-hotels that do not offer the amenities of a large hotel but have their own charm.

★ One star (up to 6)

Special Category

PLANS. Hotels may offer one or more of the following plans: • All-inclusive, which includes food, drinks and most activities • European Plan: no meals • American Plan: breakfast and either lunch or dinner included • Continental Plan: Continental breakfast included.

⌘ All-inclusive

PE European Plan

PA American Plan

PC Continental Plan

SERVICES: • The majority of Deluxe and 5-star hotels offer the following services, with the exception of golf, disco and a spa, which are marked in the lists when applicable. • The majority of 4-star hotels and 3-star hotels in Cancún Hotel Zone offer services 1-9, additional services are included in the lists when applicable. • The amenities offered by the remaining 3-star hotels and hotels in other categories are featured in the listings • At the end of the line of symbols for each hotel a figure denotes the number of rooms, villas or suites.

1. Restaurant
2. Bar
3. Air-conditioning
4. Television
5. Pool
6. Gift shop
7. Car rental
8. Travel agency / trips
9. Laundry
10. Convention rooms
11. Evening entertainment
12. Beauty parlor
13. Gym
14. Kids club
15. Disco
16. Spa
17. Tennis
18. Golf
19. Marina
20. Wedding /Honeymoon programs
21. Babysitters
22. Social activities

AREA CODES

DOMESTIC

- Domestic long distance operator assisted calls 020
- Domestic long distance 01 + area code + 7 digits
- Long distance to Mexico City 01 + 55 + 8 digits

INTERNATIONAL

- International operator assisted calls 090
- International calls from Mexico 00 + country code + city code + number
- Long distance calls from Mexico to the U.S. or Canada 001 + city code + number
- International calls to Mexico 00 + 52 + area code + number
- Calls to Mexico from U.S. or Canada 011 + 52 + area code + number

QUINTANA ROO AREA CODES

Akumal	984
Bacalar	983
Cancún	998
Chetumal	983
Chemuyil	984
Cobá	985
Cozumel	987
Felipe Carrillo Puerto	983
Holbox	984
Isla Mujeres	998
Kantenah	984
Kohunlich	983
Majahual	983
Paamul	984
Playacar	984
Playa del Carmen	984
Playa del Secreto	984
Playa Paraíso	984
Puerto Aventuras	984
Puerto Morelos	998
Punta Bete	984
Punta Brava	998
Punta Maroma	984
Punta Solimán	984
Tankah	984
Tulum	984
Xcalak	983
Xcaret	984
Xel-Há	984
Xpu-Há	984

DISTANCES

This chart shows major cities, towns and sites of interest in the state and the distances between them. Miles are shown in blue and kilometers in black type.

	1	2	3	4	5	6	7	8	9	10	11	12	13	14	15	16	17	18	19
1	•	146	65	42	34	171	75	123	69	91	190	151	23	43	135	126	16	216	188
2	235	•	212	156	181	24	71	238	216	227	43	60	170	190	130	121	130	70	98
3	105	340	•	108	53	236	141	109	4	76	256	216	42	22	133	141	81	282	254
4	68	251	173	•	76	181	85	81	111	48	200	161	65	85	103	112	26	226	198
5	55	290	86	123	•	205	111	163	57	130	225	186	11	31	170	161	51	251	224
6	274	39	379	290	329	•	95	262	240	251	43	85	194	214	155	146	155	69	122
7	121	114	226	137	178	153	•	166	145	134	115	75	98	118	59	50	59	141	113
8	198	381	175	130	261	420	267	•	112	32	281	242	151	131	128	137	107	307	280
9	111	346	6	179	92	385	232	181	•	80	260	220	46	26	136	145	85	286	258
10	146	329	123	78	209	402	215	52	129	•	270	230	119	99	96	105	75	275	268
11	305	70	410	321	360	69	184	451	416	433	•	104	213	233	174	165	174	88	129
12	242	97	347	258	299	136	121	388	353	370	167	•	174	194	135	126	135	130	37
13	37	272	68	105	18	311	158	243	74	191	342	279	•	20	158	149	39	240	211
14	69	304	36	137	50	343	190	211	42	159	347	311	32	•	155	164	59	260	231
15	216	209	213	166	273	248	95	206	219	154	279	216	253	249	•	8	118	200	172
16	202	195	227	180	259	234	81	220	233	168	265	202	239	263	14	•	110	191	163
17	26	209	131	42	83	248	95	172	137	120	279	216	63	95	190	176	•	200	172
18	347	112	452	363	402	11	226	493	458	441	142	209	384	416	321	307	321	•	168
19	302	157	407	318	359	196	181	448	413	430	207	60	339	371	276	262	276	269	•

1. Akumal
2. Bacalar
3. Cancún
4. Cobá
5. Cozumel
6. Chetumal
7. Felipe Carrillo Puerto
8. Holbox
9. Isla Mujeres
10. Kantunil
11. Kohunlich
12. Majahual
13. Playa del Carmen
14. Puerto Morelos
15. Tepich
16. Tihosuco
17. Tulum
18. Unión
19. Xcalak

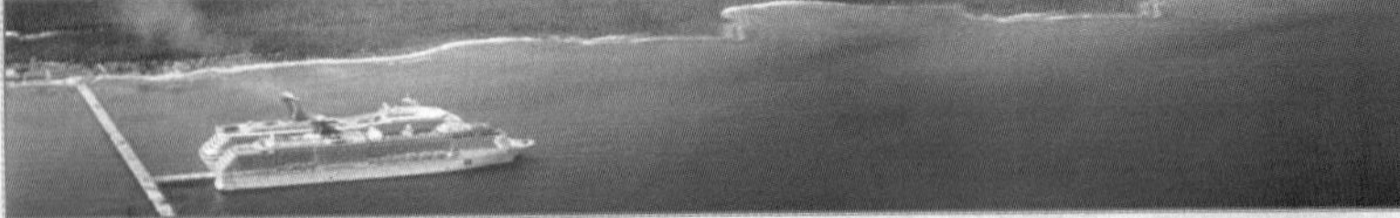

IMPORTANT NUMBERS

Wake up calls	031
Emergencies	060
Exact time	030
Area code information	040
Am. Express	01 800 502 0600
Master Card	001 800 307 7309
Visa	01 800 847 2911

THE MAJORITY OF DELUXE AND 5-STAR HOTELS OFFER MEDICAL SERVICES AND BABYSITTING ON REQUEST.

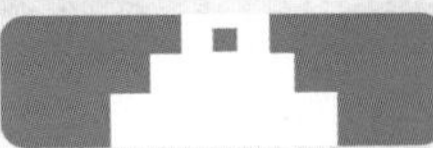

ARCHAEOLOGICAL SITES

FREE ENTRANCE ON SUNDAYS FOR MEXICANS.

TIME

DAYLIGHT SAVING TIME: ON APRIL 1 THE CLOCKS GO BACK 1 HOUR, ON THE THIRD SUNDAY OF SEPTEMBER THEY RETURN TO NORMAL. HOW MEXICO COMPARES INTERNATIONALLY:

Nueva York .... + 1 HR.
Paris, Roma, Berlín .. + 7 HRS.
Londres .... + 6 HRS

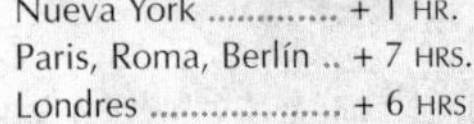

MEASUREMENTS

1 meter .... 3.28 feet
1 meter .... 39.4 inches
1 kilometer .... 0.62 miles
1 kilogram .... 2.2 pounds
Fahrenheit ºF = (ºC x 1.8) +32
Centigrade ºC = (ºF - 32) .5555

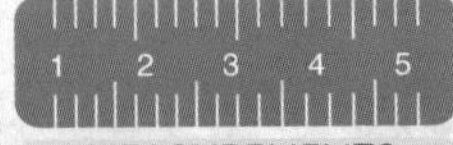

This is a guide to important national and regional holidays, not to mention events, fiestas and tournaments celebrated in Quintana Roo. The dates on which some fiestas and events are celebrated may vary.
*Sportfishing season: April to August: Marlin, sailfish, bonito, jurel, dorado and tuna. All year round: Barracuda, coronado, grouper, jack, sierra and snapper.

Fishing tournaments
Sportfishing season in the Mexican Caribbean runs from April to August and attracts large numbers of aficionados. International fishing tournaments are staged in Cancún and Isla Mujeres, Puerto Aventuras, Playa del Carmen and other communities along the Riviera Maya, Cozumel, Holbox and Puerto Morelos. Isla Mujeres also hosts the Amigos del Sol sailing regatta at the end of April.

• National Fiestas	Date	Place & description
New Year	January 1	
Three Kings Day	January 6	Children traditionally receive gifts on this day and a sweetbread called *rosca de reyes* is served.
Easter Week	Variable	Reenactment of the Passion.
All Saints Day	November 1	
Day of the Dead	November 2	Fiesta for the "deceased," Altars erected and offerings made in their honor.
Posadas	December 16-24	Reenactment of Mary & Joseph's search for lodging before the birth of Jesus.
Christmas, Eve & Day	December 24-25	

• Local Fiestas	Date	Place & description
Carnival	Variable Feb-Marzo	Cozumel, Chetumal & Cancún. Fiesta features processions, dances & music.
Spring fair	March 16-21	José María Morelos.district. Traditional dances, rodeos & fair.
Equinox	March 21 & Sept 22	The play of light and shadow on the Pyramid of Kukulcán at Chichén Itzá represents the return of the god Kukulcán.
Cancún Hip Hop Festival	March 21-26	Hip Hop concerts given by well-known performers
Anniversary of Cancún	April	Music, dance and cultural events staged in Cancún.
San Thelmo fair	April 9-15	Holbox Island. Masses, processions & traditional dances.
El Cedral Fiesta	End of April	Cozumel. Agricultural fair, fair rides and dances
Santa Cruz	May 1-3	Felipe Carrillo Puerto & Cozumel. Masses, processions, offerings, bull fights & traditional dances.
Founding of Payo Obispo	May 5	Chetumal. Parades.
Cancún Jazz Festival	May	Talented musicians from the International jazz world
Día del Bosque y del Árbol	Julio 1	Felipe Carrillo Puerto.
Fiesta of San Joaquín	August 13-16	Bacalar. Bull fights, rodeo, parades & regattas.
Founding of Isla Mujeres	August 17	Isla Mujeres. Parades, music and open air events.
Viva Mexico Festival	September 1-22	Cancún. Mexican cuisine, music and fiestas
San Miguel fair	September 24-29	Cozumel. Masses, parades & tradicional dances.
Triathlon World Championship	November 1-10	International athletes compete in two official ITU championships: the Aquathlon and the Triathlon.
Music for the Earth Festival	November 4-7	Cancún. Concerts for conservation.
Isla Mujeres Festival	Nov. 29 - Dec. 8	Fiesta to honor the island's patron saint. Processions & dances
Feria Expo Cancún	December	Trade show, exhibitions, cock fights, concerts, shows.
Celebration of the Conception	December 3-6	Kantunilkín. Masses.
La Vaquería	Variable	Ceremony involving the cutting down of a yaxché or ceiba tree, sacred tree of the Maya in order to obtain good harvests. Dances.

• National holidays: February 5, Constitution Day; February 24, Flag Day; March 21, Birthday of ex-President Benito Juárez; May 1, May Day; June 1, Navy Day; September 16, Independence Day; October 12, Anniversary of Columbus' discovery of the New World; November 1, Presidential State of the Union address; November 20, Mexican Revolution Day.• Important days in the religious calendar: February 2, Candlemass; June 29, Fiesta of St. Peter & St. Paul (Cozumel); December 12, Day of the Virgin of Guadalupe.

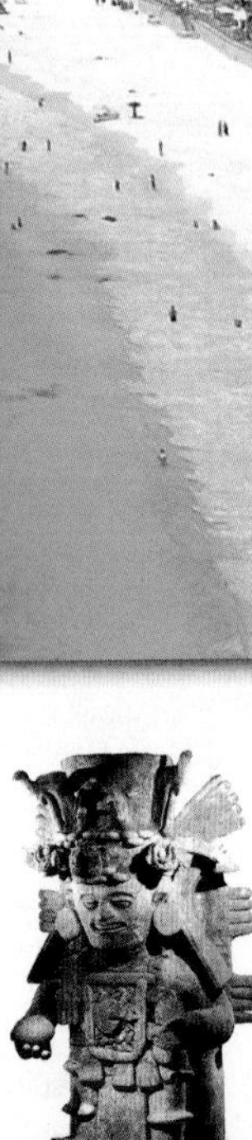

CANCÚN

This cosmopolitan city has every vacation service you could possibly need. There are currently around 26,200 rooms in 140 hotels ranging from deluxe and five-star beachfront resorts to downtown inns. Shopping centers, over 200 restaurants, nightclubs, marinas, travel agencies, transport companies, sport and entertainment options make Cancún one of the world's most popular resorts.

AIRLINES

C-09 ***Aerocaribe***
SPECIALISTS IN MUNDO MAYA, CANCÚN-COZUMEL.
AIR SHUTTLE.
Av. Cobá No. 5 Sm. 4
Plaza América L. B-1
Tels.: 884 2000
01 800 623 4518
Fax: 884 1364
www.aerocaribe.com

F-05 ***Aerocosta***
AIR TAXI, CHARTER FLIGHTS TO AIRPORTS IN QUINTANA ROO, YUCATÁN AND CAMPECHE.
Av. Tulum No. 29 Sm. 5
Tel./Fax: 884 0383
aerocosta2001@hotmail.com

C-09 ***Aerocozumel***
AIR SHUTTLE BETWEEN CANCÚN AND COZUMEL.
Av. Cobá No. 5 Sm. 4
Plaza América L B-1 y B-3
Tels.: 884 2000, 884 2111
Fax: 884 1364
www.aerocaribe.com.mx

B-08 ***Aeroméxico***
Av. Cobá No. 80 Sm. 3
Tels.: 884 3571, 884 1186
01 800 237 6639
01 900 021 4000
Fax: 884 7005
cunjd@prodigy.net.mx
www.aeromexico.com

B-02 ***American Airlines***
Blvd. Kukulcán km 9.5
Hotel Coral Beach
Tels.: 886 0129, 883 4461
01 800 904 6000
www.aa.com

Amerijet
INTERNATIONAL AIR CARGO.
International Airport
Tels.: 886 0197, 886 0198
Fax: 886 0199
amerijetcancun@aol.com
www.amerijet.com

C-09 ***Aviacsa***
Av. Cobá No. 37 Sm. 4
Tels.: 887 4211, 887 4214
01 800 006 2200
Fax: 884 6599
www.aviacsa.com.mx

Aviateca
International Airport
Tels.: 886 0008
01 800 711 1963
www.taca.com

Avioquintana
AIR TAXI, CARGO.
International Airport
Tels.: 886 0422, 886 0648
Fax: 886 0555
avioquin@prodigy.net.mx

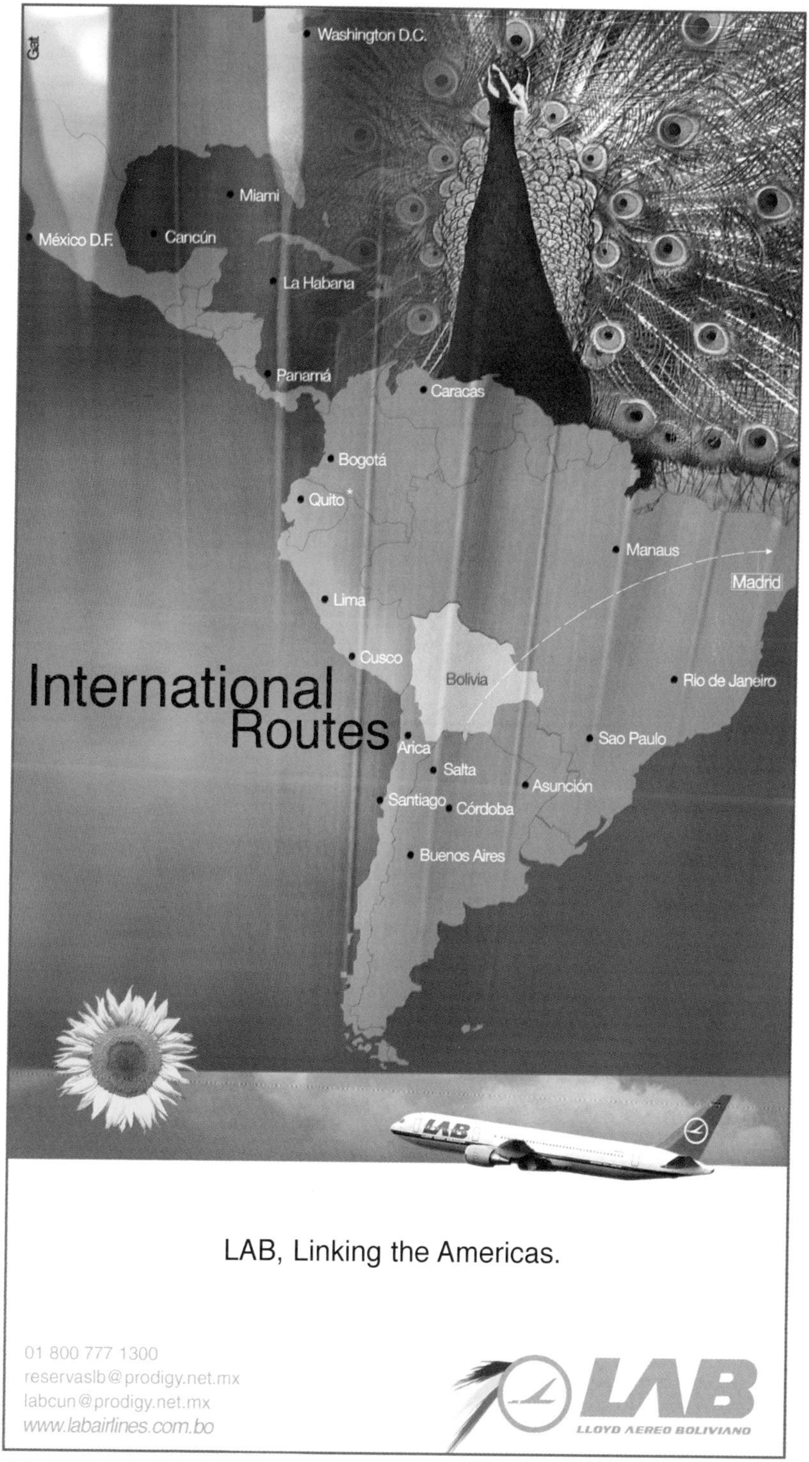

C-09 ***Azteca***
Av. Cobá No. 5 Sm. 4
Plaza América L. B-2
Tels.: 892 3126, 892 3128
Fax: 892 3127
www.azteca.com.mx

Continental Airlines
INTERNATIONAL PASSENGER, CARGO AND MAIL TRANSPORT.
International Airport
Tels.: 886 0169, 886 2106
Fax: 886 0007
www.coair.com

Copa Airlines
FLIGHTS TO 19 DESTINATIONS IN CENTRAL AND SOUTH AMERICA AND THE CARIBBEAN VIA PANAMA.
International Airport
Tels.: 886 0652, 886 0653
Fax: 886 0650
copacun@prodigy.net.mx
www.copaair.com

C-12 ***Cubana de Aviación***
ONE DAILY FLIGHT HAVANA-CANCÚN-HAVANA.
Av. Tulum 231, Sm. 4
Tels.: 887 7210, 887 7017
International Airport
Tel.: 886 0355
www.cubana.com.mx

Delta Airlines
International Airport
Tels.: 886 0368
01 800 902 2100
Fax: 886 0661
www.delta.com

D-08 ***Eurolatino***
REPRESENTATIVES OF LTU AND LANCHILE.
Av. Cobá No. 12 Sm. 5
Edificio Venus L. 2
Tels.: 887 2406, 884 8236
Fax: 887 2405
eurocoba@prodigy.net.mx

Iberia
International Airport
Tels.: 886 0243, 886 0158
www.iberia.com

C-12 ***LLoyd Aero Boliviano***
PASSENGER FLIGHTS TO CENTRAL AND SOUTH AMERICA.
Av. Tulum No. 232 Sm. 4
Mz. 12 L. A-2 y A-4
Tels.: 887 1299, 887 1300
Fax: 884 0311
International Airport
Tel.: 886 0524
www.labairlines.com.bo

D-16 ***Magic Sky & Sea Adventures***
TOURIST AIR SERVICES THROUGHOUT THE MAYA REGION, THE YUCATÁN PENINSULA AND PRIVATE INTERNATIONAL FLIGHTS.
Blvd. Kukulcán km 14.1
Tels.: 885 1720, 885 1716
Fax: 885 1613
reservations@magic-sea.com
www.magic-sea.com

C-08 ***Magnicharters***
PLANE TICKETS, TRIPS, GROUPS, BUS AND VAN RENTALS, PACKAGES.
Av. Náder No. 94 Sm. 3
Tel.: 884 0600
Fax: 884 0212

Martinair Holland
International Airport
Tel.: 886 0070
Fax: 886 0128
sales-cun@aerocharter.com.mx
www.martinair.com

B-16 ***Mexicana de Aviación***
Av. Tulum No. 269, 2° piso
Tels.: 881 9090
01 800 502 2000
Fax: 881 9041
www.mexicana.com

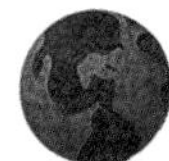

United Airlines
01 800 003 0700

US Airways
01 800 007 8800

C-11 ***Varig***
Av. Tulum No. 200
Plaza México Suite 300
Tels.: 887 4377
01 800 907 8800
Fax: 887 2398
www.varig.com.mx

TRAVEL AGENCIES

TRAVEL AGENCIES ABOUND IN CANCÚN AND MANY HOTELS HAVE TRAVEL DESKS MANNED BY STAFF FROM LOCAL AGENCIES AND TOUR OPERATORS. EXCURSIONS TO PARKS AND RESERVES AND THE PRINCIPAL ARCHAEOLOGICAL SITES ARE INDICATED WITH SYMBOLS IN THE LISTS, AS ARE OTHER SERVICES AND THE LANGUAGES SPOKEN BY STAFF.

H-01 ***Almayab***
SPANISH, ENGLISH, ITALIAN, PORTUGUESE.
Chacá Plaza 23 L. 32 Sm. 23
Tels.: 892 0514, 892 0516
Fax: 892 0514
almayab@prodigy.net.mx
www.almayab.com.mx

DESTINATION MANAGEMENT COMPANY
Land Operator • Charters
Groups • Incentive Trips
Archaeological, cultural and ecological tours, day and night cruises, fishing, diving and snorkeling, parks, swimming with dolphins. Offers the best destinations, products and services so that you can make your dreams come true!

Blvd. Kukulcán km. 5.5, Cancún, Quintana Roo, Mexico. Tel.: (998) 881 1361
www.bestday.com

Your window onto the Mexican Caribbean

On-line reservations
• Hotels • Tours •

Information on activities, nightlife, restaurants, shopping and more about the best destinations.

www.cancun.com

J-10 ***Always Cancún Travel***

ENGLISH, SPANISH.
Andador Ah Canul No. 30
Sm. 26 Mz. 16
Tel./Fax: 884 1483
www.cancunviajes.com

C-11 ***American Express***

ENGLISH, FRENCH, SPANISH.
Av. Tulum 208 Sm. 4
Tels.: 881 4068, 881 4000
Fax: 884 6942

Amstar Destination Management Company

SPANISH, ENGLISH, FRENCH, GERMAN, ITALIAN.
Av. Palenque Mz. 5
L. 1-4 Sm. 29, 2° piso
Tel.: 881 9590
Fax: 881 9594
pmc@amstarmexico.com
www.amstarmexico.com

G-02 ***AWT All World Travel***

SPANISH, ENGLISH, FRENCH.
Av. Tulum 19 y 20 Sm. 2
Plaza Galerías L. 38 y 39
Tel.: 884 7172
Fax: 884 8791
www.cancunviajes.com

K-03 ***Best Day Tours***

ENGLISH, SPANISH, FRENCH, RUSSIAN, ITALIAN, PORTUGUESE, GERMAN.
Blvd. Kukulcán km 5.5
Hotel Riu Caribe
Tel.: 881 1361
bestday@bestday.com
www.bestday.com

H-06 ***Betanzos***

SPANISH, ENGLISH, FRENCH, DUTCH, GERMAN.
Yaxchilán No. 39 esq.
Jazmínes Sm. 22 Mz. 19
Tel.: 884 1057 Fax: 884 1254
www.betanzos.com.mx

E-04 ***Cancún DMC Connection***

SPANISH, ENGLISH, FRENCH.
SPECIALIST SERVICE FOR GROUPS AND CONVENTIONS.
Plaza Quetzal
Tel.: 883 0970
Fax: 883 0238
sales@dmcconnection.com
www.dmcconnection.com

J-09 ***Cancún Kanko***

ENGLISH, SPANISH, JAPANESE.
Av. Tankah Sm. 25 Mz. 19
L. 25-26 Planta alta
Tels.: 884 8937, 884 3605
Fax: 884 3605
takeda@mexicokanko.co.jp

Cancún Line

ENGLISH, SPANISH.
Blvd. Luis D. Colosio km 5
Expo Plaza Los Álamos
Tel.: 881 7121 Fax: 887 0792
karoline@cancunline.com.mx

C-11 ***Cancún • Yucatán Incentive Services***

DIVING AND SNORKELING TRIPS TO COZUMEL. EXPERIENCE IN DMC.
Av. Tulum No. 192 Sm. 4
Plaza Tropical L. 47
Tels.: 898 1041, 898 1042
01 800 500 6276
Fax: 890 1042
www.cancunincentiveservices.com

D-11 ***CHE Travel***

SPANISH, ENGLISH, FRENCH, JAPANESE, ITALIAN, PORTUGUESE.
Blvd. Kukulcán km 12.5,
Hotel Sheraton
Tel.: 883 1828 ext. 4160
Fax: 883 1828
chetravelcancun@yahoo.com

J-07 ***Colors Travel***

SPANISH, ENGLISH.
Xel-Há No. 115 Sm. 25
Tels.: 887 4979, 887 4716
Fax: 892 0756
colorstr@hotmail.com

C-11 ***Connex Caribe México***

SPANISH, ENGLISH, GERMAN.
Av. Tulum No. 192 Sm. 4
Plaza Tropical
Tels.: 884 1085, 884 1090
connex@prodigy.net.mx

C-11 ***Consejeros de Viajes México***

SPANISH, ENGLISH, GERMAN.
Av. Tulum No. 200
Plaza México L. 308
Tels.: 884 3528, 884 3120
Fax: 887 1272
covimex@prodigy.net.mx

E-11 ***Eurolatino***

SPANISH, ENGLISH, GERMAN, FRENCH, DUTCH, ITALIAN.
Tejón No. 17 Sm. 20
Tels.: 887 3373, 887 4640
Fax: 887 4671
www.eurolatino.com.mx

G-06 ***Expo Cancún***

Paseo Pok Ta Pok,
Green 16, Mezzanine, HZ
Tels.: 883 3150, 883 5088
expocancun@expomarketingdmc.com

P-04 ***Global Incentive***

SPANISH, ENGLISH, ITALIAN, FRENCH.
COMPLETE DMC SERVICES.
Blvd. Kukulcán km 3.5,
Plaza Nutilus, HZ
Tels.: 849 5100, 849 5101
Fax: 849 5103
www.incentivemanagement.com

P-04 ***Gray Line Cancún***

SPANISH, ENGLISH.
Blvd. Kukulcán km 3.5
Plaza Nautilus
Tel.: 849 4545
Fax: 849 5151
grayline@cancun.com.mx
www.graylinecancun.com

C-09 ***His Cancún***

ENGLISH, JAPANESE, SPANISH. SPECIALISTS IN JAPANESE TOURISM, TICKETS TO ASIA.
Av. Cobá No. 5 Sm. 4
Plaza América L. A-8
Tels.: 884 6501, 887 9928
Fax: 887 3681
hiscancun@hotmail.com

F-07 ***Hotel Beds Accommodation & Destination Services***

SPANISH, ENGLISH, FRENCH, ITALIAN, PORTUGUESE, GERMAN.
Av. Tulum 318 Altos
Sm. 22, Mz. 5
Tel.: 881 7500
Fax: 881 7501
www.hotelbeds.com

C-11 ***Iberoservice México***

SPANISH, ENGLISH, GERMAN, DUTCH, ITALIAN.
Av. Tulum No. 200
Plaza México L. 213-215
Tels.: 887 4357, 884 7266
Fax: 887 4437, 884 8519

J-04 ***Incentive Leisure Travel***

Punta Pulticub 27 Sm. 24
Tels.: 884 2706, 884 8895
Fax: 887 5088
ilt@cancun.com.mx

D-11 ***Infratours***

Pecarí No. 16 Sm. 20
Tel.: 887 3771, 887 0482
Fax: 884 7784
yumbocaribe@prodigy.net.mx

C-12 ***Intermar Cancún Caribe IMC***

SPANISH, ENGLISH, FRENCH, ITALIAN, RUSSIAN, POLISH, PORTUGUESE, JAPANESE.
GROUPS & CONVENTIONS, ISO 9002
Av. Tulum No. 225
esq. Jabalí, Sm. 20
Tels.: 881 0000, 884 4266
Fax: 881 0001
intermar@travel2mexico.com
www.travel2mexico.com

C-11 ***International Incentive Travel***

ENGLISH, SPANISH. 18 YEARS OF EXPERIENCE WELCOMING GROUPS.
Av. Tulum No. 192 Sm. 4
Plaza Tropical
Tel.: 884 7880
Fax: 884 7914
iitravel@cancun.com.mx
www.cancuntravel.com.mx

IVI Cancun´s DMC

ENGLISH, SPANISH, FRENCH, GERMAN, ITALIAN, RUSSIAN.
GROUPS & CONVENTIONS, ISO 9002.
Acanceh No. 1-01 Sm. 15
Tel.: 887 1578
Fax: 884 4026, 884 7736
www.ivimarketing.com.mx
www.ivi-mexico.com

D-03 ***Jumbo Tours México***

SPANISH, ENGLISH, ITALIAN.
Blvd. Kukulcán km 8.5
Centro Comercial
Costa Blanca, HZ
Tel.: 883 3537 Fax: 883 3539
www.jumbotours.com

D-03 ***Kiddie Travels***

ENGLISH, SPANISH.
RIVIERA MAYA SPECIALISTS.
Blvd. Kukulcán km 8.5
Plaza Mayafair L. 48, 68-69
Tels.: 883 1333, 883 1332
www.kiddietravels.com

Lomas Travel

ENGLISH, SPANISH.
WHOLESALER REPRESENTATIVES.
Av. Los Colegios No. 75
Fracc. Bonfil
Tel.: 881 9400
USA 1 800 334 1197
Fax: 881 9401
sales@lomas-travel.com
www.lomas-travel.com

C-08 *Magnicharters*

SPANISH, ENGLISH.
Av. Náder No. 93 Sm. 3
esq. Cobá
Tel.: 884 0600
Fax: 884 0212
info.@magnitur.com
www.magnitur.com

C-11 *Mansur Travel*

SPANISH, ENGLISH, PORTUGUESE.
Av. Tulum No. 192 Sm. 4
Plaza Tropical L. 20
Tels.: 884 7540, 887 4062
manzurtravel@infosel.net.mx

Maritur

SPANISH, ENGLISH, FRENCH, ITALIAN. INCENTIVES, CONGRESSES.
Pabellón Caribe,
Av. Nichupte No. 22
Suite 111 Sm. 19 Mz. 2
Tels.: 892 8929, 898 0640
01 800 696 7080
Fax: 898 0641
maritur@cancun.com.mx
www.maritur.com

C-11 *Maritz Cancún*

ENGLISH, SPANISH.
INCENTIVE MARKET.
Av. Tulum 192 Sm. 4,
Plaza Tropical L. 20-B
Tel.: 887 7556
Fax: 884 8230
mpvcancun@webtelmexnet.mx
www.maritzgroupgetaways.com

C-08 *Mayaland Tours*

ENGLISH, FRENCH, SPANISH. PORTUGUESE.
Robalo No. 30 Sm. 3
Tels.: 884 4512, 887 2450
01 800 719 5465
USA 1 800 235 4079
Fax: 884 4510
info@mayaland.com
www.mayaland.com

E-08 *Maya World Expeditions*

PROFESSIONAL CONSULTANTS SPECIALIZING IN TOURISM TO MUNDO MAYA. ENGLISH, FRENCH, SPANISH, ITALIAN, GERMAN.
Av. Cobá No. 5 & 7 Sm. 22
Hotel Soberanis
Tels.: 884 4564
01 800 101 0101
Fax: 887 5138
infomaya@mayaworld.cc
www.mayaworld.cc

E-05 *Mex Atlántica Tours*

SPANISH, GERMAN, ENGLISH, FRENCH.
Rubia 38 Sm. 3 Mz. 2
Tels.: 884 2738, 884 2726
Fax: 884 8797
www.mexatlanticatours.com

Olympus Tours

ENGLISH, FRENCH, ITALIAN, GREEK, PORTUGUESE, SPANISH.
GROUPS, CONVENTIONS AND INCENTIVES, PACKAGES, EXPORTATION AND TICKETING; DAILY TRIPS TO THE ARCHAEOLOGICAL SITES.
Av. Yaxchilán
L. 13, Mz. 2, Sm. 17
Oposite Costco
Tel.: 881 9030
Fax: 887 7006
customerservice@olympus-tours.com
www.olympus-tours.com

C-09 *R.C. Tours*

SPANISH, ENGLISH.
RECEPTIVE, GROUPS AND INCENTIVES.
Av. Cobá No. 5 Sm. 4
Plaza América L. A-9
Tels.: 887 4663
01 800 216 5000
Fax: 887 4661
ventas@rctourscancun.com
www.rctourscancun.com

E-07 *Royal Holiday Travel*

SPANISH, ENGLISH, ITALIAN, FRENCH.
Av. Tulum esq. Claveles
No. 33 Sm. 22
Tels.: 887 3400, 887 1695

F-08 *Royale Tours*

SPANISH, ENGLISH, ITALIAN, PORTUGUESE, FRENCH, GERMAN.
Alcatraces No. 74 Sm. 22
Tel.: 881 7100 Fax: 884 9940
info@royaletours.com.mx
www.royaletours.com.mx

D-11 *Rumbos México*

SPANISH, ENGLISH.
CIRCUITS IN YUCATÁN, CHIAPAS AND CENTRAL MEXICO.
Pecarí No. 16 Sm. 20
Tels.: 884 2644, 884 5512
Fax: 884 2800
rumbos@prodigy.net.mx

C-09 *Sistema Mundial de Viajes*

ENGLISH, SPANISH, FRENCH.
Av. Cobá No. 5 Sm. 4
Plaza América L. A-19
Tels.: 884 3817, 887 2116
Fax: 884 4981
www.sistemamundial.com.mx

STP Caribe Wholesaler Tour Operator

WHOLESALER AND TOUR OPERATOR SPECIALIZING IN THE FIVE COUNTRIES OF THE MAYA WORLD, GSA FOR THE TACA GROUP AIRLINE IN SOUTHEAST MEXICO.
Av. La Costa No. 134
Sm. 30 Mz. 8 L. 13
Tels.: 883 9828, 883 9830
01 800 640 7505
USA 1 800 538 6802
Fax: 884 8629
stp@cancun.com.mx
www.stpguatemala.com

C-03 *Tours Network*

ENGLISH, SPANISH, FRENCH, ITALIAN. PRIVATE SERVICES FOR ANY NUMBER OF PASSENGERS. QUALIFIED STAFF.
Blvd. Kukulcán km 8.5
Hotel Clipper Club
Tel./Fax: 883 1222
www.cancuntravelcenter.com

B-16 *Tropical Incentives DMC*

ENGLISH, SPANISH.
TRANSPORT, THEME PARTIES, CULTURAL SEMINARS, GOLF AND FISHING TOURNAMENTS, AUDIOVISUAL EQUIPMENT RENTAL, ETC.
Centro Empresarial
EKIN'OX Av. Tulum,
Mz. 3, Lote 2-01, Sm. 15-A
Tels.: 884 7577, 887 2793
Fax: 884 6924
tropical@tihcancun.com.mx
www.tropicalincentives.com.mx

C-09 *Turimex*

SPANISH, ENGLISH.
CIRCUITS IN VANS AND BUSES, TRIPS TO CUBA, ETC.
Av. Cobá No. 5
Plaza América Suite 8-7
Tels.: 887 4090, 887 4038
Fax: 887 1936
turimex@prodigy.net.mx

F-11 *Turismo Aviomar*

SPANISH, ENGLISH.
Venado No. 30 Sm. 20
Tels.: 884 6433, 884 8988
Fax: 884 6935
aviomar@cancun.com.mx

C-09 *Uniexpress*

JAPANESE, SPANISH. RECEPTIVE SERVICES FOR JAPANESE TOURISM.
Av. Cobá No. 5 Sm. 4
Plaza América L. A-27
Tel.: 887 1730
Fax: 887 1766
unicun@prodigy.net.mx

D-12 *Uniterra Travel*

GERMAN, SPANISH, ENGLISH, FRENCH.
CIRCUITS IN THE MEXICAN MAYA WORLD.
Gacela No. 25 Sm. 20
Tels.: 884 8606, 884 9161
Fax: 884 6342
uniterra@prodigy.net.mx

C-08 *VI Travel*

SPANISH, ENGLISH, PORTUGUESE.
22 YEARS OF EXPERIENCE, PERSONALIZED TRIPS.
Av. Náder No. 148 Sm. 3
Edif. Barcelona Suite 201
Tel.: 884 8494
Fax: 884 8099
vitravel2@prodigy.net.mx

H-04 *Viajes Caribe Maya*

ENGLISH, SPANISH, PORTUGUESE, ITALIAN, FRENCH.
Blvd. Kukulcán
Cenzontle L. 1 Edif. Oasis
Tel.: 848 9999
Fax: 849 9952
www.caribemaya.com.mx

A-12 *Viajes Chemuyil*

SPANISH, ENGLISH.
Fuego No. 5 Sm. 4
Tels.: 884 2047, 884 9855
Fax: 887 4859
chemuyil@yahoo.com.mx

C-09 *Viajes Divermex*

SPANISH, ENGLISH.
TOUR PACKAGES TO CUBA.
Av. Cobá No. 5 Sm. 4
Plaza América L. B-6
Tels.: 887 5489, 887 5487
Fax: 884 2325
viajesdivermex@prodigy.net.mx
www.divermex.com

G-11 *Viajes Liberación*

SPANISH, ENGLISH.
Av. Yaxchilán L. 99 Sm. 20
Tels.: 887 6532, 887 7979
info@liberacion.com.mx
www.liberacion.com.mx

C-15 *Viajes México con Amistad*

ITALIAN, FRENCH, ENGLISH, PORTUGUESE, SPANISH.
Acanceh No. 3 Sm.15-A
Plaza San Ángel Inn L. 6
Tel.: 884 8369
Fax: 884 8370
www.viajesmeca.com

D-22 *Viajes Thomas Moore*

SPANISH, ENGLISH, FRENCH.
WHOLESALERS WITH PACKAGES TO MIAMI, ORLANDO AND LAS VEGAS. TRIPS TO RÍO LAGARTOS, EK BALAM, MÉRIDA AND UXMAL.
Blvd. Kukulcán km 16
Tels.: 885 0266, 884 4211
Fax: 885 0516
vtm@royalresorts.com
www.thomasmoretravel.com

C-09 *Viñales Tours*

ENGLISH, SPANISH.
PACKAGES TO CUBA, CANCÚN AND THE MEXICAN CARIBBEAN.
Av. Cobá No. 5 Sm. 4
Plaza América L. B-15
Tels.: 884 0326
01 800 202 2937
Fax: 884 0396
vtcun@vinalestours.com
www.vinalestours.com

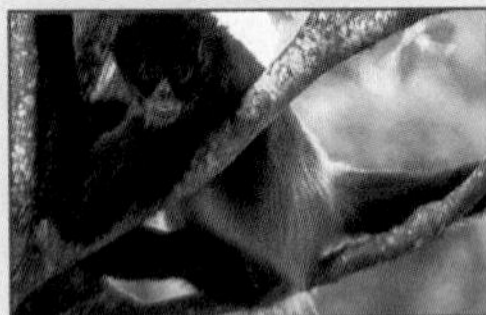

ECOTOURISM

Amigos de Sian Ka´an

FOR THE CONSERVATION OF THE STATE'S NATURAL RESOURCES.
Crepúsculo 18 Sm. 44
Fracc. Alborada, Centro
Tels.: 880 6024, 884 9580
sian@cancun.com.mx
www.amigosdesiankaan.org

EcoColors

BIKING, KAYAK, BIRD WATCHING, DIVING AND ECOTOURISM TRIPS IN THE MAYA WORLD.
Camarón No. 32 Sm. 27
Tels.: 884 3667, 884 9580
Fax: 884 9214
info@ecotravelmexico.com
www.ecotravelmexico.com

L-09 *Mayaquest*

SPANISH, ENGLISH, FRENCH, GERMAN.
ECOTOURISM TRIPS, INCLUDE BIRD WATCHING, ARCHAEOLOGY AND ADVENTURE, EXPERT GUIDES.
AREA: MESOAMERICA, COSTA RICA AND PANAMA.
Xpuhil No. 3 - 1 Sm. 27
Tels.: 898 1641
01 800 557 3532
Fax: 898 1641
aortiz@mayanquest.com
www.mayanquest.net

A-11 *Sun and Folklore by México*

ADVENTURE TOURISM.
Av. Bonampak 221 Sm. 4
Tels.: 892 4971, 884 7552
sunbymexico@hotmail.com

TOURIST ASSISTANCE

Car Rental Association

MON. - FRI. 9 AM. -2 PM., 5 PM. - 7 PM.
Av. La Costa 128 Sm. 30
Tels.: 884 9197, 884 9931
arvqroo@hotmail.com

F-01 *Quintana Roo A.C. Hotel & Motel Association*

SPANISH, ENGLISH.
CONSULTANT AND BUSINESS MANAGEMENT FOR HOTEL OWNERS
MON. - FRI. 9 AM. -2 PM., 4 PM. - 7 PM.
Av. García de la Torre
No. 6, Sm. 1
Tels.: 881 8730, 881 8732
Fax: 887 7683
amopa@ahqr.com.mx
www.ahqr.com.mx

D-07 *Cancún Water Sport Association*

MON. TO FRI. 9 AM. - 4 PM.
Blvd. Kukulcán km 10.3 ZH
Tels.: 849 4036, 849 5800
nauticos@cancunwatersports.com
www.cancunwatersports.com

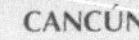

B-09 ***Mexican Caribbean Restaurant Association***
Av. Cobá 18 Sm. 4 Mz. 3
Tel./Fax: 898 1247
info@restaurantscaribemx.com
www.restaurantscaribemx.com

C-11 ***Travel Agency Association*** (AMAV)
MON. - FRI. 9 AM. - 2 PM.,
4 PM. - 7 PM.
Av. Tulum No. 200 Plaza
México L. 303 Sm. 4
Tels.: 887 4992, 887 1670
Fax: 884 3738
amavcun@prodigy.net.mx

Chamber of Commerce (CANACO)
MON. TO FRI. 9 AM. - 5 PM.,
SAT. 9 AM. - 1 PM.
Av. José López Portillo
Región 98 Mza. 66 Lote 1
Tels.: 886 8200, 886 9655
Fax: 886 9721
canacun@prodigy.net.mx
www.canacocancun.org.mx

H-05 ***Restaurant Association*** (CANIRAC)
MON. TO FRI. 9 AM. - 2:30 PM.,
5 PM. - 7 PM.,
SAT. 9:30 AM. - 1 PM.
Sm. 22 L. 20 Dpto. 1
Tel.: 887 1142
Fax: 884 3315
caniraccun@terra.com
www.cancunrestaurantes.com.mx

E-03 ***Rotary Club***
TUESDAY 9 PM.
Hotel Presidente, HZ
WEDNESDAY 9 PM.
Hotel Oasis América

D-05 ***Mexican Federation of Businessmen*** (COPARMEX)
MON. - FRI. 9 AM. - 2 PM., 3 - 7 PM.
Cazón No. 16 Sm. 3
Tels.: 887 6618, 884 7596
www.coparmexqroo.org.mx

E-06 ***Quintana Roo Tourist Information Office***
SPANISH, ENGLISH, FRENCH, ITALIAN.
MON. TO FRI. 9 AM. - 2 PM., 5 - 8 PM.
Av. Tulum No. 5 Sm. 5
City Hall
Tels.: 887 4329, 887 9876
Fax.: 887 4329
turismo@cancun.gob.mx
www.cancun.gob.mx

D-08 ***National Fund for Tourism Development*** (FONATUR)
MON. TO FRI. 8:30 AM. - 3 PM., 4:30 - 6 PM. THE SALE OF LAND AND THE DEVELOPMENT OF THE TOURIST AREA OF CANCÚN.
Av. Náder con Cobá Sm. 5
Tels.: 884 0610, 892 2377
01 800 800 1020
Fax: 884 2747
www.fonatur.gob.mx

E-04 ***Immigration Office***
MON. TO FRI. 9 AM. - 3 PM., 4 PM. - 9 PM. DOCUMENTS RECEIVED, 9 AM. – NOON.
Av. Náder esq. Uxmal
Sm. 5, L. 1
Tels.: 884 1404, 884 1658
Fax: 884 0918
www.inami.gob.mx

C-03 ***Visitors & Convention Office*** (OVC)
MON. TO FRI. 9 AM. - 6 PM.
PROMOTION OF THE RESORT AND PUBLIC RELATIONS FOR THE VISITORS & CONVENTIONS BUREAU.
Blvd. Kukulcán km 9 ZH
Tels.: 881 0400, 884 6531
Fax: 881 0402
ovccancun@sybcom.com
www.cancun.info

F-08 ***Consumer Protection Agency*** (PROFECO)
MON. TO FRI. 8:30 AM. - 3 PM.
ADVICE, COMPLAINTS, INSPECTIONS AND MONITORING OF PRICES IN THE STATE. ISSUES INFORMATION ON PRICES FOR THE COMMUNITY.
Av. Cobá No. 9 Sm. 22
Tels.: 884 2701, 884 2634,
887 2877, 884 2369
Fax: 884 2744
cancun@profeco.gob.mx
www.profeco.gob.mx

More information:
www.caribbeanmex.com

D-07 ***Mexican State Department Office***
MON. TO FRI. 8AM. - 1 PM.
ISSUES MEXICAN PASSPORTS AND PERMITS ACCORDING TO ARTICLE 27 OF THE MEXICAN CONSTITUTION, CITIZENSHIP AND NATURALIZATION APPLICATIONS, GRANTS FOR STUDY OVERSEAS.
Av. Náder No. 8 Sm. 5
Tel.: 884 7594
Fax: 884 8014
www.sre.gob.mx

C-03 ***State Tourism Board***
MON. TO FRI. 9 AM. - 5 PM.
Blvd. Kukulcán km 9
1er piso
Convention Center
Tel.: 881 9000
Fax: 881 9020
dir-prom@qroo.gob.mx
www.qroo.gob.mx

Taxi Union
MON. TO FRI. 9 AM. - 5 PM.
Región 92, Zona 6
No. 5, Ruta 4
Tels.: 888 6990, 888 6982
Radiotaxi: 840 2358
Fax: 888 6985

CHURCHES

CATHOLIC

G-06 ***Cristo Rey***
SUNDAY MASS: 8 & 10:30 AM., 12, 5, 6, & 8 PM.
Parque Las Palapas, Sm. 22
Tel.: 884 0513

P-04 ***La Resurrección***
Blvd. Kukulcán km 3.5
Tel.: 883 5005

MASS IN HOTELS

A-02 ***Dreams Cancún***
SUNDAY 11 AM.
Tel.: 848 7000

B-02 ***Fiesta Americana Coral Beach***
SUNDAY 12 NOON.
Tel.: 881 3200

C-08 ***Gran Caribe Real***
SUNDAY 12 NOON.
Tel.: 881 7300

D-18 ***Marriott CasaMagna***
SUNDAY, 10 AM.
ST. MICHAEL & ALL ANGELS EPISCOPAL
Tel.: 881 2000

D-11 ***Sheraton***
SUNDAY, 10:30 AM.
Tel.: 891 4400

PROTESTANT

Seventh Day Adventists
SATURDAY, 10 AM.
6 Oriente Sm. 64

PRESBYTERIAN

F-08 ***Puerta del Cielo***
9:15 AM.,10:45 AM & 6:30 PM.
Crisantemos 15, Sm. 22
Tel.: 884 2362

SHOPPING CENTERS

HOTEL ZONE

C-04 ***Coral Negro***
SPECIALIZES IN HANDICRAFTS.
Blvd. Kukulcán km 9.5
Tel./Fax: 883 0758

C-04 ***El Zócalo***
MEXICAN AMBIANCE, HANDICRAFTS AND ENTERTAINMENT.
Blvd. Kukulcán km 9.5
Tels.: 883 3698, 883 3722
Fax: 883 3723

D-09 ***Flamingo Plaza***
THIS WATERFRONT MALL HAS A FOOD COURT, RESTAURANTS, 70 SHOPS STOCKING DESIGNER CLOTHING, SPORTSWEAR, ETC.
Blvd. Kukulcán km 11.5
Tel.: 883 2855
Fax: 883 2954
www.flamingo.com.mx

B-04 ***Forum by the Sea***
SHOPS, FAST FOOD, RESTAURANTS, NIGHTLIFE.
Blvd. Kukulcán km 9
Tel.: 883 4425
Fax: 883 2485

D-12 ***La Isla Shopping Village***
LOCATED ON THE SHORES OF THE LAGOON, THIS MALL SHOWCASES 148 INTERNATIONAL BRAND SHOPS AND RESTAURANTS, JEWELRY STORES, BOUTIQUES AND ENTERTAINMENT CENTERS.
Blvd. Kukulcán km 12.5
Tel.: 883 5025
Fax: 883 5666
www.laislacancun.com.mx

D-03 ***La Mansión Costa Blanca***
SPECIALTY RESTAURANTS AND CRAFTS.
Blvd. Kukulcán km 8.5
Tel.: 883 0888
Fax: 884 4207
aeropolis@prodigy.net.mx

D-03 ***Mayafair***
SERVICES AND DIVERSE GOODS.
Blvd. Kukulcán km 8.5

C-02 ***Plaza Caracol***
RESTAURANTS, JEWELRY STORES, SHOPS, BOUTIQUES, CRAFTS, ETC.
Blvd. Kukulcán km 8.5
Tel.: 883 0905
Fax: 883 2529
www.grupocaracol.com.mx

C-03 ***Plaza Caribeña / Party Center***
CRAFTS, SERVICE CENTER, SHOWS.
Blvd. Kukulcán km 9
Tel.: 883 0356
Fax: 883 0398
partycenter@prodigy.net.mx

C-04 ***Plaza Dady'O***
Blvd. Kukulcán km 9.5

C-03 ***Plaza El Parian***
Blvd. Kukulcán km 8.8

C-03 ***Plaza Fiesta***
Blvd. Kukulcán km 8.8

D-13 ***Plaza Kukulcán***
MORE THAN 180 STORES AND BOUTIQUES, SPECIALTY RESTAURANTS, FOOD COURT, ATMS, A BANK, CRAFTS, LUXURY AVENUE, BOWLING AND AN ART GALLERY.
Blvd. Kukulcán km. 13
Tel.: 885 2200
Fax: 885 0926
www.kukulcanplaza.com

D-03 ***Plaza Lagunas***
Blvd. Kukulcán km 8.3

E-22 ***Plaza Marina***
Blvd. Kukulcán km 16.2

P-04 ***Plaza Nautilus***
Blvd. Kukulcán km 3.5

E-04 ***Plaza Quetzal***
Blvd. Kukulcán km 8

D-02 ***Plaza Terramar***
Blvd. Kukulcán km 8.5

DOWNTOWN

K-07 ***Plaza Bonita***
CRAFTS, RESTAURANTS, BOUTIQUES, MEXICAN AMBIANCE AND LIVE SHOWS.
Av. Xel-Há Sm. 28 L. 1
Tel.: 884 6812 Fax: 884 7105
plazabonita@prodigy.net.mx
www.plazabonita.com.mx

Plaza Cancún 2000
SERVICES AND DIVERSE GOODS.
Av. Tulum esq. Av. L. Portillo
Tel./Fax: 884 9988

H-10 ***Plaza Chinatown***
RESTAURANT, BANK, NIGHTCLUB, SHOPS, BEAUTY SALON, PATISSERIE, NURSERY, CAMERA AND COMPUTER STORES.
Av. Xcaret esq. Labná Sm. 35
Tel.: 887 6315 ext. 322
Fax: 884 3334
chinatown@prodigy.net.mx

A-14 ***Plaza Las Américas***
DEPARTMENT STORES, BOUTIQUES, RESTAURANTS, FOOD COURT, CINEMAS, BARS.
Av. Tulum Sur Sm. 7
Tels.: 887 4839, 887 4840
america@prodigy.net.mx

G-10 ***Plaza Las Avenidas***
SHOPS, RESTAURANTS AND BARS.
Av. Cobá y Yaxchilán Sm. 35
Tel.: 892 4749 Fax: 887 7552
plazaavenidas@prodigy.net.mx

A-10 ***Plaza Nayandéi***
Av. Bonampak Sm. 4

SUPERMARKETS

Carrefour
- Av. Cobá Sm. 31
  Tel.: 881 7570
- Av. López Portillo Reg. 98
  Tel.: 881 7580

Chedraui
- **E-08** Av. Tulum esq. Cobá, Sm. 22; Tel.: 887 3633

• A-15 Plaza Las Américas
Tel.: 887 2190

Comercial Mexicana
• F-04 Av. Tulum esq. Uxmal, Sm. 22; Tel.: 884 4528
• Libramiento Kabah, Sm. 21; Tel.: 880 9164
• Av. López Portillo, Sm. 59; Tel.: 886 5711

Costco
Av. Kabah; Tel.: 881 0250

Gigante
• Av. Tulum, Sm. 63
Tel.: 887 3077
• Av. Nichupté, Sm. 48
Tel.: 848 1608

G-11 ***Sam's Club***
Av. Xcaret, Sm. 21
Tel.: 881 0200

San Francisco de Asís
• E-04 Blvd. Kukulcán esq. Calle Quetzal, Zona Hotelera
Tel.: 883 4681
• K-08 Av. Xel-Há, Sm. 28

Soriana
• Av. Andrés Q. Roo esq. Av. Kabah, Sm. 37
Tels.: 206 2205 al 10

Walmart
• H-11 Av. Xcaret esq. Labná, Sm. 21; Tel.: 884 0653
• Av. Andrés Q. Roo
Tel.: 883 7143

Markets

In Downtown Cancún you'll find craft markets such as Ki-Huic and Plaza Garibaldi on Tulum Av. and traditional markets selling food, fresh produce, crafts and more.

K-08 ***Mercado 28***
Av. Xel-Há, Sm. 28

H-02 ***Mercado 23***
Calle Cedro, Sm. 23

CINEMAS

D-12 ***Cinemark I***
La Isla Shopping Village, HZ

G-03 ***Cinemas Tulum I a VI***
Av. Tulum, Sm. 2, Centro

A-14 ***Cinépolis I a X***
Plaza Las Américas, Centro

A-14 ***Cinépolis VIP***
Plaza Las Américas, Centro

SPORTS

Most Cancún hotels have tennis courts and gyms. You can use the bike path in the Hotel Zone for biking, roller skating or walking, go jogging on the Downtown track or visit the following:

GOLF COURSES

F-05 ***Cancún Golf Club***
18-HOLE, PAR 72.
Blvd. Kukulcán km 7.5
Tel.: 883 1230
Fax: 883 3358
poktapok@sybcom.com
www.cancungolfclub.com

E-23 ***Hilton Cancún Golf Club***
18-HOLE, PAR 72.
Blvd. Kukulcán km 17
Tel.: 881 8016

D-19 ***Gran Meliá Cancún***
9-HOLE, PAR 3.
Blvd. Kukulcán km 15
Tel.: 881 1100 ext. 6119

D-21 ***Grand Oasis Resort***
9-HOLE.
Blvd. Kukulcán km 16.5
Tel.: 881 7000 ext. 6277

MINI GOLF

D-17 ***Cancún Palace***
Blvd. Kukulcán km 14.5
Tel.: 881 3600 ext. 6655

BOWLING

D-13 ***Bol Kukulcán***
10 AM. TO 2 PM.
Plaza Kukulcán, L. 201
Tel.: 885 3425

C-14 ***Wol-Ha***
2 PM. TO MIDNIGHT
Av. Tulum esq. Labná
L. 1-3, Sm. 15-A
Tel.: 887 6379

BUS COMPANIES

G-04 ***ADO***
Pino btwn. Uxmal & Tulum
Tel.: 884 4352
www.grupoado.com.mx

Autotur
Chimal, Zona Industrial
Tels.: 882 0491, 882 0492
lgongora@grupoado.com.mx

Expressos
SERVICE THROUGHOUT MEXICO.
Blvd. L. Donaldo Colosio
km 6.5, Airport Hwy.
Tel./Fax: 882 0343
expressos@expressos.com.mx
www.expressos.com.mx

F-01 ***Nuevos Horizontes (Elite)***
Hotel Radisson, Downtown
Tel.: 887 4455 ext. 574

G-04 ***Riviera***
DEPARTURES TO PLAYA DEL CARMEN EVERY 15 MINUTES,
TO THE AIRPORT EVERY HOUR.
Pino btwn. Uxmal & Tulum
Tel.: 884 1365 Fax: 881 4352

CAR RENTALS

D-11 ***Advantage Rent a Car***
Av. Tulum Sm. 20
Pecarí No. 46
Tels.: 887 3929, 884 9931
cars@advantage-cancun.com
www.advantage-cancun.com

Álamo Rent a Car
International Airport
Tel.: 886 0168
Fax: 886 0159
alamocun@prodigy.net.mx

D-28 ***Autosel Rent a Car***
Lobby Crown Paradise
Blvd. Kukulcán km 18.5
Tels.: 885 1618, 883 0017
Fax: 887 5642
autosel@usa.net

F-06 ***Autoxpress***
Tulipanes L. 14 Int. 6-8
Sm. 22 Centro
Tel.: 843 5250
Fax: 892 2324
doradostar@terra.com.mx
www.autoxpresscancun.com

D-10 ***Avant Rent a Car***
Av. Tulum esq. Brisas
Hotel Oasis América
Tels.: 842 3521, 842 3522
Fax: 892 1158
www.avantrentacar.com

F-05 ***Avicar Rental***
Azucenas 2 Ret. 1 Sm. 22
Tel.: 887 2389
Fax: 884 9635
info@avicar.com.mx
www.avicar.com.mx

Avis
International Airport
Tels.: 886 0221, 883 4583
Fax: 886 0238
www.avis.com.mx

C-12 ***Budget Car Rental***
Av. Tulum No. 231 Sm. 20
Tels.: 884 6955, 884 0204
Fax: 884 5011
info@budgetcancun.com
www.budgetcancun.com

P-04 ***Buggy Car Rental***
Plaza Nautilus
Tel.: 849 5555
buggy-car-rent@yahoo.com

P-04 ***Buster Rent a Car***
Plaza Nautilus
Tels.: 849 7221, 849 2525
Fax: 849 4394
www.busterrentacar.com

B-09 ***Econo Car Rental***
Edif. Atlántis Sm. 4 L. 7
Tels.: 887 0142, 887 6487
econo@econocarrental.com
www.econocarrental.com

Elite
Royal Resorts
Tel.: 881 0100
www.elitecarentals.com

O-05 ***Eros Rent a Car***
Calle del Pescador, HZ
km 4.5, L. D-8-3 Depto. 1
Tel.: 849 7640
Fax: 849 4337
erosrent@terra.com.mx

Europcar
- Cancún International Airport
- Plaza Centro

Tel.: 886 0920
Fax: 886 0919

F-10 ***Executive Car Rental***
Av. Yaxchilán 160 Sm. 20
Tels.: 881 6880
01 800 216 7700
01 800 300 7368
Fax: 887 5012
rentacar@executive.com.mx
www.executive.com.mx

F-05 ***Fresh Rent a Car***
Av. Tulum esq. Azucenas
Ret. 1 L. 2 Sm. 22
Tels.: 884 9635, 887 2389
avicar-rental-@hotmail.com

F-10 ***Hertz Rent a Car***
Reno No. 35 Sm. 20
Tel.: 884 1326
Fax: 884 4692

I-09 ***Holiday Rent a Car***
Guaya 36 Sm. 25
Tel.: 884 1061
Fax: 887 7485

D-03 ***Jovisa***
Plaza Mayafair
Tel.: 883 3575

B-03 ***L. J. Vegas Car Rental***
Hotel NH Krystal km 9 HZ
Tels.: 885 2465, 848 9800
Fax: 880 9876

Localiza Rent a Car
Av. La Costa 128 Sm. 30
Tels.: 885 1199, 849 4680
Fax: 887 3109
localiza@cancun.com.mx
www.localizarentacar.com

Master Car
Airport - Cancún Hwy.
km 12.5
Tels.: 886 2024
01 800 710 7241
Fax: 886 2025
www.mastercar.com.mx

H-06 ***Monaco Rent a Car***
Av. Yaxchilán 65 Mz. 6
Tels.: 884 6540, 884 7843
Aeropuerto Internacional
Tel.: 886 0239
www.monacorentacar.com

National Car Rental
International Airport
Tel.: 886 0152
Fax: 886 0153
natrent@prodigy.net.mx
www.nationalcar.com

E-04 ***Payless Car Rental***
Plaza Quetzal, HZ
Tel.: 880 3506
Fax: 880 3737
paycar@prodigy.net.mx

D-07 ***Promocaribe Rent a Car***
Av. Náder No. 18
Plaza Centro L. 309
Tel.: 884 4741 Fax: 884 4714
sales@promocaribe.com
www.promocaribe.com

C-03 ***Royal Rent a Car***
Plaza El Parian, HZ
Tel.: 883 5764

G-05 ***Speed Car Rental***
Av. Uxmal L. 28 Sm. 22
Tel.: 892 0224
Fax: 892 0225

Thrifty Car Rental
International Airport
Tels.: 886 0333, 886 0555
01 800 021 2277
Fax: 886 0318
www.thrifty.com

C-16 ***Top Car Rental***
Blvd. Kukulcán km 14.5
Ret. El Rey, Villas Tropical
Tels.: 885 0094, 885 1893
01 800 719 1990
Fax: 885 1893
www.toprentacar.com

D-17 ***Travesías Rent a Car***
Blvd. Kukulcán km 14.5
Tel.: 881 6100 ext. 4058
www.palaceresorts.com

C-29 ***Veloz Rent a Car***
Hotel Solymar km 17.5
Tels.: 885 1811, 880 7432
www.solymarcancun.com

H-04 ***Ventura Car Rental***
Av. Uxmal 21, Sm. 23
Int. Hotel Alux
Tel.: 887 6020
www.venturacarrental.com

Vip Rent a Car
Airport - Cancún Hwy.
Fracc. Bonfil 2000 Mz. 3
Col. Alfredo Bonfil
Tels.: 886 2391, 886 2392
vip@caribe.net.mx
www.cancunrentacar.com

H-04 ***Ximba***
Av. Uxmal 19 Sm. 23
Tels.: 887 1410, 842 3218
Fax: 883 9083
www.ximba-rentacar.com

BANKS

YOU CAN FIND ATMS AT THE BRANCHES OF DIFFERENT BANKS AND AT OTHER LOCATIONS.

E-06 ***Banamex***
MON. TO FRI. 9AM. - 4 PM., SAT. 9:30 AM. - 2 PM.
Av. Tulum No. 19 Sm. 5
Tels.: 881 6403
01 800 111 3030
Fax: 881 6405
www.banamex.com.mx

- DOWNTOWN ATMS: BUS STATION, SAMS CLUB, PLAZA LAS AMÉRICAS, WALMART, AV. TULUM ESQ. JALEB SM. 20, COMERCIAL MEXICANA MEGA.

- HOTEL ZONE ATMS IN THE FOLLOWING MALLS: TERRAMAR, CARACOL, FLAMINGO, LA ISLA SHOPPING VILLAGE & PLAZA MARINA.

E-07 ***BBV Bancomer***
MON. TO FRI. 8:30 AM. - 4 PM, SAT. 10 AM. -2 PM.
Av. Tulum No. 20 Sm. 5
Tels.: 884 4400
01 800 112 1111
Fax: 884 3600
www.bancomer.com.mx

• Downtown ATMs: Plaza 2000, Costco, Sams Club, Walmart, Plaza Portales.

• Hotel Zone ATM: Plaza El Parián.

D-10 *Bancrecer Banorte*
Mon. to fri. 9 am. - 5 pm.,
Sat. 10 am. - 2 pm.

Av. Tulum No. 214 Sm. 4
Tel.: 887 6935
Fax: 887 6938
www.banorte.com.mx

• Downtown ATMs: Plaza Las Américas, Av. Xel-Há L.1 Sm. 25, Av. Tulum No. 214 Sm. 4, Av. Tulum L. 1 Sm. 22.

• Hotel Zone ATMs in the following malls: Flamingo, Coral Negro.

F-02 ***Bancomext***
MON. TO FRI. 9 AM. - 1 PM.
INVESTMENT DEVELOPMENT BANK.
Av. Náder No. 28 Sm. 2
Tel.: 887 1131
Fax: 887 3332
www.bancomext.com.mx

C-10 ***HSBC***
MON. TO SAT. 8 AM. - 7 PM.
Av. Tulum No. 192 Sm. 4
Tels.: 881 4103
01 800 712 4825
Fax: 881 4106
www.bital.com.mx

- DOWNTOWN ATMS: PLAZA LAS AVENIDAS, PLAZA 2000, PLAZA LAS AMÉRICAS, DRUGSTORES PARÍS ON AV. TULUM & AV. YAXCHILÁN, MERCADO 28, WALMART.
- HOTEL ZONE ATMS IN THE FOLLOWING MALLS: CARACOL, LA ISLA SHOPPING VILLAGE, FORUM BY THE SEA, KUKULCÁN.

F-05 ***Scotiabank Inverlat***
MON. TO FRI. 9 AM. - 5 PM., SAT. 10 AM. - 2 PM.
Av. Tulum No. 26 Sm. 5
Tels.: 884 1376, 884 1373
Fax: 884 0993
www.scotiabankinverlat.com

- DOWNTOWN ATMS: COMERCIAL MEXICANA ON AV. TULUM, PLAZA CHINATOWN.
- HOTEL ZONE ATM: OXXO CLOSE TO COCO BONGO.

D-10 ***Santander Serfin***
MON. TO FRI. 9 AM. - 4 PM., SAT. 10 AM. - 2 PM.
Av. Tulum No. 173 Sm. 20
Tels.: 884 0629
01 800 711 2211
Fax: 884 0718
www.santander.com.mx

- DOWNTOWN ATMS: AV. TULUM ESQ. AV. COBÁ, BUS STATION, PLAZA LAS AMÉRICAS.
- HOTEL ZONE ATMS: PLAZA LAGUNAS, HOTEL OMNI, PLAZA CARACOL, HOTEL GRAN MELIÁ CANCÚN.

MARINAS & DIVING

MARINA STAFF USUALLY SPEAK ENGLISH AND SPANISH, WE SPECIFY WHERE ADDITIONAL LANGUAGES ARE SPOKEN.

E-22 ***Aqua Fun Marina***
SPANISH, ENGLISH, ITALIAN.
TOP QUALITY INSTALLATIONS, FAMILY AMBIANCE. TRIPS TO THE REEFS AND AROUND THE LAGOON.
Blvd. Kukulcán km 16.2
Tels.: 885 3260, 885 2930
01 800 667 6572
Fax: 885 1943
operaciones@aquafun.com.mx
www.aquafun.com.mx

E-19 ***Aquaworld***
STAFF SPEAK UP TO 20 LANGUAGES.
ATTRACTIONS: TAKE THE PLUNGE, CERTIFIED DIVERS, ISLA MUJERES DAYTRIP, CANCUN´S UNDERWATER ADVENTURE, SEA WALKER, THE ROCKET, BIG GAME FISHING, CANCÚN QUEEN, FLY TOGETHER, COZUMEL DAYTRIP ADVENTURE.
Blvd. Kukulcán km 15.2
Tels.: 848 8327, 848 8326
Fax: 848 8326
info@aquaworld.com.mx
www.aquaworld.com.mx

I-04 ***Bluewater Adventures***
ENGLISH, SPANISH, FRENCH, ITALIAN, JAPANESE.
TRIPS TO ISLA MUJERES. JUNGLE TOURS TO PUNTA NIZAC IN FAST, TWO-SEATER LAUNCHES.
Blvd. Kukulcán km 6.5
Tels.: 849 4444, 849 7171
Fax: 849 4411
info@bluewateradventures.com.mx
www.bluewateradventures.com.mx

L-04 ***Bob Cancún***
INDIVIDUAL BOB SUBMARINES.
Hotel Cancún Marina
Blvd. Kukulcán km 5.5
Tel.: 849 4440
Fax: 849 7284
bobmex@prodigy.net.mx
www.bobcancun.com.mx

P-04 ***Club de Catamaranes***
SPANISH, ENGLISH, GERMAN, ITALIAN, FRENCH.
EXCLUSIVE YACHT CHARTERS FOR GROUPS. TRIPS TO ISLA MUJERES.
Blvd. Kukulcán km 3.5
Hotel Club Carrousel
Tel.: 849 7556
Fax: 849 4169

C-32 ***El Manglar***
SPANISH, ENGLISH.
Blvd. Kukulcán km 19.8
in front of Sun Palace hotel
Tel./Fax: 885 4030

I-04 ***Fishing Charters***
ENJOYABLE LEISURE TRIP AROUND CANCÚN BAY, ISLA MUJERES, CONTOY.
Blvd. Kukulcán km 6.5
Bluewater Marina
Tels.: 849 4038, 849 4766
marina@cancun.com.mx
www.fishingcharters.com.mx

Grand Turk
YACHT TRIPS FOR SMALL GROUPS. LUNCH BAR & SNORKELING INCLUDED.
Camarón No. 10 Sm. 27
Tel.: 884 3212
Fax: 884 9247
tropicalheat@prodigy.net.mx

P-03 ***Jungle Tours Neptuno***
TRIMARAN EXCURSIONS, SNORKELING IN PUERTO MORELOS.
Blvd. Kukulcán km 3.5
Hotel Blue Bay Getaway
Tels.: 849 4709, 849 4023
Fax: 849 5972

S-02 ***Lemon Divers***
DIVE TRIPS TO THE REEFS OF COZUMEL AND TO CENOTES.
Hotel Imperial Las Perlas
Tels.: 884 9184, 845 0977
lemondiv@prodigy.net.mx
www.lemondivers.com.mx

I-04 ***Manta Divers***
GERMAN, SPANISH, ENGLISH.
TRAINING AND GUIDES FOR CAVE DIVING. TRIPS TO REEFS IN THE CANCÚN AND COZUMEL AREA. SMALL GROUPS.

Playa Tortugas km 6.5 ZH
Tel.: 849 4050
Fax: 849 4612
dive@mantadivers.com
www.mantadivers.com

D-16 *Magic Sky & Sea Adventures*

English, spanish, italian, french, german.
Helicopter and hydroplane excursions.
Blvd. Kukulcán km 14.1
Tels.: 885 1720, 885 1716
Fax: 885 1613
reservations@magic-sea.com
www.magic-sea.com

D-16 *Marina Barracuda*

Aqua Safari: Punta Nizuc, Nichupté lagoon, Bahía de Mujeres (bay), Isla Mujeres.
Great Barracuda fishing boat.
Jungle Cruise to Punta Nizuc, private trips, snack bar.
Blvd. Kukulcán km 14.1
Tel.: 885 2444 Fax: 885 3444
baracuda@prodigy.net.mx

R-02 *Marina Club Lagoon*

Trips to Isla Mujfres.
Blvd. Kukulcán km 5.8
Hotel Sunset Lagoon
Tels.: 849 4739, 881 4500
Fax: 849 4745
marinacl@prodigy.net.mx

Marina Hacienda del Mar

Km 1.5 Puerto Juárez-Punta Sam Hwy.
Tel.: 880 2280 Fax: 880 1070
marina@cancun.com.mx

E-21 *Marina del Rey*

English, spanish, french, german.
Blvd. Kukulcán km 15.6
Tels.: 885 0363, 885 0300
Fax: 885 0332
mardelrey@prodigy.net.mx

D-07 *Marina Punta del Este*

Spanish, english, french.
Elite jungle tour to Punta Nizuc, diving, different skill levels.
Blvd. Kukulcán km 10.3
Tel.: 883 1210
Fax: 883 1309
www.mpuntaeste.com

L-04 *Marina Scuba Cancún*

Spanish, english, french, italian, Hungarian, japanese.
Five-star Golden Palm PADI center.
Blvd. Kukulcán km 5 HZ
Tels.: 849 5225, 849 5226
Fax: 849 4736
scuba@cancun.com.mx
www.scubacancun.com.mx

E-17 *Marina Sunrise*

Spanish, english, mayan.
Blvd. Kukulcán km 14.7 ZH
Tels.: 885 3909, 885 3910

Marinos and Marinos
Av. Tankah No. 21 Sm. 27
Tel.: 887 3460
Fax: 887 2967
nauticos@prodigy.net.mx

K-04 *Mundo Marino*

Spanish, english, german.
Sport fishing, charters and 25 years of experience.
Blvd. Kukulcán km 5.5
Tels.: 849 7259, 849 7258
mmarino@cancun.com.mx

A-02 *Sólo Buceo*

Spanish, english, japanese.
Blvd. Kukulcán km 9.5 Int.
Hotel Dreams Cancún
Tels.: 883 3979, 848 7070
Fax: 883 4852
scuba@solobuceo.com
www.solobuceo.com

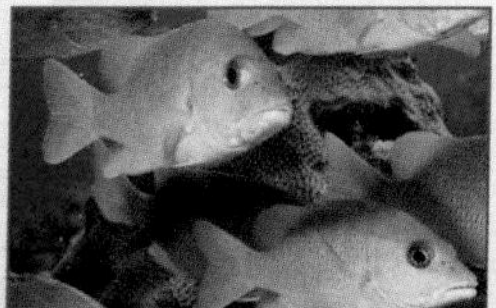

BOAT TRIPS

E-19 *Aqua World Cancún Queen*
Spanish, mayan, english, french, italian, german, japanese.
Gourmet cuisine, lobster and steak special; live music, games, dancing and open bar.
Marina Aqua World
Blvd. Kukulcán km 15.2
Tels.: 848 8327, 848 8326
Fax: 848 8326
manager@aquaworld.com.mx
www.aquaworld.com.mx

C-04 *Aquabus*
Cruises on Nichupté lagoon aboard boats with capacity for 48 and 60 passengers.
Blvd. Kukulcán km 9
Plaza Zócalo L. 2-A
Tels.: 883 3155, 883 5649
Fax: 883 3715
aquabus@cancun.com
www.aquabuscancun.com

I-04 *Asterix Tours*
Trips to Contoy, night fishing, snorkeling, sunset and evening cruises, private charters, party fishing, exclusive dinners.
Blvd. Kukulcán km 6.5
Bluewater Marina
Tel.: 886 4270
Fax: 886 4755
asterix1@prodigy.net.mx

M-03 *Aventuras Discovery*
Trips to Cozumel, Riviera Maya, Puerto Aventuras, Isla Mujeres; swimming with dolphins, snorkeling and diving.
Blvd. Kukulcán km. 5
Playa Langosta
Tels.: 849 4039, 849 4042
01 800 713 8862
USA 1 800 417 1736
Fax: 849 4758
www.dolphindiscovery.com

Colón Tours
Spanish, english, french, italian, dutch, german.
Two galleons straight from the history books, trips to Contoy and Isla Mujeres.
Punta Conoco 36 Sm. 24
Tels.: 884 1598, 884 5333
01 800 715 3375
Fax: 887 1283
sales@kolumbustours.com
www.kolumbustours.com

D-22 *Columbus Lobster Dinner Cruise*
Royal Mayan Marina,
Blvd. Kukulcán km 16.5
Tel.: 883 1488
hook@cancun.com.mx
www.capitanhook.com

I-04 *Caribbean Funday Tour*
DEPARTURES AT 9:30 AM., 4:45 PM. TRIP INCLUDES DOMESTIC DRINKS, BUFFET, SHOPPING TOUR, BIKES, FUN AND GAMES AT THE BEACH CLUB.
Blvd. Kukulcán km 6.5
Playa Tortugas
Tels.: 884 3760
01 800 021 8179
Fax: 887 2184
caribbeancarnavalvt@prodigy.net.mx

I-04 *Carnaval Caribeño*
DEPARTURES: 7 PM. & 11:30 PM. TRIP INCLUDES DOMESTIC DRINKS, BUFFET, THEME SHOWS AT THE BEACH CLUB: MEXICAN FIESTA, BACHELOR PARTY, CASINO, CARIBBEAN NIGHT.
Blvd. Kukulcán km 6.5
Playa Tortugas
Tels.: 884 3760
01 800 021 8179
Fax: 887 2184
caribbeancarnavalvt@prodigy.net.mx

N-04 *El Embarcadero*
QUAY, TRIPS TO ISLA MUJERES, WATER TAXIS. ACTIVITY CENTER: MEXICAN CRAFTS MUSEUM, SCENIC TOWER, THEATER AND MORE.
Blvd. Kukulcán km 4.5
Playa Linda
Tels.: 849 5580, 849 7777
Fax: 849 5581
elembarcadero@terra.com.mx
www.elembarcadero.com

N-04 *Garrafón Cruise*
DAILY DEPARTURES FOR EL GARRAFÓN PARK AT 9:30 AND 11 AM., RETURN: 4:30 & 5:30 PM. THE EL GARRAFÓN PACKAGE ($29 US) INCLUDES TRANSPORT, TRIP TO THE VILLAGE ON ISLA MUJERES, ADMISSION TO THE PARK, THE MARINE MUSEUM, THE SCENIC TOWER AND THE COAST PATH FOR PANORAMIC VIEWS. OTHER PACKAGES AVAILABLE INCLUDING BUFFET LUNCH, OPEN BAR AND SNORKELING GEAR.
Blvd. Kukulcán km 4.5
Playa Linda
Tels.: 849 5580, 849 7777
Fax: 849 5581
elembarcadero@terra.com.mx
www.elembarcadero.com

M-03 *Galeón Capitán Hook*
SPANISH, ENGLISH, ITALIAN. VOYAGE AROUND CANCÚN BAY, INCLUDES A LOBSTER DINNER AND A PIRATE SHOW.
Blvd. Kukulcán km 4.5
Playa Langosta
Tels.: 848 4451 al 53
Fax: 849 5086
hook@cancun.com.mx
www.capitanhook.com

M-03 *Golden Cruise*
DEPARTURES: 9:30 AM. & 5 PM. TRIP INCLUDES LIVE MUSIC, CONTINENTAL BREAKFAST, BUFFET LUNCH AND DOMESTIC BAR.
Blvd. Kukulcán km 4.5
Playa Langosta
Tels.: 849 4451 al 53
Fax: 849 5086
hook@cancun.com.mx
www.capitanhook.com

FERRIES

Cancún-Isla Mujeres

PUNTA SAM (CARS)
7:45, 10:15 AM., 12:30, 3, 5:30, 8:15 PM.

PUERTO JUÁREZ
EVERY 30 MIN FROM 6 AM. TO 9 PM.

Isla Mujeres-Cancún

PUNTA SAM (CARS)
6:30, 9:30 AM., 12:45, 1:45, 4:15, 7:15 PM.

PUERTO JUÁREZ
EVERY 30 MIN FROM 6 AM. TO 7 PM.

Punta Sam-Isla Mujeres
9:30, 11 AM., 2:45, 5:30, 8:15 PM.
EXTRA DEPARTURES DURING PEAK TIMES: 8 AM.

Isla Mujeres-Punta Sam
6:30, 9:30 AM., 12:45, 4:15, 7:15 PM.

MUSEUMS

C-03 *Anthropology & History Museum*
TUE.-FRI. 9 AM. - 8 PM, SAT. & SUN.: 10 AM. -7 PM.
ENTRY FEE: $32 PESOS.
ROOM FOR WORKSHOPS AND CONFERENCES, TEMPORARY EXHIBITIONS. GUIDED VISITS, COURSES, LECTURES AND EDUCATIONAL WORKSHOPS. SPECIALIZED LIBRARY, BOOKSTORE.
SUNDAYS FREE OF CHARGE.
Convention Center
Tel/Fax.: 883 0305
macqr@prodigy.net.mx
www.inahqr.gob.mx

O-04 *Museum of Mexican Popular Art*
MON. - SAT. 9 AM. - 9 PM, SUN. 9 AM. - 7 PM.
ENTRY FEE: $10 US ADULT, $5 US CHILDREN FROM 5 TO 11 YEARS.
El Embarcadero
Blvd. Kukulcán km 4
Tels.: 849 4332, 849 4848
www.elembarcadero.com

PARKS & AMUSEMENTS

IN CANCÚN

D-12 *Interactive Aquarium*
A GLIMPSE OF THE UNDERWATER WORLD AND THE CREATURES THAT INHABIT IT. SWIM WITH DOLPHINS, RAYS AND SHARKS PROGRAMS OFFERED. GROUP SERVICES, ENGLISH-SPANISH BILINGUAL GUIDES. RESTAURANT, BAR AND BOUTIQUE.
ENTRY FEE: $130 PESOS, $90 PESOS CHILDREN UNDER 10 YEARS.
10 AM - 9 PM.
Blvd. Kukulcán km 12.5
La Isla Shopping Village
Tels.: 883 5068, 883 0411
Fax: 883 1773
www.aquariumcancun.com.mx

BULL RING CANCÚN

Enjoy the art of bullfighting in a unique atmosphere. Find out why this tradition is so enduring and exciting. Admire the brave bulls and toreros or bullfighters with their beautiful suits.

EVERY WEDNESDAY AT 3:30 p.m.

The mulicolored charreria is a genuinely Mexican tradition. The charro show is a cultural mosaic of beautiful costumes and graceful riders from several Mexican states.

The bullring is totally covered.

Tickets at the bullring
Bonampak Ave. on the corner
of Sayil Ave.
Or call your travel agent
Tels./Fax:
(998) 884 8372, 884 8248
Cancún, Quintana Roo

O-04 *El Embarcadero*

This activity center is a little corner of Mexico. Enjoy the Museum of Mexican Popular Art, and Cancún Theater. Cruises and water taxis bound for Isla Mujeres depart from the quay.
Blvd. Kukulcán km 4, HZ
Tels.: 849 5580, 849 7777
Fax: 849 5581
www.elembarcadero.com

F-35 *Parque Nizuc*

Slides, pools and water games, swimming with the dolphins, Shotover Jet and more.
Entry fee: $27 US adult, $21 US children under 12 years.
🕓 10 am. - 5:30 pm.
Blvd. Kukulcán km 25
Tels.: 881 3000, 881 3030
Fax: 881 3003
info@parquenizuc.com
www.parquenizuc.com

A-12 *Plaza de Toros*

Bullfights, rodeos & mexican folklore.
Wednesday 3:30 pm.
Admission $300 pesos.
Av. Bonampak Sm. 4
Tel.: 884 8248
bull@prodigy.net.mx

O-04 *Teatro de Cancún*

Exhibitions, conventions and concerts.
Blvd. Kukulcán km 4, HZ
El Embarcadero
Tel.: 849 5580
Fax: 849 5581
www.elembarcadero.com

N-05 *Cancún Scenic Tower*

The best view of Cancún.
🕓 9 am. - 11 pm.
Cost: $9 US adult, $4.50 children under 11 years.
Blvd. Kukulcán km 4, HZ
El Embarcadero
Tels.: 849 4848, 849 7777
Fax: 849 5581
www.elembarcadero.com

Trips from Cancún

Aktun Chén

Cave, cenote, serpentarium and regional wildlife corner.
Entry fee $18 US adult $10 US children under 12 years.
🕓 8:30 am. - 5 pm. winter; 8:30 am. - 4:30 pm. summer.
Cancún-Tulum Hwy. km 107
Tel.: (984) 877 8550
grutas@aktunchen.com
www.aktunchen.com

CrocoCún Zoo

Crocodile and regional wildlife park.
🕓 8:30 am. - 5:30 pm.
Entry fee $144 pesos adult, $86 pesos children under 12.
Tel.: 850 3719
www.crococun.com

Dolphin Discovery

A company offering Swim and Dive with Dolphins programs on Isla Mujeres and Cozumel and in Puerto Aventuras. Entry fee: $64 US adult, $54 US children under 12. Departures 11:15 am. & 1:15 pm. Round trip transportation $15 US. Swim with dolphins $119 US, departures: 10 am., 12, 2 & 3:30 pm. Swim with dolphins $165 US, Sat. 8:45 am.
Playa Langosta
Blvd. Kukulcán km 5
Tels.: 849 4748, 849 4749
Fax: 849 4758
www.dolphindiscovery.com

El Garrafón

Marine park on Isla Mujeres. The El Garrafón package ($29 US) includes transport, trip to the village on Isla Mujeres, admission to the park, the Marine Museum, the Scenic Tower and the coast path for panoramic views. Other packages available including buffet lunch, open bar and snorkeling gear.
Daily departures from El Embarcadero at 9:30 and 11 am.
Garrafón Hwy. km 6 Sm. 9
Tels.: 884 9422, 884 9455
Fax: 887 0083
www.garrafon.com

Kantun Chi

Cave, cenotes and areas with regional fauna.
Entry fee: $10 US adult, $6 US children under 12 years
🕓 9 am. - 5 pm.
9 am. - 6 pm. summer.
Cancún-Tulum Hwy. km 100
Tel.: (984) 873 0021
info@kantunchi.com
www.kantunchi.com

Rancho Loma Bonita

Motor bike, horseback riding and boat trips. Minimum consumption $10 US. Individual motor bike $600 pesos, for two $450 pesos; horses $605 pesos adult, children from 6 to 11 years $550 pesos; boats $450 pesos adult, $270 pesos children from 6 to 11 years.
Departures: 8, 10:30 am. & 1 pm.
🕓 8am - 6 pm.
Cancún-Tulum Hwy. km 40.5
Cancún Reservation Office: 7 am. - 10 pm.
Av. Uxmal 88 Sm. 24
Tels.: 887 5465, 887 5723
Fax: 887 1708
lomabonita@infosel.net.mx
www.lomabonitamex.com

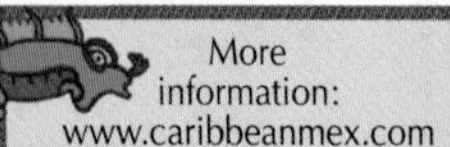

clinc
CANCÚN
CANCÚN
THE WORLD'S BEST VIEW
Only from the Rotating Scenic Towers in the Mexican Caribbean.
Garrafón Park, Isla Mujeres.
El Embarcadero, Cancún.
Xcaret, Riviera Maya.
Puerta Maya, Cozumel.
OPEN DAILY • INFORMATION (998) 849 7777 • CONSULT YOUR TRAVEL AGENT.

Tres Ríos
Ecotourism & adventure park featuring rivers and cenotes; kayaks and bikes available.
9 am. - 5 pm.
Transport to park leaving from the Cancún hotel zone and Playa del Carmen from 7:30 onwards.
Entry fee: 19 us adults, $15 us children under 12 years
$418 pesos transport included
$770 pesos all-inclusive
$670 pesos without transport
Prices may change.
Cancún-Tulum Hwy. km 54
Park tel: 850 4774
Offices in Cancún:
Av. Náder No. 29 Sm. 2
Edif. Madrid 4º piso
Tels.: 887 8077, 887 8078
01 800 714 3643
Fax: 887 8077
info@tres-rios.com
www.tres-rios.com

Xel-Há
Aquatic and nature park.
9 am. - 6 pm.
Entry fee: Sat. & Sun. $19 us adult, $10 us children under 12 years. Trips and packages including admission, transport and meals are available through the travel agency/marina in your hotel.
Cancún-Tulum Hwy. km 122
Tel. 01 (984) 875 6000
Offices in Cancún:
Av. Náder No. 28 Sm. 2
Edificio Popolná
Tel.: 884 9422
ventas@xel-ha.com.mx
www.xelha.com.mx

Xcaret
Eco-archaeological park.
Entry fee: $49 us adult, $24.50 us children under 12 years, with meal $69 us adult, $34.50 children

under 12 years, Transport Cancún-Parque 7 us, with dinner $68 us adult, $43.50 children under 12 years.
Cancún-Tulum Hwy. km 74
Tel. 01 (984) 871 4000
Departures from Cancún (Playa Caracol):
Mon.-Sat. 9, 11:30, 3 pm.
Return: 5:20 & 9:30 pm.
Sundays 9:30 & 10:30 am.
Return: 5:20 & 9 pm.
Xcaret offices in Cancún:
Blvd. Kukulcán Edif. Bahía
Tels.: 881 2400, 883 3143
Fax: 881 2424
grupos@xcaret.net
xcadir@sybcom.com
www.xcaret.net

NIGHTLIFE

Hotel Zone

B-02 *Azúcar*
Caribbean nightclub. Cuban orchestra plays live, beachfront bar.
Mon.-Sat. 9:30 pm. -3 am.
Blvd. Kukulcán km 9
Tels.: 848 7000, 848 7081
Fax: 848 7003

C-05 *Batachá*
Dance floor, live salsa, merengue and tropical music.
Tue.-Sun. 10 pm. - 5 am.
Group performs from 11 pm. - 3 am. Entry fee: $45 pesos.
Blvd. Kukulcán km 9.5
Hotel Miramar Misión
Tels.: 883 1755, 883 1920
Fax: 883 1136
reservascancun@prodigy.net.mx

B-03 *Bull Dog Café*
A VIP area with Jacuzzi, stage, live music. Private rooms for groups.
Thurs. - Sun. 10 pm. - 5 am.
Open nightly during high season.
Entry fee: $120 pesos,
Open bar $250 pesos.
Hotel NH Krystal
Blvd. Kukulcán km 9
Tel./Fax: 848 9850
www.bulldogcafe.com

L-04 *Carlos'n Charlie's*
Dance floor. Live music in English and Spanish.
From midday onwards
Plaza Forum by the Sea
Tels.: 883 4467, 849 4468
www.carlosandcharlies.com

B-04 *Coco Bongo*
Disco, live music and entertainment.
10:30 pm. - 5 am.
Entry fee: $12 us,
Open bar $25 us.
Plaza Forum by the Sea
Tels.: 883 5061, 883 5062
Fax: 883 2231
sales@cocobongo.com.mx
www.cocobongo.com.mx

C-04 *Dady' O*
Disco. Theme parties.
10 pm. - 5 am.
Entry fee: $12 us,
Open bar $25 us.
Blvd. Kukulcán km 9.5
Conjunto Coral Negro
Tel.: 883 3333 Fax: 883 3762
caviza@dadyo.net
www.dadyo.net

C-04 *Dady Rock*
Live rock music, theme nights.
6 pm. - 5 am.
Open bar $22 us.
Blvd. Kukulcán km 9.5,
Conjunto Coral Negro
Tels.: 883 3333, 883 3134
caviza@dadyo.net
www.dadyo.net

I-04 *Fat Tuesday*
American Daiquiri Bar.
8 pm. - 2 am.
Blvd. Kukulcán km 6.5
Tels.: 849 7199, 849 7200
Fax: 849 7201
www.fat-tuesday.com

D-12 *Glazz*
Disco. Theme parties.
6:30 pm. -2 am.
Blvd. Kukulcán km 12
La Isla Shopping Village
Tels.: 883 1855, 883 1881
Fax: 883 1881
glazzclub@prodigy.net.mx

D-07 *G - Spot*
Disco. Theme parties.
10 pm. - 2 am.
Blvd. Kukulcán km 10.3
Tels.: 883 2201, 883 2186

O-05 *La Boom Club*
Two entertainment centers under one roof: a bar playing Hip Hop, R&B and Rap and a disco with trans, progressive, dance, tecno and house music. Light show, theme parties.
9 pm. - 5 am.
Entry fee: $12 us,
Open bar $25 us.
Blvd. Kukulcán km 3.5
Tels.: 849 7587, 849 7588
Fax: 849 7589
www.laboom.com.mx

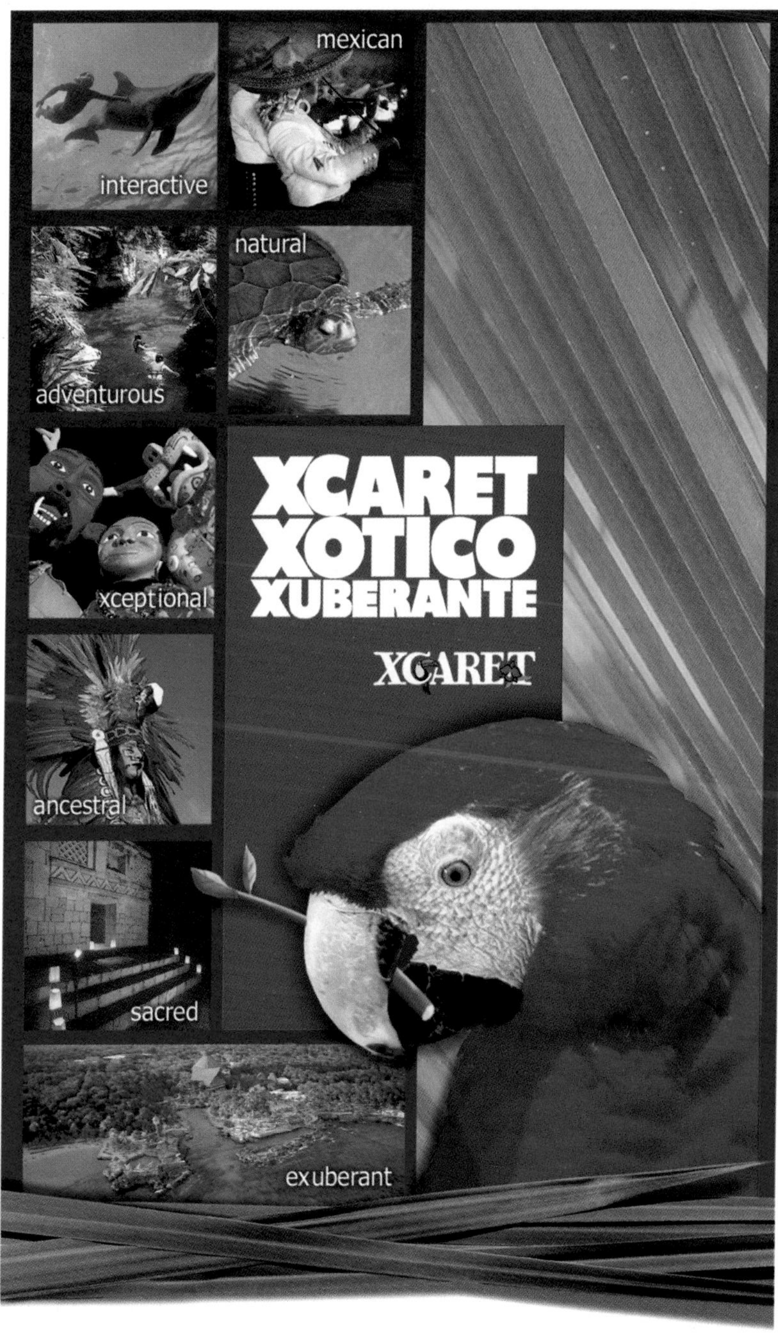
interactive
mexican
adventurous
natural
xceptional
XCARET
XOTICO
XUBERANTE
XCARET
ancestral
sacred
exuberant

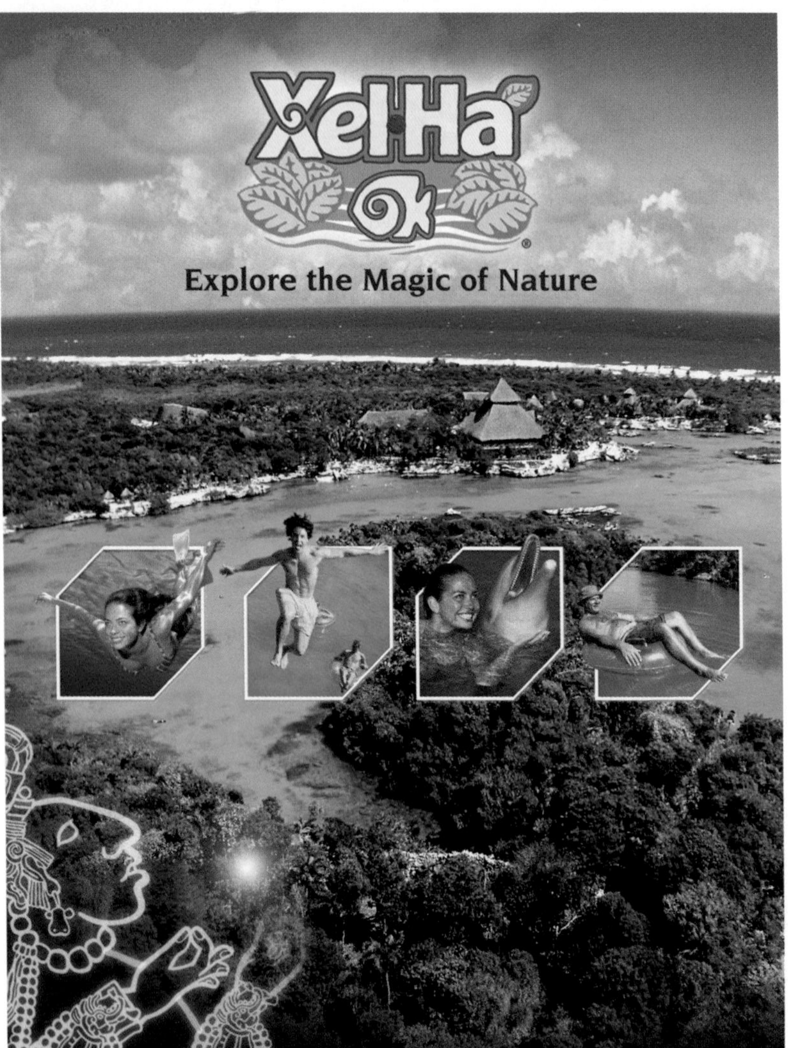
Xel-Há
Explore the Magic of Nature

D-20 *Lobby Bar*
5:30 PM. - 1 AM.
Fiesta Americana Condesa
Tel.: 881 4200 ext. 4430
Fax: 885 2005

C-04 *Nectar Bar*
LIVE MUSIC, DANCE FLOOR.
Blvd. Kukulcán km 8.5
Plaza Zócalo, local 2
Tels.: 883 3716, 883 3129

D-14 *The Royal Bandstand*
LIVE MUSIC, DANCE FLOOR.
RESTAURANT 5-11 PM.,
BAR 5-1 PM. CLOSED SATURDAY.
Next to The Royal Sands
Tel.: 848 8220

C-04 *Señor Frog's*
DANCE FLOOR, BAR, LIVE MUSIC, WAITERS PERFORM A SHOW. MEXICAN AND INTERNATIONAL CUISINE.
NOON - 3 AM.
ENTRY FEE: $4 US.
Blvd. Kukulcán km 10
Tels.: 883 2188, 883 3454
www.senorfrogs.com

D-12 *Thai Lounge*
PAD THAI, GREEN CURRY.
6-2 PM.
La Isla Shopping Village
Tel./Fax: 883 1401

B-03 *The City*
24 HRS.
Blvd. Kukulcán km 9
Tels.: 883 4187, 883 2452
www.thecitycancun.com

C-04 *O Ultralounge*
LIVE MUSIC, LOUNGE, HOUSE. FUSION COOKING.
9-6 PM.
Blvd. Kukulcán km 9.5
Tel.: 883 3333, ext. 106
Fax: 883 3702
www.oultralounge.com

DOWNTOWN

E-04 *El Camarote*
ROMANTIC MUSIC, INTERNATIONAL CUISINE.
10 PM. - 4 AM.
ENTRY FEE THURS.-SAT: $30 PESOS.
Av. Uxmal No. 26 Sm. 2-A
Plaza Kokai
Tel.: 884 3218 Fax: 884 4335

G-06 *Roots Jazz Club*
LIVE JAZZ. EUROPEAN CUISINE, CHEESE PLATTERS AND MORE.
6 PM. - 1 AM.
Tulipanes No. 26 Sm. 22
Tel.: 884 2437 Fax: 884 5547
roots@cancun.com
www.cancun.com/nightlife/roots

H-06 *Los Cuatro Elementos*
LIVE TROVA, ROCK AND BOLERO MUSIC. MODERN-BOHEMIAN AMBIANCE.
TUE. - SAT. 7 PM. - 4 AM.
Hotel Xbalamqué
Av. Yaxchilán, Centro
Tel./Fax: 884 9690

A-14 *Mambo Café*
INTERNATIONAL GROUPS PLAY LIVE, DANCE FLOOR, CARIBBEAN AMBIANCE.
10 PM. - 5 AM.
ADMISSION: MEN $50 PESOS, WOMEN $30 PESOS.
Plaza Las Américas
Tels.: 887 7894, 887 7891
ventas@mambocafe.com.mx

F-06 *Over 30´s*
LIVE MUSIC FROM THE 1970S AND 1980S, INTERNATIONAL CUISINE, SEAFOOD AND APPETIZERS.
5 PM. - 4 AM.
Av. Tulum Sm. 22
Retorno Tulipanes
Tel.: 892 0060
Fax: 887 9899
over30club@hotmail.com

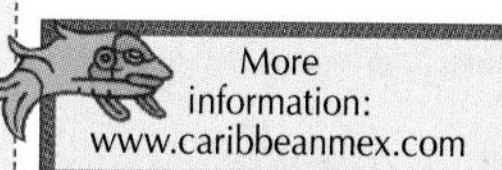

RESTAURANTS

The range of prices is given in dollars ($US) and is given for a meal including a drink, starter, main course, dessert or coffee.

- UP TO $8
- BETWEEN $8 & $15
- BETWEEN $15 & $25
- BETWEEN $25 & $35
- MORE THAN $35

- Air-conditioning
- Bar
- Groups
- Live music
- Dance floor
- Reservations

- Show
- Formal dress

Credit cards

VI VISA MC MASTER CARD AE AMERICAN EXPRESS

- House specialty
- Opening hours

HOTEL ZONE

AMERICAN

D-12 *Chilis Grill & Bar*
AE VI MC
HAMBURGERS.
MON. - THURS. 11 AM. - MIDNIGHT
FRI. - SAT. 11 AM. - 1 AM.
La Isla Shopping Village
Tels.: 883 5513, 883 5515

B-04 *Hard Rock Café*
AE VI MC
LIVE ROCK MUSIC.
HAMBURGERS, BBQ RIBS.
11PM. - 1 AM.
Plaza Forum by the Sea
Tel.: 881 8120
Fax: 881 8121
www.hardrock.com

D-12 *Johnny Rockets*
AE VI MC
HAMBURGERS, HOT DOGS, CHICKEN WINGS, MILK SHAKES, PIES.
8 AM. - MIDNIGHT

La Isla Shopping Village
Tels.: 883 5574, 883 5575
Fax: 883 5576

D-09 *Planet Hollywood*
AE VI MC
HAMBURGERS.
11PM. - 2 AM.
Flamingo Plaza
Tels.: 885 3022, 883 0527, 885 3044, 885 3033
Fax: 883 0656

C-04 *T.G.I. Friday´s*

AE VI MC

Jack Daniel´s, Grill Buffalo Wings. More than 600 cocktails, lively atmosphere.
Noon - 11 pm.
Blvd. Kukulcán km 9
Tels.: 883 3542, 883 3543
Fax: 883 2861
tgifcun@prodigy.net.mx
www.fridays.com.mx

C-08 *Tony Roma's*

AE VI MC

BBQ a la BBQ, onion rings, The original Baby Back.
Noon - 11 pm.
Blvd. Kukulcán km 11.5
Hotel Gran Caribe Real
Tel.: 883 0084
Fax: 883 0085
www.tonyromas.com.mx

Argentinian

B-04 *Cambalache*

AE VI MC

Fine imported steaks.
1 pm. - 2 am.
Plaza Forum by the Sea
Tels.: 883 0902, 883 0485
Fax: 883 0897
www.grupocambalache.com

D-18 *La Capilla Argentina*

AE VI MC

Special grill on Saturdays, Caesar Salad.
6 pm. - midnight.
Marriott CasaMagna
Blvd. Kukulcán km 15
Tel.: 881 2000
Fax: 848 9614

Brazilian

P-04 *Río Churrascaría*

AE VI MC

Steaks & exotic meat.
Noon - midnight.
Blvd. Kukulcán km 3.5
Tels.: 849 9040 al 42
Fax: 849 9043
riochurrascaria@hotmail.com

Caribbean

B-02 *Isla Contoy*

AE VI MC

Seafood.
11:30 am. - 5:30 pm.
Blvd. Kukulcán km 9.5
Hotel Fiesta Americana
Grand Coral Beach
Tel.: 881 3200
Fax: 881 3283

D-16 *Mango Tango*

AE VI MC

Parties, special events, groups, boat trip to restaurant.
Dressings & sauces made from fruit: such as mango, tamarind, kiwi, etc.
7 pm. - midnight.
Blvd. Kukulcán km 14.2
Tels./Fax: 885 0313, 885 0312
mangotango@probusiness.com.mx
www.mangotango.com.mx

Chinese

C-02 *Hong Kong*

Dumpling, woltip Hong Kong lomein.
Noon -10 pm.
Plaza Caracol
Tels.: 883 0581, 883 0582
Fax: 883 1134
www.hongkong.com.mx

Fast Food

Burger King

AE VI

- Plaza Caribeña
  11 am. - 3 am.
  Tel.: 883 3940
- Plaza Forum by the Sea
  10 am - midnight.
  Tel.: 883 0300

D-12 *Come´n Eat*

AE VI MC

16 kinds of cuisine.
Noon - 11 pm.
La Isla Shopping Village
Tel.: 883 3939

More information:
www.caribbeanmex.com

Dominos Pizza

VI

- Marina Royal Mayan
  10 am. - midnight
  Blvd. Kukulcán km 16.5
  Tel.: 885 2020
- Plaza Dady'O
  10 am. - midnight
  Tel.: 883 3666

D-03 *KFC & Pizza Hut*

11 am. - midnight
Plaza Lagunas
Tel.: 883 2277

McDonald's

7 am. - midnight.
- Plaza Marina
- Plaza Dady'O
- Flamingo Plaza
- La Isla Shopping Village
- Plaza Caracol
  Tel.: 881 7700

D-13 *Papa John's Marina*

11 am. - midnight
Blvd. Kukulcán km 12.5
Int. Paradise Tiere Marina
Tel.: 883 3040

D-21 *Pizza Hut*

11 am. - 11 pm.
Blvd. Kukulcán km 15
Tel.: 885 1885

Subway

- Plaza Forum by the Sea
  9 am. - 1 am.
  Tel.: 887 3300
- Plaza Marina
  9 am. - 10:30 pm.
  Tel.: 887 3300
- Plaza Kukulcán
  9 am. - 10:30 pm.
  Tel.: 887 3300
- Plaza Dady'O
  9 am. - 5 hrs.
  Tel.: 883 1313
- Plaza Caracol
  9 am. - 10:30 pm.
  Tel.: 887 3300
- Flamingo Plaza
  8 am. - 10 pm.
  Tel.: 885 1331

CAMBALACHE

ARGENTINIAN BIG STEAK HOUSE

A member of the largest chain of Argentinian restaurants in Mexico, collectively serving 45 tons of prime beef every month. "The charcoal grill makes all the difference." Set menus are available for groups. Rustic but refined décor and a relaxed ambiance.
Open: 1 p.m. – until the last diner leaves (call for reservations).

HOUSE SPECIALTIES: rib eye, tenderloin, roast pork, lamb and suckling pig, a variety of salads, homemade pastries and desserts. The selection of wines from Mexico, Argentina, Chile, Europe and California is excellent.
Seating for 250 people.

Forum by the Sea
Blvd. Kukulcán, km 9.5
Cancún, Q. Roo, Mexico.

Tel.: (998) 883 0902

info@grupocambalache.com
www.grupocambalache.com

STEAKS / STEAK HOUSE

D-09 *Outback Steak House*
AE VI MC
SPORTS BAR WITH A GIANT SCREEN.
PRIME RIB AND US QUALITY CHOICE STEAKS, FRESH SALMON, GRILLED LOBSTER, DESSERTS.
2 PM. - MIDNIGHT.
Flamingo Plaza
Tel.: 883 3350
Fax: 883 3385
www.outback.com.mx

B-04 *Porterhouse Grill*
AE VI MC
AMERICAN CUTS.
1 PM. - MIDNIGHT.
Blvd. Kukulcán km 9
Tel.: 848 8390
Fax: 848 8381

D-13 *Ruth´s Chris Steak House*
AE VI MC
AHÍ TUNA, NEW YORK STEAKS.
1 PM. - 11 PM.
Plaza Kukulcán
Tels.: 885 0500, 855 3301
Fax: 885 0500
www.ruthschris.com.mx

CREOLE / CAJUN

C-07 *Blue Bayou*
AE VI MC
LIVE JAZZ.
SEAFOOD.
6 PM. - 10:30 PM.
Blvd. Kukulcán km 10.5
Hyatt Cancún Caribe
Tel.: 848 7800 Fax: 883 2715

D-09 *Margarita Ville*
AE VI MC
80'S & 90'S LIVE MUSIC.
MAHI MAHI.
NOON - 2 AM.
Blvd. Kukulcán km 11.5
Plaza Flamingo L. 213
Tel.: 885 2376 Fax: 885 1079

BUFFET BREAKFAST

B-02 *Viña del Mar*
AE VI MC
SEAFOOD GRILL.
6:30 AM. - 11:30 AM.
Blvd. Kukulcán km 9.5
Fiesta Americana
Grand Coral Beach
Tel.: 881 3200
Fax: 881 3283

SPANISH

P-04 *Correo Español*
AE VI MC
7 AM. - 11 PM.
Blvd. Kukulcán km 4
Tel./Fax: 849 7114

FRENCH

E-04 *La Palapa*
VI MC
MUSSEL CASSEROLE, BEEF FILLET WITH THREE PEPPER SAUCE.
7:30 AM. - 11 PM.
Calle Quetzal No. 13
Hotel Imperial Laguna
Tel./Fax: 883 5454
lapalapa@cancun.com.mx

B-02 *Le Basilic*

DUCK PATÉ.
MON.-SAT. 6:30 PM. - 11 PM.
Blvd. Kukulcán km 9.5
Fiesta Americana
Grand Coral Beach
Tel.: 881 3200
Fax: 881 3283

INTERNATIONAL

C-09 *Avanti*
AE VI MC
AVANTI FISH FILLET, LOBSTER.
7 AM - 11 PM.
Blvd. Kukulcán km 11.5
Baccará Resort
Tels.: 881 3900, 883 2077
Fax: 881 3900

B-03 *Bogart´s*
AE VI MC
LIVE PIANO AND SAXOPHONE.
LOBSTER THREE WISHES, CASABLANCA SUPREME.
6 PM. - 11:45 PM.
Blvd. Kukulcán km 9
Tel.: 848 9800
Fax: 848 9860
www.bogartscancun.com

C-02 *Café du Soleil*
AE VI MC
TAMARIND SHRIMP, FOCACCIA.
10 AM. - 11 PM.
Plaza Caracol
Tel.: 883 0459
Fax: 883 2529

D-22 *Captain´s Cove*
AE VI MC
CARIBBEAN SEAFOOD PLATE, COCONUT SHRIMP.
7 AM. - 11 PM.
Blvd. Kukulcán km 16.5
Tel.: 885 0016
Fax: 881 0100 ext. 62204

L-04 *Carlos'n Charlie's*
AE VI MC
LIVE GROUP.
BBQ RIBS.
11 AM. - MIDNIGHT
Plaza Forum by the Sea
Tels.: 883 4467, 883 4468

B-03 *Cilantro*
AE VI MC
SEAFOOD.
6:30 PM. - MIDNIGHT.
Blvd. Kukulcán km 8.5
Hyatt Regency Cancún
Tel.: 891 5555 ext. 1556
Fax: 883 1694

D-18 *Champions*
AE VI MC
GAMES AND SPORTING EVENTS SCREENED,
40 BIG SCREEN TVS.
HAMBURGERS.
NOON - 2 AM.
Blvd. Kukulcán km 15
Marriott CasaMagna
Tel.: 881 2000 ext. 6343
Fax: 848 9614

C-33 *El Palmar*
AE VI MC
6 AM. - 11 PM.
Blvd. Kukulcán km 20
Westin Regina Resort
Tel.: 848 7422
Fax: 885 0074

D-12 *Hippos*
AE VI MC
INTERNET CAFÉ AND HUGE VARIETY OF CDS AND CASSETTES FOR SALE.
FAJITAS, FONDUES AND FLAMBÉES.
11 AM. - 1 AM
La Isla Shopping Village
Tels.: 883 5518, 883 5648
Fax: 883 5518
www.hippos.com.mx

D-13 *Houlihan´s Cancún*
AE VI MC
LEMON CHICKEN AND LETTUCE ROLLS.
11 AM. - 11 PM.
Plaza Kukulcán
Tels.: 885 0203, 885 0441
Fax: 885 0203

D-20 *Kalmia*
AE VI MC
INTERNATIONAL BUFFET BREAKFAST, THEME NIGHTS, MEXICAN AND CARIBBEAN SHOWS.
6:30 AM.- 11 PM.
Blvd. Kukulcán km 16.5
Fiesta Americana Condesa
Tel.: 881 4200
Fax: 885 2005

D-09 *Pat O´Brien´s*
AE VI MC
LIVE POP AND ROCK FROM THE 80S & 90S FRIDAYS-SUNDAYS.
NEW ORLEANS-STYLE CUISINE.
7 AM. - 2:30 AM.
Flamingo Plaza
Tels.: 883 0418, 883 0832
Fax: 883 0994
www.patobriens.com

B-04 *Rainforest Café*
AE VI MC
SALMON COOKED ON CEDAR GRILL, SURF & TURF FAJITAS, ORIENTAL GRILL, SAUTÉED BEEF.
10 AM. - 1 AM.
Plaza Forum by the Sea
Tel.: 881 8130 Fax: 881 8131
www.rainforestcafe.com

D-14 *The Royal Bandstand*
VI MC
MEXICAN & CARIBBEAN SPECIALTIES.
REST. 5 PM. - 11 AM.
BAR 5 PM. - 1 AM. LIVE MUSIC. CLOSED SAT. The Royal Sands
Tel.: 848 8220

C-04 *Sr. Frog´s*
AE VI MC
LIVE MUSIC.
GRILLS, SEAFOOD, MEXICAN CUISINE.
NOON - 2 AM.
Blvd. Kukulcán km 9.5
Tel./Fax: 883 1092
www.senorfrogs.com

C-33 *Sunset Grill*
AE VI MC OT
SEAFOOD.
10 AM. - 5 PM.
Blvd. Kukulcán km 20
Westin Regina Resort
Tel.: 848 7400
Fax: 885 0074

M-04 *The Cove*
VI MC
SEAFOOD.
7:30 AM. - 11:30 PM.
Blvd. Kukulcán km 5
Playa Langosta
Tels.: 849 4682, 849 4683
Fax: 849 4694

D-15 *The Club Grill*
AE VI MC
LIVE JAZZ.
TEQUILA DUCK.
7 PM. - 11 PM.
Blvd. Kukulcán km 14
The Ritz Carlton Cancún
Tel.: 881 0808 ext. 5803

B-03 *Vip´s*
AE VI MC
SUN. - THURS. 7 AM. - MIDNIGHT, FRI. - SAT. 7 AM. - 2 AM.
Blvd. Kukulcán km 9
Convention Center
Tel.: 883 0165
www.vips.com.mx

ITALIAN

C-33 *Arrecifes*

AE VI MC

LIVE PIANO.

6 PM. - MIDNIGHT.

Blvd. Kukulcán km 20
Westin Regina Resort
Tel.: 848 7400
Fax: 885 0074

C-02 *Casa Rolandi*

AE VI MC

NORTHERN ITALIAN AND SWISS-ITALIAN CUISINE.

FISH COOKED IN SALT, RAVIOLI STUFFED WITH ZUCCINI, TUNA TAGLIATA, VEAL CHEEKS.

1 PM. - 11:30 PM.

Plaza Caracol
Tels.: 883 1817, 883 2557
Fax: 883 1817
www.rolandi.com

L-03 *Dolcemente*

AE VI MC

LASAGNA RAGU, CHICKEN CACCIATORA, ICE CREAM.

NOON - MIDNIGHT.

Blvd. Kukulcán km 5.5
Pez Volador No. 7
Tel./Fax: 849 4006

D-13 *El Cenácolo*

AE VI MC

HOMEMADE PASTA, SHRIMP & VODKA PENNE.

1:30 PM. - MIDNIGHT.

Plaza Kukulcán
Tel.: 885 3603
Fax: 885 3706

D-15 *Fantino*

AE VI MC

LIVE PIANO.

GRAPPA, OSSOBUCCO, TRUFFLE RISOTTO, PASTAS.

7 PM. - 11 PM.

Blvd. Kukulcán km 14
Retorno del Rey 36
The Ritz Carlton Cancún
Tel.: 881 0808 ext. 5803
Fax: 885 1045

D-18 *Gustino*

AE VI MC

LIVE INSTRUMENTAL MUSIC, TUESDAYS TO SATURDAYS.

PIZZA TOWER.

6 PM. - 11 PM.

Blvd. Kukulcán km 14.5
Hotel JW Marriott
Tel.: 848 9600 ext. 6849
Fax: 848 9614

D-25 *Italian Pizza & Pasta*

AE VI MC

PASTA.

NOON - 5 PM., 6 PM. - 11 PM.

Retorno Lacandones km 17
Hotel Hilton Cancún
Tels.: 881 8397, 881 8000
Fax: 881 8031

D-18 *La Dolce Vita*

AE VI MC

LIVE SOFT JAZZ.

LOBSTER AND SHRIMP MEDALLIONS, BOQUINETE FISH WITH SHRIMP AND MUSHROOMS.

NOON - 11:30 PM.

Blvd. Kukulcán km 14.5
Tels.: 885 0150, 885 0161
Fax: 884 0461
dolcevita@sybcom.com

D-12 *La Madonna*

AE VI MC

SWISS-ITALIAN CUISINE. LIVE JAZZ ON FRIDAYS.

FLAMBÉES, LOBSTER, EXTENSIVE WINE CELLAR, MARTINIS.

REST. NOON - MIDNIGHT, BAR 6 PM. - 2 AM.

La Isla Shopping Village
Tels.: 883 4837, 883 2222
Fax: 883 3687
lamadonna@prodigy.net.mx
www.lamadonna.com.mx

C-02 *Savio´s*

AE VI MC

LIVE SOFT JAZZ.

FETTUCCINI NEPTUNO.

10 AM. - 11:30 PM.

Plaza Caracol
Tel.: 883 2085 Fax: 884 0461

JAPANESE

C-03 *Campay Sushi Bar*

AE VI MC

SURF & TURF TEPPANYAKI

1 PM. - 11 PM.

Plaza Caribeña
Tels.: 883 1151, 883 0356

D-18 *Mikado*

AE VI MC

MEALS PREPARED BY THE CHEF BEFORE YOUR VERY EYES.

6 PM. - 11 PM.

Blvd. Kukulcán km 15
Marriott CasaMagna
Tel.: 881 2000, ext. 6265
Fax: 848 9614

D-25 *Mitachi*

AE VI MC

SUSHI BAR, SEAFOOD.

NOON -5 PM., 6 PM. - 10 PM.

Retorno Lacandones km 17
Hotel Hilton Cancún
Tels.: 881 8047, 881 8000
Fax: 881 8031

D-12 *Shokuni Master Sushi Chef*

AE VI MC

SHOKUNI ROLLS.

1 PM. - 11 PM.

La Isla Shopping Village
Tel.: 883 5183

SEAFOOD

E-18 *Crab House*

AE VI MC

LIVE TRIO AND SAXOPHONE.

SEAFOOD, KING CRAB, CRAB CLAWS, SALADS.

1 PM. - MIDNIGHT.

Blvd. Kukulcán km 14.8
Tels.: 885 3936, 885 0722
Fax: 885 0726

C-03 *Chocko´s & Tere*

AE VI MC

LIVE MARIMBA.

SEAFOOD GRILL, TERE STUFFED FILLET.

8 AM. - MIDNIGHT.

Plaza Party Center
Tels.: 883 1156, 883 0356
Fax: 883 0358
www.cancunpartycenter.com

D-16 *Faro's*

AE VI MC

LOBSTER REINA, SHRIMP XTABENTÚN.

2 PM. - 11 PM.

Blvd. Kukulcán km 14.2
Tels./Fax: 885 0303, 885 0312
mangotango@probusiness.com.mx
www.mangotango.com.mx

B-02 *Isla Contoy*

AE VI MC

NOON - 11:30 PM.
LIVE TRIO 7 PM. - 9 PM.
Blvd. Kukulcán, Km. 9.5
Tel.: 881 3309

C-02 *La Fishería*

AE VI MC

SEAFOOD GRILL, TERE STUFFED FILLET.
SEAFOOD CASCADE, SQUID STEAK WITH SALMON AND CAPER SAUCE.
11 AM. - 11:30 PM.
Blvd. Kukulcán km 8.5
Tel.: 883 1395 Fax: 884 0461

D-21 *Laguna Grill*

AE VI MC

BAR WITH HOUSE MUSIC.
GYOSA MARTINIS, CHILEAN SEA BASS.
2 PM. - MIDNIGHT.
Blvd. Kukulcán km 15.6
Tels.: 885 0320, 885 0267
Fax: 885 0320
lagunagrill@prodigy.net.mx

D-08 *Lorenzillos*

AE VI MC

LOBSTER.
NOON - MIDNIGHT.
Blvd. Kukulcán km 10.5
Tel.: 883 1254 Fax: 883 3088
www.lorenzillos.com.mx

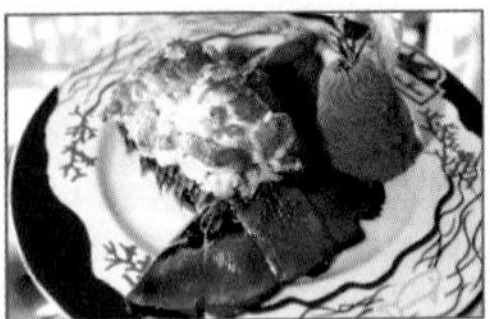

D-18 *Lorito Joe´s*

AE VI MC

LIVE TRIO.
SEAFOOD.
11 AM. - 11 PM.
Blvd. Kukulcán km 14.6
Tel.: 885 1547
Tel./Fax: 885 1536
www.loritojoes.com

B-03 *Mezquite Grill La Brisa*

AE VI MC

LIVE LATIN JAZZ.
SEAFOOD, FISH AND DISHES COOKED ON A MESQUITE GRILL.
NOON - MIDNIGHT.
Punta Cancún, next to the Hotel Dreams Cancún
Tels.: 848 7000, 848 7081
Fax: 848 7003

C-02 *Mocambo*

AE VI MC

MOCAMBO GRILL, MANGO FLAVOR MARGARITA.
NOON TO MIDNIGHT.
Blvd. Kukulcán km 9.5
Tel.: 883 0398
Fax: 287 8118
rpublicas@laparrilla.com.mx

D-15 *Puerto Madero*

AE VI MC

MADERO RIB STEAK, ALASKAN CRAB.
1 PM. - 1:30 AM.
Blvd. Kukulcán km 14
Tels.: 885 2829, 885 2831
Fax: 885 2830
www.puertomaderocancun.com

L-04 *Shrimp Bucket*

AE VI MC

SHRIMP BUCKET.
NOON - 11:30 PM.
Blvd. Kukulcán km 5.5
Tels.: 849 7341, 849 7339
Fax: 849 7340
www.shrimpbucket.com

D-07 *The Plantation House*

AE VI MC

LAGOONSIDE GRILL. LIVE PIANO AND CARIBBEAN MUSIC.
MAYAN GRILL, FISH, LOBSTER.
5 PM. - MIDNIGHT.
Blvd. Kukulcán km 10.5
Tels.: 883 1433, 883 1455
www.plantationhouse.com.mx

B-03 *The Seafood Market*

AE VI MC

SEAFOOD GRILL.
5 PM.- 11 PM.
Blvd. Kukulcán km 8.5
Hyatt Regency Cancún
Tel.: 883 1234 ext. 1815
Fax: 883 1349

MEDITERRANEAN

D-16 *Aioli*

AE VI MC

CAESAR SALAD, BOQUINETE FISH FILLED WITH MUSHROOMS, 5TH ELEMENT DESSERT.
6:30 AM. - 11 AM., 6 PM. - 11 PM.
Blvd. Kukulcán km 14.5
Retorno del Rey
Hotel Le Meridien
Tel.: 881 2260
Fax: 881 2201

D-20 *Rosato*

AE VI MC

WINNER OF THE PRESTIGIOUS AAA 4 DIAMOND AWARD.
ROSATO TRIO: LOBSTER TAIL, GRILLED SHRIMP AND BEEF FILLET WITH MASHED POTATO.
6:30 PM. - 11 PM.
Blvd. Kukulcán km 16.5
Fiesta Americana Condesa
Tel.: 881 4200 ext. 4421
Fax: 885 2005

B-04 *U´Mediterráneo*

AE VI MC

SHRIMP BOCCELLI.
NOON - MIDNIGHT
Plaza Forum by the Sea
Tel.: 883 4848
Fax: 883 4847

MEXICAN

D-18 *Café Salsa*

AE VI

LOBSTER BUFFET, WEDNESDAYS & FRIDAYS.
6:30 AM. - 11 PM.
Blvd. Kukulcán km 14.5
Hotel JW Marriott
Tel.: 848 9600 ext. 6646
Fax: 848 9614

D-21 *Careyes*

AE VI MC

GRILLED LOBSTER AND STEAKS.
6 PM. - 10 PM.
Blvd. Kukulcán km 16.5
Gran Oasis
Tel.: 885 0867 ext. 6492
Fax: 885 1210

D-15 *El Café Mexicano*

AE VI MC

LOBSTER BUFFET ON FRIDAY EVENING, MEXICAN NIGHT ON SATURDAYS.
7 AM. - 11 PM.
Blvd. Kukulcán km 14
Retorno del Rey 36
The Ritz Carlton Cancún
Tel.: 881 0808 ext. 5303
Fax: 885 1045

B-03 *Hacienda El Mortero*

AE VI MC

LIVE MARIACHI MUSIC.
SHRIMP AL PASTOR, CHEMITA FILLET, SEAFOOD, STEAK AND MIXED GRILLS.
6 PM. - 11:45 PM.

Blvd. Kukulcán km 9
Tel.: 848 9800
Fax: 848 9860
www.elmorterocancun.com

C-02 *Iguana Wana*
AE VI MC
LIVE MEXICAN MUSIC.
FAJITAS.
8 AM. - MIDNIGHT.
Plaza Caracol
Tel.: 883 0829
Fax: 883 2529

D-20 *K'ambú*
AE VI MC
BUFFET FEATURING NEW WORLD, CARIBBEAN, ORIENTAL AND MEXICAN CUISINE.
11 AM. - 6 PM.
Blvd. Kukulcán km 16.5
Fiesta Americana Condesa
Tel.: 881 4200
Fax: 885 2005

D-12 *La Casa de Las Margaritas*
AE VI MC
LIVE MUSIC: MARIMBA, JAROCHO, MARIACHI AND GUITAR.
SUNDAY BUFFET.
LAS MARGARITAS CHICKEN, TLAYUDAS, MARGARITA BAR.
NOON - MIDNIGHT.
Blvd. Kukulcán km 12
La Isla Shopping Village
Tels.: 883 3222, 883 3054
Fax: 883 2725
www.lacasadelasmargaritas.com

D-13 *La Destilería*
AE VI MC
LIVE MARIACHI MUSIC.
MOLCAJETE ARRACHERA.
12:30 PM. - MIDNIGHT.
Blvd. Kukulcán km 12.5
Tel.: 885 1086
Fax: 885 1087
www.ladestileriacancun.com

B-02 *La Joya*
AE VI MC
LIVE MARIACHI MUSIC.
FOLKLORIC BALLET.
6:30 PM - 11 PM.
Blvd. Kukulcán km 9.5
Fiesta Americana
Grand Coral Beach
Tel.: 881 3200
Fax: 881 3283

D-15 *La Placita*
AE VI MC
LIVE MARIACHI MUSIC, FRI-SUN.
11 PM. - 1 PM.
Blvd. Kukulcán km 13.5
Tel.: 885 0626

B-02 *María Bonita*
AE VI MC
LIVE MARIACHI, JAROCHO AND LATIN MUSIC.
MELTED CHEESE CASA FUERTE, BEEF FILLET WITH FOUR CHILES, TAMARIND SHRIMP.
6 PM. - 1 AM., BUFFET SUN. NOON - 4 PM.
Punta Cancún, next to Dreams Cancún Hotel.
Tels.: 848 7000, 848 7081
Fax: 848 7003

More information:
www.caribbeanmex.com

D-13 *OK Maguey*

AE VI MC

LIVE MARIACHI AND MARIMBA MUSIC.
STEAKS,
TIKIN XIK FISH.
7 AM. - 11 PM.
Plaza Kukulcán
Tels.: 885 0503, 885 2325
Fax: 885 0503
okmagueycun@hotmail.com

D-10 *Quetzal*

AE VI MC

THEME NIGHTS
7 AM. - 11 PM.
Blvd. Kukulcán km 11.5
Hotel Meliá Turquesa
Tel./Fax: 881 2500

D-03 *Sanborns Café*

AE VI MC

SWISS ENCHILADAS,
MOLLETES, CHILAQUILES.
6:30 AM. - 2 AM.
Plaza Mayafair
Tels.: 883 3226, 883 3240

D-09 *Sanborns Café*

AE VI MC

ENCHILADAS SUIZAS.
24 HRS.
Plaza Flamingo
Tels.: 885 1069, 885 1150

D-25 *Spices Cafeteria & Taco Bar*

AE VI MC

6:30 AM. - 11:30 AM.,
5:30 PM. - 11:30 PM.
Retorno Lacandones km 17
Hotel Hilton Cancún
Tels.: 881 8049, 881 8000
Fax: 881 8031

NATURAL

D-02 *100% Natural*

VI MC

7 AM. - 11 PM.
• Plaza Terramar
Tels.: 883 3636, 883 1180
• Plaza Terramar
Tels.: 883 3636

SNACKS

D-25 *Galileo Lounge Bar*

AE VI MC

LIVE JAZZ.
6 PM. - 2 AM.
Retorno Lacandones km 17
Hotel Hilton Cancún
Tels.: 881 8043, 881 8000
Fax: 881 8031

C-09 *Kelly´s Sport Bar*

AE VI MC

5 PM. - 1 AM.
Blvd. Kukulcán km 11.5
Avalon Grand
Tels.: 848 9300, 848 9339
Fax: 849 9300

C-09 *Studebaker*

AE VI

HAMBURGERS, MILK SHAKES.
7 AM. - 11 PM.
Blvd. Kukulcán km 11.5
Tel.: 881 3900 Fax: 881 3902

YUCATECAN

D-26 *El Rey Mundo Maya*

VI MC

LIVE PRE-HISPANIC MUSIC.
GUIDED TOUR OF THE ARCHAEOLOGICAL ZONE, VISIT TO THE MAYAN VILLAGE, DINNER & SHOW
7 PM. - 10 PM.
Blvd. Kukulcán km 18.5
Tels.: 885 2019, 885 2009
Fax: 883 2080, 883 2088

D-03 *Pacal*

AE VI MC

YAX HA DUCK.
1:30 PM. - MIDNIGHT
Blvd. Kukulcán km 8.5
Tels.: 883 2113, 883 2184
Fax: 884 9401

DOWNTOWN

LEBANESE

Byblo´s

ARAB-STYLE TACOS SERVED AT THE TERRACE. KEEPE, TABBOULEH.
RESTAURANT: 1 PM. - 6 PM.,
TERRACE: 6 PM. - MIDNIGHT.
Av. Palenque 108 Sm. 26
Tel.: 887 4041

A-12 *El Árabe*

LEBANESE CUISINE
NOON - MIDNIGHT.
Av. Bonampak 61 Sm. 4
esq. Sayil
Tel.: 845 4992

ARGENTINIAN

C-05 *Grillo´s*

AE VI MC

GRILLED STEAKS,
ARGENTINIAN CHURRASCO,
BIFECHORIZO, ASADO DE TIRA.
1 PM. - MIDNIGHT.
Av. Bonampak 113 Sm. 3
Tels.: 884 1871, 884 2585
Fax: 884 2585
grillos1@prodigy.net.mx

B-09 *La Patagonia*

GRILLED STEAKS, EMPANADAS,
SEAFOOD.
MON. - SAT. 1 PM. - 10 PM.,
SUN. 2 PM. - 10 PM.
Av. Cobá No. 18 Sm. 4
Tel./Fax: 884 1860
lapatagonia@hotmail.com
www.lapatagonia.com.mx

FAST FOOD

Burger King

AE VI

- Plaza Las Avenidas
  7 AM. - 1 AM.
  Tel.: 887 8811
- Plaza Las Américas
  10 AM. - 10 PM.
  Tel.: 884 4290
- Tulipanes 15 Sm. 22
  9 AM. -11 PM.
  Tel.: 887 6733

G-04 *Chicken Factory*

7 AM. - 11 PM.
Av. Tulum con Av. Uxmal
Tels.: 884 4868, 884 4880

G-09 *Dominos Pizza*

VI

9 AM. - MIDNIGHT.
- Plaza Las Avenidas
  Tel.: 884 7512
- Av. López Portillo 1000
  Plaza Esmeralda
  Tel.: 880 4343

I-04 *KFC*

10 AM. - MIDNIGHT.
Av. Uxmal L. 12 Sm. 24
Tel.: 887 1022

J-12 ***Papa John´s***

🕐 10 AM. - MIDNIGHT.
Av. Cobá Loc. 1 Sm. 36
Tel.: 892 0000

F-03 ***McDonald's***

🕐 7 AM. - MIDNIGHT.
Av. Tulum L. 15 Sm. 2
Tel.: 881 7701

F-06 ***Pizza Hut***

🕐 NOON - MIDNIGHT.
Av. Tulum Sm. 22
Mza. 4 L.25, Planta Alta
Tel.: 884 4847

I-04 ***Pizza Hut***

🕐 11 AM. - MIDNIGHT.
Av. Uxmal No. 14 Sm. 24
Tel.: 887 3838

G-10 ***Subway***

🕐 24 HRS.
Plaza Las Avenidas Sm. 35
Tel.: 887 5616

STEAKS

G-04 ***Tío Filete***
AE VI MC

CHUCHO FILLET, GRILLED SKIRT STEAK.
🕐 7 AM. - 11:30 PM.
Av. Tulum con Av. Uxmal
Best Western Plaza Caribe
Tel.: 884 1377 ext. 312
Fax: 884 6352

CHINESE

H-10 ***Hong Kong***
AE VI

CAN ACCOMMODATE 350 PEOPLE, BANQUETS CAN BE CATERED IN THE RESTAURANT, DELIVERY SERVICE.
PIEDRA VOLCÁNICA, SHANGHAI SHRIMP.
🕐 1 PM. - 11 PM.
Plaza Chinatown
Av. Xcaret esq. Av. Labná
Tels.: 892 3456, 887 6315
Fax: 887 4896
www.hongkong.com.mx

INDIAN

K-08 ***Taj Mahal***

🕐 NOON - 10 PM.
Mercado 28
Sm. 28 Mz. 7 L. 2
Tels.: 887 6758, 887 6759

INTERNATIONAL

B-13 ***Casa Angelus***
AE VI MC

SUPERVISED KIDS' PLAYGROUND.
SNAIL CARPACCIO, GRILLED SALMON, ANGELUS PORK TENDERLOIN.
🕐 OPEN: 1:30 PM., CLOSES MON. - THURS. 11:30 PM., FRI.- SAT. - MIDNIGHT.
Av. Sayil No. 10 Sm. 4
Tel./Fax: 887 9444

H-06 ***El Jardín***
AE VI MC

BUFFETS ON WED., SAT & SUN. PIZZAS 2 x 1.
🕐 7 AM. - 11 PM.
Av. Yaxchilán Sm. 22
Mza. 22 L. 41 y 43
Tel.: 884 9333

E-04 ***El Mesón del Vecindario***
AE VI MC

VEGETABLE LASAGNA, FONDUES, PASTAS AND EMPANADAS.
🕐 RESTAURANT 8 AM. - MIDNIGHT, BAR OPEN UNTIL 1 AM.
Av. Uxmal No. 23 Sm. 3
Tel./Fax: 884 8900

H-10 ***La Pasteletería***
AE VI MC

CREPES & DESSERT.
🕐 8 AM. - 11 PM.
Av. Cobá No. 7 Sm. 25
Tels.: 884 3420, 884 1918
www.pasteleteria.com

F-07 ***La Tosca***
VI MC

STEAKS, AZTEC-STYLE MOLCAJETE.
🕐 10 AM. - MIDNIGHT.
Av. Tulum No. 107 Sm. 22
Tels.: 884 1838, 884 1659

D-04 ***Los Balcones***
AE VI MC

ARGENTINIAN STEAKS.
🕐 7 AM. - 11 PM.
Av. Uxmal No. 26 Sm. 2-A
Hotel Kokai
Tels.: 884 3218, 884 4335

G-05 ***Sanborn´s Café***
AE VI MC

ENCHILADAS, CAKES AND PASTRIES. BOOKS, MAGAZINES, GIFTS, CDS AND DRUGSTORE.
🕐 24 HRS.
Av. Uxmal esq. Av. Tulum
Tel.: 884 0002 Fax: 884 0532

A-14 ***Sanborn´s***
AE VI MC

LIVE MUSIC FROM 8 PM. - MIDNIGHT.
ENCHILADAS SUIZAS, COFFEE.
🕐 7 AM. - 1 AM.
Plaza Las Américas
Tel.: 887 7547

HONG KONG

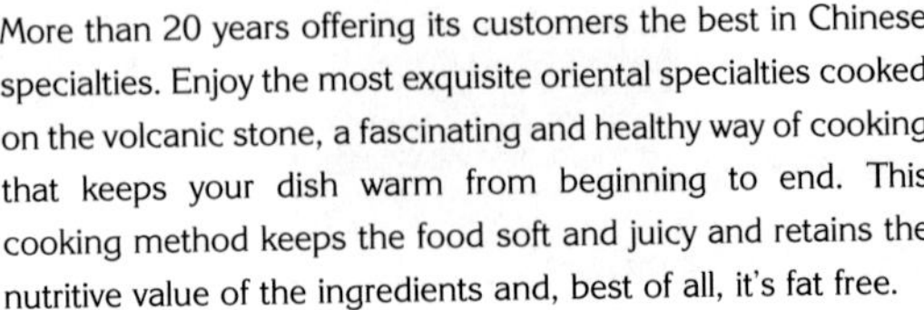

More than 20 years offering its customers the best in Chinese specialties. Enjoy the most exquisite oriental specialties cooked on the volcanic stone, a fascinating and healthy way of cooking that keeps your dish warm from beginning to end. This cooking method keeps the food soft and juicy and retains the nutritive value of the ingredients and, best of all, it's fat free.

The restaurant also offers service for special events and banquets

Plaza Chinatown
Av. Xcaret esq. Av. Labná
Cancún Quintana Roo, Mexico.
Tel.: 892 3456

www.hongkong.com.mx

C-14 ***Vip's***

AE VI MC

Thurs. - Sat. midnight,
Sun. - Wed. 7 am. - 2 am.
Av. Acanceh Sm. 15
Tel./Fax: 887 8031
www.vips.com.mx

ITALIAN

F-06 ***Casa Italiana***

Pasta & pizzas.
8 am. - midnight.
Av. Tulum No. 9 Sm. 22
Tel./Fax: 884 5762

C-08 ***La Dolce Vita***

AE VI MC

Lobster medallions.
1:30 pm. - 1 am.
Av. Cobá No. 87 Sm. 3
Tels.: 884 3393, 884 1384

C-07 ***Locanda Paolo***

AE

Veal, pasta & seafood.
1:30 pm. - midnight.
Av. Bonampak 145 Sm. 3
Tel.: 887 2627
locandapaolo@hotmail.com

Lucky Luciano

AE

Pasta.
2 pm. - 11 pm.
Av. Tlaquepaque Sm. 45
Tel./Fax: 880 5858

A-14 ***Mama Roma***

AE VI MC

Modo Mío breast of chicken.
7:30 am. - midnight.
Av. Tulum Sur
Plaza Las Américas
Tel.: 887 4540
Fax: 887 9692

D-08 ***Rolandi´s Restaurant Bar Pizzería***

AE VI MC

Four Seasons Pizza, Shrimp Pasta with Vodka Sauce. Dishes cooked in a wood-burning oven.
1 pm. - 12:30 am.
Av. Cobá No. 12 Sm. 5
Tel.: 884 4047
Fax: 884 3994
www.rolandi.com

JAPANESE

D-04 ***Yamamoto***

AE VI MC

Sushi bar.
Mon. - Sat. 1:30 pm. - 11 pm.,
Sun. 1:30 pm. - 8 pm.
Av. Uxmal No. 31 Sm. 3
Tel.: 887 3366
Fax: 884 7848
www.yamamotocancun.com

SEAFOOD

Alta Vista

AE VI MC

Located on a 60 meter high viewing tower.
Boquinete fillets El Faro, hollandaise crab meat.
Noon - midnight.
Av. López Portillo Sm. 84
Mz. 5 L. 6, Puerto Juárez
Tels.: 843 2146, 843 2011

G-05 ***Calamar***

VI MC

Tikin Xik Fish.
Noon - 8 pm.
Margaritas No. 65 Sm. 22
Tel./Fax: 884 0190

F-07 ***Carrillo´s***

AE VI MC

LIVE MEXICAN DUET.
SEAFOOD SPECIAL, LOBSTER IN GARLIC BUTTER.
1 PM. - 10 PM.
Claveles No. 33 Sm. 22
Tel.: 884 1227 Fax: 884 2371
www.cancuncarrillos.com

K-08 ***El Cejas***

10 AM. - 8 PM.
Mercado 28, Sm. 28

F-06 ***El Pescador***

AE VI MC

HUACHINANGO IN GARLIC BUTTER (AZTEC-STYLE SNAPPER), GRILLED LOBSTER, SEAFOOD SERENADE.
11 AM. - 11 PM.
Tulipanes No. 28 Sm. 22
Tel.: 884 2673
Fax: 884 3639

Flamingos

AE VI MC

LIVE TRIO MUSIC.
FISH & SEAFOOD.
NOON - 9 PM.
Hwy. Puerto Juárez-Punta Sam km 3.5
Tel.: 843 0505
Fax: 843 0405

H-02 ***Isla Contoy***

10 AM. - 8 PM
Flamboyanes & Cedro No. 16, Mz. 37 Sm. 23
Tel.: 884 0172

G-06 ***La Habichuela***

AE VI MC

CEBICHE PARAÍSO, LOBSTER, COCOBICHUELA.
NOON - MIDNIGHT.
Margaritas No. 25 Sm. 22
Tel.: 884 3158
Fax: 884 1716
www.lahabichuela.com

H-06 ***Mariscos Villa Rica***

AE VI MC

LIVE JAROCHO MUSIC, THU. - SAT.
TUMBADA SEAFOOD RICE.
11 AM. - 11 PM.
Av. Yaxchilán 35 Sm. 22
Tel.: 884 7992
Tel./Fax: 887 8514

MEXICAN

Bisquets Obregón

AE VI MC

BREADED BEEF, BISCUITS, HOMEMADE BREAD AND PASTRIES.
7 AM. - 1 AM.

A-14 • Plaza Las Américas
Tel.: 887 4852
F-03 • Av. Náder Sm. 2 L.9
Tel.: 887 6877
• Plaza Las Palmas Sm. 36
Tel.: 892 2727

I-09 ***Café Club***

MOLE POBLANO, STUFFED CHILES.
7 AM. - 11 PM.
Av. Tankah No. 72 Sm. 25
Tel.: 884 2088
Fax: 887 7263

California

AE VI MC

BUFFET.
7 AM. - 11 PM.
• Libramiento Kabah
Tel.: 848 2870
F-04 • Av. Uxmal Sm. 2
Tel.: 892 0330

L-08 ***Checándole***

MOLE ENCHILADAS, BREADED BEEF
NOON - 9 PM.
Av. Xpuhil No. 6 Sm. 27
Tels.: 884 7147, 887 9323
Fax: 884 5099
checandole@hotmail.com

E-06 ***El Café de la Náder***

AE VI MC

STEAKS, COFFEES AND BAKERY.
7 AM. - 11 PM.
Av. Náder No. 5 Sm. 5
Tel.: 884 1584
Fax: 884 4347

F-08 ***El Tacolote***

AE VI MC

LIVE MARIACHI MUSIC.
STEAK COOKED ON A TABLE GRILL, TACOS.
1 PM. - 1 AM.
Av. Cobá No. 19 esq. Alcatraces Sm. 22
Tels.: 887 3045, 892 1000
Fax: 887 3260
www.tacolote.com

A-14 ***El Tumba Burros***

AE VI MC

TUMBA BURROS, GIANT TACOS.
11 AM. - 1 AM.
Plaza Las Américas
Tel.: 884 9174
Fax: 887 6374

La Curva

VI MC

SKIRT STEAK COOKED WITH CHILES.
1 PM. - 1 AM.
Plaza Las Hadas Sm. 44
Tel.: 848 0458
Fax: 848 0033

A-12 *La Faena*
AE VI MC
MARIACHI, NORTHERN AND TRIO MUSIC.
LAMB MIXIOTE, STEAK TARTARE WITH SHERRY.
1 PM. - 10 PM.
Av. Bonampak Sm. 4-A
Plaza de Toros
Tel.: 884 4197
Fax: 887 1783

A-12 *La Guadalupana*
AE VI MC OT
LIVE TRIO AND MARIACHI MUSIC.
STEAK SERVED IN ITS OWN JUICES.
1 PM. - 11 PM.
Av. Bonampak Sm. 4-A
Plaza de Toros
Tels.: 887 0660, 887 3208
Fax: 887 3208

H-05 *La Parrilla*
AE VI MC
LIVE MARIACHI MUSIC IN THE EVENING.
CHARCOAL GRILLED STEAKS, SEAFOOD; BUFFET, FRI. - SUN.
MON. - SAT. 1 PM. - 4 AM.
SUN. NOON - 2 AM.
Av. Yaxchilán 51 Sm. 22
Tel.: 884 5398
Fax: 887 9141

H-05 *La Placita*
AE VI MC
ARRACHERA.
1:30 PM. - 4 AM.
Av. Yaxchilán 12 Sm. 22
Tel.: 884 0407
Fax: 887 6315

D-10 *La Ronda*
AE VI MC
7 PM. - 11 PM.
Av. Tulum esq. Brisa Sm. 4
Hotel Oasis América
Tel.: 848 8600
Fax: 848 8604

F-07 *Los Huaraches*
7:30 AM. - 6:30 PM.
Claveles esq. Alcatraces
No. 31 Sm. 22
Tels.: 884 3918, 884 2528

H-07 *Pericos*

AE VI MC
RESTAURANT - CANTINA - ENTERTAINMENT. LIVE MARIMBA AND MARIACHI.
PANCHO VILLA BEEF MEDALLIONS, ZAPATA-STYLE FISH, MADERO CHICKEN BREAST, ADELITA BROCHETTE.
NOON - 1 AM.
Av. Yaxchilán 61 Sm. 25
Tels.: 884 3152, 887 4884
Fax: 884 0415
www.pericoscancun.com

F-07 *Rosa Mexicano*
AE VI MC
LIVE MARIACHI MUSIC.
SEAFOOD.
5 PM. - 11 PM.
Claveles No. 4 Sm. 22
Tel.: 884 2371
Fax: 884 6313

A-15 *So Good!*
AE VI MC
SALADS & HAMBURGERS.
NOON - MIDNIGHT.
Av. Tulum No. 260 Sm. 7
Plaza Las Américas
Tel.: 884 8798, 884 8537
Fax: 884 8537

NATURAL

J-07 *100% Natural*
AE MC
LIVE TRIO MUSIC AT THE WEEKEND.
7 AM. - 11 PM.
Av. Sunyaxchén Sm. 25
Tels.: 884 0102, 884 3617

F-06 *Roots Jazz Club*
AE VI MC
LIVE JAZZ.
SALADS AND PASTAS.
TUE. - SAT. 6 PM. - 1 AM.
Tulipanes No. 26 Sm. 22
Tel.: 884 2437
Fax: 884 5547
roots@cancun.com

YUCATECAN

K-08 *Antojitos Emara*
POC CHUC, COCHINITA PIBIL.
11 AM. - 11:30 PM.
Av. Xel-Há Sm. 27 L. 2 y 3
Tel.: 884 3904

G-06 *Labná*
AE VI MC
UNIQUE AMBIANCE, PRE-HISPANIC FOLK BALLET, LIVE TRIO AND BOLERO MUSIC.
RELLENO NEGRO.
NOON - MIDNIGHT.
Margaritas No. 29 Sm. 22
Tel.: 892 3056
Fax: 884 0940
www.labna.com

H-02 *Los Almendros*
AE VI MC
CREATORS OF POC CHUC.
11 AM. - 10 PM.
Av. Tulum L. 66 Sm.23
Tel.: 887 1332
Fax: 884 0942

HOTELS

CATEGORY: Hotels are classified in a range between one and six stars (deluxe) and the Special Category refers to small hotels that do not offer the amenities of large resorts but have their own charm.

★ One star (up to 6)

Special Category

HOTELS. Rates (subject to change) are given in dollars and are intended as an approximate guide to the daily cost of a standard double room.

LOW SEASON	HIGH SEASON
Up to $50	Up to $50
Between $50 & $100	Between $50 & $100
Between $100 & $180	Between $100 & $180
Between $180 & $250	Between $180 & $250
Between $250 & $350	Between $250 & $350
More than $350	More than $350

SERVICES: • The majority of Deluxe and 5-star hotels offer the following services, with the exception of golf, disco and a spa, which are marked in the lists when applicable. • The majority of 4-star hotels and 3-star hotels in Cancún Hotel Zone offer services1-9, additional services are included in the lists when applicable. • The amenities offered by the remaining 3-star hotels and hotels in other categories are featured in the listings • At the end of the line of symbols for each hotel a figure denotes the number of rooms, villas or suites.

1. Restaurant
2. Bar
3. Air-conditioning
4. Television
5. Pool
6. Gift shop
7. Car rental
8. Travel agency / trips
9. Laundry
10. Convention rooms
11. Evening entertainment
12. Beauty parlor
13. Gym
14. Kids Club
15. Disco
16. Spa
17. Tennis
18. Golf
19. Marina
20. Wedding program
21. Babysitters
22. Social activities

All-inclusive Plan

HOTEL ZONE

DELUXE ★★★★★★

66 D-17 *Cancún Palace*

580

MINI GOLF.

Blvd. Kukulcán km 14.5
Tel.: 881 3600
Fax: 881 3601
relpubcp@palaceresorts.com
www.palaceresorts.com

40 A-02 *Dreams Cancún Resort & Spa*

PE 415

Punta Cancún
Tels.: 848 7000
01 800 122 2200
USA 1 866 237 3267
Fax: 848 7001
info@dreamsresorts.com
www.amresorts.com

57 B-02 *Fiesta Americana Grand Aqua*

PE 371

Blvd. Kukulcán km 12.5
Tels.: 881 7600
01 800 504 5000
USA 1 800 FIESTA 1
Fax: 881 7635
www.fiestaamericana.com

39 B-02 *Fiesta Americana Grand Coral Beach*

PE 602

GOLF PROGRAM.

Blvd. Kukulcán km 9.5
Tels.: 881 3200, 881 3284
01 800 504 5000
USA 1 800 FIESTA 1
Fax: 881 3276
www.fiestaamericana.com

70 D-20 *Fiesta Americana Condesa*

PE 502

Blvd. Kukulcán km 16.5
Tel.: 881 4200
USA 1 800 FIESTA 1
Fax: 885 1800
www.fiestaamericana.com

69 D-19 *Gran Meliá Cancún*

PE 700

Blvd. Kukulcán km 16.5
Tels.: 881 1100, 885 1085
Fax: 881 1740
www.solmelia.com

76 D-25 *Hilton Cancún Beach and Golf Resort*

PE 442

Blvd. Kukulcán km 17
Retorno Lacandones
Tel.: 881 8000 Fax: 885 2437
sales@hiltoncancun.com
www.hiltoncancun.com

67 D-18 *JW Marriott Cancún*

PE 524

Blvd. Kukulcán km 14
Tels.: 848 9600
01 800 888 0888
USA 1 888 813 2776
Fax: 848 9601
www.marriott.com

★★★★★★

A tradition of hospitality that combines comfort, elegance and service with style. Recently remodeled, Fiesta Americana Condesa Cancún combines beautiful scenery with first-rate service.

Its 502 attractive rooms and deluxe suites offer a spectacular view of the Mexican Caribbean, Internet connection, video games, 24-hour room service and more. Kids can entertain themselves in the Fiesta Kids Club and games area and babysitters are available on request. Facilities include fabulous waterfall-shaped pools, 3 indoor tennis courts, a gym, spa, sauna, 3 Jacuzzis, a marina and shopping area.

The hotel has a Business Center with 3,144 square meters for meetings and events, as well as outdoor areas, state-of-the-art technology and trained staff.

Its 3 restaurants offer everything from international fare and delicious breakfasts at Kalmia to seafood and appetizers at K'ambu and Italian specialties at Rosato while The Lounge, the Splash Bar and the beach bar offer everything you need in the way of drinks.

Blvd. Kukulkán Km 16.5
Hotel Zone, Cancún,
Quintana Roo, Mexico 77 500
Tel.: + 52 (998) 881 4200
Fax: + 52 (998) 881 1800
From Mexico: 01 800 504 5000
From US: 1 800 FIESTA1

reserv@posadas.com
www.fiestamericana.com

An exclusive paradise with impeccable service

Located just 20 minutes from Cancún's International Airport on one of the loveliest beaches and opposite one of the most modern and exclusive malls.

Enjoy a well-earned rest in one of its 371 rooms with access to high-speed, wireless Internet, minibar, DVD-VD-MP3 and Home Theater, while you take in the view of the Caribbean from the balcony.

Eight pools, two tennis courts, a gym and spa with 11 cabins and temazcal are just some of the facilities available, together with a Kids' Fiesta Club for the children.

Seventeen halls, equipped with the latest technology and multilingual staff, are available for events. Business Center and Vip executive services.

Its restaurants offer the most refined avant-garde cuisine: MB (New American Cuisine), Siete (Pop Art fusion with Mexican haute cuisine), Azur (seafood, pastas and snacks), Deli (snacks), The Lounge, Citric, Shore Club, Pool Club or if you prefer, *In-Room Dining*, with 24-hour service.

Blvd. Kukulkán Km 12.5
Hotel Zone, Cancún,
Quintana Roo, Mexico 77 500
Tel.: + 52 (998) 881 7600
Fax: + 52 (998) 881 7635
From Mexico: 01 800 504 5000
From US: 1 800 FIESTA1

reserv@posadas.com
www.fiestamericana.com

★★★★★★

Blvd. Kukulcán km 9.5
Hotel Zone, Cancún
Quintana Roo, Mexico 77500
Tel.: (998) 881 3200
Fax: (998) 881 3276
MEX 01 800 504 5000
US 1 800 FIESTA 1

www.fiestamericana.com

When you're looking for something a little out of the ordinary, make sure you choose an elegant, refined resort. The winner of Five Diamonds from the AAA for the past ten years, Fiesta Americana Grand Coral Beach Cancún provides unbeatable service. It has 602 suites facing the sea, with one of the most attractive beaches in Cancún, within easy reach of sophisticated malls and entertainment centers.

Enjoy the spectacular multi-level pool, the sophisticated Le Basilic restaurant with its superb cuisine and a courtesy game of golf* at the nearby Pok-Ta-Pok Golf Club (par 72) designed by Robert Trent Jones Jr.

Fiesta American Grand Coral Beach Cancún also offers an area of 26,000 square meters for groups and conventions with a dance hall with a capacity for 1,800 and lively theme-based parties.

520 Junior Suites • 80 Master Suites • 2 Presidential Suites • Grand Club

Guaranteed to exceed your wildest expectations!

* Restrictions apply

65 D-16 ***Le Meridien Cancún Resort & Spa***

213

Blvd. Kukulcán km 14
Retorno del Rey
Tels.: 881 2200
01 800 715 1829
USA 1 800 225 5843
Fax: 881 2201
sales@meridiencancun.com.mx
www.meridiencancun.com.mx

31 E-03 ***Presidente Inter - Continental Cancún***

PE 307

Blvd. Kukulcán km 7.5
Tel.: 848 8700
Fax: 883 0414
cunhc@interconti.com
www.interconti.com

63 D-15 ***The Ritz Carlton***

PE 415

Blvd. Kukulcán km 14
Retorno del Rey 36
Tels.: 881 0808, 881 0731
01 800 019 5300
USA 1 880 241 3333
Fax: 885 1045
www.ritzcarlton.com

86 C-33 ***The Westin Regina Resort Cancún***

PE 305

Blvd. Kukulcán km 20
Tels.: 848 7400
01 800 902 2300
USA 1 800 WESTIN 1
Fax: 885 0479
recan@westin.com
www.westin.com

72 D-22 ***Omni Cancún Hotel & Villas***

PE 376

Blvd. Kukulcán km 16.5
Tels.: 881 0600, 848 8900
01 800 215 1200
USA 1 800 843 6664
Fax: 885 0059
omnicun@cancun.com.mx
www.omnihotels.com

FIVE STAR ★★★★★

32 E-03 ***Ambiance Villas & Club***

PA PE PC 230

Blvd. Kukulcán km 8.5
Tel.: 883 1100
01 800 640 6288
USA 1 866 340 9082
Fax: 883 1101
sales1@ambiancevillas.com
www.ambiancevillas.com

51 C-09 ***Avalon Baccará***

PE 27

Blvd. Kukulcán km 11.5
Tels.: 881 3900
01 800 713 8170
Fax: 881 2173
www.avalonvacations.com

52 C-09 ***Avalon Grand***

PE 115

Blvd. Kukulcán km 11.7
Tel.: 848 9300
01 800 261 5014
Fax: 883 5370
www.avalonvacations.com

53 C-10 ***Beach Palace***

205

Blvd. Kukulcán km 11.5
Tel.: 891 4110
Fax: 891 4119
relpubbp@palaceresorts.com
www.palaceresorts.com

61 C-14 ***Casa Turquesa***

PA PE 34

Blvd. Kukulcán km 13.5
Tels.: 885 2924, 885 2925
01 800 215 7700
USA 1 888 528 8300
Fax: 885 2922
info@casaturquesa.com
www.casaturquesa.com

17 L-03 ***Casa Maya Cancún***

275

Blvd. Kukulcán km 5.5
Tels.: 849 4555
1 800 848 8794
1 800 207 9280
Fax: 849 4377

16 N-04 ***Club Internacional***

PE 201

GOLF PROGRAM.
Blvd. Kukulcán km 4.5
Tels.: 881 5100, 885 0032
Fax: 881 5180
bcenters@royalresorts.com
www.royalresorts.com

78 D-28 ***Crown Paradise Club***

699

Blvd. Kukulcán km 18.5
Tels.: 848 9000, 848 9045
01 800 361 3300
USA 1 800 882 8215
Fax: 848 9095
ventas@crownparadise.com
www.crownparadise.com

49 C-08 ***Caribe Real Cancún***

PE 638

Blvd. Kukulcán km 11.5
Tels.: 881 7340
01 800 216 5500
USA 1 800 543 7556
Fax: 881 7314
reservations@realresorts.com.mx
www.realresorts.com.mx

34 D-02 ***Fiesta Americana Cancún***

PA PE 281

Blvd. Kukulcán km 8.5
Tels.: 881 1400, 881 1401
Fax: 881 1404
www.fiestaamericana.com

★★★★★

Meliá Turquesa

All Inclusive Beach Resort

Located on the shores of the Caribbean next to Laguna Nichupté, 20 minutes from the International Airport and just a few yards from the main malls, restaurants and nightlife. It has 450 rooms, 3 restaurants, 3 bars with unlimited drinks, snack bar, daily activities program, nightly entertainment, Mini Club (6-12), Club 4 (0-4 years) and group & convention facilities.

Blvd. Kukulcán km 12, Zona Hotelera, 77500, Cancún, Q. Roo, México 77500; Tel.:+ 52 (998) 881 2500
Fax:+ 52 (998) 881 2501 • *melia.turquesa@solmelia.com* • *www.solmelia.com*

(64) D-15 *Golden Crown Paradise Spa*

214

ADULTS ONLY. MINI GOLF.
Blvd. Kukulcán km 14.5
Retorno San Miguelito 37
Tels.: 885 0909
01 800 361 3300
USA 1 800 882 8215
Fax: 885 1919
reservgcp@crownparadise.com
www.crownparadise.com

(14) O-04 *Gran Costa Real Cancún*

PE 354

Blvd. Kukulcán km 4.5 ZH
Tels.: 881 7340, 881 7311
01 800 216 5500
USA 1 800 543 7556
Fax: 881 7399
reservations@realresorts.com.mx
www.realresorts.com.mx

(71) D-21 *Grand Oasis Resort*

PE 318

OFFERS A PROGRAM WITH CANCÚN GOLF CLUB.
Blvd. Kukulcán km 16.5
Tel.: 881 7000
USA 1 800 906 8300
Fax: 885 1210
www.oasishoteles.com.mx

(48) C-07 *Hyatt Cancún Caribe*

PE 223

Blvd. Kukulcán km 10.5
Tels.: 848 7800, 848 7815
01 800 005 0000
USA 1 800 233 1234
Fax: 883 1514
hyattcancuncaribe@hyattintl.com
www.cancun.hyatt.com

(41) B-03 *Hyatt Regency*

PA 304

OFFERS A PROGRAM WITH CANCÚN GOLF CLUB.
Blvd. Kukulcán km 8.5
Tel.: 881 1234
USA 1 800 233 1234
Fax: 883 1694
sales.hrcancun@hyattintl.com
www.cancun.regency.hyatt.com

(68) D-18 *Marriott CasaMagna Cancún Resort*

PE 450

Blvd. Kukulcán km 15
Retorno Chac
Tels.: 881 2000, 881 2003
USA 1 800 223 6388
Fax: 881 2052
cancunmarriott@infosel.net.mx
www.marriott.com

(54) D-10 *Meliá Turquesa*

PA PE 450

Blvd. Kukulcán km 12
Tels.: 881 2500, 881 2601
Fax: 881 2501
www.solmelia.com

(45) C-05 *Miramar Misión*

PA PE 283

Blvd. Kukulcán km 9.5
Tels.: 883 1755
01 800 215 1333
USA 1 800 669 0221
Fax: 883 1136
ventascancun@prodigy.net.mx
www.hotelesmision.com.mx

(42) B-03 *NH Krystal Cancún*

PE 328

Blvd. Kukulcán km 9
Tels.: 848 9800, 848 9811
01 800 903 3300
USA 1 800 231 9860
Fax: 883 1790
ventas@krystalcancun.com.mx
www.krystal.com.mx

(15) N-04 *Oasis Beach*

PE 471

Blvd. Kukulcán km 4.5
Tel.: 849 4510
Fax: 849 4506
roxanap@oasishoteles.com
www.oasishoteles.com

(79) C-29 *Oasis Playa Resort*

456

Blvd. Kukulcán km 19.5
Tel.: 891 5000
Fax: 891 5050
cplaya@oasishotels.com.mx
www.oasishoteles.com

(19) K-03 *Riu Caribe Resort & Spa*

PA PE PC 506

Blvd. Kukulcán km 5.5
Tel.: 848 7850
Fax: 848 7867
hotel.caribe@riu.com
www.riu.com

(37) D-02 *Riu Cancún*

569

Blvd. Kukulcán km 8.5
Tels.: 848 7151, 881 4300
01 888 668 816
Fax: 881 4310
www.riu.com

(36) D-02 *Riu Palace*

468

Blvd. Kukulcán km 8.5
Tels.: 891 4300
01 888 668 816
Fax: 891 4301
www.riu.com

★★★★★

GOLDEN CROWN PARADISE SPA

Introducing Cancún's latest All-Inclusive Adults Only club. This intimate retreat is ideal for honeymoons or a romantic getaway in the Mexican Caribbean. The friendly staff will keep you supplied with drinks by the pool or in the four bars and serve you delicious meals in four different restaurants. The Crown Club Suites are the perfect option for couples looking for that extra-special treatment.

Facilities include meeting rooms for business travelers.

Adults only • 4 restaurants • 4 bars • Spa • Business Center

Ret. San Miguelito No. 37,
Hotel Zone, Cancún
Quintana Roo, Mexico, 77500;
Tels.: (998) 885 0909
Mexico 01 800 361 3300
USA 1 800 882 8215
Fax: (998) 885 1919

reservgcp@crownparadise.com
www.crownparadise.com

★★★★★

CROWN PARADISE CLUB & SPA CANCÚN

This resort takes the All-Inclusive vacation to new levels for couples, families and groups. Enjoy the good life 24 hours a day. Savor fine cuisine and drinks at seven different restaurants or in your ocean-view room. There are four entertainment areas with live music and a Kids Club with supervised activities. The resort offers couples privacy and a romantic ambiance, facilities for business travelers and excellent service for all guests.

Spa • 7 restaurants • 6 bars • Kids' Club • Groups and Conventions

Blvd. Kukulcán km 18.5,
Hotel Zone, Cancún
Quintana Roo, Mexico, 77500;
Tels.: (998) 848 9000
Mexico 01 800 361 3300
Fax: (998) 848 9045

ventas@crownparadise.com
www.crownparadise.com

★★★★★

Superb beach location, with Deluxe rooms and Junior Suites with luxury amenities, all beautifully appointed. 4 restaurants and 4 bars, including our 24-hour All-Inclusive Club, group and convention halls, Spa, Internet in rooms, recreational activities, water sports center and much, much more.

• 354 deluxe rooms • www.realresorts.com.mx

Sales & Marketing
Tel. + 52 (998) 881 7311
sales@realresorts.com.mx
Groups
Tel. + 52 (998) 881 7312
groups@realresorts.com.mx
Reservations
Tel. + 52 (998) 881 7340
Mex. 01 800 216 5500
EUA & CAN 1 800 543 7556
Fax: + 52 (998) 881 7399
reservations@realresorts.com.mx

★★★★★

Enjoy the blue Caribbean in sumptuous Mediterranean installations with a unique blend of excellent European service and warm Mexican hospitality. We take care of all the details to guarantee you excellent vacations with the best all-inclusive concept in this destination.

• 638 Standard and Junior Suites • www.realresorts.com.mx

Sales & Marketing
Tel. + 52 (998) 881 7311
sales@realresorts.com.mx
Groups
Tel. + 52 (998) 881 7312
groups@realresorts.com.mx
Reservations
Tel. + 52 (998) 881 7340
Mex. 01 800 216 5500
EUA & CAN 1 800 543 7556
Fax: + 52 (998) 881 7399
reservations@realresorts.com.mx

★★★★★

HYATT REGENCY CANCÚN

Located at the heart of the Hotel Zone, a short distance from major malls, restaurants and nightclubs. Enjoy aquatic games in two pools with waterfalls, relax in the hammocks overlooking the sea and on the island sundeck in the Caribbean or savor exquisite cuisine in the Seafood Market specialty restaurant.

For greater privacy, check into the Regency Club which also has a Presidential and Governor's Suite.

• 300 Rooms + 4 Suites • 2 Restaurants • 4 Bars

Blvd. Kukulcán km 8.5
Hotel Zone
Cancún, Q. Roo, Mexico, 77500
Tel.: (998) 883 1234,
Fax: (998) 883 1694

sales.hrcancun@hyattintl.com
www.cancun.regency.hyatt.com

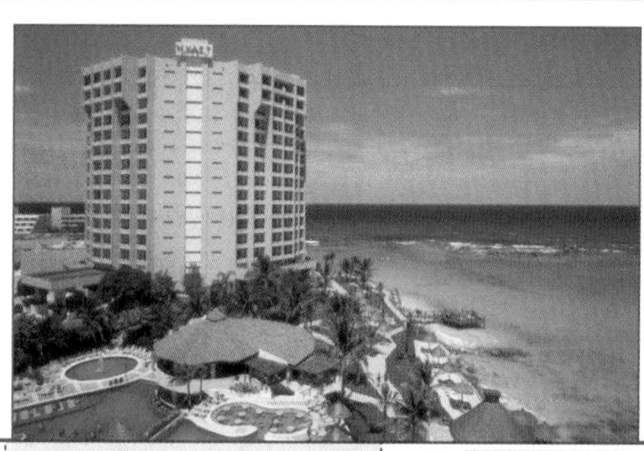

★★★★★

HYATT CANCÚN CARIBE VILLAS & RESORT

Just five minutes from all the major malls, this elegant boutique resort is nestled on half a kilometer of secluded beach and surrounded by extensive gardens. The 223 rooms have terraces or balconies with spectacular views of the Caribbean. A bonus is the exclusive area of villas, each with two bedrooms and a suite, direct access to the beach, pool area and an open air Jacuzzi. Ideal for honeymooners.

Services: Tennis courts, running track, masseuse, water sports, a nearby golf course and a variety of restaurants and bars including the highly acclaimed Blue Bayou with its menu of Cajun and Creole specialties.

• 223 deluxe, beachfront rooms

Blvd. Kukulcán km 10.5,
Hotel Zone
Cancún, Q. Roo, Mexico, 77500
Tel. (998) 848 7800,
Fax: (998) 883 1514

hyattcancuncaribe@hyattintl.com
www.cancuncaribe.resort.hyatt.com

(82) C-30 ***Royal Solaris Cancún Resort Marina & Spa***

500

MINI GOLF.
Blvd. Kukulcán km 20.5
Tels.: 848 8400, 848 8415
01 800 215 2800
USA 1 866 8 SOLARIS
Fax: 848 8418
www.hotelessolaris.com

(56) D-11 ***Sheraton Cancún Resort & Towers***

PE 326

Blvd. Kukulcán km 12.5
Tels.: 891 4400, 891 4492
01 800 903 2500
Fax: 885 0204
infocancun@sheraton.com
www.sheraton.com/cancun

(47) C-06 ***Sierra (Le Blanc)***

269

MINI GOLF.
Blvd. Kukulcán km 10
Tels.: 883 2444, 883 3655
01 800 509 9960
Fax: 883 3486
www.palaceresorts.com

(85) B-32 ***Sun Palace***

237

Blvd. Kukulcán km 20
Tels.: 891 4100, 891 4109
01 800 672 5223
USA 1 800 346 8225
Fax: 881 6001
www.palaceresorts.com

(46) C-06 ***Sunset Royal***

204

Blvd. Kukulcán km 10
Tels.: 881 4500, 849 4906
1 800 221 5333
Fax: 881 4694
www.royalsunsetcancun.com

(74) D-23 ***The Royal Caribbean***

PE 206

GOLF PROGRAM.
Blvd. Kukulcán km 17.5
Retorno Gucumatz
Tels.: 881 0100, 881 5160
Fax: 885 0032
bcenters@royalresorts.com
www.royalresorts.com

(75) D-24 ***The Royal Islander***

PE 179

GOLF PROGRAM.
Blvd. Kukulcán km 17.5
Retorno Gucumatz
Tels.: 881 0100, 881 5160
Fax: 885 0032
bcenters@royalresorts.com
www.royalresorts.com

(73) D-22 ***The Royal Mayan***

PE 200

GOLF PROGRAM.
Blvd. Kukulcán km 17.5
Retorno Gucumatz
Tels.: 881 0100, 881 5160
Fax: 885 0278
bcenters@royalresorts.com
www.royalresorts.com

(62) D-14 ***The Royal Sands***

PE 340

GOLF PROGRAM.
Blvd. Kukulcán km 13.5
Tels.: 881 0100, 881 5160
Fax: 848 8230
bcenters@royalresorts.com
www.royalresorts.com

(21) J-04 ***Villas Tacul Boutique Hotel***

23

Blvd. Kukulcán km 5.5
Tels.: 849 7060, 883 0000
01 800 215 2000
USA 1 800 842 0193
Fax: 849 7070
vtacul@cancun.com.mx
www.villastacul.com.mx

FOUR STAR ★★★★

(10) O-04 ***Aquamarina Beach***

172

Blvd. Kukulcán km 4.5
Tels.: 849 4606
01 800 201 2742
Fax: 849 4600
www.aquamarina-beach.com

(38) C-03 ***Best Western Cancún Clipper Club***

PE PC 35

TIMESHARING.
Blvd. Kukulcán km 8.5
Tels.: 891 5999, 891 5977
01 800 904 7500
USA 1 800 9378 376
Fax: 891 5989
bestwestern@clipper.com.mx
www.clipper.com.mx

(5) P-04 ***Blue Bay Getaway***

396

ADULTS ONLY.
Blvd. Kukulcán km 3.5
Tels.: 848 7900, 848 7942
Fax: 848 7906
www.bluebayscancun.com

(58) D-12 ***Caribbean Village***

300

Blvd. Kukulcán km 13.5
Tels.: 848 8000
01 800 858 2258
Fax: 848 8003
www.occidental-hoteles.com

(7) P-04 ***Club Carrousel***

158

Blvd. Kukulcán km 3.5
Tels.: 848 7170
01 800 800 8480
Fax: 848 7179, 849 4140
www.hotelescarrousel.com

(9) P-05 ***Club Las Velas***

PE 312

Blvd. Kukulcán km 3.5
esq. Galeón
Tels.: 891 4080, 891 4087
01 800 215 2100
USA 1 888 273 9814
Fax: 849 4575
clbvelas2@prodigy.net.mx
www.clublasvelas.com.mx

(50) C-08 ***Flamingo Cancún Resort and Plaza***

PA 234

Blvd. Kukulcán km 11.5
Tels.: 883 1544, 883 1547
Fax: 883 1029
ventas@flamingocancun.com
www.flamingocancun.com

(24) F-06 ***Holiday Inn Express***

PE PC 119

Paseo Pok Ta Pok L. 21- 22
Tels.: 883 2200
01 800 009 9900
USA 1 800 4654 329
Fax: 883 2532
cancunsales@prodigy.net.mx
www.hiexpress.com/cancunmex

★★★★

Perfect for enjoying your holidays in a family atmosphere offering privacy and tranquillity. Located in the beach area, 30 minutes from the International Airport and 5 minutes from the city, malls and nightlife. We offer All-Inclusive and European Plan packages as well as events halls with first-rate services for our guests.

Blvd. Kukulcán km 4.5, Cancún, Q. Roo, Tel.: (998) 849 4606, Mexico 01 800 201 2742, USA/ Canada: 1 877 615 7194
Fax: (998) 849 4600 reservations@aquamarinabeach.com • www.aquamarinabeach.com

★★★

EL PUEBLITO ALL INCLUSIVE MEXICAN VILLAGE

Its totally Mexican architecture and colonial style make this the most Mexican corner of the Caribbean. Enjoy its restaurants and bars as well as its activities and nightlife. 350 rooms, beach, 5 pools, water slide, theater and more. The only hotel in Cancún with a chapel for religious celebrations.

Blvd. Kukulcán km 17.5, Cancún, Q. Roo, México Tel.: (998) 881 8800, llame sin costo al: 01 800 003 0000; Fax: (998) 885 2066
reservas@pueblitohotels.com • *www.pueblitohotels.com*

★★★★

HOTETUR BEACH PARADISE

ALL-INCLUSIVE. This All-Inclusive resort with 170 rooms and suites is located on a lovely beach, a 15-minute drive from the airport, and close to shopping centers, bars, restaurants, nightclubs and two golf courses.

Blvd. Kukulcán km 19.5, Cancún Q. Roo, México 77500, Tel.: (998) 885 2222, Fax: (998) 885 2526
• www.catalog.hotetur.com • www.hotetur.com

(84) C-30 ***Hotetur Beach Paradise***

PE 170
Blvd. Kukulcán km 19.5
Tel.: 885 2222
Fax: 885 2526
www.hotetur.com
www.catalog.hotetur.com

(26) G-07 ***Ocean Club Cancún***

PE 39
Paseo Pok Ta Pok L. 2
Tels.: 883 3300, 883 3211
Fax: 883 3773
gerencia@oceanclub.com.mx
www.oceanclub.com

(22) J-04 ***Maya Caribe***

PE 40
Blvd. Kukulcán km 6
Tels.: 848 9300, 883 5370
contactus@maya-caribe.com

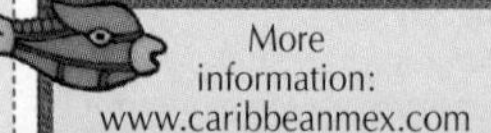

More information:
www.caribbeanmex.com

55 D-10 ***Park Royal Pirámides***

294

TIMESHARING.
Blvd. Kukulcán km 12.5
Tel.: 885 1333 Fax: 885 1498
www.parkroyalhotels.com.mx

80 D-29 ***Solymar Beach Resort***

PE 119
Blvd. Kukulcán km 18.7
Tels.: 885 1811, 885 1905
Fax: 885 1689
solysales@prodigy.net.mx
www.solymarcancun.com

20 K-04 ***Sunset Lagoon Hotel & Marina***

104
Blvd. Kukulcán km 5.8
Tels.: 883 1111, 883 1145
01 800 221 5333
USA 1 305 599 2124
Fax: 883 4959
www.royalsunsetcancun.com

8 P-04 ***The Caribbean Princess***

PE 84
Galeón D-9-5
Blvd. Kukulcán km 3.5
Tels.: 849 4770, 849 7084
01 800 712 8714
Fax: 849 7082
sales@tcpcun.com
www.thecaribbeanprincess.com

60 D-13 ***TucanCun Beach Resort & Villas***

321
Blvd. Kukulcán km 13.5
Tels.: 885 0568, 885 0818
Fax: 885 1850
ventascd@cancun.com.mx
www.tucancunbeach.com

Q-03 ***Villa Deportiva Juvenil***

Blvd. Kukulcán km 3
Tel.: 883 1337

THREE STAR ★★★

11 O-05 ***Acquasol Club***

PA
PE PC 90
FAT TUESDAY BEACH CLUB.
Pescador L. D-8-3
Blvd. Kukulcán km 4
Tels.: 849 4707, 849 4721
01 800 523 7421
USA 1 877 358 5721
Fax: 849 4722
acquasolclub@prodigy.net.mx
www.acquasolclubcancun.com

60 C-31 ***Aristos Cancún Plaza***

PE PA PC 139
Blvd. Kukulcán km 20.5
Tels.: 885 3333
01 800 503 3399
USA 1 800 5-ARISTO
Fax: 885 0236
ariscunventas@prodigy.net.mx
www.aristoshotels.com

2 R-03 ***Barceló Club Las Perlas***

PE 194
Blvd. Kukulcán km 2.5
Tels.: 848 9100, 848 9111
Fax.: 848 9110
bookings@clublasperlas.com
www.barcelo.com

33 E-03 ***Oasis Viva Cancún***

PE 212
Blvd. Kukulcán km 8.5
Tels.: 883 0800, 883 0019
Fax.: 843 2087
www.oasishoteles.com

18 L-04 ***Cancún Marina Club***

PE PA 88
Blvd. Kukulcán km 5.5
Tels.: 849 4999, 849 7072
01 800 719 5523
01 800 216 7222
Fax: 849 7071
hmarinac@prodigy.net.mx

4 Q-03 ***Club Verano Beat***

PE 77
Blvd. Kukulcán km 3.5
Tels.: 849 4800, 849 7427
Fax: 849 7233
www.club-verano-beat-cancun.com

43 C-04 ***Condominios Carisa y Palma***

PA 120
Blvd. Kukulcán km 9.5
Tels.: 883 0211, 883 0265
01 800 215 0400
USA 1 866 521 1787
Fax: 883 0932
ventas@carisaypalma.com
www.carisaypalma.com

43 C-04 ***Condominios Salvia***

96
Blvd. Kukulcán km 9.5
Tels.: 883 2286, 883 2568
01 800 509 9296
Fax.: 01 800 509 9286
salviacondos@yahoo.com
www.salviareservaciones.com

23 I-04 ***Dos Playas Cancún***

PE 111
Blvd. Kukulcán km 6.5
Tel.: 849 4920
Fax: 849 4921
amanon@dosplayas.com
www.dosplayas.com

28 E-04 ***Grand Royal Lagoon***

PA PE PC 36
Blvd. Kukulcán km 7.5
Quetzal L. 8-A
Tels.: 883 2899, 883 2749
01 800 552 4666
Fax: 883 0003
promocion@grlagoon.com
www.grlagoon.com

1 S-02 ***Imperial Las Perlas***

PA PE PC 118
Blvd. Kukulcán km 2.5
Tels.: 849 5200, 883 3448
Fax: 849 4269
hipc@cancun.com.mx
www.hotelimperialcancun.com

77 D-27 ***El Pueblito Beach Hotel Cancún***

350
Blvd. Kukulcán km 17.5
Tels.: 881 8800, 881 8842
01 800 003 0000
Fax: 885 2066
pueblito@pueblitohotels.com
www.pueblitohotels.com

35 D-03 ***Suites Costa Blanca***

PE 21
Blvd. Kukulcán km 8.5
Centro Comercial
La Mansión Costa Blanca
Tels.: 883 0888, 883 0659
Fax: 883 3384
aeropolis@prodigy.net.mx

13 O-05 ***Torre Dorada***

PA PE PC 80
Blvd. Kukulcán km 4
Tels.: 849 4400, 849 7056
Fax: 849 7055
www.hoteltorredorada.com

TORRE DORADA CANCÚN

★★★

Its 148 Mexican-style suites have air-conditioning, cable TV and a balcony overlooking the bay and the lagoon. It has two pools, a games area, gardens, billiards, volleyball and a restaurant.

Blvd. Kukulcán km 4, L. D-8-0, Cancún, Q. Roo, Mexico
Tel.: +52 (998) 849 4400, Fax: +52 (998) 849 7055
info@hoteltorredorada.com • www.hoteltorredorada.com

30 E-05 ***Suites Sina***
PE 32
Quetzal No. 33
Fracc. Club de Golf
Tels.: 883 1017, 883 1018
01 800 712 6104
Fax: 883 2459
sinasuit@cancun.com.mx
www.cancunsinasuites.com.mx

TWO STAR ★★

29 E-04 ***Imperial Laguna***
PE 61
Quetzal No. 11
Fracc. Club de Golf
Tels.: 883 0070, 849 5200
Fax: 849 4269

SPECIAL CATEGORY

87 A-34 ***Club Med***
428
Blvd. Kukulcán km 21.5
Tels.: 881 8200, 881 8204
01 800 901 7000
USA 305 925 9000
Fax: 881 8280
www.clubmed.com

27 G-09 ***Coral Mar***
TIMESHARING.
41
Paseo Pok Ta Pok 23
Tels.: 883 0188, 883 0077
clubcoralmar@yahoo.com

DOWNTOWN

FIVE STAR ★★★★★

F-01 ***Radisson Hacienda***
PA PE 247
TIMESHARING.
Av. Náder No. 1 Sm. 2
Tels.: 881 6500
01 800 201 7647
USA 1 800 333 3333
Fax: 884 7954
ventas@radissoncancun.com
www.radissoncancun.com

FOUR STAR ★★★★

G-04 ***Best Western Plaza Caribe***
PA PE 139
Av. Tulum y Uxmal L. 19
Tels.: 884 1377, 887 6763
01 800 215 1500
USA 1 800 528 1234
Fax: 884 6352 ext.364
plazacbe@cancun.com.mx
www.hotelplazacaribe.com

D-10 ***Oasis América***
PE PA 190
HAS A BEACH CLUB.
Av. Tulum esq. Brisa
Tel.: 848 7500
Fax: 849 4506
www.oasishoteles.com

G-05 ***Cancún Rosa***
PE 20
Margaritas No. 2 Sm. 22
Tel.: 848 0623
Fax: 848 1294

H-06 ***Margaritas***
PE 101
HAS A BEACH CLUB.
Av. Yaxchilán 41, Sm. 22
Tels.: 884 9333
01 800 640 7473
Fax: 884 1324
margaritas@sybcom.com

E-04 ***Plaza Kokai Cancún***
PE 48
Av. Uxmal No. 26 Sm. 2-A
Tels.: 884 3218
01 800 719 5627
Fax: 884 4335
ventas@hotelkokai.com
www.hotelkokai.com

H-06 ***Suites Caribe Internacional***
PA PE PC 105
Av. Yaxchilán 36-37 Sm. 24
Tels.: 884 3999, 884 3243
01 800 713 0167
Fax: 884 1993
caribeinternacional@caribeinternacional.com
www.caribeinternacional.com

H-06 ***Xbalamqué***
PE 92
Av. Yaxchilán 31 Sm. 22
Tels.: 884 9690, 887 3828
Fax: 892 0699
xbalamque@prodigy.net
www.xbalamque.com

THREE STAR ★★★

F-07 ***Antillano***
PE 48
Av. Tulum & Claveles No. 1
Sm. 22 L. 20, 37 & 39
Tels.: 884 1532, 884 1132
01 800 288 7000
Fax: 884 1878
reserva@hotelantillano.com
www.hotelantillano.com

A-11 ***Bonampak***
PE 80
Av. Bonampak 225 Sm. 4
Tels.: 884 0280, 887 3158
Fax: 887 5793
bonampac@prodigy.net.mx

D-10 ***Cancún Handall***
PE 42
Av. Tulum esq. Jaleb Sm. 20
Tel.: 842 6664
Fax: 884 5731
www.hotelhandall.com

H-06 ***Canto***
PE 30
Av. Yaxchilán Sm. 24 L. 31
Tels.: 884 1267, 884 5793
Fax: 884 9262
www.hotelcanto.com

F-07 ***Carrillo´s***
43
Claveles No. 33
Tels.: 884 1227, 884 4922
Fax: 884 2371
carrillos@ww2.net.mx

I-02 ***El Batab***

68

Av. Chichén Itzá 52 Sm. 23
Tels.: 884 3822, 884 3720
01 800 215 5100
Fax: 884 3821
batab@prodigy.net.mx
www.hotelbatab.com

E-04 ***El Rey del Caribe***

24

TRANSPORTATION AIRPORT-HOTEL-AIRPORT.
Av. Uxmal No. 24 Sm. 2-A
Tels.: 884 2028, 887 9099
01 800 508 1864
Fax: 884 9857
reycaribe@reycaribe.com
www.reycaribe.com

I-06 ***Hacienda Cancún***

36

Av. Sunyaxchén 39 Sm. 24
Tel.: 884 3672
Fax: 884 1208

G-08 ***María de Lourdes***

57

Av. Yaxchilán 80 Sm. 22
Tels.: 884 4744, 884 1721
01 800 215 6000
Fax: 884 1242
www.hotelmariadelourdes.com

F-05 ***Parador***

66

Av. Tulum No. 26 Sm. 5
Tels.: 884 1043, 884 1922
Fax: 884 9712
www.hotelparador.com.mx

E-08 ***Soberanis***

66

Av. Cobá No. 5 y 7 Sm. 22
Tels.: 884 4564
01 800 101 0101
Fax: 887 5138
www.soberanis.com.mx

F-07 ***Suites Cancún Center***

44

Alcatraces No. 32 Sm. 22
Tels.: 884 2301, 884 7270
Fax: 884 7270
www.suitescancun.com

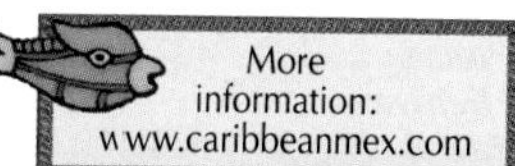

C-12 ***Suites La Maison***

15

SPECIALIZED SERVICE FOR EXECUTIVES.
Av. Tulum No. 227
Tel.: 892 0392 Fax: 892 0393
lamaisonsuites@prodigy.net.mx

TWO STAR ★★

H-04 ***Alux***

32

Av. Uxmal L. 21 Sm. 23
Tels.: 884 0556, 884 3065
Fax: 884 3046
www.hotelalux.com

C-15 ***Farallon Inn***

18

Av. Acanceh 13 - 1 Sm. 15
Tel./Fax: 887 4458

F-05 ***Kin Mayab***

42

Av. Tulum No. 75 Sm. 22
Tels.: 884 2999, 884 0176
Fax: 884 9162
www.novotelcancun.com

K-06 ***Tankah***

38

Av. Tankah L. 69-70 Sm. 24
Tels.: 884 4446, 884 4844
Fax: 884 3065
www.hoteltankah.com

E-04 ***Villa Maya***

16

Av. Uxmal No. 20
esq. Rubia Sm. 3
Tels.: 884 2829, 884 2918
Fax: 884 1762

ONE STAR ★

H-04 ***Cotty***

28

Av. Uxmal No. 44 Sm. 22
Tels.: 884 0550, 884 1319
www.hotelcotty.com

SPECIAL CATEGORY

D-07 ***Suites Alborada***

9

Av. Náder No. 5 Sm. 5
Tel./Fax: 884 4347
suitesalborada@hotmail.com

PUERTO JUÁREZ

FOUR STAR ★★★★

Blue Bay Club

161

Puerto Juárez Hwy. km 1.5
Tel.: 881 7900
Fax: 881 7999
www.bluebayresorts.com

MEDICAL SERVICES

H-09 ***Centro Radiológico***
Av. Cobá esq. Caimito
Tels.: 884 1944, 884 8483

O-05 ***Clínica Amerimed***
GENERAL PRACTICE, ENGLISH AND SPANISH SPOKEN.
Blvd. Kukulcán km 4, ZH
Tel.: 849 4911
www.amerimed-hospital.com

G-11 ***Red Cross***
GENERAL PRACTICE, EMERGENCIES.
Prol. Av. Yaxchilán No. 2
Tels.: 884 1616, 884 7466
Urgencias: 065

F-04 ***Hospital Amat***
LABORATORY, ULTRASOUND, X RAYS, 24-HOUR SERVICE.
Av. Náder No. 13 Sm. 2
Tels.: 887 4422, 887 4423
887 4429, 884 3823
Fax: 887 4435, 887 7539
hosamat@prodigy.net.mx

B-11 ***Hospital Americano***
EMERGENCIES, THERAPY, PEDIATRICS, LABORATORY, X RAYS, HOSPITAL.
Ret. Viento No. 15 Sm. 4
Tel.: 884 6133

A-16 ***Hospital Amerimed***
LABORATORY, ULTRASOUND, X RAYS, THERAPY, EMERGENCIES, DRUGSTORE, HOSPITAL, GENERAL PRACTICE.
ENGLISH & SPANISH.
Av. Tulum Sur Sm. 7
Tel.: 881 3434
www.amerimed-hospital.com

Hospital General
GYNECOLOGY, ORTHOPEDICS, X RAYS, LABORATORY, HOSPITAL.
Andador No. 5 Sm. 65
entre Calles 12 y 13
Tels.: 884 2666, 884 2967

F-07 ***Hospital Total Assist***
EMERGENCIES, ANAESTHESIA, CRITICAL MEDICINE, SCANS, ULTRASOUND, DECOMPRESSION CHAMBER, LABORATORY.
Claveles 5 Sm. 22 Mz. 5
Tel.: 884 8082
htotal@prodigy.net.mx
www.totalassist.com

Hospiten Cancún
HOSPITAL, EMERGENCIES.
Av. Bonampak L. 7
Mz. 2 Sm. 10
Tels.: 881 3700
01 800 900 90009
Fax: 881 3737
cancun@hospiten.es
www.hospiten.com

E-09 ***IMSS***
EMERGENCIES & HOSPITAL.
Av. Cobá esq. Tulum
Tels.: 884 1108, 884 1963
Fax: 884 1907
imss@gob.mx
imss.gob.mx

IMSS
GYNECOLOGY, PEDIATRICS, EMERGENCIES.
Av. López Portillo y Kabah
Tels.: 888 7200, 888 7201
imss@gob.mx
imss.gob.mx

SPECIALISTS

THE FOLLOWING DOCTORS SPEAK ENGLISH AND SPANISH.

A-16 ***Gastroenterologist***
DR. FÉLIX RIVAS.
Hospiten Cancún
Tel.: 881 3700

F-10 ***Gynecologist***
DRA. REBECA MALIS.
GYNECOLOGY, OBSTETRICS, UROLOGY.
Venado No. 21-3 Sm. 20
Tels.: 884 5066, 887 3382

F-07 ***Internist***
DR. SERGIO A. CARDOSO.
GENERAL PRACTICE, HOUSE CALLS BY APPOINTMENT.
FRI. 10 AM.-1:30 PM. & 5-7:30 PM.; SAT. 10 AM. -2 PM.
Hospiten Cancún
Tel.: 881 3700

C-12 ***Dentist***
DR. JOAQUÍN BERRÓN OSOMO.
Av. Tulum 232-5 C
Sm. 4
Tel.: 887 3979
Fax: 887 2579
jberron@cablered.net.mx

F-04 ***Orthopedist***
DR. JOSÉ MARROQUÍN.
ORTHOPEDICS, GENERAL AND ALTERNATIVE MEDICINE, NEURAL AND BIOMAGNETIC THERAPY.
LANGUAGES: SPANISH, ENGLISH, FRENCH, GERMAN, FINNISH.
Av. Náder L.5 Sm. 2
Tels.: 887 4646, 892 0054
jmarroquín@caribe.net.mx

E-04 ***Pediatrics***
DR. HORACIO NOLASCO.
Av. Náder No. 13 Sm. 2
First floor
Tels.: 884 4041, 884 4108
drnolasco@caribe.net.mx

I-08 ***Quiropractor / Sport Medicine***
DR. MOISÉS REZNICK.
BODY REPROGRAMMING AND PURIFICATION, ALLERGY TREATMENTS.
Nance No. 19 Sm. 25
Tels.: 884 1814, 884 8294

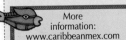

More information:
www.caribbeanmex.com

G-08 ***Veterinarian***
DR. LUIS MANUEL MARTÍNEZ GONZÁLEZ.
MON-SAT. 10 AM -2 PM.
Av. Cobá No. 35 Sm. 22
Tel.: 884 0679

DRUGSTORES

H-06 ***Canto***
MON. - SAT. 8 AM. - MIDNIGHT, SUN. 9 AM. - 11 PM., HOUSE CALLS.
Av. Yaxchilán
L. A-D Sm. 24 Mz. 27
Tels.: 884 4083, 887 9370
Fax: 884 9330

A-14 ***Farmacias Similares***
8 AM. - 9 PM.
Plaza Las Américas
Tel.: 898 0190

H-06 ***París***
24-HOUR SERVICE, HOUSE CALLS 8 AM. - 11 PM.
Av. Yaxchilán 32 Sm. 22
Tels.: 884 0164, 884 3005

Yza
24-HOUR SERVICE, HOUSE CALLS.
Av. Kabah Sm. 59 L. 7-8
Tels.: 886 6034, 884 6035
Fax: 886 6890
www.farmaciasyza.com.mx

EMERGENCIES

Customs	886 0073
Fire Brigade	887 8606
	884 1913
Red Cross	884 1616
Wake-up call	031
Emergencies	066
Exact Time	030
Immigration	884 1404
Police	887 8606
Highway Patrol	884 1107

CONSULATES

J-05 ***Germany***
MON. - FRI. 9 AM. - NOON.
Punta Conoco 36, Sm. 24
Tels.: 884 5333, 884 1898
Fax: 887 1283
Embassy 0155 5283 2200

D-11 ***Austria***
MON. - FRI. 9 AM. - 2 PM., 5 PM. - 8 PM., SAT. 9 AM. - 2 PM.
Pecarí No. 37 Sm. 20
Tels.: 887 5383, 884 1700
Fax: 884 9591

C-11 ***Belgium***
MON. - FRI. 9 AM. - 2 PM., 4 PM. - 7 PM.
Av. Tulum 192
Plaza Tropical L. 59
Tel.: 892 2512
Fax: 892 2097
Embassy 0155 5280 0758

E-03 ***Belize***
MON. - FRI. 9 AM. - 1 PM.
Av. Náder 34 esq. Lima
Tels.: 887 8417, 887 8631
Fax: 887 8631
Embassy 0155 5520 1274

C-02 ***Canada***
MON. - FRI. 9 AM. -5 PM.
Plaza Caracol
3º Piso, L. 330
Tel.: 883 3360
Fax: 883 3232
Embassy 0155 5724 7900

B-09 ***Casa Argentina***
MON. - FRI. 10 AM.-1 PM., 5 PM. - 8 PM.
Av. Cobá 18 Sm. 4, Mz. 3
Tel./Fax: 887 1814
cargentina@hotmail.com

D-11 ***Cuba***
MON. - FRI. 8 AM. - 1 PM.
Pecarí 17 Sm. 20
Tel./Fax: 884 3423
Embassy 0155 5280 8563

D-22 ***Denmark***
MON. - FRI. 8 AM. - 6 PM.
Hotel Omni, HZ
Blvd. Kukulcán km 16.5
Tels.: 881 0670, 881 0600
Fax: 885 0059
Embassy 0155 5255 3405

H-04 ***Spain***
MON. - FRI. 10 AM. - 1 PM.
Blvd. Kukulcán km 6.5
esq. Cenzontle
Tel.: 848 9900
Fax: 848 9946
Embassy 0155 5280 4383

C-02 ***United States***
MON. - FRI. 9 AM. - 1 PM.
Plaza Caracol II,
3º piso, HZ
Tel.: 883 0272
Fax: 883 1373
Embassy 0155 5080 2000

F-03 ***Finland***
MON. - FRI. 8 AM. - 2 PM., 5 PM. - 8 PM.
Av. Náder No. 28 Sm. 2
Edif. Popol-Ná
Tel.: 884 1643
Fax: 887 8995
Embassy 0155 5540 6036

A-12 ***France***
MON. - FRI. 9 AM. - 1 PM.
Av. Bonampak 239, Sm. 4
Tel.: 887 8141
Fax: 887 7842
Embassy 0155 9171 9840

D-14 ***Great Britain***
MON. - FRI. 9 AM. - 3 PM.
The Royal Sands
Tel.: 881 0100 ext. 65898
Fax: 848 8229
Embassy 0155 5525 1581

C-08 ***Guatemala***
MON. - FRI. 9:30 - 1 PM.
Av. Náder No. 148,
L. 90-92, Sm. 3
Tels.: 884 8286, 884 8185
Fax: 884 4370
Embassy 0155 5540 7520

The Netherlands
MON. - FRI. 9 AM. - 1 PM.
International Airport
Tel.: 886 0070
Fax: 886 0128
Embassy 0155 5258 9921

More information:
www.caribbeanmex.com

F-07 ***Italy***
MON. - FRI. 9 AM. - 2 PM.
Alcatraces 39 Sm. 22
Tel.: 884 1261
Fax: 884 5415
Embassy 0155 5596 3655

F-11 ***Norway***
MON. - FRI. 9 AM. - 1 PM.
Venado No. 30 Sm. 20
Tel.: 884 6433
Fax: 887 7106
Embassy 0155 5540 3487

E-03 ***Poland***
MON. - FRI. 9 AM. - 4 PM.
Av. Náder No. 42 Sm. 2-A
Edif. Marruecos
Tel.: 884 7020
Fax: 887 3399
Embassy 0155 5550 4878

H-04 ***Sweden***
MON. - FRI. 9 AM. - 2 PM.
Cenzontle No. 2, ZH
Tel.: 849 7144
Embassy 0155 5540 6393

D-08 ***Switzerland***
MON. - FRI. 9 AM. - 1 PM.
Av. Cobá No. 12, L. 214
Tel./Fax: 884 8446
Embassy 0155 5520 3003

BOOKSTORES

A-14 ***Dalí***
Plaza Las Américas
Tel.: 887 7541

H-06 ***El Pabilo***
Hotel Xbalamqué

F-06 ***Fama***
Av. Tulum 105 Sm. 22
Tel.: 884 6586

E-04 ***Lettera Libros***
Av. Uxmal y Náder Sm. 3

Plaza Arte
Av. del Sol No. 11 Sm. 45
Tel.: 848 2759
www.plazarte.info

ISLA MUJERES

Intimate beachfront retreats, restaurants serving up seafood, Italian and Mexican specialities, craft shops and water sports are the essence of Isla. Diving and fishing are excellent and the island boasts a dolphin center and an eco-park.

TRAVEL AGENCIES

F-06 ***Caribbean Reality Travel***

ENGLISH, SPANISH.
Av. Abasolo No. 6
Tels.: 877 1371, 877 1372
Fax: 877 1373
www.caribbeanrealitytravel.com

E-06 ***Mundaca Travel***

ENGLISH, SPANISH.
PACKAGES TO CUBA, BUS TICKET SALES AND RIVIERA MAYA TOURS.
Av. Hidalgo No. 15-A
Tels.: 877 0025
01 800 714 3817
Fax: 877 0076
www.mundacatravel.com

ASSOCIATIONS

E-07 ***Isla Mujeres Hotel Association***
Av. Hidalgo No. 110
btwn. Madero & Abasolo
Tel.: 877 0430
Fax: 877 0429
hotel.belmar@caribe.net.mx

E-08 ***Restaurant Association*** (CANIRAC)
Av. Hidalgo No. 5
Tel.: 877 0627
Fax: 877 0541
gomar1@prodigy.net.mx

E-07 ***Chamber of Commerce*** (CANACO)
Av. Abasolo No. 16
Tel.: 877 0563
canacoim@prodigy.net.mx

G-08 ***Tourist Office***
Av. Rueda Medina No. 130
Tels.: 877 0307, 877 0767
infoisla@prodigy.net.mx
www.isla-mujeres.com.mx

G-08 ***Tourist Promotion Trust***
Av. Rueda Medina No. 130
Tels.: 877 0767, 877 0307
Fax: 877 0307
infoisla@prodigy.net.mx
www.isla-mujeres.com.mx

G-08 ***Immigration***
Av. Rueda Medina
Tel./Fax: 877 0189
migracun@qroo1.telmex.net.mx

G-08 ***National Parks***
PARK ASSISTANCE AND TOURIST DEVELOPMENT MAINTENANCE.
Av. Rueda Medina No. 7
Tel./Fax: 877 0118
pncontoy@prodigy.net.mx

F-09 ***Police***
Morelos esq. Hidalgo
Tel.: 877 0458

BANKS

G-08 ***Banamex***
ATM.
Morelos esq. Juárez

G-09 ***HSBC***
ATM MACHINES AT THE GARRAFÓN PARK AND AT SAN FRANCISCO DE ASÍS SUPERMARKET.
Av. Rueda Medina No. 3
Tels.: 877 0005
01 800 712 4825
www.bital.com

BARS

A-04 ***Disco Castaway***
AE VI MC
REGIONAL DANCE SHOW ON SATURDAYS.
9 PM. - 1 AM.
Roca El Yunque next to Avalon Reef Club
Tel.: 999 2050
www.avalonvacations.com

E-05 ***Nitrox Club VIP***
DISCO.
Guerrero 14
esq. Matamoros
nitroxclub@hotmail.com

H-06 ***La Taberna***
VI MC
SNACK BAR.
YACHT CLUB DOCK, PANORAMIC VIEW OF THE BAY.
Av. Rueda Medina

E-02 ***Palapa Chimbos***
Av. Guerrero esq. Playa Nte.

SHOPPING

F-07 ***Arco Iris***
HANDICRAFT SHOPS.
Av. Juárez No. 3
Tel.: 877 0378

G-07 ***El Paso***
HANDICRAFT SHOPS, BEACHWEAR.
Av. Rueda Medina btwn.
Abasolo & Av. Madero
Tel.: 877 0140

E-06 ***Librería Cosmic Cosas***
INTERNET ACCESS, NEW AND USED BOOKS IN DIFFERENT LANGUAGES, TRAVEL GUIDES AND TOURIST INFORMATION.
9 AM. - 10:30 PM.
Av. Matamoros No. 82
btwn. Hidalgo & Guerrero
Tel.: 877 0806
cosmiccosas@yahoo.com

G-08 ***Poco Loco***
BEACHWEAR.
Av. Rueda Medina
Tel.: 877 0140

G-09 ***Rachat & Romero***
FINE JEWELRY.
Av. Juaréz esq. Morelos
Tels.: 877 0331, 877 0299
Fax: 877 0476

G-08 ***Rob & Eli***
HANDICRAFT SHOPS, CIGARS.
Av. Benito Juárez No. 2 L.1
Tel.: 877 1345

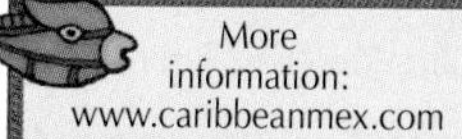

F-09 ***T-Shirt-Manía Isla***
HANDICRAFT SHOPS, CLOTHING.
Av. Benito Juárez
esq. Av. Morelos
Tel.: 877 0036

G-08 ***The Silver Factory***
FINE JEWELRY.
Av. Juaréz esq. Morelos
Tels.: 877 0331, 877 0299
Fax: 877 0476

G-09 ***Villa del Mar***
HANDICRAFT SHOPS.
Av. Rueda Medina No. 1
Tel.: 887 0031

INTERNET

G-07 ***Casa España***
Av. Madero btwn. Rueda Medina & Av. Juárez
Cel.: 044 998 577 0363
antodent@hotmail.com

ENTERTAINMENT

G-08 ***Amigos de Isla Contoy***
NON-GOVERNMENT ORGANIZATION PROMOTING CONSERVATION AND TOURIST DEVELOPMENT OF CONTOY NATIONAL PARK.
Av. Rueda Medina No. 7
Tel.: 877 0118
aicontoy@prodigy.net.mx
www.islacontoy.org

Dolphin Discovery
SWIMMING WITH DOLPHINS, DIVING, AND A ROMANTIC DINNER ABOARD THE SPANISH GALLEON, COLUMBUS.
Villa Pirata L. 98-102
Tels.: 877 0875
01 800 713 8862
www.dolphindiscovery.com.mx

Garrafón
9 AM. - 5 PM.
ENTRY FEE: $150 PESOS ADULTS.
Garrafón Hwy. km. 6
Punta Sur
Tel.: 877 1101
Fax: 877 0083
marketing@garrafon.com
www.garrafon.com

Hacienda Mundaca
9 AM. - 5 PM.
ENTRY FEE: $20 PESOS ADULTS, $10 PESOS CHILDREN.
Garrafón Hwy. km 6

Parque Escultórico
ENTRY FEE: $50 PESOS.
Garrafón Hwy. km. 6
Punta Sur
Tel.: 877 1100

FERRIES

H-09 ***Naviera Contoy***
CARS AND PASSENGER FERRY TRANSPORTATION.
ISLA MUJERES - PUNTA SAM.
Av. Rueda Medina
Tel./Fax: 877 0065
maritima@prodigy.net.mx

ISLA MUJERES-PUNTA SAM	PUNTA SAM-ISLA MUJERES
6:30 AM.	8:00 AM.
9:30 AM.	11:00 AM.
12:45 PM.	2:45 AM.
4:15 PM.	5:30 AM.
7:15 PM.	8:15 AM.

F-09 ***Marítimos Magaña***
DEPARTURES EVERY 30 MINUTES, FROM 6 AM. - 9 PM., FROM PUERTO JUÁREZ TO ISLA MUJERES AND VICE VERSA.
Av. Juárez 14-B
Tel.: 877 0382

H-08 ***Marítimos del Caribe***

CANCÚN PLAYA TORTUGAS-ISLA MUJERES	ISLA MUJERES-CANCÚN PLAYA TORTUGAS
9:00 AM.	10:00 AM.
11:15 AM.	12:00 PM.
1:30 PM.	2:00 PM.
4:00 PM.	5:00 PM.
6:00 PM.	7:00 PM.

H-08 ***Ultramar***
FROM GRAN PUERTO CANCÚN, PUERTO JUÁREZ TO ISLA MUJERES FROM 6 AM. TO MIDNIGHT. FROM ISLA MUJERES TO GRAN PUERTO CANCÚN, PUERTO JUÁREZ, FROM 6 AM. TO 1AM. DEPARTURES THROUGHOUT THE DAY.

MARINAS & SCUBA DIVING

F-08 ***Aerobanana***
ENGLISH, SPANISH.
TOURIST TRANSPORTATION, SCENIC FLIGHTS AND TRIPS TO ARCHAEOLOGICAL ZONES.
Av. Morelos esq. Juárez
Tel.: 877 0331
Fax: 877 0250

G-10 ***Buceo Bahía***
SPANISH, ENGLISH, ITALIAN.
Av. Rueda Medina No. 166
Tel.: 877 0340
Fax: 877 0587
bahiaislamujeres@hotmail.com

G-06 ***Club de Yates***
AGENCY, GAS STATION, TELEPHONE AND RADIO ACCESS, TOURS TO CHICHÉN ITZÁ AND TULÚM.
Av. Rueda Medina
esq. Abasolo
Tel.: 877 0086 Fax: 877 0156

G-06 ***Contoy Express Tour***
ENGLISH, SPANISH, PORTUGUESE.
Av. Rueda Medina btwn. Matamoros & Av. Abasolo
Tel.: 877 1367
sales@contoyisland.com

F-05 ***Coral Scuba Dive Center***
ENGLISH, FRENCH, ITALIAN, SPANISH.
Av. Matamoros No. 13-A
Tels.: 877 0763, 877 0572
Fax: 877 0371
www.coralscubadivecenter.com

G-05 ***Cruise Divers***

ENGLISH, SPANISH.
Av. Rueda Medina
por Matamoros
Tel.: 877 1190
cruisedivers@hotmail.com

C-02 ***Delfín Diving***
ENGLISH, SPANISH, FRENCH, ITALIAN, GERMAN.
Playa Norte, Hotel Na Balam
Tel./Fax. 877 0305
www.delfindiving.com

GARRAFÓN

Your dreams of the Tropics come true in Garrafón Park on Punta Sur, the southern headland of lovely Isla Mujeres, just a 25-minute boat ride from Cancún. The park is renowned for its 200-meter-long coral reef, breathtaking views of the endless Mexican Caribbean, a Mayan temple, an exhibition of modern sculptures, paths to the area's only cliff, hammocks and a variety of water sports and services.

If Eden exists visitors would find it in Garrafón-Punta Sur.

G-10 *Dive Shop Bahía*

ENGLISH, SPANISH, FRENCH, ITALIAN.
Av. Rueda Medina No. 166
Tel.: 877 0340
Fax: 877 0587
bahiaislamujeres@hotmail.com
www.islamujeres.net/shops/bahia/home.htm

Marina Isla Mujeres

ENGLISH, SPANISH.
Fracc. Laguna Mar L. 52-54
Sac Bajo Hwy., Hotel Marina
Tels.: 877 0594
01 800 718 5945

Marina Paraíso

ENGLISH, SPANISH.
Av. Rueda Medina 491-A
Tel/Fax: 877 0252
www.marinaparaiso.com

Marina Puerto Isla Mujeres

Puerto de Abrigo, Prol. Aeropuerto Laguna Macax
Tels.: 877 0485, 877 0330
01 800 216 9800
USA 1 800 960 ISLA
Fax: 877 0093
www.puertoislamujeres.com

E-08 *Mundaca Divers*

ENGLISH, SPANISH, FRENCH.
TOURS AROUND THE ISLAND: DOLPHINS AND REEFS.
Francisco I. Madero No. 10
Tel.: 877 0607
www.mundacadivers.com

D-03 *Sea Hawk Divers*
Calle Carlos Lazo
Tel.: 877 0296
hawkdivers@hotmail.com

F-01 *Tarzán*

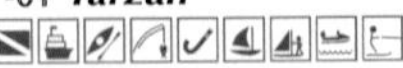

ENGLISH, SPANISH.
Playa Norte
Tel.: 877 0679

TRANSPORT

MOPED, BIKE AND GOLF CART RENTALS.

Cárdenas	877 0079
Caribe	877 0242
Ciro's	877 0568
D-07 *El Sol*	877 0791
El Zorro	877 0937
Garrafón de Castilla	877 0508
Gomar	877 0604
Gomar II	877 0627
Isla	877 1212
Juroca	877 0006
Kan-kin	877 0071
G-07 *María José*	877 0130
Pepe's	877 0019
Prisma	877 0938
G-09 *Rafer*	877 0541

TAXIS

H-08 *Taxi Driver Union*
Av. Rueda Medina
Tel./Fax: 877 0066

RESTAURANTS

CAFES

G-04 *Color de Verano*

COFFEE SHOP, CERAMICS AND FURNITURE ON SALE.
DESSERTS.
TUE.-SUN. 3 PM. - 11 PM.
Av. Adolfo López Mateos
Tels.: 877 1264
colordeverano@prodigy.net.mx
www.colordeverano.com

E-06 *Mañana*

BAGUETTES AND MIDDLE EASTERN CUISINE.
Av. Matamoros esq. Guerrero
Cel.: 044 998 860 4347

INTERNATIONAL

E-05 *Bamboo*

SHRIMP SATAY, PHAD THAI, CHICKEN CURRY.
7 PM. - 2 AM.
Av. Hidalgo
Plaza los Almendros
Tel.: 877 1355

F-06 *Bistro Francés*

LOBSTER, STEAKS.
7 AM. - MIDNIGHT.
Av. Matamoros No. 29
Cel.: 044 998 143 2119

F-07 *El Mesón del Bucanero*

VI MC

BUCANERO FISH FILLET IN A WHITE WINE SAUCE.
7:30 AM. - 10:30 PM.
Av. Hidalgo No. 11
Tels.: 877 1222, 877 0126
Fax: 877 0210
reserve@bucaneros.com
www.bucaneros.com

E-08 *El Sombrero Gomar*

VI MC

VARIETY OF SEAFOOD DISHES.
7 AM. - 11 PM.
Av. Hidalgo esq. Madero
Tel.: 877 0627

F-05 *Faynes*

LIVE TROPICAL MUSIC.
VARIETY OF SEAFOOD DISHES.
3 PM. - MIDNIGHT.
Av. Hidalgo No. 12
Tel.: 877 0528

G-04 *Jax Bar & Grill*

VI MC

LIVE GROUP.
SUSHI.
10 AM. - 2 AM.
Av. Rueda Medina esq. López Mateos
Tel.: 877 1218
Fax: 877 1253

F-04 *Seso Loco*

SESO LOCO PIZZA, SESO LOCO SEAFOOD.
5 PM. - 1 PM.
Av. Hidalgo.
Plaza Isla Mujeres
Tel.: 877 1446

G-01 *Sunset Grill*

VI MC

LIVE CARIBBEAN MUSIC.
SEAFOOD.
8 AM. - 11 PM.
Av. Rueda Medina
Playa Norte
Tel.: 877 0785

ITALIAN

E-05 ***Angelo - Piccolo Budda-***

Seafood zuppeta, lasagna.
4 pm. - 11:30 pm.
Av. Hidalgo
Tel.: 877 1273
angeloisla@yahoo.com

Casa Rolandi

AE VI MC
Live music from Thursday to Sunday.
Tuna Tataki, rack of lamb au jus cooked in a wood burning oven.
8 am. - 10:30 pm.
Fracc. Laguna Mar
Sac Bajo Hwy.
Tels.: 877 0500, 887 0700
Fax: 877 0100
casarolandi@villarolandi.com
www.rolandi.com

E-05 ***El Olivo Pizzería***

1 pm. - 10 pm.
Av. Matamoros No. 7
Cel.: 044 998 731 0036

F-04 ***Pizza Rock***

5 pm. - 1 am.
Av. Hidalgo
Plaza Isla Mujeres
Tel.: 877 0660

E-07 ***Rolandi's Restaurante Bar Pizzería***

AE VI MC
Seafood pizza, noodles with clams and white wine. Wood burning oven.
1 pm. - 12:30 am.
Av. Hidalgo btwn. Madero & Abasolo
Tel.: 877 0430 Fax: 877 0429
pizzeriaisla@rolandi.com
www.rolandi.com

SEAFOOD

E-06 ***Amigos***

VI MC
Live music all day.
7 pm. - 11 pm.
Av. Miguel Hidalgo btwn. Matamoros & Abasolo
Tel.: 887 0624

H-08 ***Brisas del Caribe***

Live marimba music.
7 am. - 10:30 pm.
Av. Rueda Medina No. 8

D-02 ***Buho's***

VI MC
Romantic wedding services on the beach.
Buho's shrimp.
7 am. - 9:30 pm.
Av. Carlos Lazo No. 1
Tels.: 877 0301, 877 0179
Fax: 877 0213

F-02 ***La Palapa***

Tikin xik fish and in papillote.
10 am. - 6 pm.
Playa Norte
esq. Av. Miguel Hidalgo
Tel.: 877 0024

 # 8 ***La Palapa del Huinic***

VI MC
7 am. - 11 pm.
Hotel Cristal Mar
Laguna Mar Macax L.16
Tels.: 877 0398, 877 0399

G-05 ***Manolo's***

Live music all day.
Tikin xik fish.
7 am. - 11 pm.
Av. Matamoros No. 5 entre Juárez y Rueda Medina

H-08 ***Miramar***

Grilled seafood selection.
7 am. - 11 pm.
Av. Rueda Medina
Tel.: 877 0363

Playa Lancheros

Tikin xik fish.
10 am. - 6 pm.
Playa Lancheros km. 4.6
Hwy. to Garrafón
Tel.: 877 0340

H-06 ***Velázquez***

Grilled specialties.
7am. - midnight.
Av. Rueda Medina btwn. Abasolo & Matamoros
Cel.: 044 998 844 6763

MAYA

C-02 ***Zazil Ha***

AE VI MC
Seafood soup with coconut in Xtabentún, salmon with banana and chaya.
6 pm. - 11:30 pm.
Zazil Ha No. 118
Playa Norte
Tels.: 877 0058, 877 0279
Fax: 877 0446
nabalam2@prodigy.net.mx
www.zazilha.com

MEXICAN

E-05 ***Brisa Mexicana***

Mexican Breeze Shish Kebab, Yucatecan snacks.
7 pm. - 1 am.
Av. Hidalgo
esq. Matamoros
Cel.: 044 998 846 7028

F-04 ***Chiles Locos***

Shrimp with coconut, Chile Loco.
8 am. - 11 pm.
Av. Hidalgo btwn. López Mateos & M. Matamoros
Tel.: 877 1219

Discovery

AE VI MC
Buffet.
9:30 am. 5:30 pm.
Villa Pirata
Sac Bajo Hwy.
Tel./Fax: 877 0875

E-07 ***Don Chepo***

AE VI MC
Grilled steaks, grilled skirt steak.
2 pm. - 10:30 pm.
Madero btwn. Hidalgo & Vicente Guerrero
Tel.: 877 0503

F-04 ***Fredy's***

Baked shrimp, pork chops.
3 pm. - 11 pm.
Av. Hidalgo No. 1
Tel.: 877 1339

G-06 ***Galar's***

8 am. - 6 pm.
Av. Rueda Medina btwn. Abasolo & Av. Matamoros
Tels.: 877 0200, 877 0209

E-09 ***La Cazuela***

7 am. - 2:30 pm.
Av. Nicolás Bravo, next to Hotel Rocamar
Tel.: 877 0975

G-05 ***Los Portales***

Live trio every day.
12:30 pm. - 4 pm.
Av. Juárez No. 32
Tel.: 877 0094

F-04 ***Taquería Medina***

Tacos al Pastor.
5 pm. - 4 am.
Av. Hidalgo No. 64
Tel.: 877 0829

G-09 ***Mirtita***

Breakfasts.
7 am. - 3 pm.
Av. Rueda Medina
Tel.: 877 0232

Playa Tiburón

VI MC
Lobster, steaks.
Tropical Music 1 pm. - 5 pm.
10 am. - 10 pm.
Laguna Mar L. 17 y 18
Tels.: 888 0660, 888 0284

G-04 ***Pinguino's***

AE VI MC
Lobster.
7 am. - 11 pm.
Hotel Posada del Mar
Av. Rueda Medina 15-A
Tels.: 877 0770, 877 0771
Fax: 877 0266

G-07 ***Snack René & Renée***

Seafood.
8:30 am. - 6 pm.
Av. Francisco I. Madero 12
Tel.: 877 0294

Natural healthy food

F-05 ***Cafe-Cito***

Crepes & waffles.
7 am. - 2 pm., 6 pm. - 10 pm.
Av. Matamoros No. 42
esq. Juárez
Cel.: 044 998 257 8064

Tex-Mex

E-06 ***Isla Tequila***

Karaoke.
Burritos & chimichangas.
10 am. - 2 am.
Av. Hidalgo No. 19-A
Cel.: 044 998 860 3495
islatequila@yahoo.com

CHURCHES

E-09 ***Inmaculada Concepción***

7 am. - 9 pm.
Mass: 7 am. & 8 pm.
Downtown, across from the Municipal Palace

Virgen de Guadalupe

7 am. - 6 pm.
Sundays and feast days: 8 am.
Col. Salinas

MEDICAL SERVICES

Red Cross
Tel.: 877 0280

E-08 ***Health Center***
Tel.: 877 0117

D-05 ***IMSS***
Av. Carlos Lazo
Tels.: 877 0530, 877 0091

Naval Hospital
Av. Rueda Medina
Tel.: 877 0001

Drugstores

G-07 ***La Mejor***
9 am. - 10 pm.
Francisco I. Madero 18
Tel.: 877 0116

F-09 ***Farmacia Isla Mujeres***
Mon.-Sat. 9 am. - 10 pm., Sun. 9 am. - 3 pm.
Av. Juárez No. 8
Tel.: 877 0178

HOTELS

Five star ★★★★★

\# 1 ***Avalón Reef Club***

PE 146
Located on an islet.
Zazil-Ha Zona Norte
Islote El Yunque
Tels.: 999 2050
1 888 497 4325
Fax: 999 2052
reservations@avalonmail.net
www.avalonvacations.com

\# 11 ***La Casa de los Sueños***

PE 9
Garrafón Hwy.
Fracc. Mar Turquesa L. 9
Tel.: 877 0651
Fax: 877 0708
info@wayakc.com
www.wayakc.com

A-04 ***Secreto***

PC 9
Private boat, transfer to airport.
Sección Rocas L. 11
Punta Norte
Tels.: 877 1039
01 800 508 7923
Fax: 877 1048
reserv@hotelsecreto.com
www.hotelsecreto.com

\# 4 ***Villa Rolandi***

20
Breakfast & dinner included.
Fracc. Laguna Mar Makax
Sm. 7 Sac Bajo Hwy.
Tels.: 877 0500, 877 0700
Fax: 877 0100
info@villarolandi.com
www.rolandi.com

Four star ★★★★

G-01 ***Condominios Nautibeach***

PE 30
Pets allowed.
Av. Rueda Medina
esq. Playa Norte
Tel.: 877 0606
Fax: 877 0606, 877 1894
www.nautibeach.com

\# 8 ***Cristalmar Resort & Beach***

PE 38
Fracc. Paraíso Laguna Mar
Makax L. 16
Tels.: 877 0390, 877 0397
01 800 719 5609
USA 1 888 571 3239
Fax: 877 0401
cristalm@cancun.com.mx
www.cristalmarhotel.com

C-02 ***Na Balam***

PE 31
Yoga, meditation, massages.
Calle Zazil Ha No. 118
Playa Norte
Tels.: 877 0058, 877 0279
Fax: 877 0446
nabalam@nabalam.com
www.nabalam.com

\# 5 ***Villas Allure@Hinaha***

PE 17
Fracc. Paraíso Laguna Mar
Sac Bajo Hwy. L. 55-56
Tel./Fax: 877 0615
www.hinaha.com

HOTEL VILLA ROLANDI GOURMET & BEACH CLUB

An enchanting and intimate beachfront hideaway offering guests 20 deluxe suites. Built in Mexican-Mediterranean style, the hotel blends perfectly in to the magnificent setting of pearly white beaches. Casa Rolandi restaurant is famous for its gourmet tradition, sterling service and the delicious Swiss and Northern Italian dishes it serves.

Fracc. Laguna Mar Makax, Sm. 7
Isla Mujeres, Q. Roo, Mexico;

Tel.: (998) 877 0700,
Fax: (998) 877 0100

info@villarolandi.com
www.rolandi.com

THREE STAR ★★★

E-07 *Belmar*
12
Hidalgo No. 110
btwn. Madero & Abasolo
Tel.: 877 0430 Fax: 877 0429
hotel.belmar@caribe.net.mx

D-02 *Cabañas María del Mar*
PE 73
Av. Carlos Lazo No. 1
Tels.: 877 0179, 877 0213
01 800 223 5695
Fax: 877 0156
www.cabanasdelmar.com

E-07 *Francis Arlene*
23
Guerrero No. 7
Tels.: 877 0310, 877 0861
hfrancis@prodigy.net.mx

 # 14 *Garrafón de Castilla*
PE PC 12
Punta Sur Hwy. km 6
Tels.: 877 0107, 877 0508
Fax: 877 0508

D-07 *Mar Azul Beach & Town Resort*
PA PE 90
Madero No. 1 & 2
Tels.: 877 0120, 887 1122
gpomarazul@prodigy.net.mx

 # 12 *María Elena*
PE 28
Garrafón Hwy. km 5.5
Tel./Fax: 888 0471

 # 9 *Maria's Kankin*
PE 13
Garrafón Hwy. km 4
Tels.: 877 0015, 877 0733
Fax: 877 0395
maria@sibcom.com

 # 6 *Marina Isla Mujeres*
12
Fracc. Laguna Mar Makax
L. 52-54, Sac bajo Hwy.
Tel./Fax: 877 0594
01 800 718 5945
hotelmarinaim@prodigy.net.mx

C-03 *Playa La Media Luna*
PC 18
Sección Rocas L. 9-10
Punta Norte Sm. 1
Tels.: 877 0759
01 800 223 5695
Fax: 877 1124
reserv@playamedialuna.com
www.playamedialuna.com

E-09 *Rocamar*
25
Nicolás Bravo
esq. Guerrero
Tel./Fax: 877 0101

F-06 *Suites Los Arcos*
PA 12
Av. Hidalgo No. 58 Centro
Tels.: 877 1343, 877 1344
Fax: 877 0236
suiteslosarcos@hotmail.com
www.suiteslosarcos.com

TWO STAR ★★

G-06 *Berny*
PE 32
Av. Juárez con Abasolo
Tels.: 877 0132, 884 3672

B-02 *Casa Maya Zazil Ha*
PE 20
CABINS AND BUNGALOWS.
Zazil Ha No. 129 Mz. 30
esq. Playa Norte
Tels.: 877 0045, 877 1024
Fax: 877 0045
casamayalodge@hotmail.com
www.kasamaya.com.mx

G-09 *D'Gomar*
17
Av. Rueda Medina No. 150
Tel.: 877 0541
gomar1@prodigy.net.mx

E-05 *El Caracol*
18
Matamoros No. 5
Tel.: 877 0150

G-04 *Posada del Mar*
PE PA PC 62
Av. Rueda Medina 15-A
Tels.: 877 0044, 877 0770
Fax: 877 0401
hotel@posadadelmar.com

F-07 *El Marcianito*
13
Av. Abasolo No. 10
Tels.: 877 0111, 877 0327

F-07 *El Mesón del Bucanero*
PA 18
Av. Hidalgo No. 11
Tels.: 877 1222, 877 0126
01 800 712 3510
USA 1 888 646 8431
Fax: 877 0210
reserve@bucaneros.com
www.bucaneros.com

G-04 *Posada San Jorge*
12
Av. Juárez; Tel.: 877 0155

 # 7 *Su Casa de la Isla*
PE 9
Hwy. Sac Bajo L. 44
Tel.: 877 0180

G-06 *Vistalmar*
PE 36
Av. Rueda Medina
Tel.: 877 0209

E-04 *Xul-Há*
PE 19
Av. Hidalgo Norte No. 6
Tel.: 877 0075

ONE STAR ★

E-07 *Carmelina*
29
Guerrero No. 4
Tel.: 877 0006

E-07 *Isleño*
PE 20
Francisco I. Madero No. 8
Tel.: 877 0302

G-07 *Maria José*
PE 14
Francisco I. Madero
Tel.: 877 0245

G-10 *Mirtita*
PE 5
Av. Ignacio Allende
con Av. Juárez
Tel.: 877 0157 Fax: 877 0048

G-07 *Osorio*
PE 32
Francisco I. Madero
Tel.: 877 0294

G-01 *Casa Chez Magali*
PE 6
Av. Rueda Medina
Playa Norte No. 8
Tel.: 877 0259
Fax: 877 0487
mymar@prodigy.net.mx

 # 13 *Villas Punta Sur*
PE 6
Hwy. to Garrafón km 6
Tel.: 877 0572
Fax: 877 0371
vps@villaspuntasur.com
www.villaspuntasur.com

 # 2 *Villas Rotundo*
PE 5
Fracc. Laguna Mar Makax
Nte. L. 73 y 75
Hwy. Sac Bajo
Tel.: 877 0357

F-07 *Rocateliz*
PE 5
Av. Hidalgo No. 93
Tel.: 877 0407

OTHERS

G-07 *Casa España*
PE
KITCHENETTE, JACUZZI.
Francico I. Madero btwn.
Rueda Medina & Av. Juárez
josericha@hotmail.com

E-07 *Caribe Maya*
PE 25
Francico I. Madero No. 9
Tel.: 877 0684

G-05 *Cielito Lindo*
APARTMENT WITH KITCHENETTE.
ADULTS ONLY.
PE 2
Av. Rueda Medina No. 78-B
Tel.: 877 0585
joy@cancun.com.mx

G-05 *Hostel Posada del Mar*
PE 7
Av. Juárez btwn. Matamoros
& López Mateos
Tels.: 877 0212, 877 0044

Fax: 877 0266
hotel@posadadelmar.com
www.posadadelmar.com

F-05 *María Leticia*
PE 10
APARTMENTS.
Av. Juárez No. 28
Tel.: 877 0832 Fax: 887 0394

E-04 *Las Palmas*
PE 15
Guerrero No. 20
Playa Norte
Tel.: 877 0965

F-07 *Posada Isla Mujeres*
PE 15
Av. Juárez Norte Sm. 1
Mz. 14 L. 20
Tel.: 877 0122

F-07 *Posada Edelmar*
PE PA PC 5
KITCHENETTE.
Av. Hidalgo No. 12-A
Tel./Fax: 877 0488

C-06 *Poc Na Hostel*
PC 19
DISCOUNT WITH INTERNATIONAL STUDENT CARD.
Matamoros No. 15
Tel./Fax: 877 0090
www.pocna.com

G-05 *Posada Suemy*
PE 15
Matamoros No. 12
Tel.: 877 0122

E-05 *Urban Hostel*
PE 10
Matamoros esq. Guerrero
Tels.: 879 9342, 877 1560
urbanhostel@yahoo.com

SPECIAL CATEGORY

 # 10 *Playa Gaviota*
PE 10
Hwy. to Garrafón km 4.5
Tel./Fax: 877 0216
www.playagaviotasuites.com

 # 3 *Villa Vera Puerto Isla Mujeres*
PE 24
Laguna Makax
Tels.: 877 0330, 877 0413
Fax: 877 0093
isilva@clubregina.com

HOLBOX

The Mexican Caribbean's northernmost island, Holbox is a quiet retreat on the Gulf coast, popular with birdwatchers, fishermen and travelers looking for the simple pleasures in life. The sandy streets in this picturesque village converge on a white beach lined with rustic bungalows, attractive small hotels and restaurants serving delicious seafood.

HANDICRAFTS

A-13 ***Doña Doris***
Villas Delfines

C-06 ***Doña Leila***
Benito Juárez

B-09 ***La Bodeguita***
Calle Palomino

A-06 ***La Bambina***
Calle Morelos

D-08 ***Gisela***
Calle Palomino

B-04 ***Lalo. Com***
Av. Abasolo No. 139

MONEY EXCHANGE
C-09 ***Dinero Rápido***

DRUGSTORE
D-06 ***Pepe's***

INTERNET & LONG DISTANCE
B-07 ***El Parque***

MINI SUPER
D-06 ***Besa***

TOURIST ASSISTANCE

I-08 ***Port Office***
Tel.: 875 2099

C-08 ***Post & Telegraph Office***
Tel.: 875 2053

F-07 ***Health Center***
Tel.: 875 2164

TRANSPORT

MOPED, BIKE AND GOLF CART RENTALS.
(CALLE BENITO JUÁREZ).

C-05 ***Glendy***	875 2093
B-06 ***Moguel***	875 2028
D-06 ***Monkey's***	875 2029
B-09 ***Puesta del Sol***	875 2143
D-06 ***Willy's***	875 2008

TRANSPORT TO THE ISLAND

Transporte Marítimo 9 Hermanos
Tels. 875 2010, 875 2067

Departures from Holbox	***Departures from Chiquilá***
5:00 AM.	6:00 AM.
7:00 AM.	8:00 AM.
10:30 AM.	11:30 AM.
11:00 AM.	12:00 PM.
1:00 PM.	2:00 PM.
3:00 PM.	4:00 PM.
4:00 PM.	5:00 PM.
6:00 PM.	7:00 PM.

REGULAR DEPARTURES DURING VACATION PERIODS.

TOURS AND FISHING

IT IS POSSIBLE TO ARRANGE TOURS TO SURROUNDING AREAS AT MOST HOTELS.

G-07 ***Cooperativa Punta Mosquito***
Tel.: 875 2126

A-13 ***Delfines***
Tel.: 875 2196

C-09 ***Liliyelén***
Tel.: 875 2189

E-06 ***Monkey's Group***
Tel.: 875 2029
www.holboxmonkeys.com

D-06 ***Willy's Tours***
Tel.: 875 2008

A-06 ***Faro Viejo***
SPANISH, ENGLISH, FRENCH. ECOLOGICAL TOURS IN SMALL GROUPS, DOCK WITH WATER AND ELECTRICAL HOOKUPS.
Hotel Faro Viejo
Tel.: 875 2217
Fax: 875 2186
www.faroviejoholbox.com.mx

B-06 ***Moguel***
Tel.: 875 2028

A-12 ***Posada Mawimbi***
UNDERWATER SAFARI.
Tel.: 875 2003

A-14 ***Villas Flamingo***
Tel.: 875 2167

A-12 ***Xaloc***
Tel.: 875 2160

HORSE BACK RIDING

A-01 ***Los Potrillos***
Tel.: 875 2183

RESTAURANTS

INTERNATIONAL

D-06 ***Colibrí***
COLIBRÍ SPECIALS.
7:30 AM. - 3 PM., 6 - 11 PM.
Av. Benito Juárez btwn. Avs. Porfirio Díaz & M. Escobedo
Tel.: 875 0162

C-09 ***Edelyn***
LOBSTER PIZZA.
9 AM. - 11:50 PM.
Av. Porfirio Díaz esq. Palomino
Tels.: 875 2024, 875 2331

A-13 ***El Canguay***
VI MC AE
GRILLED SURF AND TURF SELECTION, PIBIL-STYLE CHICKEN.
7 AM. - 10 PM.
Villas Delfines
Tels.: 875 2196, 875 2197
www.holbox.com

A-06 ***Faro Viejo***
VI MC
TROPICAL DRINKS, SEAFOOD ZARZUELA, FARO VIEJO-STYLE LOBSTER.
8 AM. - 10 PM.
Hotel Faro Viejo
Tel.: 875 2217 Fax: 875 2186
www.faroviejoholbox.com.mx

A-14 ***Flamingos***
VI MC
FISH & SEAFOOD.
1 PM. - 3 PM., 7 PM. - 9:30 PM.
Villa Flamingos
Tel.: 875 2167
Fax: (998) 887 9605
www.villaflamingos.com

A-12 ***Maja'Che***
AE VI MC
FISH & SEAFOOD.
NOON - 10 PM.
Xaloc Resort
Tels.: 875 2160, 875 2154
www.holbox-xalocresort.com

D-08 ***Pelícano's***
SURF AND TURF (LOBSTER & FILET MIGNON), GRILLED SEAFOOD.
10 AM. - 11 PM.
Palomino esq. Porfirio Díaz
Tel.: 875 2205

B-06 *Viva Zapata*

Seafood & steak.
6 pm. - 1 am.
Calle Igualdad btwn.
Avs. Juárez & Morelos
Tel.: 875 2330

Italian

C-06 *La Cueva del Pirata*

Fish & seafood.
11 am. - 9 pm.
Benito Juárez,
across from the park
Tel.: 875 2183

Seafood

A-06 *Buena Vista*

Grilled seafood.
Posada Playa Bonita
Tel.: 875 2102

A-07 *Villamar*
Benito Juárez

D-09 *Zarabanda*
AE VI MC
Saraband Shish Kebab, stuffed squid.
8:30 am. - 9 pm.
Palomino No. 248
esq. Escobedo
Tel.: 875 2094

HOTELS

Four star ★★★★

A-06 *Faro Viejo*
PA PE 14
Benito Juárez & beach
Tel.: 875 2217 Fax: 875 2186
faroviejo@prodigy.net.mx
www.faroviejoholbox.com.mx

A-13 *Villas Delfines*
PA PE PC 20
Calle Igualdad across from
the High School, Playa Norte
Tel.: 875 2196 Fax: 875 2197
Cancún: 884 8606
Cel.: 044 998 874 4014
delfines@holbox.com
www.holbox.com

A-12 *Villas Paraíso del Mar*
PE 36
Boutique hotel.
Calle Igualdad across from
the High School, Playa Norte
Tel.: 875 2062 Fax: 875 2077
dirparaiso@hmhotels.net
www.paraisodelmar.com

Three star ★★★

A-11 *Casa Las Tortugas*
PE PC 11
Cabins, kitesurf, water sport center.
Igualdad esq. Justo Sierra
Tel./Fax: 0875 2129
info@holboxcasalastortugas.com
www.holboxcasalastortugas.com

A-13 *Esmeralda*
PE 28
Information and reservations in Cancun:
Tel.: (998) 847 5620
Fax: (998) 882 7187
esmeralda@esmeralda-hotel.com
www.esmeralda-hotel.com

A-11 *Holbox Paraíso*
PA PE 8
Playa Norte km 2
Tel.: 875 2171
holboxparaiso@hotmail.com

A-14 *Villa Flamingos*
PA PE 10
Plutarco Elías Calles
Tel.: 875 2167
Offices in Cancun:
Tel./Fax: (998) 887 9605
villaflamingos@hotmail.com
www.villaflamingos.com

A-12 *Xaloc Resort*
PA PE PC 18
Chacchí esq. Playa Norte
Tels.: 875 2160, 875 2154
xalocresort@prodigy.net.mx
www.holbox-xalocresort.com

Others

A-05 *La Palapa*
PE 6
Morelos No. 231
Tel./Fax: 875 2121
www.hotellapalapa.com

A-08 *Mi Capricho*
PA 9
Villas. Adults only.
Playa Norte btwn. Avs.
Benito Juárez & Palomino
Cel.: (998) 845 0171
(998) 845 1108
micaprichoholbox@yahoo.com
www.micapricho-holbox.com

C-09 *Posada Amapola*
PE 11
Palomino, across from the park
Tels.: 875 2020, 875 2076
Fax: 875 2075

A-05 *Posada Careyes*
PE 5
Av. Pedro Joaquín
Coldwell esq. Abasolo
Tel.: 875 2029

B-05 *Posada D'Ingrid*
PE 10
Morelos esq. Av. Pedro
Joaquín Coldwell
Tel.: 875 2070

C-06 *Posada Los Arcos*
PE 20
Av. Benito Juárez btwn.
Avs. Igualdad & Porfirio D.
Cel.: (01 984) 875 2043
www.holboxlosarcos.com

A-12 *Posada Mawimbi*
PE 11
Calle Igualdad across from
the High School, Playa Norte
Tels.: 875 2003, 8752348
Fax.: 875 2348
www.mawimbi.com.mx

A-06 *Posada Playa Bonita*
PE 10
Six cabins.
Av. Pedro Joaquín Coldwell
esq. Benito Juárez
Tel.: 875 2102

A-01 *Puerto Holbox*
PE 4
Av. Pedro Joaquín Coldwell
in front of airstrip
Tel.: 873 0804 Fax: 873 0501
www.holboxisland.com

A-01 *Villas Chimay*
PE 7
Ecological concept.
Playa Noroeste
Tel./Fax: 875 2220
chimay@holbox.info
www.holbox.com

A-03 *Villa Los Mapaches*
PE 9
Av. Pedro Joaquín Coldwell
Tel./Fax: 875 2090
losmapaches@prodigy.net.mx
www.losmapaches.com

COZUMEL

Dive mecca and cruise ship destination Cozumel has much to offer. Deluxe and five-star beachfront hotels stretch north and south of San Miguel, the island capital, and there are smaller inns in town. Restaurants and shops line the streets. Diving is the number one activity on Cozumel and dive centers cater to every skill level and interest. They also work with the Reef Park authorities to conserve the coral.

AIRLINES

Domestic and international flights

Aerocozumel
International Airport
Tel./Fax: 872 3456

B-18 ***Aerolamsa***
30 Av. Sur No. 509
Av. Pedro Joaquín Coldwell
Tels.: 872 1781, 872 2252
Fax: 872 4387
cozumel@aeroferinco.com

Continental Airlines
International Airport
Tel./Fax: 872 0487
01 800 900 5000

Mexicana
International Airport
Tels.: 872 0133
01 800 502 2000
Fax: 872 0405

ASSOCIATIONS

F-09 ***Hotel & Motel Association***
2 Norte 299-C
btwn. 10 & 15 Av.
Tels.: 872 3132, 872 5098
Fax: 872 2809
ahoteles@cozunet.com
www.islacozumel.com.mx

Dive Operator Association (ANOAAT)
Calle 21 Sur esq. 20 Av.
Tel./Fax: 872 0640
anoaat@prodigy.net.mx

G-20 ***Restaurant Association*** (CANIRAC)
11 Av. Sur No. 100
Edificio El Forum
Tels.: 872 3490, 872 7850
Fax: 872 3490
caniraccozumel@prodigy.net.mx

D-22 ***Chamber of Commerce***
20 Av. Sur No. 916
btwn. Calles 13 & 15
Tels.: 872 3391, 872 5014
Fax: 872 0583
canacocz@prodigy.net.mx

G-10 ***Tourist Promotion Fund***
2 Norte 299-C
btwn. 10 & 15 Av.
Tel.: 872 7585 Fax: 872 7636
www.islacozumel.com.mx

CONSULATES

A-04 ***United States***
35 Norte No. 750
btwn. 12 Bis & 14
Tel.: 872 4574

SHOPPING CENTERS

Plaza Chedraui
Av. Rafael Melgar
In front of Cozumel Palace
Tel.: 872 5406

G-11 ***Plaza del Sol***
5a Av. Sur No. 51

I-14 ***Plaza Orbi***
Rafael Melgar No. 27
Tel.: 872 2520

J-17 ***Plaza Punta Langosta***
Rafael Melgar No. 599
btwn. Calles 7 & 11
Tels.: 869 1360, 869 1127

Jewelry

Diamond International
Rafael Melgar No. 149-C, No. 99-C, 161 & Rafael Melgar btwn. Calles 8 & 6
Tels.: 872 4237, 872 6169
872 1154, 872 7589
vcaczm@prodigy.mx

Emerald Mines
Rafael E. Melgar No. 54
Tel.: 872 3236

Maraf
Rafael E. Melgar No. 20
Tel.: 869 0396
www.maraf.com

Pama
Rafael E. Melgar No. 9
Tel.: 872 0090
luisa@pamacozumel.com

Plaza del Sol Palancar
Rafael E. Melgar No. 15
btwn. Calles 2 & 4 Norte
Tel.: 872 1468

Rachat & Romero
Rafael E. Melgar No. 101
Tel.: 872 0224

Silver Center
Rafael E. Melgar No. 101-A
btwn. Calles 2 & 4 Norte
Tel.: 872 0316

Tanzanite Internacional
Rafael E. Melgar No. 261
btwn. Calles 8 & 6
Tel.: 872 3696

CHURCHES

Catholic

G-11 ***San Miguel***
Av. Juárez esq. Av. 10
Tel.: 872 1087

E-22 ***Corpus Cristi***
Av. 20 btwn. Calles 15 & 17
Tel.: 872 1053

PRESBYTERIAN

A-06 *Eben Ezer*
30 Av. esq. Calle 10 Norte
Tel.: 872 3400

Iglesia de Jesucristo de Todos los Santos
Calle 4 esq. Av. 40 Norte
Tel.: 872 4167

BANKS

H-12 *Banamex*
WITH ATM MACHINES AT BANK BRANCHES, AT THE TOURIST DOCK AND AT THE AIRPORT.
9 AM. - 4 PM.
5a. Av. Sur No. 8 btwn.
1a Av. & Av. Rosado Salas
Tels.: 872 3411, 872 0814
01 800 111 3030
www.banamex.com.mx

G-11 *BBV Bancomer*
8:30 AM. - 4 PM.
5a Av. Sur No. 51
Plaza del Sol
Tels.: 872 1550, 872 0550
01 800 112 1111
Fax: 872 2949
www.bancomer.com.mx

B-11 *Banorte Bancrecer*
• Av. Joaquín Coldwell 2
Tels.: 872 4906, 872 4727
• 5a Av. No. 9
btwn. Juárez & 2 Norte
Tels.: 872 0718, 872 6768
www.banorte.com

G-12 *HSBC*
ATM MACHINES AT CARLOS'N CHARLIE'S, CITY HALL & SAN FRANCISCO DE ASÍS.
Calle 1a Sur esq. 5a Av.
Tels.: 872 0142, 872 3080
01 800 712 4825
Fax: 872 0142
www.hsbc.com.mx

F-14 *Santander Serfín*
10a Av. No. 198
esq. Calle 3a Sur
Tels.: 872 2853, 872 0807
01 800 704 0400
Fax: 872 2853
www.santander.com.mx

Scotiabank Inverlat
ATM MACHINES AT AV. JUÁREZ.

TRAVEL AGENCIES

Fantasy Travel Experts
TOURS IN VANS OR BUSES.
20 Av. Sur 1200 close to 19 Av. Col. Gonzalo Guerrero
Tels.: 872 6138, 872 7361
Fax: 872 4081
fantasytravel@prodigy.net.mx

B-17 *Ferinco Travel & Tours*
SPANISH, ENGLISH, FRENCH.
Av. Pedro Joaquín Coldwell
No. 509 esq. 5a Sur
Tels.: 872 1781, 872 2252
Fax: 872 4387
cozumel@ferinco.com
www.travel.ferinco.com

B-20 *Fiesta Holidays*
11 Sur No. 598 close to 30 Av. Col. Gonzalo Guerrero
Tel.: 872 0433 Fax: 872 1044
morgan@fiestaholidays.com.mx
www.fiestaholidays.com.mx

G-09 *Intermar Cozumel*
SPANISH, ENGLISH.
Calle 2 Norte No. 101-B
Tels.: 872 1535, 872 1098
Fax: 872 0895
cozumel@travel2mexico.com
www.travel2mexico.com

H-22 *Lomas Travel*
SPANISH, ENGLISH.
5a Av. No. 961
btwn. Calles 13 & 15 Sur
Tel.: 872 3609 Fax: 872 3710
cozumel@lomas-travel.com
www.lomas-travel.com

F-09 *Olympus Tours*
SPANISH, ENGLISH.
4 Norte No. 272-B
btwn. 10 & 15 Av.
Tel.: 872 2454 Fax: 872 2478
cozumel@olympus-tours.com
www.olympus-tours.com

G-12 *Royale Tours*
FOUR-WHEEL DRIVE TOURS THROUGH THE JUNGLE.
SPANISH, ENGLISH.
Av. 1a Sur 164-218
Tel./Fax: 872 2497
cozumel@royaletours.com.mx
www.royaletours.com.mx

H-09 *Turismo Aviomar*
ENGLISH, FRENCH, SPANISH.
5a Av. Norte No. 8-A
btwn. Calles 2 & 4
Tels.: 872 5445, 872 4622
Fax: 872 5144
aviomarviajes@prodigy.net.mx
www.aviomar.com.mx

G-20 *Viajes Liberación*
ENGLISH, SPANISH, PORTUGUESE, ITALIAN.
Calle 11, Edificio Portales
Tels.: 872 6501
01 800 800 5072
Fax: 872 6401
ventasczm@liberacion.com
www.viajesliberacion.com

WATER SPORTS

MOST MARINAS AND DIVE SHOPS PROVIDE SERVICE IN ENGLISH AND SPANISH ONLY, UNLESS OTHERWISE INDICATED.

I-15 *Aldora Divers*
5 Sur No. 37
Tel.: 872 3397 Fax: 872 4048
www.aldoradivers.com

I-15 *Aqua Safari*
Rafael Melgar No. 427
btwn. 5 & 7 Sur
Tel.: 872 0101 Fax: 872 0661
dive@aquasafari.com
www.aquasafari.com

Aquatic Sports
GERMAN.
21 Sur esq. 20
Tel./Fax: 872 0640
scubaco@scubacozumel.com
www.scubacozumel.com

Aquaworld
SEVERAL LANGUAGES.
"SEA WALKER" TOUR.
Costera Sur Hwy. km 3.7
Playa Paraíso
Tels.: 872 1210, 872 0700
www.aquaworld.com

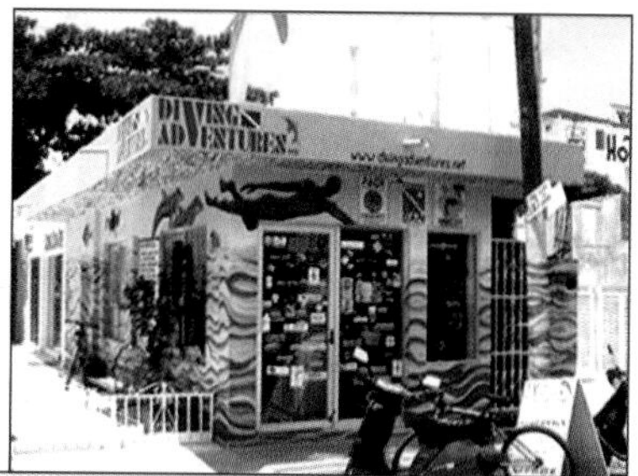

G-13 ***Black Shark***

SPANISH, ENGLISH, MAYA.
5a Av. Sur No. 231 btwn. Av. Rosado Salas & 3 Sur
Tel./Fax: 872 5657
www.blackshark.net
info@blackshark.net

H-14 ***Blue Bubble Divers***

3 Sur No. 33 btwn. Rafae Melgar & 5a Av.
Tel./Fax: 872 1865
USA 1 866 405 5749
www.bluebubbledivers.com

Blue Note

ENGLISH, FRENCH, ITALIAN, GERMAN, PORTUGUESE, JAPANESE.
2 Norte btwn. Av. 40 & 45
Tel.: 872 0312
cozumel@bluenotescuba.com
www.bluenotescuba.com

H-15 ***Buceo Médico***

GERMAN.
DECOMPRESSION CHAMBER.
5 Sur No. 21-B btwn. Rafael Melgar & 5a Av. Sur
Tels.: 872 2387, 872 1430
Fax: 872 1848

F-12 ***Caballito del Caribe***

GERMAN, FRENCH.
SUNSET BOAT TOUR.
10 Av. Sur No. 115, btwn. 1a & Av. Rosado Salas
Tel.: 869 1034 Fax: 872 1449
caballito@cozumel.com.mex
www.seahorsecozumel.com

J-19 ***Caribbean Divers***

FRENCH.
Calle 3 Sur esq. 5a Av.
Tel.: 872 1080 Fax: 872 1426
cdivers@prodigy.net.mx
www.caribbbeandiverscozumel.com

J-20 ***Cozumel Equalizer***

FRENCH, GERMAN. DINNERS ABOARD A SPANISH GALLEON.
Rafael Melgar esq. 11 Av.
Tel.: 872 3511 Fax: 872 6751
equalizer@prodigy.net.mx
www.cozumelequalizer.com

F-13 ***Deep Blue***

10 Av. Sur & Av. Rosado Salas No. 200
Tel./Fax: 872 5653
www.deepbluecozumel.com

Del Mar Aquatics

DEPARTURES FROM 8 AM. - 7 PM.
Costera Sur Hwy. km 4
Tel./Fax: 872 5949
sales02@delmaraquatics.net
www.delmaraquatics.net

G-13 ***Dive Cozumel***

PORTUGUESE, ITALIAN.
TECHNICAL DIVING, "SUNSET" BOAT TOUR.
Av. Rosado Salas No. 85
Tel.: 872 4567 Fax: 872 7558
USA 1 866 319 2649
www.divecozumel.net

Dive House

JAPANESE.
Fiesta Americana Cozumel Dive Resort
Tel.: 872 1953 Fax: 872 3068
dive@divehouse.com
www.divehouse.com

Dive Palancar

SCUBA DIVING DEPARTURES: 8:30 AM. - 3 PM., NIGHT DIVES: 6 PM.
San Francisco Palancar Hwy. km 16.5
Tel.: 872 9770 Fax: 872 5094
divepal@prodigy.net.mx
www.divepalancarcozumel.com

I-15 ***Diving Adventures***

ITALIAN.
Calle 5 No. 22
Tels.: 872 3009, 872 2519
MEX 01 800 849 7150
USA 1 888 338 0388
dive@divingadventures.net
www.divingadventures.net

Dressel Divers

FRENCH, ITALIAN, PORTUGUESE, DUTCH, GERMAN.
Costera Sur Hwy. km 17.8
Tel.: 872 9900
sales1@dresseldivers.com
www.dresseldivers.com

F-11 ***Eco Divers***

10a Av. close to 1a Sur
Tel./Fax: 872 5628
ecodivers@cozumel-diving.net

Emerald Dolphin

19 Sur No. 1134
Tel./Fax: 872 3270
eddscozumel@prodigy.net.mx
www.cozumel-diving.net/edds

Fury Catamarans Cozumel

SUR HWY. km 3.5
Tel.: 872 0333 Fax: 872 7478
cozumelfury@webtelmex.net.mx
www.furycat.com

E-20 ***Island Adventurs***

11 Av. No. 349
btwn. 15 & 20
Tel.: 872 5858 Fax: 872 5848
islandadventurs@usa.net

Kuzamil Snorkeling Center

SUNSET BOAT TOUR.
50 Av. Sur Bis No. 565
Col. Adolfo López Mateos
Tels.: 872 0539, 872 4637
sales@kuzamil.com
www.kuzamil.com

La Tortuga

Calle 17 esq. 5a Av.
Tel.: 872 5381
Cel.: 044 987 100 2393
scubatortuga@yahoo.com

Manta Sports

65 Av. No. 216 btwn. 4 & 6
Tel.: 872 6157 Fax: 872 6156
info@mantasports.com
www.mantasports.com

Marina Playa Sol

PARASAILING.
Costera Sur km. 15
Club Playa Sol
Tel.: 872 9042 Fax: 872 5121

Ocean Tours

PARASAILING.
Hotel Isleño
& Hotel Cozumeleño
Tel.: 872 0050 Fax: 872 1379
ocean@dicoz.com

Pepe Scuba

ITALIAN.
Costera Norte Hwy. km 2.5
Hotel Coral Princess Club
Tel.: 872 6293
Fax: 872 2800
pepe@cozumel.net
www.cozumel-diving.net/pepe

Sand Dollar Sports

JAPANESE.
PRIVATE PARTIES.
65 Av. No. 216-B
Col. 10 de Abril
Tel.: 872 6157
USA 1 888 737 6399
info@sanddollarsports.com
www.sanddollarsports.com

Scuba Cozumel

Av. Rafael Melgar
Prol. 1251
Tels.: 872 1133
01 800 847 5708
Fax: 872 1977
www.scubaclubcozumel.com

Scuba Du

Hwy. to Chankanaab km 6.5
Hotel Presidente
Tels.: 872 9505, 872 9506
Fax: 872 4130
scubadu@cozumel.net
www.scubadu.com

Scuba Shack

Hwy. to Chankanaab km 3.5
Tel./Fax: 872 4240
scubas@cozunet.com

G-11 ***Scuba Staff Divers***

JAPANESE, PORTUGUESE.
DEPARTURES: 8:30 AM. & 2 PM.
10 Av. No. 99
btwn. 1a Sur & Juárez
Tels.: 876 1210
01 800 101 2650
Fax: 872 7734
diverczm@prodigy.net.mx
www.cozumel-mx.com

F-11 ***Sea Scuba***

Av. Juárez btwn. Avs. 10 & 15
Tel.: 872 5744 Fax: 872 3778
seascuba@cozumel.com.mx

H-09 ***Snorkel Center***

5a Av. Norte No. 8
btwn. Calles 2 & 4
Tels.: 872 6364, 869 0538
Fax: 872 6364
snorkcen@prodigy.net.mx

Wild Cat Divers

Costera Hwy. km 6.5
Tel.: 872 1028
wildcatcozumel@hotmail.com

G-13 ***Yucab Reef***
Av. Rosado Salas 85 Altos
Tel.: 872 4110

E-12 ***Yucatech Expedition***

FRENCH.
15 Av. Sur No. 144 btwn.
1a Av. & Rosado Salas
Tel.: 872 5659 Fax: 872 1417
yucatech@prodigy.net.mx

SUBMARINE

Atlantis Submarine
MON. - SAT. 10, 11 AM., 12, 1 & 2 PM.
COST: $76 USD ADULT, $39 USD CHILDREN FROM 3 - 11 YEARS.
Hwy. to Chankanaab km 4
Southern Hotel Zone
Tel./Fax: 872 5671
01 800 715 0804
cozumel@atlantisadventures.net
www.atlantisadventures.net

FERRIES

Car Ferries Cozumel-Puerto Morelos
FERRY SERVICE FOR CARS AND PASSENGERS.

- FROM COZUMEL TO PUERTO MORELOS: 9 & 10:30 AM.
- FROM PUERTO MORELOS TO COZUMEL 4 & 8 AM.
- FROM COZUMEL TO PUNTA VENADO 7, 11 AM. & 4 PM.
- FROM PUNTA VENADO TO COZUMEL 9AM., 1 PM. & 6 PM.

Hwy. to Chankanaab km. 4.5
Tels.: 872 0916, 857 1326
Fax: 872 0950

Cruceros Marítimos del Caribe

- FROM COZUMEL TO PLAYA DEL CARMEN: 5, 7, 8, 9, 10 AM., 12, 2, 4, 5, 6, 8 & 10 PM.
- FROM PLAYA DEL CARMEN TO COZUMEL: 6, 8, 9, 10, 11 AM., 1, 3, 5, 6, 7, 9 & 11 PM.

ROUND TRIP: $146 PESOS,
ONE WAY: $80 PESOS.
6 Norte No. 14
Tels.: 872 1508, 872 1588
www.crucerosmaritimos.com.mx

TAXIS

Taxi Stand
6 AM. - 10 PM
Rosado Salas
Col. López Mateos
Tels.: 872 0041, 872 5770

CAR RENTALS

Aguilar	872 1809
Aeroferinco	872 1781
Águila	872 0729
Álamo	872 2100
Autorent	872 3532
Avis	872 0099
Budget	872 0903
Canto	872 2233
Chac	872 3325
Cozumel	872 3488
Discovery	869 0516
Dollar	869 4446
El Dorado	872 2383
España	872 5657
Executive	872 1308
Fiesta	872 4333
Hertz	872 3955
Isis	872 3367
Island Adventures	872 5848
Isleña	872 0788
JB Car Rental	872 7580
JE de Cozumel	872 4959
Less Pay	872 4744
Localiza	872 2111
Margon	872 1318
Marlin	872 1586
Masha	872 1096
National	872 3263
Olé	872 5858
Pelícanos (MOPEDS)	872 6579
Rent a Matic	872 4101
Tommy's (MOPEDS)	872 2111
Tucán (MOPEDS)	872 4525
2000	872 2679

EMERGENCIES

Police	872 0409
Fire Brigade	872 0800
Red Cross	872 1058
Navy Office	872 1229
Immigration	872 0071
Customs	872 2005
Emergencies	060

MEDICAL SERVICES

I-15 *Mexican Dive Medical Service*
Calle 5 Sur No. 21 btwn.
Rafael Melgar & 5a Av.
Tel.: 872 1430

Centro de Salud
Calle 11 btwn. Avs. 15 & 20
Tel.: 872 5182

CMC
Calle 1 Sur esq. Av. 50
Tel.: 872 5370

Centro Médico de Cozumel
Av. 1a Sur btwn. 50 & 50
bis. No. 101
Tels.: 872 5370, 872 5664
Fax: 872 5370

F-08 *Clínica Villanueva*
Av. 10 btwn. Calles 4
& 6 Norte
Tel.: 872 0395

Consultorio Médico de Análisis
Calle 3 Sur No. 296
btwn. Avs. 10 & 15
Tel.: 872 1467

Res Cross
Av. 20 esq. Adolfo
Rosado Salas
Tel.: 872 1058

D-20 *Hospital General*
11 Av. Sur & Calle 20
Tel.: 872 0525

A-20 *IMSS*
24 HOUR SERVICE.
11 Sur Av. No. 60
Col. Independencia
Tels.: 872 0222, 872 0639
www.imss.gob.mx

ISSSTE
60 Av. con 1a Sur
Tel.: 872 0359

Médica General y Partos
Av. 10 Sur No. 612
Tel.: 872 4068

G-07 *Médica San Miguel*
6 Nte. No. 132 esq. Calle 5
Tels.: 872 0103, 872 5850
Fax: 872 6155

DRUGSTORES

Dori
5a Av. esq. Calle 7 Sur
Tel.: 872 5519

El Kiosco
5a Av. esq. Calle 1 Sur
Tel.: 872 5519

La Placita
Av. Juárez btwn. Avs. 5 & 10
Tel.: 872 5132

Los Colores de Dori
Calle 2 Norte btwn.
Av. Rafael Melgar & 5a Av.
Tel.: 872 2238

París
Calle 6 Norte btwn. Avs. 5 & 10
Tel.: 872 3552

Portal del Parque
5a Av. Sur btwn. Av. Juárez
& Calle 1 Sur
Tel.: 869 2119

Portales
- Calle 11 btwn. Av. Rafael Melgar & 5a Av.
Tel.: 872 0936
- Av. 10 No. 101 esq. Av. Juárez
Tel.: 872 1048

Yza
5a Av. No. 50 btwn.
Av. Juárez & Calle 2 norte

Joaquín
5a Av. esq. Plaza del Sol
Tel.: 872 0195

BARS

J-20 *Disco Bar Neptuno*
VI MC
LIVE DJS.
9 PM. - 1 AM.
Rafael Melgar & 11 Sur
No. 798
Tels.: 872 1537, 872 4374
Fax: 872 4347
www.neptunodisco.com

Karaoke Brisas
AE VI MC
KARAOKE ON WEEKENDS FROM
10 PM. - 2 AM.
BEEF LINGUINI.
7 AM. - 11 PM.
Costera Sur Hwy. km 1.7
Hotel Brisas Cozumel
Tel.: 872 2900 Fax: 872 2154

H-13 *Bar Karaoke Show Time*
8 PM. - 5 AM.
Rosado Salas 30-A
Tel.: 872 0899

H-13 *Snack Bar Viva México*
AE VI MC
10 AM. - 4 AM., WEEKEND
CLOSING TIME AT 5 AM.
Rafael Melgar No. 199 Sur
Tel./Fax: 872 0799
www.vivamex.com.mx

I-12 *Tequila Bar Kiss My Cactus*
VI MC
MARGARITAS.
300 DIFFERENT TEQUILAS.
8 AM. - 10 PM.
Av. Rafael Melgar btwn.
1a & Rosado Salas
Tel.: 872 5793

RESTAURANTS

CAFES

J-17 *Café Rock & Java*
SALADS.
7 AM. - 11 PM.
Av. Rafael Melgar No. 602
Tel.: 872 4405

G-13 *Cocos Cozumel*
BREAKFASTS.
6 AM. - NOON
5a Av. Sur No. 180
Tel.: 872 0241

H-08 *Del Museo*
BREAKFASTS.
7 AM. - 2 PM.
Av. Rafael Melgar
esq. 6 Norte
Tel.: 872 0838

I-14 *The Coffee Bean*
8 AM. - 11 PM.
Av. 3 Sur No. 9

CAJUN

H-13 *French Quarter*
AE VI MC
JAMBALAYA CAJUN LOBSTER.
4:30 PM. - 11 PM.
5 Av. btwn. Rosado Salas
& Calle 3
Tel.: 872 6321

CARIBBEAN

G-09 *La Veranda*
VI MC
LIVE CONTEMPORARY FLAMENCO
GUITAR MUSIC.
PEPPER STUFFED WITH SEAFOOD.
4 PM. - 11 PM.
4 Nte. No. 140
btwn. 5a & 10a Av. Nte.
Tel.: 872 4132

J-19 *Lobster Cove*
AE VI MC
LIVE LATIN JAZZ.
LOBSTER, COCONUT SHRIMP,
LEMON PIE.
8 AM. - 11 PM.
Av. Rafael Melgar No. 790
Tel./Fax: 872 4022

STEAK HOUSES

H-13 *Pepe´s Grill*
AE VI MC
LIVE CARIBBEAN AND 'TROVA'
MUSIC, MON.-SAT.
PRIME RIB, CAESAR SALAD.
5 PM. - 11 PM.
Av. Rafael Melgar
esq. Rosado Salas
Tel.: 872 0213

More information:
www.caribbeanmex.com

F-10 *Sonora Grill*
VI MC
GRILLED STEAKS.
10 AM. - 10 PM.
Av. Juárez & Calle 15
Tel.: 872 3620

INTERNATIONAL

G-09 *All Sports Bar*
HAMBURGERS.
10 AM. - 1:30 AM.
5a Av. No. 3 esq. 2 Norte
Tel./Fax: 869 2246

Casa Misión
AE VI MC
JUMBO SHRIMP,
KING CRAB.
STARTING FROM 3 PM.
Av. 55 btwn. Juárez & 1a Sur
Tels.: 872 1641, 872 3248

El Galeón
AE VI MC
FLAMBEED SPECIALTIES.
7 AM. - 11 PM.
Costera Norte Hwy. km 2.5
Hotel Coral Princess
Tel.: 872 3200 Fax: 872 2800

H-10 *Hard Rock Café*
AE VI MC
LIVE ROCK MUSIC.
HAMBURGERS, RIBS.
9 AM. - 2 AM.
Av. Rafael Melgar No. 2-A
Tel.: 872 5273
Fax: 872 5272
www.hardrock.com

La Cocay
6:30 AM. - 11 PM.
17 Sur & 25 Av.
Tel.: 872 5533

La Palapa
AE VI MC
SEAFOOD.
7:30 AM. - MIDNIGHT.
Hwy. to Chankanaab km 4
Hotel Casa del Mar
Tel.: 872 1900 Fax: 872 1588

H-11 *Las Palmeras*
AE VI MC
LIVE CARIBBEAN AND TROVA MUSIC.
FAJITAS.
7 AM. - 11 PM.
Av. Rafael Melgar Sur
Across from the pier
Tel.: 872 0532

H-10 ***Los Girasoles***
AE VI MC
7 AM. - 4 PM.
Calle 2 Norte No. 3
Hotel Plaza Cozumel
Tel.: 872 2700 Fax: 872 0066

F-07 ***Manatí***
2 PM. - 11 PM.
8 Norte esq. 10 Norte
Cel.: 044 987 710 0787

Palma Azul
AE VI MC
7 AM. - 11 PM.
Hwy. to San Juan km 4
Hotel Playa Azul
Tels.: 872 0199, 872 0033
Fax: 872 0110

Playa Sol
VI MC
PLAYA SOL FISH, BUFFET.
9 AM. - 6 PM.
Costera Sur Hwy. km 15
Tels.: 872 9030, 872 9040
Fax: 872 9045

H-13 ***Tony Rome***
CHICKEN PARMESAN, BBQ RIBS.
8 AM. - MIDNIGHT, SUN. 3 PM. - MIDNIGHT.
5a Av. btwn. Rosado Salas & Calle 3 Sur
Tel.: 872 0131
www.tonyrome.com

ITALIAN

G-10 ***Azul Cobalto***
11 AM. - 11 PM.
Av. Juárez No. 181
Tel.: 872 3318

J-17 ***Mama Roma***
AE VI MC
NEW YORK PIZZA, SALADS.
10 AM. - MIDNIGHT.
Av. Rafael Melgar No. 551
Plaza Punta Langosta
Tel.: 869 1641 Fax: 869 1642

SEAFOOD

J-19 ***Acuario***
AE VI MC
LIVE CARIBBEAN MUSIC, THU-SAT.
SHRIMP & LOBSTER.
NOON - MIDNIGHT.
11 Sur No. 798 &
Av. Rafael Melgar
Tel.: 872 1097 Fax: 872 4374

G-17 ***El Capi Navegante***
VI MC
KING CRAB.
11 AM. - 11 PM.
Av. 10 Sur No. 312
Tel.: 872 1730

La Cabaña del Pescador
6 PM. - 10:30 PM.
Costera Norte Hwy. km 4.5

Playa Azul
AE VI MC
LOBSTER, SHRIMP.
10 AM. - 6 PM.
San Juan Hwy. km 4
Hotel Playa Azul
Tels.: 872 0199, 872 0043
Fax: 872 0110
www.playa-azul.com

MEXICAN

J-17 ***Carlos'n Charlie's***
AE VI MC OT
BBQ RIBS & SHRIMP.
MON.-FRI. 10 AM-1:30 AM.
SAT. 11 AM. - 1:30 AM.,
SUN. 5 AM. - 1:30 AM.
KITCHEN CLOSES AT MIDNIGHT.
Av. Rafael Melgar No. 551
Plaza Punta Langosta
Tel.: 869 1646

F-10 ***El Abuelo Gerardo***
SEXY CHICKEN FAJITAS, SEXY SHRIMP.
8 AM. - 10 PM.
10a Av. Norte No. 21
Tel./Fax: 872 1012

F-13 ***La Choza***
AE VI MC
MOLE POBLANO, STUFFED CHILES.
7 AM. - 11 PM.
Rosado Salas 200 esq. 10a
Tel.: 872 0958 Fax: 872 3417

Las Tortugas
VI MC
SEAFOOD GRILL.
11 AM. - MIDNIGHT; TUE.- SUN.
Av. Joaquín Coldwell
& Calle 19 No. 1200
Tel./Fax: 872 1242
tugas@prodigy.net.mx

H-13 ***La Misión Downtown***
AE VI MC
NOON - MIDNIGHT.
Rosado Salas
Tel.: 872 6340

H-12 ***Los Dorados de Villa***
TAMPIQUEÑA-STYLE MEAT, ROYAL SHRIMP.
8 AM. - MIDNIGHT.
1a Sur No. 72
Tel./Fax: 872 0196

I-06 ***Pancho's Backyard***
AE VI MC
LIVE REGIONAL MUSIC.
FILLET IN CHIPOTLE SAUCE, FLAMBÉED SHRIMP.
10 AM. - 11 PM.
Av. Rafael Melgar No. 27
Inside Los Cinco Soles
btwn. Calles 8 & 10
Tels.: 872 2141, 872 1106
Fax: 872 1950
www.loscincosoles.com

B-12 ***Plaza Leza***
VI MC
PLAZA LEZA BEEF TIPS.
7 AM. - 11 PM.
1a Sur No. 58
Tel.: 872 1041

J-17 ***Sr. Frogs***
AE VI MC
NATURAL FRUIT DAIQUIRI.
11 AM. - 2 AM.
Plaza Punta Langosta
Tels.: 869 1650, 869 1651
Fax: 869 1652

B-09 ***Tacos La Misión***
AE VI MC
BEEF SHISH KEBAB.
NOON - MIDNIGHT.
Av. Joaquín Coldwell
Tel.: 869 2463

H-13 ***Viva México***
AE MC
9 AM. - 4 PM.
Av. Rafael Melgar Sur 199
Tel.: 872 0799

REGIONAL

G-12 *Casa Denis*

SNACKS.
7 AM. - 11 PM.
1a Sur No. 132
Tel.: 872 0067
www.casadenis.com

El Turix

PIBIL-STYLE CHICKEN AND PORK.
WED. - SUN. 6 PM. - 1 AM.
Calle 17 btwn. 20 Bis & 25 Sur
Tel.: 872 5234
Fax: 872 5533

El Moro
VI MC
SEAFOOD PLATE, LOBSTER.
FRI. - WED. 1 PM. - 11 PM.
75 Av. Bis No. 124 btwn. Calles 2 & 4
Tel.: 872 30 29

Los Girasoles-Beach Club
AE VI MC
FISH, CEVICHE.
NOON - 6 PM.
Costera Sur Hwy. km 1.7
Hotel Brisas Cozumel
Tels.: 872 2500, 872 2899

SNACK & GRILL

F-05 *Baby Reef*
AE VI MC
HAMBURGERS, NACHOS.
9 AM. - MIDNIGHT.
5 Av. Norte esq. Av. Juárez
Hotel Reef Club
Tel.: 872 0584

H-10 *Fat Tuesday*

9 AM. - 1 AM.
Av. Juárez por 2 Norte
Tel.: 872 5130

La Palapa Grill
AE VI MC
7 AM. - 11 PM.
Costera Norte Hwy. km. 2.5
Hotel Coral Princess
Tels.: 872 3200
01 800 215 2200
Fax: 872 2800

FAST FOOD

Burger King
AE VI
9 AM. - 11 PM.
- Plaza Punta Langosta
Tel.: 869 1817
- Plaza Chedraui
Tel.: 869 1879

J-15 *McDonald's*

8 AM. - 11 PM.
Av. Rafael Melgar No. 415
Tel.: 869 2199

DAYTIME ACTIVITIES

Dolphin Discovery
7 AM. - 6 PM.
4 DOLPHIN PROGRAMS: SWIMMING $119 USD, SNORKELING $89 USD, INTERACTIVE $75 USD, SCUBA DIVING $165 USD.
Costera Sur Hwy. km 9.5
Parque Chankanaab
Tels.: 872 9701, 872 9702
www.dolphindiscovery.com

Playa Sol
9 AM. - 6 PM.
ADMISSION: $8 USD.
Costera Sur Hwy. km 15
Tels.: 872 9030, 872 9040
www.playasol.com.mx

Torre Escénica Giratoria
Puerta Maya Terminal
RESERVATIONS IN CANCUN:
Tels.: 884 9422, 884 9455

Wild Tours
FOUR-WHEEL DRIVES, KAYAK TOURS; INCLUDES TRANSPORTATION.
DEPARTURES: 9 AM., 1 PM. & 5 PM.
THREE PACKAGES: $89.99 USD, $69.99 USD, $59.99 USD.
15 Av. Norte No. 300
Tels.: 872 6747, 872 2244
01 800 202 4990
Fax: 872 5876
www.wild-tours.com

GOLF

Cozumel Country Club
18 HOLE GOLF COURSE, INSTRUCTORS & RESTAURANT.
Costera Norte Hwy. km 6.5
Indoor Clubhouse
Tel.: 872 9570 Fax: 872 9590
info@cozumelcountryclub.com.mx
www.cozumelcountryclub.com.mx

PARKS

San Gervasio Tourist Center
7 AM. - 5 PM.
ADMISSION: $50 PESOS, CHILDREN UNDER 8, FREE
SERVICES: BILINGUAL GUIDES, HANDICRAFT SHOPS, BOOKSTORE, COZUMEL'S LARGEST ARCHEOLOGICAL SITE.

Chankanaab Park
8 AM. - 6 PM.
ADMISSION: $150 PESOS, CHILDREN UNDER 8, FREE.
SERVICES: BILINGUAL GUIDES, SNACK BAR, SNORKEL EQUIPMENT RENTAL, HANDICRAFT SHOPS.
Av. Joaquín Coldwell 70 btwn. Av. Juárez & 1a Sur
Tels.: 872 0914, 872 2940
Fax: 872 0093
www.cozumelparks.net.mx

Playa Mía Grand Beach Park
WEEKDAYS 9 AM TO 6 PM
WEEKENDS 9:30 TO 5:30 PM
CLOSED ON THURSDAYS
RESTAURANT, MAYA RUINS, BEACH, SNORKELING, DIVING, KAYAKING, SPECIAL EVENTS, ENTRANCE TICKET INCLUDES FOOD.
Costera Sur Hwy. km. 15 Southern Hotel Zone
Tels.: 872 9030, 872 9040
Fax.: 872 9045
www.playamia.com

Parque Punta Sur & Ecological Reserve
7 AM. - 6 PM.
ADMISSION: $100 PESOS, CHILDREN UNDER 8, FREE.
INCLUDES GUIDES, VISIT TO ARCHEOLOGICAL SITE, MUSEUM ENTRANCE, BOTANICAL GARDEN AND BEACH AREAS.

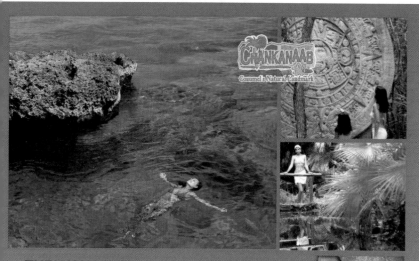

MUSEUMS

H-08 *Cozumel Museum*
9 AM. - 5 PM. : $3 USD.
Rafael Melgar & 6 Norte
Tels.: 872 1475, 872 0914
www.cozumelparks.net.mx

G-20 *Mexican Music Museum*
FROM 6 PM. ON.
ADMISSION: $5 USD ADULTS, CHILDREN FREE. ARRANGED IN ADVANCE. PRE-HISPANIC AND CONTEMPORARY PIECES FROM SEVERAL DIFFERENT SITES. TOUR IN ENGLISH AND SPANISH.
Calle 11 Sur No. 101-9
Tels.: 872 5269, 872 0514

Navegation Museum
9 AM. - 4 PM.
Reserva Ecológica Parque Punta Sur
Tels.: 878 8462, 872 0914
www.cozumelparks.net.mx

HOTELS

FIVE STAR ★★★★★

 # 8 *Coral Princess*
139
Costera Norte Hwy. km 2.5
Tels.: 872 3200, 872 5122
Fax: 872 2800
ventas@coralprincess.com
www.coralprincess.com

 # 10 *Cozumel Palace*
174
Av. Rafael Melgar km 1.5
Southern Hotel Zone
Tels.: 872 2400, 872 2000
Fax: 872 1937
www.palaceresorts.com

 # 17 *El Cid La Ceiba*
71
Costera Sur Hwy. km 4.5
Tel.: 872 0844 Fax: 872 0065
USA 1 800 435 3240
cozumel@elcid.com.mx
www.elcid.com.mx

 # 19 *Fiesta Americana Cozumel Dive Resort*
226
Hwy. to Chankanaab km 9.5
Tel.: 872 9600 Fax: 872 2666
www.posadas.com

 # 23 *Iberostar Cozumel*
300
Costera Sur Hyw. km 17.8
El Cedral
Tels.: 872 9900
01 800 007 3572
Fax: 872 9909
www.iberostar.com

 # 1 *Meliá Paradisus Cozumel*
150
Costera Norte Hwy. km 5.8
Tel.: 872 9870
01 800 901 7100
Fax: 872 1599
www.solmelia.com
melia.cozumel@solmelia.com

 # 22 *Occidental Grand*
253
Costera Norte Hwy. km 17.5
Tels.: 872 9730, 872 9740
01 800 907 9500
Fax: 872 9745
www.occidentalgrand.com

 # 5 *Playa Azul Golf and Beach Hotel*
46
GOLF INCLUDED.
Hwy. to San Juan km 4
Northern Hotel Zone
Tels.: 872 0199, 872 0033
01 800 017 1819
Fax: 872 0110
playazul@playa-azul.com
www.playa-azul.com

 # 18 *Presidente Intercontinental*
253
Costera Sur Hwy. km 6.5
Tels.: 872 9500
01 800 904 4400
USA 1 800 327 0200
Fax: 872 9528, 872 9501
cozumel@interconti.com
www.cozumel.interconti.com

More information: www.caribbeanmex.com

FOUR STAR ★★★★

 # 11 *Cozumel Resort*
178
Costera Sur Hwy. km 1.7
Tels.: 872 2900, 872 2811
01 800 696 6966
USA 1 877 454 4355
Fax: 872 2154
reserv@hotelcozumel.com.mx
www.hotelcozumel.com.mx

 # 16 *Casa del Mar*
106
Hwy. to Chankanaab km 4
Tels.: 872 1900, 872 1877
01 800 667 0066
Fax: 872 1811
sales@casadelmarcozumel.com
www.casadelmarcozumel.com

J-15 *Casa Mexicana*
98
Av. Rafael Melgar No. 457
Tels.: 872 9090
01 800 227 2639
1 877 228 6747
Fax: 872 9073
reservaciones@casamexicanacozumel.com.mx
www.casamexicanacozumel.com

 # 3 *El Cozumeleño*
254
Playa Santa Pilar km 4.5
Northern Hotel Zone
Tels.: 872 9350,
01 800 437 3923
Fax: 872 9544
salescoz@cozumel.com.mx
www.elcozumeleno.com

 # 6 *Fontán*
49
Costera Norte Hwy. km 2.5
Tels.: 872 0300, 872 0194
Fax: 872 0105
www.hotelesfontan.com.mx

★★★★★

Meliá Cozumel

All Inclusive Golf & Beach Resort

The best resort for nature lovers on the island of Cozumel and just 10 minutes from the airport. 147 comfortable rooms, 3 restaurants with buffet or à la carte service, 5 bars, 2 pools, Mini Club and activities program for the whole family. The only all-inclusive plan offering attractive packages of unlimited golf at the Cozumel Country Club, the only 18-hole golf course on the island.

Carretera Costera Norte km 5.8, Isla de Cozumel, 77600, Q. Roo, México. Tel. + 52 (987) 872 9870, Fax: + 52 (987) 872 1599
melia.cozumel@solmelia.com • *www.solmelia.com*

★★★★★

PLAYA AZUL GOLF AND BEACH HOTEL

The only boutique oceanfront hotel that offers unlimited golf included in the room rate! Cart is paid directly at the golf course. Friendly staff, cozy deluxe rooms and suites. Intimate, magic, run by owners. Upscale cuisine. A wide array of activities: deep sea and fly fishing, diving and snorkeling... or just beach, sun and margaritas.

Highway to San Juan km 4, Northern Hotel Zone, Cozumel, Quintana Roo, Mexico 77600, P.O.Box 31.
Tels. (987) 872 0199, 872 0043, 872 0033 Fax: (987) 872 0110 • playazul@playa-azul.com • www.playa-azul.com

★★★★

COZUMEL RESORT

All inclusive resort with an excellent location, 10 minutes from downtown. 178 beautiful and spacious rooms, the largest swimming pool in Cozumel and facilities for divers in a very pleasant environment.

HOTEL COZUMEL ★★★★

Costera Sur Hwy. Km 1.7, Cozumel, Q. Roo, Mexico 77600; Tels.: 52 (987) 872 2811, 872 2900, Fax: (987) 872 2154, Call toll free EUA 1 877 454 4355, Mexico 01 800 696 6966 reserv@hotelcozumel.com.mx • www.hotelcozumel.com.mx

★★★★

REEF CLUB COZUMEL BEACH & DIVE RESORT

The Most Fun All Inclusive in Cozumel.

Its relaxed atmosphere makes it ideal for families, honeymooners, scuba divers and golfers. Wide range of activities available.

Costera Sur Hwy. km 12.9, Tel.: (987) 872 9300, Fax: (987) 872 9315
USA 1 888 773 4349, MEX 01 800 001 7333 www.reefclubcozumel.com

 # 21 *Occidental Allegro*
294
San Francisco Palancar
Southern Hwy. km 16.5
Tels.: 872 9770
USA 1 800 858 2258
Fax: 872 9792
www.allegroresorts.com

H-10 *Plaza Cozumel*
PE 60
2 Norte No. 3 btwn.
Av. Rafael Melgar & 5a Av.
Tels.: 872 2700, 872 2722
Fax: 872 0066
www.hotelplazacozumel.com

 # 20 *Reef Club Cozumel*
306
Costera Sur Hwy. km 12.9
Tels.: 872 9300
01 888 001 7333
Fax: 872 9315
dirventas@reefclubcozumel.com
www.reefclubcozumel.com

 # 2 *Sol Cabañas del Caribe*
PE 52
Costera Sur km 5.1
Northern Hotel Zone
Tels.: 872 9871, 872 0411
01 800 341 5993
Fax: 872 9315
www.solmelia.com

THREE STAR ★★★

H-14 *Aguilar*
PE 32
3 Sur No. 98 btwn. 5a Av.
& Av. Rafael Melgar
Tel.: 872 0307 Fax: 872 0769
www.cozumel.hotel.net/aguilar

J-19 *Barracuda*
PE 44
Av. Rafael Melgar No. 628
Tels.: 872 0002, 872 1243
Fax: 872 0884, 872 3633
barracud@cozumel.com.mx

 # 13 *Caribe Blue*
PE 22
Costera Sur Hwy. km 2.2
Tel./Fax: 872 0188

 # 7 *Condominios Condumel*
PE 10
Costera Norte Hwy. km 1.5
Tel.: 872 0892 Fax: 872 0661
www.condumel.com.mx

E-20 *Days Inn Villa Iguanas*
PE 40
11 Sur No. 460
Tels.: 872 1600, 872 1788
Fax: 870 1692
daysinn@cozumel.com.mx
www.cozumel-villaiguanas.com

H-13 *El Marqués*
PE 39
5a Av. Sur No. 180
Tels.: 872 0677, 872 0537
Fax: 872 0537
cozumel-hotels.net/el_marques

H-08 *Flamingo*
PE 18
6a Norte No. 81
Tel/Fax: 872 1264
www.hotelflamingo.com

H-10 *Mesón San Miguel*
PE 102
Av. Juárez No. 2 Bis
Tels.: 872 0352, 872 0233
Fax: 872 4463
hmeson@prodigy.net.mx
www.mesonsanmiguel.com

H-07 *Hacienda San Miguel*
PE 11
10 Norte No. 500 btwn.
5a Av. & Av. Rafael Melgar
Tels.: 872 1986, 872 7043
USA: 1 866 712 6387
Fax: 872 7036
info@haciendasanmiguel.com
www.haciendasanmiguel.com

 # 14 *Park Royal Cozumel*
141
Costera Sur Hwy. km 3.5
Tel.: 872 0700 Fax: 872 1301
www.parkroyalhotels.com.mx

J-15 *Safari Inn*
PE 12
Av. Rafael Melgar No. 429
btwn. Calles 5 & 7
Tel.: 872 0101 Fax: 872 0661
www.aquasafari.com

I-14 *Suites Bahía*
PE 25
Rafael Melgar & 3 Sur
Tels.: 872 1791
01 800 227 2639
Fax: 872 9073
www.reservaciones@suitesbahia.com

H-14 *Suites Colonial*
PE 25
5 Av. Sur No. 9
Tel./Fax: 872 0211
01 800 227 2639
www.suitescolonial.com

 # 9 *Scuba Club Cozumel*
61
Av. Rafael Melgar
Prol. Sur km 1.15
Tels.: 872 1133, 872 0853
01 800 847 5708
Fax: 872 1800

 # 15 *Villa Blanca Garden Beach*
PE 72
Costera Sur Hwy. km 3
Tel.: 872 0730 Fax: 872 0865
USA 1 800 DIVE-MEX
info@villablanca.net
www.villablanca.net

J-15 *Vista del Mar*
PE 12
Av. Rafael Melgar No. 45
btwn. Calles 7 & 5 Sur
Tel.: 872 4145 Fax: 872 7043
info@hotelvistadelmar.com
www.hotelvistadelmar.com

TWO STAR ★★

C-06 *Al'Marestel*
PE 11
10 Nte. No. 498 esq. 25 Av.
Tel./Fax: 872 0822
almarestel@prodigy.net.mx

E-10 *Caribe*
PE 14
2 Norte btwn. 15 & 20
Tel./Fax: 872 6122

H-08 *Cozumel Inn*
PE 27
4a Norte No. 3
Tel.: 872 0314 Fax: 872 3156

G-12 *El Pirata*
PE 27
5a Av. Sur No. 121-A
Tel./Fax: 872 0051

H-13 ***Flores***
PE · 26
Rosado Salas No. 72 btwn. Av. Rafael Melgar & 5a Av.
Tels.: 872 1429, 872 1120
Fax: 872 2475

H-12 ***López***
PE · 30
1a Av. Sur No. 86
Tel.: 872 0108

G-13 ***Mary Carmen***
PE · 14
5a Av. Sur No. 132
Tel.: 872 0581
Fax: 872 7561

H-15 ***Maya Cozumel***
PE · 32
5a Sur No. 4
Tel.: 872 0011

H-13 ***Palma Dorada Inn***
PE · 24
Rosado Salas No. 44
Tel./Fax: 872 0330
pdinn@prodigy.net.mx

ONE STAR ★

E-12 ***Pepita***
PE 27
15 Av. Sur No. 120
Tel.: 872 0098

PROVINCIA MAYA

FELIPE CARRILLO PUERTO

THREE STAR ★★★

 # 4 ***Esquivel "La Casona"***
34
REGIONAL SHOW.
Calle 65 No. 746
Across from the Principal Park
Tel.: 834 0344
Fax: 834 0313

TWO STAR ★★★

 # 3 ***Chan Santa Cruz***
PE 10
Calle 68 No. 782
esq. Calle 67
Tel.: 834 0274

 # 1 ***El Faisán y El Venado***
PE 35
Av. Juárez No. 781
Tels.: 834 0043, 834 0702

 # 2 ***San Ignacio***
PE 12
Av. Juaréz No. 761
Tel.: 834 0122

Los Barandales ★
ECOTOURISTIC TOURS.
PE 16
Calle 57 close to Av. Juárez
Tel.: 834 0109

RIVIERA MAYA

Accommodation options along the coast run the gamut from huge resort villages with every service to smaller beachfront hotels, quiet inns and tropical-style cabañas or cottages. There are restaurants and water sports centers in the different resorts and area capital Playa del Carmen offers a wealth of travel services. The eco-parks in the Riviera Maya are day trip options.

HOTELS. Rates (subject to change) will give you a rough idea of the daily cost of a standard double room. Rates vary according to the season. "Off" season is generally considered to run from April 15 to December 15 while high season encompasses Christmas, New Year, January, February, March, Easter week and breaks for national holidays. Some hotels offer special group rates and packages. Rates are given in dollars.

LOW SEASON	HIGH SEASON
Up to $50	Up to $50
Between $50 & $100	Between $50 & $100
Between $100 & $180	Between $100 & $180
Between $180 & $250	Between $180 & $250
Between $250 & $350	Between $250 & $350
More than $350	More than $350

CATEGORY. The classification system used in Mexico by most hotels has categories that run from one to six stars (Deluxe). We have also included a special category, which would cover small and exclusive hotels or eco-hotels that do not offer the amenities of a large hotel but have their own charm.

★ One star (up to 6) — Special Category

PLANS. Hotels may offer one or more of the following plans: • All-inclusive, which includes food, drinks and most activities • European Plan: no meals • American Plan: Breakfast and either lunch or dinner included • Continental Plan: Continental breakfast included.

⌘ All-inclusive — PE European Plan

PA American Plan — PC Continental Plan

SERVICES: • The majority of Deluxe and 5-star hotels offer the following services, with the exception of golf, disco and a spa, which are marked in the lists when applicable. • The majority of 4-star hotels offer services 1-9, additional services are included in the lists when applicable. • The amenities offered by the remaining 3-star hotels and hotels in other categories are featured in the listings • At the end of the line of symbols for each hotel a figure denotes the number of rooms, villas or suites.

1. Restaurant
2. Bar
3. Air-conditioning
4. Television
5. Pool
6. Gift shop
7. Car rental
8. Travel agency / trips
9. Laundry
10. Convention rooms
11. Evening entertainment
12. Beauty parlor
13. Gym
14. Kids club
15. Disco
16. Spa
17. Tennis
18. Golf
19. Marina
20. Wedding /Honeymoon programs
21. Babysitters
22. Social activities

HIGHWAY 307 GOES FROM CHETUMAL TO PUERTO JUÁREZ AND VICE VERSA, STRETCHING THE LENGTH OF THE RIVIERA MAYA AND PASSING THROUGH CANCÚN (AT KILOMETER 356 FROM CHETUMAL). KILOMETERS ARE GIVEN STARTING FROM CHETUMAL, PUERTO JUÁREZ, TULUM OR CANCÚN.

FROM CANCÚN TO PUERTO MORELOS

DELUXE ★★★★★★

 # 1 *Moon Palace Sunrise*
⌘ 1300
Chetumal-Cancún km 339
Tels.: 881 6000, 881 6088
01 800 672 5223
USA 1 800 346 8225
Fax: 881 6095
relpub@palaceresorts.com
www.palaceresorts.com

 # 1 *Moon Palace Nizuc*
⌘ 731
Chetumal-Cancún km 339
Tels.: 881 6000, 881 6088
01 800 672 5223
USA 1 800 346 8225
Fax: 881 6001
relpub@palaceresorts.com
www.palaceresorts.com

 # 2 *Paraíso de La Bonita Resort & Thalasso*
PE 90
THALASSO THERAPY CENTER.
Chetumal-Cancún km 328
Tels.: 872 7300, 872 8301
USA (713) 974 6500
1 800 327 0200
Fax: 872 8301
resa@paraisodelabonitaresort.com
www.paraisodelabonitaresort.com

#7 *Secrets Excellence Riviera Cancún*
440

ADULTS ONLY.
Chetumal-Cancún km 324 + 3.42
Tel.: 872 8500 Fax: 872 8501
USA 1 866 GOSECRETS
info@secretsexcellence.com.mx
www.secretsresorts.com

FIVE STAR ★★★★★

 # 6 *Paradisus Riviera Cancún*
500

LOCATED 15 MINUTES FROM THE CANCÚN INTERNATIONAL AIRPORT, 25 MINUTES SOUTH OF CANCÚN.
Chetumal-Cancún km 324
Tel.: 872 8383 Fax: 872 8385
01 800 901 7100
paradisus.riviera.cancun @solmelia.com
www.solmelia.com

 # 4 *Desire Resort & Spa*
110

CLOTHES OPTIONAL.
Chetumal-Cancún km 328
Entrance to Bahía Petempich
Tel.: 872 8280 Fax: 872 8299
info@desireresorts.com
www.desireresort.com

FOUR STAR ★★★★

 # 5 *Bahía Maya*
96

Chetumal-Cancún km 328
Entrance to Bahía Petempich
Tel.: 872 8100 Fax: 872 8106
bahiamaya@caribe.net.mx
www.royalpremierhoteles.com

 # 3 *Club Paraíso Maya*
107

TRANSPORTATION TO CANCÚN AND TO PLAYA DEL CARMEN.
Cancún-Tulum km 27.5
Bahía Petempich
Tel.: 872 8080 Fax: 872 8088
www.renthotel.com

THE ORDER OF THE CITIES AND SITES OF INTEREST IS ACCORDING TO THEIR GEOGRAPHICAL LOCATION, FROM CANCÚN TO CHETUMAL.

CROCOCÚN

LOCATED 32 KM. FROM CANCÚN.

E-02 *CrocoCún Zoo*
CROCODILE AND REGIONAL WILDLIFE PARK.
DURATION OF VISIT: 1 HOUR.
Tel.: 850 3719

PUERTO MORELOS

LOCATED 32 KM. FROM CANCÚN.

BOOKSHOPS

B-10 *Alma Libre Bookstore*
10 AM. - 4 PM., 6 PM. - 9 PM.
NEW AND USED BOOKS.
Across from the Central Park
Tel./Fax: 871 0713
info@almalibrebooks.com
www.almalibrebooks.com

STORES

DELICATESSEN

A-10 *Monchis Hanah-Kiih*
7 AM. - MIDNIGHT.
WHOLEWHEAT PRODUCTS, PRESERVES, PASTAS, COLD CUTS, ETC.
Across from the Central Park
Cel.: 044 998 860 0257

CRAFTS

C-12 *Mercado de Artesanías Hunab-Ku*
9 AM. - 8 PM.
HATS, SILVER, SHELLS, HAMMOCKS, CERAMICS, STONE AND WOOD HANDICRAFTS, TRADITIONAL CLOTHING, ETC.
Calle Rojo Gómez

MONEY EXCHANGE

B / F-10 *Morex*
8 AM. - 10 PM.
• Across from the Central Park
• Entrance to Pto. Morelos.
Tel.: 871 0162
morex@puertomorelos.com.mx
www.puertomorelos.com.mx

B-10 *Turex*
7 AM. - 10 PM.
Across from the Central Park
Tel.: 871 0000

A-10 *Cajero Red HSBC*
Across from the Central Park

PALAPA DE FÉLIX-PUERTO MORELOS-RIVIERA MAYA

National Marine Park and Cenote Route

Snorkeling Express: Incredible reef adventure. Includes visit to two reefs, light lunch, drinks and air conditioned transportation. Duration: 9 a.m. to 1:30 p.m. and noon to 4:30 p.m. Prices: adults $55 US, children $30 US.

Jungle and Sea Adventure. Includes visit to the caves, tour to the cenotes and snorkeling on the reefs, light lunch, drinks and air-conditioned transportation. Duration: 9 a.m. to 5 p.m. Prices: adults $69 US, children $40 US.

RESERVATIONS:
Palapa de Félix
from 8 a.m. to 8:30 p.m.
Tels.: 01 800 71 71 278,
01 800 67 26 230,
884 2316
fortizguerrero@hotmail.com
www.sorkelingrivieramaya.com

Snorkeling Express

Sea & Jungle Adventure

CAR RENTALS

 # 5 Avant Rent a Car
Punta Petempich
Int. Hotel Bahía Maya
Tels.: 842 3521, 842 3522
Fax: 892 1158
www.avantrentacar.com

B-13 Transportadora Turística Ortiz
VAN RENTAL WITH BILINGUAL DRIVER. TOURS TO TULUM, XEL-HÁ, COBÁ, BAHÍA SOLIMAN; CHICHÉN ITZÁ & VALLADOLID, RÍO LAGARTOS, SIAN KA'AN, FELIPE CARRILLO PUERTO, PALENQUE, UXMAL.
Calle Cozumel L. 15-A
Tel.: 884 2316
snorkeling@hotmail.com
www.snorkelingrivieramaya.com

AGENCIES & TOURS

A-10 Goyo's Info Center
TEMAZCAL (TRADITIONAL MEXICAN STEAM BATH). ENGLISH, SPANISH.
Av. Javier Rojo Gómez 16
Tels.: 871 0189, 871 0636
goyosjungle@excite.com
www.goyos.info

C-15 Kool Tours
JEWELS OF THE JUNGLE TOUR.
Hotel Rancho Libertad
Cels.: 044 998 101 7696
044 998 894 5126
info@kooltours.net
www.kooltours.net

B-10 Marand Travel
FISHING, DIVING AND SNORKELING TOURS. CAR RENTALS. SPANISH, ENGLISH, FRENCH, ITALIAN.
Av. Tulum esq. Rojo Gómez
Tels.: 871 0332, 871 0162
marand@puertomorelos.com.mx
www.puertomorelos.com.mx

A-03 Maya Echo Inc.
VISIT TO THE BOTANICAL GARDEN, CENTRAL VALLARTA (GUM HARVESTING COMMUNITY) AND NATURAL SINKHOLE. ENGLISH, SPANISH.
Calle Palapas
Tel.: 871 0136
starseed@mayaecho.com
www.mayaecho.com.mx

B-13 Palapa de Félix
SNORKELING TOURS ON THE REEF AND IN THE CENOTES.
Tels.: 884 2316
01 800 717 1278
snorkeling@hotmail.com
www.snorkelingrivieramaya.com

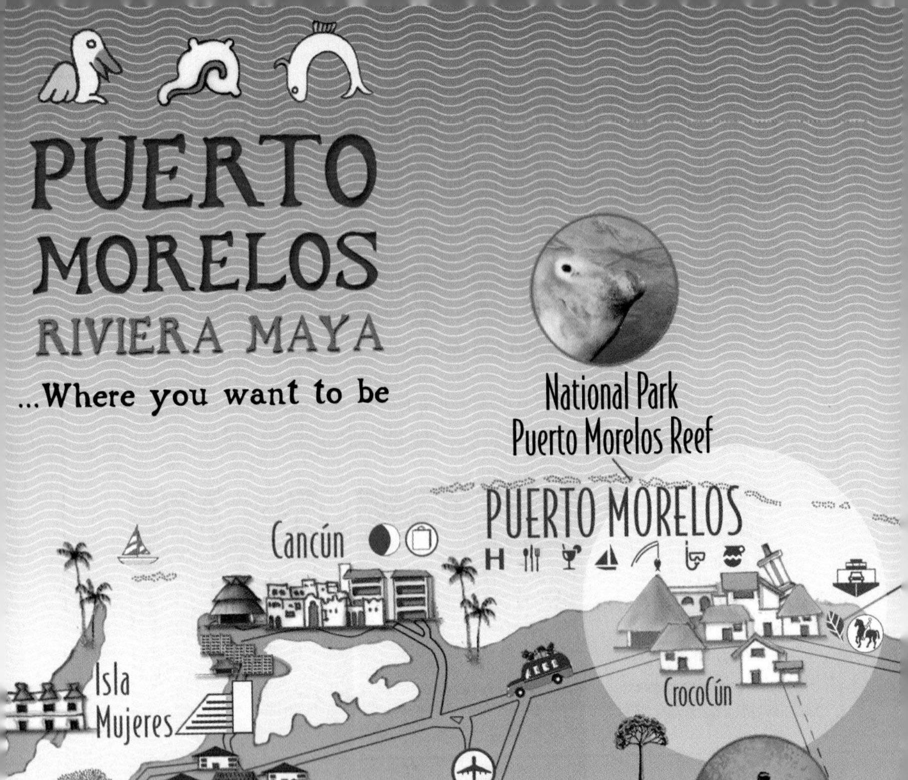

...Where you want to be

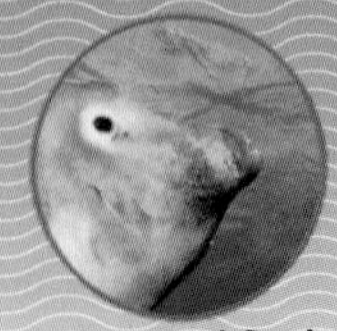

National Park
Puerto Morelos Reef

PUERTO MORELOS

Cancún

Isla
Mujeres

CrocoCún

Central Vallarta
Cenotes Route

La Isla

3 Bocas

180

Leona Vicario

Chichén Itzá, Mérida

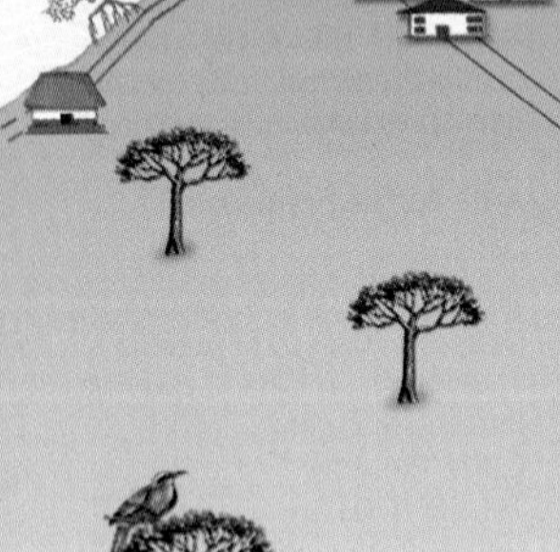

Tranquillity and harmony

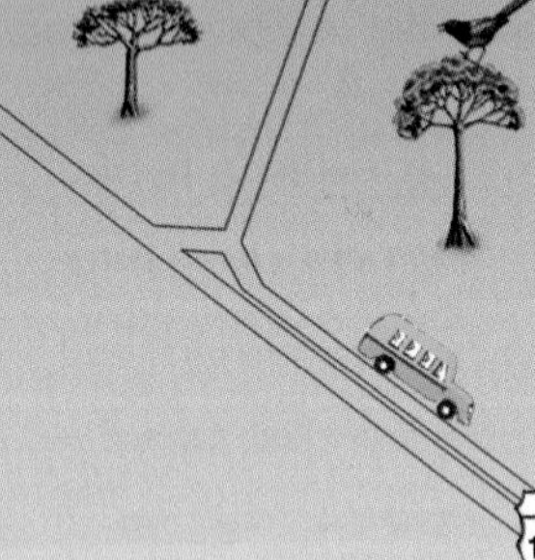

Between the sea and the jungle

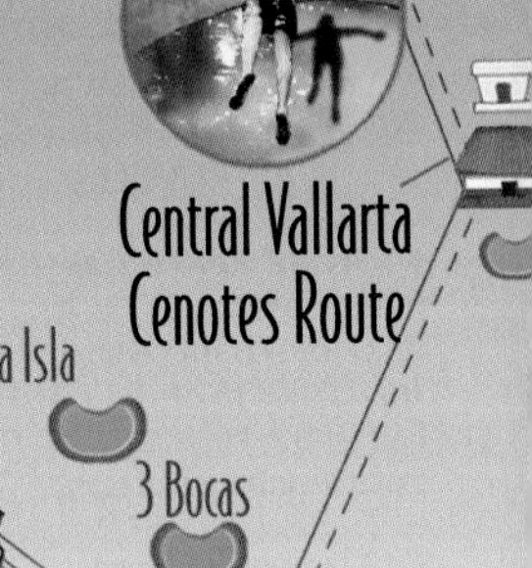

Village atmosphere

National Marine Park

Adventures in cenotes and caves

Wildlife

TOURIST ASSISTANCE

E-10 ***Information Booth***
TUE. - SUN. 9 AM. - 3 PM.
Entrance to Puerto Morelos

A-08 ***Promoción Turística de Puerto Morelos***
Av. Javier Rojo Gómez
Sm. 2, Mz. 2, L. 16
Tels.: 871 0027, 871 0507
Fax: 871 0202

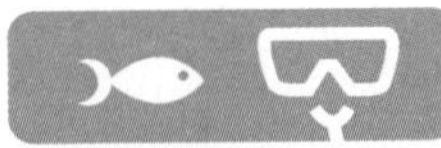

MARINAS

A-10 ***Almost Heaven Adventures***
SPANISH, ENGLISH.
José María Morelos L. 4
Tel./Fax: 871 0230
www.almostheavenadventures.com

A-06 ***Brecko's***
ENGLISH, SPANISH, MAYA.
Sm. 2 M. 15 L. 7-01
Hotel Casita del Mar
Tel.: 871 0517
shadeh@hotmail.com

A-01 ***Marina El Cid***
Sm. 20, L. 1 & 2
Tels.: 871 0185, 871 0184
www.elcid.com

A-10 ***Mystic Diving***
ENGLISH, SPANISH.
SMALL GROUPS, DIGITAL VIDEO AND PHOTOGRAPHY ON ALL TRIPS, PACKAGES.
Av. Rafael Melgar No. 2
Across from the Central Park
Tel.: 734 8002
Tel./Fax: 871 0634
mysticdiving@prodigy.net.mx
www.mysticdiving.com

A-08 ***Netos Snorkeling Tours***
SPANISH, ENGLISH.
INCLUDES TRANSFER AND GEAR.
Hotel Ojo de Agua
Tel./Fax: 871 0202

A-08 ***Nito's Divers***
SPANISH, ENGLISH.
NIGHT DIVE.
Across from the Central Park
Tel./Fax: 871 0012

FERRIES

PASSENGERS, VEHICLES AND CARGO.
Puerto Morelos dock, south of the town
Tel.: 871 0008 ext. 18 & 19

- FROM COZUMEL TO PUERTO MORELOS: 2 PM.
- FROM PUERTO MORELOS TO COZUMEL: 5 AM.
- FROM CALICA TO COZUMEL: 5, 10 AM., 12 & 4 PM.
- FROM COZUMEL TO CALICA: 7, 9 AM., 1 & 6 PM.

RESTAURANTS

BARS

B-09 ***Chip's Bar***
MON.-FRI. 4 PM. - MIDNIGHT., SAT. & SUN. 6 PM. - MIDNIGHT.
Av. Rojo Gómez
Int. Posada El Moro
Tel.: 871 0673

AMERICAN

B-07 ***Mama's Bakery***
CARROT CAKE, HANDMADE BREAD.
MON.-SAT. 7:30 AM. - 5 PM., SUN. 8:30 AM. - 1 PM.
Av. Niños Héroes
Tel.: 845 6810
stickybunsmx@yahoo.com

CAFES

A-10 ***Le Café D'Amancia***

DESSERTS.
8 AM. - 11 PM.
Across from the Central Park
Tel.: 850 4110
amancia80131@hotmail.com

CONTEMPORARY

B-09 ***John Gray's Kitchen***
DINNERS 6 PM. - 11 PM., BAR 6 PM. - 1 AM.
Av. Niños Héroes L.14
Tel.: 871 0665

INTERNATIONAL

A-11 ***Café del Puerto***
PIZZAS AND BISTRO SPECIALTIES.
11 AM. - 11 PM.
Av. Rafael Melgar No. 1
Cel.: 044 998 874 2086
gomezyayo@hotmail.com

A-03 ***Xtabay***
AE VI MC
CROAKER STEAK, STAR GRILL.
6 PM. - 11 PM.
Hotel & Spa Ceiba del Mar
Tel.: 872 8060
Fax: 872 8061
info@ceibadelmar.com
www.ceibadelmar.com

ITALIAN

A-09 ***Spaghettino***
BEEF AND FISH CARPACCIO.
8 AM. - NOON, 5 PM. - 11 PM.
Av. Javier Rojo Gómez
Mz. 15 L. 9 Sm. 2
Tel.: 871 0573
anitsirc62@hotmail.com

A-10 ***Palapa Pizza***
CHICKEN FAJITAS.
5:30 PM. - 11 PM.
Across from the Central Park
Tel.: 871 0039
Fax: 871 0041
clarita@caribe.net.mx

SEAFOOD

A-10 ***Coctelería Los Titos***
SEAFOOD PAELLA.
8 AM. - 9 PM.
Across from the Central Park
Tel.: 871 0738

B-13 *El Muelle*

Calle Cozumel L. 15-A
Tel.: 884 2316
snorkeling@hotmail.com
www.snorkelingrivieramaya.com

A-10 *El Viejo Pescador*

SEAFOOD GRILL.
11 AM. - 11 PM.
Across from the Central Park
Tel./Fax: 871 0296

A-11 *Las Palmeras*

LOBSTER IN GARLIC BUTTER.
GARLIC CREAM SOUP.
10 AM. - 10 PM.
Av. Rafael E. Melgar L. 4
Tels.: 842 4040, 871 0163

A-11 *Pelícanos*

VI MC

PELICANOS COMBINATION PLATE.
8:30 AM. - 11 PM.
Across from the Central Park
Tel.: 871 0014

B-11 *Posada Amor*

VI MC

SEAFOOD,
SUNDAY BUFFET.
7 AM. - 10 PM.
Av. Javier Rojo Gómez
Sm. 1 M. 9 L. 3
Tels.: 871 0033
01 800 234 4324
Fax: 871 0033
pos_amor@hotmail.com

MEXICAN

A-08 *Ojo de Agua*

AE VI MC

8 AM. - 10 PM.
Sm. 2 Mz. 2 L. 16
Tels.: 871 0027, 871 0507
Fax: 871 0202
info@ojo-de-agua.com
www.ojo-de-agua.com

A-10 *El Pirata*

FISH TACOS.
7 AM. - 11 PM.
Av. Javier Rojo Gómez
Across from the Central Park
Tel.: 871 0489

A-09 *Olé Don Pepe Olé*

AE MC

KARAOKE.
SPANISH PAELLA,
GRILLED, SEAFOOD.

1 PM. - 2 AM.
Av. Javier Rojo Gómez
L. 4 M. 4
Tel.: 871 0602

ORIENTAL

B-10 *Hola Asia*

AE VI MC

GENERAL TSO.
WED.-MON. 5 PM. - 11 PM.
Across from the Central Park
Tel.: 871 0679

ATTRACTIONS

A-02 *Acamaya Reef*
UNDERWATER SCULPTURE EXHIBIT.
CAMPING AREA.
Sm. 11 Mz. 5 L. 5
Tel.: 871 0131

Central Vallarta
CHICLEROS CAMP, CENOTES ROUTE. Entrance
Cancún-Chetumal
km 37

F-13 *Jardín Botánico Dr. Alfredo Barrera Marín*
DURATION OF VISIT: 2 HOURS.
Cancún-Chetumal km 37
Tel.: 044 998 850 0940

A-09 *Ikarus Kiteboarding School*
KITE-BOARDING CLINIC,
CERTIFIED WITH PASA.
Tels.: 871 0636, 871 0594
www.ikaruskiteboarding.com

HOTELS

FIVE STAR ★★★★★

 # 3 *Ceiba del Mar Hotel & Spa*

PA PE 125

TEMAZCAL (TRADITIONAL MEXICAN STEAM BATH), TERRACES WITH JACUZZI.
Costera Norte Lote 1
Sm. 10, Mz. 26
Tels.: 872 8060, 872 8068
01 800 426 9772
USA 1 877 545 6221
Fax: 872 8061
info@ceibadelmar.com
www.ceibadelmar.com

FOUR STAR ★★★★

 # 15 *Caribbean Reef Club*

32

ADULTS ONLY. CLOTHING OPTIONAL.
Playa Villa Marina
Tels.: 871 0191, 871 0168
USA 1 800 3 CANCUN
Fax: 871 0190
info@caribbeanreefclub.com
www.caribbeanreefclub.com

 # 8 *Ojo de Agua*

PE PA PC 36

SNORKELING TOURS.
Sm. 2 Av. Javier Rojo Gómez L. 16
Tels.: 871 0507, 871 0027
Fax: 871 0202
info@ojo-de-agua.com
www.ojo-de-agua.com

THREE STAR ★★★

 # 5 *Casita del Mar*

PA 19

Heriberto Frías Sm. 2
Mz. 14 L. 6
Tel./Fax: 871 0301
casitam@prodigy.net.mx
www.hotelcasitadelmar.com

 # 13 *Hacienda Morelos*

15

Rafael E. Melgar No. 5
Tels.: 871 0448, 871 0449
Fax: 871 0015

 # 12 *Posada Amor*

PC 20

Av. Javier Rojo Gómez
Sm. 1 Mz. 9 L. 3
Tels.: 871 0033
01 800 234 4324
pos_amor@hotmail.com

 # 10 *Villas Latinas*

PA 22

Av. Javier Rojo Gómez
Mz. 2 Sm. 2 L. 2
Tel./Fax: 871 0118
villaslatinas@prodigy.net.mx
www.cancun.info

★★★★

HOTEL OJO DE AGUA

Protected by the Caribbean barrier reef, this hotel has 36 large bedrooms, 12 of them with kitchenette. All rooms have direct access to the garden, which connects with the restaurant and palapa. Dive Center and kayak, surf board and snorkeling equipment rental.

Av. Javier Rojo Gómez, SM 2, Lote 16, Puerto Morelos, Quintana Roo, Mexico 77580. Tels.: (998) 871 0027, 871 0507, Fax: (998) 871 0202 *info@ojo-de-agua.com* • *www.ojo-de-agua.com*

TWO STAR ★★

 # 2 *Acamaya Reef Hotel*
7

WITH CAMPING AREA ON THE BEACH.
Sm. 11, Mz. 5, L. 5, entering at CrocoCún.
Tel.: 871 0131
Fax: 871 0132
acamayareef@avantel.net
www.acamayareef.com

 # 7 *Amar Inn*
PC 6

Av. Javier Rojo Gómez esq. Lázaro Cárdenas
Tel.: 871 0026
amar-inn@hotmail.com

 # 9 *Inglaterra*
PE 14

Av. Niños Héroes No. 29
Tel./Fax: 871 0418
hotelinglaterra@hotmail.com
www.visitpuertomorelos.com/inglaterra

 # 14 *Rancho Sak Ol*
PC 13

To the south of the dock
Tels.: 871 0181, 871 0182
Fax: 871 0181
reservations@ranchosakol.com
www.ranchosakol.com

OTHERS

 # 6 *Casa Caribe*
PE 5

Av. Javier Rojo Gómez
Tel.: 871 0459
casacaribe@cancun.com.mx

 # 4 *Motel Edén*
PE 18

Andrés Quintana Roo No. 788 Mz. 21 Sm. 2
Tels.: 871 0450, 871 0451
Fax: 871 0015

 # 11 *Posada El Moro*
PE 6

Av. Javier Rojo Gómez Sm. 2 Mz. 5 L. 17
Tel.: 871 0159
morelos-roths@att.net

EMERGENCIES

B-10 *Police, Fire & Emergencies*
Tel.: 871 0117

B-10 *Civil Protection*
Cel.: 044 998 860 5034

Dr. Carlos Taboada Olvera
CONSULTATIONS IN SPANISH, ENGLISH OR FRENCH.
Tel.: 871 0442
Cel.: 044 998 258 5351

DRUGSTORES

F-11 *Farmacia Paris*
Reg. 17 Mz. 13 Lte. 16 Local 511
Tel.: 871 0254

B-10 *San José Obrero*
Tel.: 871 0053

F-10 *Yza*
24 HRS.
Tel.: 871 0077

CHURCHES

B-10 *San José Obrero*
CATHOLIC.
Across from the Central Park

RANCHO LOMA BONITA

Rancho Grande
MOTORCYCLE, HORSE AND BOAT TOURS.
8 AM. - 6 PM.
Cancún-Tulum km 40
RESERVATIONS IN CANCÚN:
Tels.: 887 5465, 887 5723
Fax: 887 1708
lomabonita@infosel.net.mx
www.lomabonitamex.com

PUNTA BRAVA

FIVE STAR ★★★★★

 # 1 *El Dorado Royale*
384

ADULTS ONLY.
Cancún-Tulum km 45
Tels.: 872 8030, 872 8038
01 800 012 0123
Fax: 872 8033
sales@eldorado-resort.com
www.karismahotels.com

More information: www.caribbeanmex.com

PLAYA DEL SECRETO

 # 2 *Casa del Secreto*
2

LUXURIOUS VILLA WITH 3 OR 5 BEDROOMS.
Chetumal-Cancún km 312
Tel./Fax: 874 4286
USA 1 877 724 8451
info@casadelsecreto.com
www.casadelsecreto.com

PLAYA PARAÍSO

DELUXE ★★★★★★

 # 3 *Mayan Palace Riviera Maya*
PE 1098

TIMESHARING.
Cancún-Playa del Carmen km 48
Tels.: 206 4000
01 800 366 6600
USA 1 800 242 9446
Fax: 206 4050
conciergerm@mayanpalace.com.mx
www.mayanpalace.com.mx

FIVE STAR ★★★★★

 # 4 *Iberostar Paraíso Beach*
424

Chetumal-Cancún km 309
Tels.: 877 2800
01 800 007 5292
Fax: 877 2810
rvaspso@iberostar.com.mx
www.iberostar.com

 # 5 *Iberostar Paraíso del Mar*
388

DRESSEL DIVERS MARINA.
Chetumal-Cancún km 309
Tel.: 877 2800
01 800 557 4879
Fax: 877 2810
rvaspso@iberostar.com.mx
www.iberostar.com

 # 6 *Iberostar Paraíso Lindo*
466

WAVES POOL, CONVENTION CENTER.
Chetumal-Cancún km 309
Tels.: 877 2800
01 800 557 4879
Fax: 877 2810
rvaspso@iberostar.com.mx
www.iberostar.com

PUNTA MAROMA

MARINAS

Playa Maroma Beach Club & Marina
Cancún-Tulum km 55
Tel.: 881 9400
Fax: 881 9406
sales@maromaparadise.com
www.maromaparadise.com

HOTELS

DELUXE ★★★★★★

 # 7 *Maroma Resort and Spa*
PA 56

Cancún-Chetumal km 51
Tel./Fax: 872 8200
reservations@maromahotel.com
www.maromahotel.com

FIVE STAR ★★★★★

 # 8 *Venta Club Playa Maroma*
381

Chetumal-Cancún km 306
Tel.: 877 3300
Fax: 877 3312
recmaroma@webtelmex.net.mx
www.ventaglio.com

TRES RÍOS

LOCATED 54 KM. FROM CANCÚN

ECOLOGICAL PARK WITH RIVERS AND NATURAL SINKHOLES, KAYAKS AND BIKES.
9 AM. - 5 PM.
ADMISSION: $19 US ADULTS, $15 US CHILDREN UNDER 12 YEARS.
Park tel. no.: 850 4774
OFFICES IN CANCÚN:
Tels.: 887 8077, 887 0712
01 800 714 3643
www.tres-rios.com

PUNTA BETE

DELUXE ★★★★★★

 # 10 *Secrets Capri Riviera Cancún*
290

Chetumal-Cancún km 299
Tels.: 873 4880
USA 1 866 GOSECRETS
Fax: 873 4881
info@secretscapri.com.mx
www.secrethotels.net/capri

FIVE STAR ★★★★★

 # 9 *Club El Mandarín*
323

Chetumal-Cancún km 299
Tel.: 873 4700
Fax: 873 4701
mandarin.res@renthotel.org
www.clubelmandarin.com

FOUR STAR ★★★★

 # 20 *Caracol Village*
366

Chetumal-Cancún km 295
Tels.: 873 4444
01 800 614 5848
Fax: 873 4446
ventas@caracolvillage.com
www.caracolvillage.com

 # 16 *Kai-Kaana*
30

Chetumal-Cancún km 296 + 2.1
Tel.: 877 4000
reserva@kaikaanarivieramaya.com.mx
www.kaikaanarivieramaya.com.mx

 # 11 *La Posada del Capitán Lafitte*
PE 62

Cancún-Tulum km 62
Tels.: 873 0214, 873 0212
lafitte@prodigy.net.mx
www.capitanlafitte.com

 # 13 *Qualton Club Riviera Maya*
PA PC PE 30

Chetumal-Cancún km 296
Xcalacoco
Tel./Fax: 877 4000
01 800 638 3838
www.qualton.com

SPECIAL CATEGORY

 # 14 *Coco's Cabañas*
PE 5

Xcalacoco L. 2
Playa del Carmen
Tels.: 874 7056, 887 9330
USA 786 866 9512
1 866 978 4692
Fax: (998) 884 0520
info@travel-center.com
www.travel-center.com

 # 17 *Ikal del Mar*

30

10 km north
of Playa del Carmen
Tel.: 877 3002 Fax: 877 3003
info@ikaldelmar.com
www.ikaldelmar.com

 # 12 *Kailuum II*

30

BREAKFAST AND
DINNER INCLUDED.
ECOLOGICAL, NO ELECTRICITY.
Cancún-Tulum km 62
Tel.: 873 3456
Fax: 801 3502
info@turqreef.com
www.mexicoholiday.com

OTHERS

 # 19 *Bahía Xcalacoco*
Chetumal-Cancún km 296
Entrance to Punta Bete
bahia_xcalacoco@yahoo.com

 # 15 *Cabañas Juanito*
Chetumal-Cancún km 296
Entrance to Punta Bete
Tel.: 877 5400

 # 18 *Paradise Point*
CABINS.
Chetumal-Cancún km 296
Entrance to Punta Bete
Tel.: 806 0757
paradisepoint1@juno.com

PLAYA DEL CARMEN

AIRLINES

J-22 *AeroSaab*
AIR TAXI; FLIGHTS TO MÉRIDA,
UXMAL, CHICHÉN ITZÁ, HOLBOX.
PANORAMIC FLIGHT $250 PESOS
P/P. MINIMUM OF 4 PEOPLE.
7 AM. - 7 PM.
Airstrip, 20a Av. Sur
Tels.: 873 0804, 873 0501
info@aerosaab.com
www.aerosaab.com

J-22 *Aerocaribe*
MON. - FRI. 8 AM. - 8 PM.
45 Av. Sur esq. Calle 3 Sur
Downtown
Chedraui Shopping Center
Local 33ZE
Tels.: 873 0350, 803 2102
1 800 623 4518
Fax.: 873 0121
www.aerocaribe.com

I-21 *Ferinco Travel & Tours*
LAND, SEA AND AIR TOURS;
CHECK AGENCIES AND TOURS.
Tel.: 873 1919

ASSOCIATIONS

P-09 *Angel Notion*
NON PROFIT ORGANIZATION
THAT GATHERS MONEY
DONATIONS.
www.graciasplaya.com
www.angelnotion.com

P-09 *Riviera Maya Hotel Association*
28 Nte. L. 1 Mz. 4 esq.
Hwy. 307 Loc. 103-104
Edificio Profesional 28
Tels.: 859 2276, 859 2234
Tel./Fax: 859 2275
asochtls@rivieramaya.org.mx
www.rivieramaya.com

O-10 *Playa del Carmen Small Hotel Association*
MON.-FRI. 8 AM. - 4 PM.,
SAT. 8 AM. - 1 PM.
45 Av. btwn. Calles 22 & 24
Tel.: 873 3619
Fax: 873 3620
info@hotelesplayadelcarmen.com
www.hotelesplayadelcarmen.com

M-22 *Restaurant Association* (CANIRAC)
MON. - FRI. 9 AM. - 3 PM.
3 Sur btwn. 35 & 40 Av.
Tel.: 873 1033 Fax: 873 2237
canirac7@prodigy.net.mx
www.restaurantesrivieramaya.com

I-19 *Post Office*
MON. - FRI. 9 AM. - 4 PM.,
SAT. 9 AM. - 1 PM.
Av. Juárez, btwn.
15a & 20a Av.
Tel.: 873 0300

P-09 *Riviera Maya Trust Fund for the Development of Tourism*
MON. - FRI. 9 AM. - 2 PM.,
3 PM. - 5:30 PM.
28 Norte L. 1 Mz. 4
esq. Carr. 307 Loc. 200-204
Edificio Profesional 28
Tels.: 859 2173, 859 2170
Fax: 873 0003
info@rivieramaya.com
www.rivieramaya.com

I-19 *Tourist Information*
ENGLISH, FRENCH,
ITALIAN, GERMAN.
Av. Juárez con 15a Av.
Tel.: 873 0242 Fax: 873 2804
consejoturisticorivieramaya@yahoo.com.mx

BANKS

Banamex
9 AM. - 4 PM.
I-14 10a Av. & Calle 12
Tel.: 873 2947
J-19 Av. Juárez btwn. 20 & 25 Av.; Tel.: 873 0825
www.banamex.com

I-15 *Bancrecer Banorte*
MON. - FRI. 9 AM. - 4 PM.,
SAT. 10 AM. - 2 PM.
10a Av. btwn. Calles 8 & 10
Plaza Pelícanos
Tel.: 879 3606
Fax: 879 3607

J-19 *BBV Bancomer*
ATM MACHINE AT THE DOCK.
MON. - FRI. 8 AM. - 4 PM.,
SAT. 10 AM. - 2 PM.
- Av. Juárez btwn. 25 & 30 Av.; Tel.: 873 0402
- Av. Juárez btwn. 20 & 25 Av.; Tel.: 873 1507

www.bancomer.com

HSBC
ATM MACHINE AT CITY HALL.
I-19 30 Av. btwn. Calles 4 & 6
Tel.: 873 1538
L-17 Av. Juárez btwn. 10a & 15a Av.; Tel.: 873 0404

Santander Serfín
ATM MACHINE IN THE FIESTA
KANTENAH HOTEL.
K-19 Av. Juárez btwn.
20 & 25 Av.
MON. - FRI. 9 AM. - 4 PM.
Tel.: 873 2430
F-35 Fracc. Playacar
MON. - FRI. 9 AM. - 4 PM.,
SAT. 10 AM. - 2 PM.
Tels.: 873 2900 al 04

Scotiabank Inverlat
Ⓛ Mon. - Fri. 9 am. - 5 pm., Sat. 10 am. - 2 pm.
G-19 • 5a Av. esq. Juárez
Tels.: 873 1488, 873 2198
I-12 • Av. Constituyentes esq. 10a Av.
Tels.: 803 3724, 803 3725
• ATM machine in Bahia Príncipe.

H-16 ***Trans Caribbean Trust Company***
Ⓛ 9 am. - 9 pm.
5a Av. btwn. Calles 6 & 8
Cel.: 044 984 876 3025
Tel.: 873 2498
Fax: 873 2537
beaches@transcaribbeantrust.com
www.beaches-r-us.com

I-15 ***Autotur***
Buses available for charters or rent. Brand new & deluxe.
115 Av. Mz. 191 Lote 12
por Calle 10 Nte.
Col. Ejidal
Tels.: 206 1794, 206 1879
lgongora@grupoado.com.mx
www.autotur.com.mx

REAL ESTATE

H-18 ***Pimsa***
Ⓛ Mon. - Fri. 10 am. - 2 pm. & 5 pm. - 9 pm., Sat. 10 am. - 2 pm.
5a Av. Nte. btwn. Calles 2 & 4, L. D, Downtown
Tel.: 873 1070
Fax: 873 2761
pimsa2@prodigy.net.mx
www.pimsa-realty.com

H-22 ***Riviera Realtors***
Ⓛ 9 am. - 8 pm.
Plaza Antigua, suite 13, Playacar
Tels.: 803 2070, 803 1981
Fax: 803 1981
www.rivierarealtors.com

BUS COMPANIES

H-19 ***ADO***
Destinations: Yucatán, Campeche, Tabasco, Chiapas, Veracruz, Puebla, Mexico City.
- Av. Juárez esq. 5a Av.
  Tel.: 803 0944
- Av. 20 btwn. 12 & 14

gmedina@grupoado.com.mx
www.concunta.com

H-19 ***Autobuses Riviera***
Departures every 15 minutes to Cancún & the airport every hour.
Av. Juárez esq. 5a Av.
Tels.: 873 0109, 873 0455
gmedina@grupoado.com.mx
www.concunta.com

AGENCIES AND TOURS

In general, the agencies, marinas and tour operators offer their services in English and Spanish only, unless otherwise indicated.

H-05 ***Alltournative***
French, Portuguese, Dutch, German, Italian, Swedish, Maya.
Tours to exclusive sites.
Av. 38 Nte. L. 3 Mz. 200
btwn. 1a & 5a Av.
Tels.: 873 2036, 873 2715
01 800 221 5340
info@alltournative.com
www.alltournative.com

N-06 *Apple Vacations AMSTAR*

TOURS TO TULUM, XEL-HÁ, CHICHÉN ITZÁ, XCARET.
Fracc. Las Gaviotas
40 Av. btwn. Calles 38 & 34
Tel.: 873 3383
Fax: 873 3384
applevrm@prodigy.net.mx
www.applevacations.com

ATV Explorer

MAYA, FRENCH, ITALIAN, GERMAN, DUTCH. FOUR-WHEEL DRIVE TOURS, SWIMMING IN NATURAL SINKHOLES AND SNORKELING.
Rancho 3 km south
of Playa del Carmen
Tel.: 873 1626
Fax: 873 0601
info@atvexplorer.com
www.atvexplorer.com

H-22 *Barceló Viajes*

FRENCH, ITALIAN, PORTUGUESE, FINNISH, GERMAN, SWEDISH.
Plaza Antigua
Tel.: 879 3067
Fax: 879 3106
www.barcelods.com.mx

E-12 *Best Day Tours*

FRENCH, GERMAN, ITALIAN, PORTUGUESE.
Av. Constituyentes No. 1
Outside Hotel Porto Real
Tel.: 873 4013 Fax: 873 4033
bestday@real.com.mx
www.bestday.com

F-21 *Camelot Tours*

MAYA, FRENCH, ITALIAN, GERMAN, DUTCH, POLISH, JAPANESE.
PRIVATE TRANSPORTATION, ROUTES THROUGHOUT THE COUNTRY.
Calle 3 sur Mz 22 L. 4
esq. diagonal 85
Colonia Ejidal
Tels.: 206 1816, 873 3826
Fax: 206 1817
camelottours@yahoo.com
www.camelot-tours.com

H-16 *Classique Travel*

Calle 6 btwn. 5a & 10a Av.
Tels.: 873 2598, 873 0142
Fax: 803 1000
classiqueplaya@hotmail.com

M-19 *Escapes Naturales*

GERMAN, FRENCH.
TRIPS IN JEEPS AND VANS.
Diagonal 85 Sur esq. 3 Sur
Col. Ejidal
Tel./Fax: 859 2461
01 800 ESKAPES
escapes@prodigy.net.mx
www.escapesnaturales.com

N-18 *Expo Playa del Carmen*

TRANSPORTATION TO THE AIRPORT.
4 Norte No. 263
btwn. 40 & 45 Av.
Tels.: 879 3040, 879 3041
Fax: 873 0403
expoplaya@prodigy.net.mx

I-21 *Ferinco Travel & Tours*

LAND, SEA AND AIR TOURS.
Calle 3 Sur esq. 15 Av.
Tel./Fax: 873 1919
cozumel@ferinco.com

J-13 *Hola Tours & Travel*

Dutch, french, german.
Seven-day tours of Cancún, Mérida, Campeche, Palenque, Chicanná & Chetumal.
Calle 14 Bis
btwn. 15a & 20a Av.
Tels.: 873 0805, 873 2044
Fax: 873 1121
holamex@webtelmex.net.mx
www.holatours.com

I-12 *Iberoservice*

German, dutch, french.
16 Nte. btwn. 10a & 15a Av.
Tels.: 873 2745, 873 2318
Fax: 873 2459
playacar@iberoservicemexico.com
www.iberoservicemexico.com

J-09 *Iguana Boat*

Italian, french.
Calle 26 No. 150
btwn.10a & 20a Av.
Tel.: 873 1874 Fax: 873 1874
Cel.: 044 984 876 4058
iguana_boat@yahoo.com
www.iguanaboat.com

H-22 *Intermar Caribe*

French, russian, polish, portuguese, japanese.
ISO 9002.
Av. 30 Norte No. 171
esq. Calle 6 bis
Tel.: 873 1438
Fax: 873 1439

G-12 *Koox Kin Tours*

Italian, german, french.
5a Av. esq. Constituyentes
Tels.: 803 1605, 803 1606
Fax: 803 1247

K-20 *Lomas Travel*

Italian.
Receptive agency.
Av. Juárez btwn. 30 & 25 Av.
Tels.: 873 2775, 873 0370

D-34 *Maritur*

English, spanish.
Lote Hotelero 6 Playacar
Hotel Royal Hideaway
Tel.: 873 4516
www.maritur.com

I-14 *Mayaluum*

French, italian.
Tours of the Riviera Maya, Cuba and Orlando.
10a Av. Nte. esq. Calle 12
Tels.: 873 2960, 873 2961
mayaluum@prodigy.net.mx

H-22 *Olympus Tours*

French, greek. Exportation and ticketing, packages.
Plaza Antigua Loc. 28 & 7
Tel.: 809 3333
Fax: 809 3343
rivieramaya@olympus-tours.com
www.olympus-tours.com

I-14 *Playa Citizen*

German.
Av. 10 btwn. Calles 12 & 14
Tel.: 803 3300
www.playacitizen.com

I-14 *Royale Tours*

Italian, french, german.
Transportation to the airport.
10a Av. esq. Calle 12
Tels.: 803 2016, 873 0622
Fax: 873 0622
www.royaletours.com.mx

I-17 *Susie Tours*

German.
Calle 4 btwn. 10a & 15a Av.
Tel.: 873 0157
Cel.: 044 984 807 5812

H-22 *Thomas Moore*

10a Av. Sur Plaza Antigua
Tel./Fax: 879 3288
www.thomasmoretravel.com

G-17 *Tierra Maya Tours*

German. Guided tours in Mexico and the Maya World.
5a Av. btwn. Calles 4 & 6
Tel.: 873 1385
Fax: 873 1386
www.tierramayatours.com

Translamex

Tours to Chichén Itzá, Tulum, Xel-Há, Cobá, etc.
5a Av.
Tels.: 873 3085, 873 3086
www.translamexl.com

H-16 *Viajes Interactivos*

10a Av. Loc. 1
btwn. Calles 6 & 8 Norte
Tel.: 873 1374 Fax: 873 2513
plaviatu@prodigy.net.mx
www.viajes-interactivos.4t.com

L-06 *Viajes Liberación*

Av. 30 Nte. esq. Calle 38
Branch in Av. Constituyentes
Tels.: 873 2121, 873 0686
Fax: 873 0908
playa.cun@liberacion.com.mx
www.liberacion.com.mx

MARINAS

All of the following marinas offer snorkeling.

F-14 *Abyss Dive Center and Training Facility*

German, french.
Scuba diving at sunrise for certified divers.
Blue Parrot Inn
Calle 12 & the beach
Tel.: 873 2164
abyss@playadelcarmen.com
www.abyssdiveshop.com

D-32 *Barrakuda Scuba México*

Hotel Allegro Resort
Playacar L. 6
Tel.: 873 0339 Fax: 873 0710
www.barrakuda.net

Blue Tracks Caribe

Italian, french, german.
Technical scuba diving following NSS standard.
Sunset Snorkeling Tour.
Posada Capitán Lafitte
Tel.: 873 0212 ext. 21
Fax: 873 0214
www.bluetracks.com

D-05 ***Buceo Cyan-Ha***

GERMAN, FRENCH, ITALIAN.
SCUBA DIVING AT DIFFERENT LEVELS.
Hotel Shangri-La
Tels.: 873 0978, 803 0558
dive@cyanha.com
www.cyanha.com

G-18 ***Club Náutico Tarraya***

Restaurant La Tarraya
Calle 2 Nte. & the beach
Tel.: 879 3329
grafs@prodigy.net.mx
www.prodigyweb.net.mx/grafs

G-16 ***Dive Mike***

SWEDISH, NORWEGIAN, DANISH.
TECHNICAL SCUBA DIVING AND NIGHT DIVES.
Calle 8 btwn. 5a Av. and the beach. Tel.: 803 1228
dive.mike@usa.net
www.divemike.com

E-39 ***Dressel Divers***

GERMAN, ITALIAN, FRENCH, DUTCH.
Av. Xaman-Ha L. 2
Iberostar Quetzal-Tucán
Tel.: 877 2000 ext. 3402
Fax: 873 0200
clubbuceo@prodigy.net.com
www.dresseldivers.com

H-04 ***Expedition Dive***

ITALIAN.
Calle 40 btwn. 5a & 10a Av. Posada Hora Feliz
Cel.: 044 984 804 7981
expeditiondive@yahoo.com
www.expeditiondive.com

D-05 ***Explora***

FRENCH, GERMAN.
Playa Tucan Beach
Tel.: 879 7151
Cel.: 044 984 876 3151
info@exploradive.com
www.exploradive.com

G-13 ***Phantom Divers***

FRENCH, ITALIAN, MAYA.
SCUBA DIVING IN COZUMEL, CERTIFICATIONS, PARASAILING.
1a Av. esq. Calle 14
Tel.: 879 3988
Fax: 873 1974
info@phantomdivers.com
www.phantomdivers.com

G-14 ***Phocea Caribe***

UNDERWATER PHOTOGRAPHY.
FRENCH, ITALIAN, PORTUGUESE, GERMAN, MAYA.
1a Nte. btwn. Calles 10 & 12, Hotel Colibrí
Tel./Fax: 873 1024
phoceacaribe@hotmail.com
www.phoceacaribedive.com

K-18 ***Protec Advanced Training Facility***

GERMAN.
CAVE DIVING WITH GUIDE AND TRAINING.
Calle 4 btwn. 25 & 30 Av.
Tel.: 803 1168
www.protecdiving.com

Scuba Caribe

FRENCH, GERMAN, ITALIAN, DUTCH.
PARASAILING, BANANA RIDE.
• Av. Xaman-Ha Mz. 3 L. 1 Condominios Playacar
Tels.: 877 2300, 803 2066
• Riu Playacar, Riu Yucatán, Riu Tequila
Tel.: 877 2300
• Riu Palace México
Tel.: 877 4200
infomexico@scubacaribe.com
www.scubacaribe.com

E-08 ***Sealife Divers & Dive Shop***

ITALIAN, GERMAN, DUTCH, FRENCH, SWEDISH.
Calle 28, Tucán Beach Club
Tels.: 877 8727
USA 1 810 277 0957
www.travelrivieramaya.com

F-21 ***Studio Blue***

FRENCH, GERMAN.
Calle 1a btwn. 5a Av. & the beach; Tel.: 872 4414
studio-blue@cozumel.net
www.cozumel-diving.net

G-15 ***Tank-Ha Dive Center***

GERMAN, ITALIAN, FRENCH, PORTUGUESE.
5a Av. Nte. btwn. Calles 8 & 10
Tels.: 873 0302, 879 3427
Fax: 873 1355
dive@tankha.com
www.tankha.com

E-35 ***Viva Diving***

GERMAN, ITALIAN, FRENCH.
Av. Xaman-Ha, Playacar
Viva Resorts
Tels.: 873 4600
01 800 898 9968
Fax: 873 4624
www.vivaresorts.com

G-16 ***Yucatek Divers***

GERMAN, FRENCH, DUTCH, ITALIAN.
DIVE CENTER WITH 4.5-METER-DEEP TRAINING POOL AND GEAR SHOP.
5a Av. Nte. btwn. Calles 6 & 8, Downtown
Tel.: 803 1363 Fax: 803 0054
info@yucatek-divers.com
www.yucatek-divers.com

FERRIES

I-16 ***Cruceros Marítimos del Caribe***

ADULTS: $90 PESOS.
CHILDREN: $45 PESOS.
DEPARTURES FROM PLAYA DEL CARMEN TO COZUMEL: 6, 8, 9, 10, 11 AM., 1, 3, 5, 6, 7, 9 & 11 PM.
DEPARTURES FROM COZUMEL TO PLAYA DEL CARMEN: 5, 7, 8, 9, 10 AM., 12, 2, 4, 5, 6, 8 & 10 PM.
Calle 6 Norte No. 4 btwn. 10 & 15 Av.
Tels.: 872 1588, 872 1579
info@crucerosmaritimos.com.mx

DAYTIME ACTIVITIES

GOLF

F-31 ***Playacar Golf Course***

FROM 6 AM. TO SUNDOWN.
CHAMPIONSHIP COURSE.
GREEN FEE 150 US.
Paseo Xaman-Ha Mz. 26 Fracc. Playacar
Tels.: 873 0624, 873 0674
USA 1 800 635 1836
teetimes@palaceresorts.com
www.palaceresorts.com

AIR ADVENTURES

J-22 *Alas*
ENGLISH, SPANISH.
SCENIC AIR TOUR $99 US.
Departures from the airstrip
Tels.: 871 4020, 871 4021
Cel.: 044 984 804 7632
miguelvolador@yahoo.com
alas@nimbos.com

F-21 *Sky Dive*
SKYDIVING FROM 10,000 FEET WITH CERTIFIED INSTRUCTORS.
Plaza Marina No. 32
Tel.: 873 0192 Fax: 873 1015
info@skydivecancun.com
www.skydive.com.mx

KITEBOARDING

G-12 *Ikarus Kiteboarding School*
KITE-BOARDING CLINIC, CERTIFIED WITH PASA.
5a Av. btwn. Av. Constituyentes & 16 Norte
Tels.: 803 3490, 871 0748
Cel.: 044 998 100 0355
Fax: 803 2068
www.ikaruskiteboarding.com

SCHOOLS

I-11 *Playalingua*
INTENSIVE SPANISH COURSES. ENGLISH, FRENCH, GERMAN AND ITALIAN CLASSES.
Calle 20
btwn. 5a & 10a Av.
Tel.: 873 3876 Fax: 873 3877
mail@playalingua.com
www.playalingua.com

M-17 *Soléxico Language and Cultural Center*
SPANISH COURSES.
Calle 6 btwn. 35 & 40 Av.
Tel.: 873 0755
Fax: 873 0754
info@solexico.com
www.solexico.com

TRIPS

H-24 *Aviario Xaman-Ha*
200 BIRDS ON DISPLAY IN 18,000 M². SPACE.
9 AM. - 5 PM.
ADMISSION: $80 PESOS, CHILDREN ACCOMPANIED BY AN ADULT GET IN FREE.
Paseo Xaman-Ha
Tels.: 873 0318, 873 0330

H-06 *El Jardín de Los Aluxes*
BOTANICAL GARDEN, REGIONAL HANDICRAFTS MADE FROM WOOD, SEEDS AND SHELLS. FREE ENTRANCE. TOURS IN ENGLISH, SPANISH AND GERMAN.
5a Av. btwn. Calles 34 & 38

P-25 *El Tamarindo*
AMUSEMENT PARK. Across from the entrance to Playacar

Eco-Aventura Punta Venado
ECOTOURISM & ADVENTURE.
Hwy. 307,
btwn. Calica & Xcaret
Tels.: 898 1331, 898 1917
dircom@puntavenado.com
www.puntavenado.com

H-22 *Plaza Antigua*
DRUGSTORES, TRAVEL AGENCY, MONEY EXCHANGE, CONSULTANCIES, TOBACCO SHOPS, REAL ESTATE AGENCIES, IMMIGRATION OFFICES, RESTAURANTS, ETC.
Av. 10, entrance to Playacar
Tel./Fax: 873 1509

J-12 *Plaza Las Perlas*
BOOKSTORE, CDS AND CASSETTES, BOUTIQUES, GIFTS, ETC.
Av. Constituyentes
btwn. 20 & 25 Av.
Tel.: 803 0626

G-21 *Plaza Paseo del Carmen*
Av. 10, entrance to Playacar
Tel.: 803 3789
paseodelcarmen@hotmail.com

I-15 *Plaza Pelícanos*
MOVIE THEATERS, BEAUTY SALON, TOY STORE, JEWELRY STORE, BANK, SUNDRIES, OPTICAL STORE, GAMES, BOUTIQUES, RESTAURANTS, ETC.
10a Av. btwn. Calles 8 & 10
Tels.: 803 1413, 803 1425
www.plazapelicanos.com.mx

G-35 *Plaza Playacar*
BOUTIQUES, SOUVENIRS, DRUGSTORES, BANK, INTERNET, TOBACCO SHOP, BEAUTY SALON, CAR AND MOPED RENTAL, JEWELRY STORES, ETC.
Paseo Xaman-Ha Mz. 25
Fracc. Playacar
Tels.: 873 0006, 873 0008

MEDICAL SERVICES

Clinics & hospitals

K-18 *Clínica Médica del Carmen*
24-HOUR ASSISTANCE.
Av. 25 esq. Calle 2 Nte.
Tel./Fax: 873 0885

P-09 *Hospital Playa Med*
24-HOUR ASSISTANCE.
Hwy. 307, next to Telebodega
Tels.: 879 3143, 879 3147
Ambulances: 879 3154
medplaya@hotmail.com

Specialists

M-12 *Quiropractor*
NATURAL MEDICINE.
Av. 35 btwn. Calle 16 & Av. Constituyentes
Tels.: 879 3419, 876 5136
Cel.: 044 984 877 7400
info@graciasplaya.com
www.graciasplaya.com

Drugstores

L-16 *El Astillero*
30 Av. esq. Calle 8
Tel./Fax: 873 0190

Payless
I-15 5a Av. L. 2-A Plaza Rincón del Sol Tel.: 879 3296
H-22 Plaza Antigua Tel.: 879 3089
G-19 Av. Juárez Loc. 1, 5a Av. Nte. esq. la playa
G-14 5a Av. Nte., L. 227 Plaza Iguana Azul Loc. 1 Tel.: 879 3354

Farmacias París
H-19 Av. Juárez esq. Av. 10 Nte.; Tel.: 873 0535
H-18 2 Nte. Loc. C No. 114 btwn. 5a & 10a Av. Nte. Tel.: 879 3247
• 30 Av. Nte. close to Av. CTM Loc. 1 y 2, Col. Zazil Tel.: 873 1642

PUBLIC SERVICES

Fire Brigade	879 3669/70
Red Cross	873 1233
Emergencies	65
For emergencies, dial cell phone	114
Police	873 0291
Federal Highway Patrol	(998) 884 1542
Security	873 0291

CAR RENTALS

Álamo	873 1118
Avis	873 3842
Budget	873 2769
Buster	803 0521
Europcar	873 2820
Executive	873 2354
Fiesta	873 2464
Happy Rent a Car	873 1739
Hertz	873 1130
Holiday	873 0959
Localiza	873 0580
National	873 0883
Playa Car Rental	873 0240
Success	873 3970
Thrifty	873 0119
Master Car	Cel. 845 1940

BARS

Q-20 *Alux*
7 PM. - 2 AM.
Av. Juárez Mz. 12 L. 13-A Col. Ejidal
Tels.: 803 0713, 804 6933
milyunalux@hotmail.com

F-14 *Blue Parrot*
AE VI MC
LIVE GROUP. BEACH ATMOSPHERE RIGHT ON THE BEACH.
GRILLED SKIRT STEAK, FAJITAS.
11 AM. - 3 AM.
Calle 12 Nte. & the beach
Tel.: 873 0083 ext. 650
Fax: 873 0049
www.blueparrot.com

G-16 *Bourbon Street*
SPANISH SNACK BAR.
TROPICAL DRINKS, 'MOJITOS' AND MARGARITAS.
NOON - MIDNIGHT
5a Av. Loc. 13 btwn. Calles 6 & 8; Tel.: 803 3022
bourbonstreet@hotmail.com

H-14 *Cabalova*
SPORTS BAR.
SUSHI, JAPANESE FOOD.
NOON - 2 AM.
5a Av. btwn. Calles 12 & 14
Tel.: 803 2396

G-17 *Capitán Tutix*
AE
DISCO-BAR.
10 AM. - 4 AM.
Beachfront with Calle 4
Tel./Fax: 803 1595

H-09 *La Cantinita del Medio*

CUBAN CIGARS FOR SALE.
CUBAN COCKTAILS.
5a Av. esq. Calle 26

H-09 *La Hora Feliz*

VI MC
MANGO MARTINI
7 AM. - 1 AM.
5a Av. esq. Calle 26
La Nueva Quinta
(Little Italy)
Tel.: 803 3435

H-17 *La Taberna*

VI MC
WITH POOL TABLES AND TABLE GAMES.
MOLCAJETE: 3 MEATS IN A 4-CHILE SAUCE.
10 AM. - 6 AM.
10a Av. esq. Calle 4
Tels.: 803 0447, 803 0448

H-17 *Mambo Café*

CARIBBEAN & SALSA MUSIC.
TUE. - SUN. 9 PM. - 4 AM.
Calle 6 Nte. btwn.
5a & 10a Av.
Tels.: 803 2656, 803 2657

H-15 *Ranita*

CARIBBEAN COCKTAILS.
2 PM. - 2 AM.
Calle 10 btwn. 5a & 10a Av.
Tel./Fax: 873 0389
www.ranacansada.com

G-18 *Sky*

3 PM. - 2 AM.
Calle 2 btwn. 5a Av.
& the beach
Cel: 01 998 129 9632

H-14 *Tequila Barrel*

VI MC
LIVE BLUES.
LARGE SELECTION OF TEQUILAS.
11 AM. - 2 AM.
5a Av. btwn. Calles 10 & 12
Tel.: 873 1061
teqbarrel@prodigy.net.mx
www.tequilabarrel.com

H-15 *Ula-Gula*

AE VI
LIVE DJS.
6 PM. - 3 AM.
5a Av. esq. Calle 10
Tel.: 879 3725

G-21 *Viva Margarita*

LIVE DJS FROM 10 PM TO MIDNIGHT, THURSDAY, FRIDAY AND SATURDAY.
Plaza Paseo del Carmen

RESTAURANTS

GERMAN

I-18 *Manne´s Biergarten*

SCHWEINEBRATEN, PORK ROAST.
3 PM. - MIDNIGHT
Calle 4 btwn. 10a & 15a Av.

ARGENTINEAN

H-17 *Buenos Aires*

ARGENTINEAN GRILL.
5 PM. - 12:30 AM.
Calle 6 Nte. btwn.
5a & 10a Av.
Tel./Fax: 873 2751

H-13 *Sur*

ARGENTINEAN GRILL & LOUNGE.
ARGENTINEAN MEAT CUTS.
1 PM. - 1 AM.
5a Av. esq. Calle 14

H-16 *Viva La Vaca*

AE VI MC
LIVE AMBIANCE MUSIC.
ARGENTINEAN MEAT CUTS, PAELLA, ARGENTINEAN GRILL.
NOON - MIDNIGHT.
5a Av. Nte. btwn. Calles 6 & 8
Tels.: 803 2110, 803 2109

BRASILIAN

H-13 *Espadas Brazilian Steak House*

MC VI
ROTISSERIE OF 10 TYPES OF BRAZILIAN-STYLE MEAT.
3 PM. - MIDNIGHT.
5a Av. Norte No. 147
close to 14 Bis
Tel.: 803 1006 Fax: 807 5505

CAFES

THE ESTIMATED PRICE FOR SOME OF THE FOLLOWING CAFETERIAS IS RELATIVE, SINCE NOT ALL OF THEM OFFER MAIN DISHES.

G-18 *Ciao Gelato*

ITALIAN ICE CREAM & COFFEE.
5a Av. btwn. Calles 2 & 4
Tel./Fax: 873 1201
lazylizard@prodigy.net.mx

H-15 *Café Sasta*

SPECIAL GROUND COFFEE, BAKERY.
7 AM. - 11 PM.
5a Av. Loc. 9 btwn.
Calles 8 & 10
Tel./Fax: 875 1051
paamulmx@yahoo.com

G-19 *Coffee Press*

BOOK EXCHANGE, MAGAZINES.
FRESHLY GROUND GOURMET COFFEE, CAKES AND PASTRIES.
7:30 AM. - 10:30 PM.
Calle 2 btwn. 5a Av.
& the beach
Tel./Fax: 873 2272
playacoffee@excite.com
www.playacoffee.com

F-20 *Frosty El Maya*

HOMEMADE ICE CREAM.
11 AM. - 10 PM.
Plaza Marina Loc. 20

H-15 *Hot Baking Company*

SANDWICHES, OMELETTES, HOMEMADE BREAD.
6 AM. - 8 PM.
Calle 10 btwn. 5a & 10a Av.
Tel.: 876 4370
www.bestofrivieramaya.com

I-15 *Italian Coffee*

CAPPUCCINO.
10:30 AM. - 10:30 PM.
Plaza Pelícanos
Tels.: 803 1431, 803 1432
www.italiancoffee.com

G-18 *Playa Scoop*

ITALIAN ICE CREAMS AND COFFEE.
9 AM - 11 PM.
5a Av. btwn. Calles 2 & 4
Tel.: 873 1201

G-21 *Segafredo*

CAFETERIA/BAR/RESTAURANT
PANNINI, ICE-CREAM
10 AM. - MIDNIGHT
Plaza Paseo del Carmen
Tel.: 803 4035

H-09 *Three Monkeys*

INTERNET CONNECTION.
CAPPUCCINO BAR.
9:30 AM. - 1:30 PM., 4 PM. - 12:30 AM.
Calle 26 btwn. 5a & 10a Av.
threemonkeys2000@hotmail.com

INTERNATIONAL

Q-20 *Alux*

WITH A UNIQUE AMBIANCE IN A DRY NATURAL SINKHOLE.
MIL ALUX FILLET.
7 PM. - 2 AM.
Av. Juárez Mz. 12 L. 13-A
Col. Ejidal
Tels.: 803 0713, 804 6933
milyunalux@hotmail.com

H-13 *Apasionado*

VI MC
LIVE LATIN JAZZ.
APASIONADO SEAFOOD PLATE. SURF AND TURF.
6 PM. - MIDNIGHT.
5a Av. esq. Calle 14
Tels.: 803 1100, 803 1101

H-13 *Byblos*

VI MC
6 PM. - MIDNIGHT
Calle 14 btwn. 5a & 10a Av.
Tel.: 803 1790

H-20 *Carlos & Charlie's*

AE VI MC
10 AM. - 2 AM.
Plaza Paseo del Carmen
Tels.: 803 3453, 803 3454
www.grupoandersons.com

H-13 *Captain Bob & Son's*

AE VI MC
CAPTAIN BOB, COCONUT SHRIMP WITH LOBSTER AND SCALLOPS.
6 PM. - MIDNIGHT.
5a Av. No. 277 btwn.
Calles 12 & 14
Tel.: 803 1872

G-19 *Don Emilione*

AE VI MC
SEAFOOD CASSEROLE.
8 AM. - 11:30 PM.
5a Av. Nte. No. 7 btwn.
Av. Juárez & Calle 2 Nte.
Tels.: 873 2073, 873 2074
Fax: 873 2075
restaurant@donemilione.com
www.donemilione.com

G-15 *El Faro Pavilion*

AE VI MC
8 AM. - 5 PM.
Calle 10 Nte. L. 1 btwn.
5a Av. & the beach
Hotel El Faro
Tels.: 873 0970, 873 2061
Fax: 873 0968
www.hotelelfaro.com

H-12 *El Jardín*

AE VI MC
MARIBEL SHRIMP, SHRIMP STEAK IN SWEET-LIME SAUCE, AZTEC MOLCAJETE.
1 PM. - 4 PM., 7 PM. - 11 PM.
5a Av. esq. Calle 14 Bis
Condotel El Tukán
Tel.: 873 1255
www.eltukancondotel.com

H-14 *Fly Restaurant & Lounge*

AE VI MC
LIVE LOBSTER, LARGE SELECTION OF MARTINIS.
SUN. - THU. 5 PM. - MIDNIGHT, FRI. & SAT. 5 PM. - 4 AM.
5a Av. esq. Calle 12
Tels.: 803 1350, 803 1351
flyplayaoceangrill@prodigy.net.mx

H-16 *Jardín Limones*

VI MC
PALAPA SURROUNDED BY GARDENS WITH HANDICRAFT EXHIBIT.
VEGETARIAN FOOD, SEAFOOD.
4 PM. - MIDNIGHT.
5a Av. btwn. Calles 6 & 8
Tel.: 873 0848

G-21 *Johnny Rocket's*

AE VI MC
HAMBURGERS.
10 AM. - 11 PM.
Plaza Paseo del Carmen
Tel.: 803 5648

G-18 *La Casa del Agua*

AE VI MC
MADAGASCAR SHRIMP.
NOON - MIDNIGHT.
5a Av. esq. 2 Nte.
Tels.: 803 0232, 803 0233
Fax: 873 1887
www.travelbymexico.com

H-16 *La Fortuna*

SEAFOOD, SPANISH CUISINE.
NOON - 10 PM.
Av. 10 Nte. esq. Calle 8

G-14 *La Media Luna*

SEAFOOD & VEGETARIAN FOOD.
8 AM. - 11:30 PM.
5a Av. btwn. Calles 12 & 14
Tel./Fax: 873 0526

G-18 *La Ruina*

TIKIN XIC FISH.
8 AM. - 11 PM.
Calle 2 Nte. btwn. 5a Av. & the beach
Tel./Fax: 873 0405
laruina@dicoz.com

G-16 *Le Bistro*

VI MC
8 AM. - 6 PM.
Beachfront esq. Calle 8
Hotel La Alhambra
Tel./Fax: 803 0503

G-17 *Los Rancheros*

VI MC
SALSA AND MARIACHI GROUPS.
SEAFOOD, FINE STEAKS.
11 AM. - 11:30 PM.
5a Av. btwn. Calles 4 & 6
Tels.: 873 3430, 803 2538
rancheros_playa@hotmail.com

H-14 *Palapa Hemingway*

VI MC
CARIBBEAN SHRIMP, SALMON SALAD.
7 AM. - 1 AM.
5a Av. btwn. Calles 12 & 14
Tels.: 803 0003, 803 0004
palapahemingway@hotmail.com

D-09 *Playa Tukan Beach Food and Fun*

AE VI MC
SALADS, PASTA, SEAFOOD GRILL.
10 AM. - 5 PM.
Calle 28 & the beach
Tel.: 803 1961
playatukan@eltukancondotel.com
www.eltukancondotel.com

G-14 *Pokhara*

VI MC
VEGETARIAN CREPES, FONDUE.
5 PM. - MIDNIGHT.
Calle 12 No. 108
btwn. 5a & 1a Av. Nte.

F-21 *Señor Frog's*
AE VI MC
LIVE ROCK AND POP MUSIC.
FLAMBÉED DISHES.
10 AM. - 2 AM.
Playa Marina L. 17
Tel.: 879 0930 Fax: 873 0931
srfrogs@prodigy.net.mx

G-16 *T.G.I. Friday's*
AE VI MC
JACK DANIELS.
11:30 AM. - MIDNIGHT.
5a Av. No. 189
esq. Calle 8 Nte.
Tel./Fax: 879 3570
tgiplaya@prodigy.net.mx

ITALIAN

G-14 *Ambasciata d'Italia*
AE VI MC
FETTUCCINI WITH SHRIMP AND COGNAC, PIZZAS.
NOON - MIDNIGHT.
5a Av. esq. Calle 12
Tel./Fax: 873 0553
ambasciatadit@yahoo.com

I-17 *Café de la Luna*
FRIDAY: LIVE DJ, MUSIC FROM THE 70S.
LASAGNA, SEAFOOD GRILL.
Calle 4 btwn. 10a & 15a Av. Nte.; Tel.: 873 2384
www.posadabarriolatino.com

G-19 *Caffe Roma*
RENATO DI ROMA SHOW.
PESCADORA RICE, FETTUCCINI WITH LOBSTER.
10 AM. - 2 AM.
Av. Juárez No. 109
btwn. 5a Av. & the beach
Tel.: 803 2847

G-16 *Casa Mediterránea*
SEAFOOD GRILL, HANDMADE PASTA.
1 PM. - 11 PM.
5a Av. No. 173
btwn. Calles 6 & 8
Tels.: 876 3926, 879 5771

G-14 *Da Gaby*
GRILLED LOBSTER.
6 PM. - MIDNIGHT
Calle 12 Nte.
btwn. 1a & 5a Av.
Tel./Fax: 875 0048
dagaby@hotmail.com

H-14 *Glass Bar*
HOMEMADE PASTA WITH CRAWFISH.
7 AM. - 3 AM.
Calle 12 btwn. 5a & 10a Av.
Tel.: 873 1335

G-14 *Idea Pasta*
LASAGNA, CANELLONI. HOMEMADE PASTA.
12:30 PM. - 11 PM.
5a Av. btwn. Calles 12 & 14
Tel.: 873 2173

H-10 *Il Pescatore*
PASTA & FISH.
5:30 PM. - 11 PM.
Av. 10 Nte. No. 309
esq. Calle 24

G-09 *Il Portico*
PASTA, SANDWICHES, SALADS.
7:30 AM. - 11 PM.
5a Av. esq. Calle 26
Tel./Fax: 803 0267
ilporticomx@yahoo.com

G-16 *Jaguar*
AE VI MC
PIZZAS WOOD-BURNING OVEN, LOBSTER.
7 AM. - MIDNIGHT.
5a Av. close to Calle 8 Nte. L. 7
Tel./Fax: 873 0650
www.jungla-caribe.com

H-18 *Karen's Pizza*
VI MC
FAJITAS, SHRIMP.
10 AM. - 2 AM.
5a Av. Nte. btwn.
Calles 2 & 4 Nte.

G-13 *La Siesta*
PIZZAS (WOOD-BURNING OVEN).
11:30 AM. - 11:30 PM.
1a Nte. btwn. Calles 12 & 14
Tel.: 879 3982

G-13 *Mandarina's Café*
VI MC
PIZZAS.
2 PM. - 1 PM.
5a Av. esq. Calle 14 Bis
Tel.: 803 1249

H-15 *Pizza Pazza*
SPECIAL DECORATIONS, PACKAGES, HOME DELIVERY.
SHRIMP, SPINACH & GORGONZOLA PIZZA.
11:30 AM. - 11 PM.
- 10 Av. btwn. 8 & 10
- Calle 12 btwn. 10a & 5a Av.
- 5a Av. btwn. 14 & 14 bis.
- Av. Juárez btwn. 20 & 25

Tels.: 803 0903, 803 0895
www.solopizzapazza.com

G-21 *Rolandi's*
AE VI MC

Pizza and pasta cooked on a charcoal stove, fish.
Noon - midnight.
Plaza Paseo del Carmen
Tels.: 803 4121, 803 4122

SEAFOOD

G-17 *Big Lobster*
VI MC

Live lobster, flambées.
Noon - 11 pm.
5a Av. btwn. Calles 4 & 6

G-14 *Blue Lobster*
VI MC

Lobster.
8 am. - 11 pm.
5a Av. Nte. esq. Calle 12
Tel.: 873 1360

P-16 *La Floresta*

Shrimp, crab and marlin tacos.
9:30 am. - 6 pm.
Hwy. 307 km 167.5
Tel.: 879 3164

H-20 *La Bodeguita del Medio*
AE VI MC

Live Cuban music.
Cuban dishes, mojitos.
Noon - 2 am.
Plaza Paseo del Carmen
Tels./Fax: 803 3950, 803 3951
dgonzalez@gruposon.com

G-16 *La Paella*
AE VI MC

Paella, seafood & fish.
5a Av. btwn. Calles 6 & 8
Tel.: 803 2110 Fax: 803 2109

G-18 *La Tarraya*

Tikin Xic fish.
7 am. - 10 pm.
Calle 2 Nte. & the beach
Tel.: 873 2040 Fax: 873 2060
www.tarraya.com.mx

G-16 *Mocambo*

Veracruz-style seafood, seafood tacos.
Noon - midnight
Calle 8 btwn. 5a Av. & the beach

I-14 *Mr. Calin*

Seafood tacos, Calin special, shrimp in garlic butter with octopus.
9 am. - 9 pm.
- Calle 12 btwn. 5a & 10a
- Av. Juárez btwn. 35a & 40a

H-18 *Pez Vela*
AE VI MC

Riviera Maya medallions, lobster.
7 am. - midnight.
5a Av. esq. Calle 2
Tel.: 873 0999

I-13 *Wine & She's*
AE VI MC

Tapas (Spanish appetizers) Spanish omelet, soft-tough-shell crab.
2 pm. - 2 am.
Calle Corazón
Tel.: 803 2995

MEDITERRANEAN

I-13 *Ágora*
VI MC

Fish, pasta.
8 am. - noon, 5 pm. - midnight (Sun. closes early)
10 Av. btwn. Calles 12 & 14
Tel.: 873 1484

MEXICAN

H-18 *Ajúa! Maya*
AE VI MC

Pre-Hispanic, Latin, cumbia and salsa music.
Caesar salad, flambéed lobster and shrimp, Angus beef cuts, desserts.
Noon - 1 am.
Calle 4 btwn. 5a & 10a Av.
Tels.: 873 2523, 873 3000
Fax: 803 1118
www.ajuamaya.com

O-20 *Bisquets de Playa*
VI

House calls.
Homemade bread, Tampiqueña-style meat.
24 hrs.
Av. Juárez esq. 45a Av.
Tel.: 803 1616 Fax: 803 1717

H-17 *Casa Tequila*
AE VI MC

Live Mexican country music.
More than 234 kinds of tequila.
Grilled specialties & seafood.
7 am. - 1 am.
5a Av. btwn. 4 & 6 Nte.
Tels.: 873 3622, 873 0195

G-13 *Chuchis*

Home-style food.
7 am. - 10 pm.
Calle 1a Nte. btwn. 12 & 14
Tel./Fax: 873 0629

G-19 *D' Nada*

Fajitas.
7 am. - midnight
Av. Juárez btwn. 5a Av. & the beach
Tels.: 873 2641, 873 0066

H-18 *El Almendro*
VI MC

Grilled seafood.
8 am. - midnight
Calle 4 btwn. 5a & 10a Av.
Tel.: 803 1473 Fax: 873 3924

H-10 *El Asador de Manolo*
VI MC

Charcoal grilled meats and chicken, seafood.
1 pm. - midnight.
Av. 10 btwn. Calles 24 & 26
Tel.: 803 0632
capellimanolo@hotmail.com

G-19 *El Tacolote*
AE VI MC

Tacolote grilled meat and seafood selection.
11 am. - midnight
Av. Juárez btwn. 5a Av. & the beach
Tel.: 873 1363 Fax: 873 2149
www.tacolote.com.mx

H-17 ***Estas Son Las Mañanitas***
VI MC
Pasta with lobster, Mexican-style fish.
7 AM. - 11:30 PM.
5a Av. btwn. Calles 4 & 6
Tel./Fax: 873 0114

G-15 ***La Parrilla***
AE VI MC
Live mariachi music.
Meats and seafood cooked over live coals, Margaritas.
Noon - 5 PM., 5:30 PM. - 1 AM.
5a Av. esq. Calle 8
Tel./Fax: 873 0687
www.laparrilla.com.mx

G-18 ***La Patrona***
Milpa Alta fish fillet.
Calle 2 Nte. btwn. 5a Av. & the beach

H-10 ***Las Delicias***
7 AM. - 11 PM.
5a Av. Nte. esq. Calle 22 Nte.; Tel.: 803 1214

G-19 ***Las Piñatas***
Caribbean seafood plate.
8 AM. - 11 PM.
Av. Juárez btwn. 5a Av. & the beach
Tel.: 873 1196 Fax: 873 0392

H-09 ***La Vagabunda***
VI MC
Fish & seafood.
7 AM. - 11:30 PM.
5a Av. btwn. Calles 24 & 26
Tel.: 873 3753

J-15 ***Oasis Deli***
Homemade & Mexican dishes.
10AM. - 5 PM.
Av 20 Nte. esq. Calle 10 bis
Tel.: 803 1781

H-16 ***Sueño Guajiro***
Seafood tacos.
5 PM. - 1 AM.
Calle 6 Nte.
Tel.: 803 0956

H-13 ***Xlapak***
Natural juice bar.
Maya World library, slide show, Aztec dance.
8 AM. - 11 PM.
5a Av. btwn. Calles 14 & 14 Bis
Cel.: 044 984 804 0407

Natural healthy food

H-14 ***100% Natural***
VI MC
Grilled chicken with prickly pear salad.
7 AM. - 11 PM.
5a Av. btwn. Calles 10 & 12
Hotel Copacabaña
Tels.: 873 2242, 873 1941
www.100natural.com

G-15 ***Café Tropical***
AE VI MC
Falafel.
7 AM. - midnight
5a Av. btwn. Calles 8 & 10 L. 8
Tel./Fax: 873 2111
cafetropical@prodigy.net.mx

H-06 ***La Cueva del Chango***
Breakfast, fresh fruit and juices.
8 AM. - 2 PM.
Calle 38 Nte. esq. 5a Av.
Tels.: 873 2137, 804 9190

Regional

P-18 ***El Faisán y El Venado***
VI MC
Pibil-style pork, stuffed cheese ball.
7 AM. - 9 PM.
Cancún-Tulum Hwy.
Tel.: 873 0533

H-15 ***Yaxché***
AE VI MC
Live pre-Hispanic music.
Tikin Xic fish, cochinita pibil, Poc Chuc.
Noon - midnight
Calle 8 btwn. 5a & 10a Av.
Tels.: 873 2502, 873 3712
www.mayacuisine.com

Thai

H-15 ***Babes Noodle Bar***
Thai Noodle Bar.
Noon - midnight.
Calle 10 btwn. 5a & 10a Av.
www.babesnoodlesandbar.com

Fast food

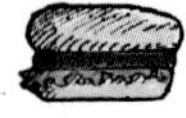

G-19 ***Burger King***
9 AM. - midnight.
1a Av. Sur btwn. 5a Av. & the beach
Tel./Fax: 873 1523

G-19 ***Dominos***
10 AM. - midnight.
5a Av. esq. Juárez
Tel.: 873 1616

G-19 ***McDonald's***
8 AM. - midnight.
5a Av. esq. Juárez
Tel.: 873 1888

I-15 ***Papa John's***
11 AM. - midnight.
Plaza Pelícanos Loc. 16
Tel.: 803 3333 Fax: 843 6117

H-09 ***Pizzas Renzo***
Noon - 11 PM.
5a Av. btwn. Calles 28 & 30

G-21 ***Subway***
8 AM. - 10 PM.
1a Sur, next to the dock
Tel.: 803 0402

H-14 ***Mayami***
Brazilian style hot dogs.
3 PM. - 2 AM.
Calle 12 btwn. 5a & 10a Av.

★★★★★★

PLAYA DEL CARMEN

Enjoy the privacy and comfort only luxury hotels can offer at this resort located on a white sand beach, in the heart of Playa del Carmen. Beautifully decorated Junior Suites with Jacuzzi and balcony or terrace, with luxury amenities. Several restaurants and bars, Spa with steam bath, sauna, immersion tank and jacuzzi, area for massages and other services, all with the highest quality.

Sales & Marketing
Tel. + 52 (998) 881 7311
sales@realresorts.com.mx

Groups
Tel. + 52 (998) 881 7312
groups@realresorts.com.mx

Reservations
Tel. + 52 (998) 881 7340
Mex. 01 800 216 5500
EUA & CAN 1 800 543 7556
Fax: + 52 (998) 881 7399
reservations@realresorts.com.mx

• 418 Royal Junior Suites • www.realresorts.com.mx

★★★★★

PLAYA DEL CARMEN

Set in the heart of Playa del Carmen, facing the sea; 271 spacious Junior Suites with hammocks on the terrace for enjoying a relaxing atmosphere. 5 restaurants and 4 bars, with 24-hour All Inclusive Club; group and convention halls, spa, recreational activities, water sports and more.

Sales: + 52 (998) 881 7311, sales@realresorts.com.mx • Reservations: + 52 (998) 881 7340, reservations@realresorts.com.mx
Mex. 01 800 216 5500, EUA & CAN 1 800 543 7556; Fax: + 52 (998) 881 7399 • **www.realresorts.com.mx**

★★★★

PLAYA DEL CARMEN

Its comfortable facilities combined with its personalized service and attractive gardens make Real Playa del Carmen unique, whether you wish to enjoy the beach or the nightlife on Quinta Avenida. It has 3 restaurants, a beach club, water sports center and tennis courts.

Sales: + 52 (998) 881 7311, sales@realresorts.com.mx • Reservations: + 52 (998) 881 7340, reservations@realresorts.com.mx
Mex. 01 800 216 5500, EUA & CAN 1 800 543 7556; Fax: + 52 (998) 881 7399 • **www.realresorts.com.mx**

HOTELS

THE STAR CLASSIFICATION OF THE FOLLOWING HOTELS IS BASED ON THE LISTINGS IN THE RIVIERA MAYA TRUST FUND DIRECTORY.

DELUXE ★★★★★★

E-12 ***Royal Porto Real***
418

Av. Constituyentes
btwn. 1a Nte. & the beach
Tels.: (998) 881 7311
01 800 216 5500
EUA 1 800 543 7556
Fax: (998) 881 7399
reservations@realresorts.com.mx
www.realresorts.com.mx

FIVE STAR ★★★★★

H-14 ***Deseo***
PE 18

ADULTS ONLY.
5a Av. esq. Calle 12
Tel.: 879 3620 Fax: 879 3621
EUA 1 866 978 0891
info@hoteldeseo.com
www.hoteldeseo.com

E-12 ***Gran Porto Real & Spa***
PE 271

Av. Constituyentes No. 1
btwn. 1a Nte. & the beach
Tels.: 873 4000
01 800 216 5500
EUA 1 800 543 7556
Fax: 873 4099
porto@realresorts.com.mx
www.realresorts.com.mx

The Reef Coco Beach
201

Costera Norte L. 1, Mz. 7
Tel.: 873 4120 Fax: 873 2001
sales@thereefcocobeach.com
www.thereefcocobeach.com

FOUR STAR ★★★★

G-09 ***Adelia María***
PE 18

Calle 1 Nte. esq. 26 Nte.
Tel./Fax: 879 3393
www.adeliamaria.com.mx

F-14 ***Blue Parrot Inn***
PE 46

Calle 12 Nte. L. 3
Tel.: 873 0083 Fax: 873 0049
USA 888 854 4498
reservations@blueparrot.com
www.blueparrot.com

H-11 ***Caribbean Paradise Resort and Spa***
PE PC 49

AGREEMENT WITH A GOLF CLUB.
5a Av. Nte.
esq. Av. Constituyentes
Tels.: 803 2032, 873 1010
Fax: 803 3033
www.caribbeanparadisenet.com

J-16 ***Colonial***
PE 17

20 Av. btwn. Calles 8 & 6
Tel./Fax: 873 0456
colonial@quintanaroo.com

F-15 ***El Faro***
PE 29

AGREEMENT WITH A GOLF CLUB.
Calle 10 Nte. & the beach
Tel.: 873 0970
Fax: 873 0968
www.hotelelfaro.com

G-17 ***El Sol del Caribe***
PE 11

WITH EQUIPPED KITCHENETTE.
5a Av. No. 156
btwn. Calles 4 & 6
Tel.: 873 0958
Fax: 873 2755
elsoldelcaribe@prodigy.net.mx

J-11 ***Gloria del Caribe***
PE 90

Av. Constituyentes No. 180
btwn. 15a & 20a Av.
Tels.: 873 1590, 873 1591
Fax: 873 1592
gloriadelcaribe@prodigy.net.mx

H-19 ***Hacienda del Caribe***
PE 34

Calle 2 Nte. No. 130
btwn. 5a & 10a Av.
Tels.: 873 3132, 873 3130
Fax: 873 1149
info@haciendadelcaribe.com
www.haciendadelcaribe.com

H-13 ***La Tortuga***
PA 45

Av. 10 esq. Calle 14
Tels.: 873 1484, 873 1967
Fax: 873 0798
info@hotellatortuga.com
www.hotellatortuga.com

E-07 ***Las Palapas***
PA PE PC 75

34 Nte. btwn. 5a Av.
& the beach
Tels.: 873 0582, 873 0616
Fax: 873 0458
info@laspalapas.com.mx
www.laspalapas.com.mx

I-17 ***Los Itzaes***
PA PE PC 16

WITH BEACH CLUB.
10a Av. No. 3
esq. Calle 6 Bis.
Tels.: 873 2398, 873 2397
Fax: 873 2373
hotellositzaes@prodigy.net.mx
www.itzaes.com

I-14 ***Mayan Paradise***
PC 44

10 Av. Nte.
btwn. Calles 10 Bis & 12
Tel.: 873 0933
Fax: 873 2015

G-20 ***Molcas***
PA 26

Calle 1a Sur btwn.
Calle 3 Sur & the beach
Tels.: 873 0070, 873 0071
Fax: 873 0135
molcas@prodigy.net.mx
www.molcas.com.mx

H-14 ***Mosquito Blue***
PE 46

ADULTS ONLY.
FREE 24-HOUR INTERNET.
Calles 12 btwn.
5a & 10a Av.
Tels.: 873 1335, 873 1336
873 1245 Fax: 873 1337
sales@mosquitoblue.com
www.mosquitoblue.com

H-11 ***Paradise***
PE 32

10a Av.
btwn. Calles 20 & 22
Tel.: 873 1397
Fax: 873 1398
info@hotel-paradise.com
www.hotel-paradise.com

F-16 ***Playa Maya***
PC 22

FREE INTERNET AND SAFES
Beachfront L. 1-1 btwn.
Calles 6 & 8 Nte.
Tel.: 803 2022
Tel./Fax: 803 2023
manager@playa-maya.com
www.playa-maya.com

★★★★

CARIBBEAN PARADISE RESORT

This Spa and Gourmet resort is located in downtown Playa del Carmen, on the famous 5th Avenue. It is surrounded by boutiques, restaurants and entertainment centres and has a unique atmosphere.

46 rooms with balcony or terrace, 9 of them with ocean view. Its beach club is located only a few steps from the hotel.

5a Av. Norte Esq. Constituyentes, Playa del Carmen, Q. Roo 77710 Tel.: 01 (984) 803 2032, Fax: 01 (984) 803 3033
• caribbeanreservaciones@prodigy.net.mx • www.caribbeanparadisenet.com •

★★★★

LAS PALAPAS

Tranquillity, turquoise blue waters, long stretches of white sand beaches and the tropical atmosphere of its palapas make for a dream vacation!

34 Nte. btwn. 5a. Ave. and the beach, Playa del Carmen; Mexico
Tel.: (984) 873 0582, Fax: 873 0458 • www.laspalapas.com

★★★★

LOS ITZAES HOTEL

Charming hotel located in the heart of Playa del Carmen. Known for its comfort and tranquility, as well as the personalized service given to guests. Boasts 14 rooms and 2 Jr. Suites; pool- Jacuzzi, solarium terrace, massages, aromatherapy and beach club. Breakfast is included.

10a. Av. No. 3, Downtown, Playa del Carmen, Quintana Roo, Mexico 77710, Tels.: (984) 873 2398, 873 2397; Fax: (984) 873 2373
• *hotellositzaes@prodigy.net.mx* • *www.itzaes.com* •

H-09 *Quinto Sol*
PA PE PC 20
WITH BEACH CLUB.
5a Av. esq. Calle 28 No. 330
Tels.: 873 3292, 873 3293
Fax: 873 3294
reservation@hotelquintosol.com
www.quintosol.com

H-07 *Real Playa del Carmen*
132
WITH BEACH CLUB.
Calle 34 btwn.
5a & 10a Av. Nte.
Tel.: (998) 881 7340
Fax: (998) 881 7314
reservations@realresorts.com.mx
www.realresorts.com.mx

I-08 *Riviera Caribe Maya*
PE 22
10a Av. Nte. esq.
Calle 30 Nte.
Tel.: 873 1193 Fax: 873 2311
info@hotelrivieramaya.com
www.hotelrivieramaya.com

G-08 *Riviera del Sol*
PE 23
1a Av. Nte.
esq. Calle 30 Nte.
Tels.: 873 3100, 873 3102
01 800 043 4343
USA 1 800 822 3274
Fax: 873 3104
stay@rivieradelsol.com
www.rivieradelsol.com

THREE STAR ★★★

G-15 *Albatros*
PE 36
Calle 8 Nte. & the beach
Tels.: 873 0001
USA 1 800 538 6802
Fax: 873 0002
albatros@playadelcarmen.com
www.mexicoholiday.com

G-16 *Alejari*
PC 30
Calle 6 Nte. btwn. 5a Av. & the beach
Tels.: 873 0374, 873 0372
Fax: 873 0005
halejari@prodigy.net.mx
www.hotelalejari.com

G-16 *Alhambra*
PE PC 24
MASSAGES, FLORAL THERAPIES AND YOGA CLASSES.
Calle 8 Nte. & the beach
Tels.: 873 0735
01 800 216 8799
USA 1 877 642 4535
Fax: 803 0503
alhambr7@prodigy.net.mx
www.alhambra-hotel.net

I-17 ***Antigua Posada Barrio Latino***
PE 16
Calle 4 btwn.
10 & 15 Av. Nte.
Tel./Fax: 873 2384
info@posadabarriolatino.com
www.posadabarriolatino.com

F-13 ***Blue Beach***
PA PE 28
Privada 1a Nte.
btwn. Calles 12 & 14
Tel.: 873 1204 Fax: 873 2075
info@bluebeachhotel.com
www.bluebeachhotel.com

H-16 ***Cabañas Bananas***
PE 24
5 Av. btwn. Calles 6 & 8
Tel./Fax.: 873 0036
cabanasbananas@hotmail.com

I-18 ***Casa Tucán***
PE 23
Pool for practicing scuba diving and a dive shop.
Calle 4 btwn. 10a & 15a Av.
Tel./Fax: 873 0283
casatucan@prodigy.net.mx
www.casatucan.de

H-09 ***Coco Río***
PE PC 15
With beach club.
Calle 26 btwn. 5a & 10a Av.
Tel.: 879 3361 Fax: 879 3362
hotelcocorio@hotmail.com
www.hotelcocorio.com

G-14 ***Cohiba***
PE 20
1a Av. esq. Calle 12
Tel.: 873 2080 Fax: 873 2090
hotelcohiba@prodigy.net.mx

G-14 ***Colibrí***
PE 33
Av. 1a Nte. btwn.
Calles 10 & 12
Tel.: 873 1833 Fax: 873 2516
hotel-colibri@prodigy.net.mx
www.hotelcolibri.com

G-16 ***Jungla Caribe***
PE 25
5a Av. esq. Calle 8 Nte. L.7
Tel.: 873 0974 Fax: 873 0650
info@junglacaribe.com
www.junglacaribe.com

G-15 ***Kinbè***
PE 19
Calle 10 Nte.
btwn. 1a & 5a Av.
Tel.: 873 0441 Fax: 873 2215
hotelkinbe@prodigy.net.mx
www.kinbe.com

J-18 ***La Paz***
PE 20
Transportation to the airport.
20 Av. btwn. Calles 2 & 4
Tel.: 873 0467 Fax: 873 3178
hotellapaz@prodigy.com.mx
www.hotellapaz.com

G-15 ***Corto Maltés***
PE 14
Calle 10 btwn. 5a Av.
& the beach
Tel./Fax: 878 0206
www.cortomaltes.com

G-14 ***Costa del Mar***
PE 38
1a Av. Nte. btwn.
Calles 10 & 12
Tels.: 873 0850, 873 0058
Fax: 873 0058
costamar@prodigy.net.mx
www.hotelcostadelmar.com

G-19 ***Don Emilione***
PE 10
5a Av. Nte. No. 7 btwn.
Av. Juárez & Calle 2 Nte.
Tel.: 873 2073 Fax: 873 2075
info@donemilione.com
www.donemilione.com

H-12 ***El Tukán Condotel***
PE 81
Natural sinkhole, beach club.
5a Av. Nte.
Tel.: 873 1255
www.eltukancondotel.com

H-08 ***Fiesta Banana***
PE PC 23
5a Av. Nte. esq. Calle 32
Tel.: 803 0201 Fax: 803 0202
fiestabanana@mail.com
www.fiestabanana.com

G-14 ***Hacienda María Bonita***
PE PC 41
10 Av. Nte. No. 215
btwn. Calles 10 & 12
Tels.: 873 2052, 873 2051
Fax: 873 2049
hmbonita@yahoo.com
www.hotelmariabonita.com

J-17 ***Hul Ku***
PE 37
20 Av. btwn. Calles 4 & 6
Tel./Fax: 873 0021
info@hotelhulku.com
www.hulku.com

H-15 ***La Rana Cansada***
PE 15
Calle 10 btwn. 5a & 10a Av.
Tel./Fax: 873 0389
mail@ranacansada.com
www.ranacansada.com

J-12 ***Las Golondrinas***
PE 50
With beach club.
Av. Constituyentes
No. 176 esq. Calle 20
Tels.: 873 2805, 873 2806
873 2807, 873 2808
USA 1 800 822 3274
Fax: 873 2463
hotellasgolondrinas@prodigy.net.mx
www.hotellasgolondrinas.com

H-16 ***Lunata***
PC PE 10
5a Av. btwn. Calles 6 & 8
Tel.: 873 0884 Fax: 873 1240
lunata@playadelcarmen.com
www.lunata.com

L-19 ***Maranatha***
PE 34
Av. Juárez btwn.
30 & 35 Av.
Tels.: 873 0143, 873 0929
Fax: 873 0038
www.hotelmaranatha.com

G-15 ***Maya Bric***
PE 29
5a Av. Nte. btwn.
Calles 8 & 10
Tels.: 873 2041, 873 2206
Fax: 873 2041
info@mayabric.com
www.mayabric.com

F-18 ***Mimi del Mar***
PE PA PC 18
1a Nte. & the beach
Lote 1-A, Mz. 2
Tels.: 873 3187, 873 2595
Fax: 873 2595
htlmimi@prodigy.net.mx
www.mimidelmar.com

L-17 ***Mom´s***
PE 26
30 Av. esq. Calle 4 Nte.
Tels.: 873 0315, 873 1269
Fax.: 873 0315
info@momshotel.com
www.momshotel.com

G-16 ***Pensión San Juan***
PC 14
5a Av. No. 165
Btwn. Calles 6 & 8 Nte.
Tel.: 873 0647
Fax: 879 3990
pensionsanjuan@prodigy.net.mx
www.pensionsanjuan.com

H-10 ***Playa Suites Hotel & Apartments***
PE 20
10a Av. No. 315
Tels.: 873 0565, 879 3374
Fax: 879 3373
info@playasuites.com
www.playasuites.com

H-15 ***Plaza***
PE 33
5a Av. Bis.
close to Calle 10 Nte.
Tels.: 873 2193, 873 2642
Fax: 873 2196

G-12 ***Plaza Mariachi***
PA PE 18
100 METERS FROM THE BEACH.
5a Av. close to Calle 16 Nte. No. 251
Tels.: 873 1518, 873 3736
Fax: 873 2482
01 800 712 0745
hotelplazamariachi@hotmail.com
www.hotelplazamariachi.com.mx

I-13 ***Posada Las Ondinas***
PE 10
10a Av. esq. Calle 14
Tel.: 873 1013
Fax: 873 1965
ondinas@playa.com.mx
www.posadalasondinas.com

I-16 ***Sahara***
PE 25
EQUIPPED KITCHENETTE.
15 Av. esq. Calle 8
Tel.: 873 2818
Fax: 873 2236
reservations@saharainplaya.com
www.saharainplaya.com

H-10 ***San Ángel***
PE 18
Calle 24 Nte. Mz. 55 L. 17
No. 124 btwn. 5a & 10a Av.
Tel./Fax: 873 2584
www.travelbymexico.com/qroo/sanangel

D-05 ***Shangri La Caribe***
PA 122
Calle 38 Nte. esq. the beach
Tels.: 873 0579, 873 0591
Fax.: 873 0500
info@shangrilacaribe.net
www.shangrilacaribe.net

H-10 ***Tierra Maya***
PE 22
TEMAZCAL, REIKI, JACUZZI.
Calle 24 Nte. btwn.
5a & 10a Av.
Tels.: 873 3958, 873 3960
Fax: 803 3381
mail@hoteltierramaya.com
www.hoteltierramaya.com

G-15 ***Treetops Hotel***
PC 18
GROUP AND DIVING PACKAGES.
Calle 8 btwn. 5a Av.
& the beach
Tel.: 873 1495 Fax: 873 0351
treetops@prodigy.net.mx
www.treetopshotel.com

G-09 ***Villa Amanecer***
PA PC 21
Calle 26 Nte. No. 286
Tels.: 873 2716, 873 3197
Fax: 873 2717
mail@villa-amanecer.com
www.villa-amanecer.com

G-17 ***Vista Caribe***
PE 35
Calle 6 Nte. btwn. 5a Av.
& the beach
Tels.: 873 0349, 803 0649
Fax: 873 0645
manager@hotelvistacaribe.com
www.hotelvistacaribe.com

TWO STAR ★★

H-10 ***Aventura Mexicana***
PC 30
FOR THOSE AGED 16 AND OVER.
10a Av. esq. Calle 22
Tels.: 873 1876, 100 2708
Fax: 873 1876
hotelaventura@prodigy.net.mx
www.aventuramexicana.com

H-20 ***Balam Nah Center***
PE 21
WITH BEACH CLUB.
1a Av. Sur Bis No. 1
btwn. 5a & 10a Av.
Tel.: 873 2116 Fax: 873 2117
hotelbalamnah@yahoo.com
www.hotelbalamnah.com

J-14 ***Casa de las Flores***
PE 12
Av. 20 Nte. No. 150
btwn. Calles 4 & 6, Downtown.
Tel.: 873 2898
Fax: 873 2534
hotelcasadelasflores@prodigy.net.mx
www.hotelcasadelasflores.com

G-12 ***Chichan Baal Kah***
PE 7
Calle 16 Nte.
Btwn. 5a Av. & 1a Nte.
Tels.: 873 1252
USA 1 800 538 6802
info@turqreef.com
www.mexicoholiday.com

G-14 ***Copa Cabaña***
PE 30
5a. Av. Nte. No. 209
btwn. Calles 10 & 12
Tels./Fax: 873 0209,
873 0218
copa_cabana@usa.net
www.copacabanaplaya.net/

G-14 ***Da Gabi***
PE 10
Calle 12 Nte.
Btwn. 1a & 5a Av.
Tel./Fax: 873 0048
dagabi@hotmail.com
www.prodigyweb.net.mx/dagabi

G-17 *Delfín*
13
5a Av. esq. Calle 6 Nte.
Tel./Fax: 873 0176
hoteldelfin@prodigy.net.mx
www.hoteldelfin.com

J-14 *El Campanario Sr. Suites*
11
WITH BEACH CLUB AND KITCHENETTE IN THE ROOMS.
15 Av. Nte. No. 218
esq. Calle 12
Tel./Fax: 873 1139
info@hotellasgolondrinas.com
www.hotellasgolondrinas.com

G-16 *Lab Nah*
33
WITH KITCHENETTE.
Calle 6 Nte. btwn. 5a Av. & the beach
Tels.: 873 2099
USA 1 800 822 3274
Fax: 873 0204, 873 2099
reservations@labnah.com
www.labnah.com

K-17 *Melodía*
20
24-HR INTERNET SERVICE.
Calle 4 btwn. 25 & 30 Av.
Tel./Fax: 873 0336
hotelmelodia@prodigy.net.mx
hotelmelodia@hotmail.com

G-13 *Moon Gate*
11
5a Av. esq. Calle 16
Tel.: 873 1949 Fax: 873 0668
www.eltukancondotel.com

I-18 *Paraíso Azul Casa de Gopala*
16
POOL FOR PRACTICING SCUBA DIVING AND A DIVE SHOP.
Calle 2 Nte. btwn.
10a & 15a Av.
Tel./Fax: 873 0054
casadegopala@prodigy.net.mx
www.casadegopala.com

I-19 *Playa del Carmen*
24
Av. Juárez No. 151
btwn. 10a & 15a Av.
Tel.: 873 0294

G-16 *Pelícano Inn*
39
Beach access between
Calles 6 & 8 Nte.
Tel.: 873 0997 Fax: 873 0998
pelicanoinn@playawireles.com
www.mayanriviera.com

H-15 *Posada Freud*
13
JUNGLE TOUR.
5a Av. btwn. Calles 8 & 10
Tel./Fax: 873 0601
reservations@posadafreud.com
www.posadafreud.com

H-18 *Posada Mayeli*
24
Calle 2 Nte.
btwn. 5a & 10a Av.
Tels.: 873 2799, 878 1002
mayeli2@prodigy.net.mx
www.mayeli.com

M-18 *Posada San Carlos*
22
Privada Calle 2 Bis. Nte.
btwn. 35 & 40 Av.
Tel.: 873 1107

L-20 *Suites Las Quintas*
31
Av. Juárez
btwn. 30 & 35 Av.
Tel./Fax: 873 0120

J-16 *Yum K'iin*
21
20 Av. Nte. No. 171
btwn. Calles 6 & 8
Tel.: 873 0173 Fax: 873 3467
yumkiin@prodigy.net.mx

ONE STAR ★

H-14 *Baal Nah Kah*
5
Calle 12 btwn. 5a & 10a Av.
Tel.: 873 0040
Fax: 873 0050
marino@playadelcarmen.com
www.playabedandbreakfast.com

G-18 *Cabañas La Ruina*
30
WITH HAMMOCKS, BATHROOMS AND CAMPING AREA.
Calle 2 & the beach
Tel./Fax: 873 0405

H-19 *Posada Cowboy*
22
Av. 10 Nte. btwn.
Calle 2 & Av. Juárez
Tels.: 879 3838, 879 3839
cowboyhotel@yahoo.com.mx

I-19 *Posada Marinelly*
16
Av. Juárez No. 147
btwn. 10a & 15a Av.
Tel.: 873 0140

H-10 *Posada Mariposa*
23
5a Av. No. 314
btwn. Calles 24 & 26
Tel./Fax: 873 3886
welcome@posadamariposa.com
www.posadamariposa.com

G-17 *Posada Sian Ka'an*
16
5a Av. btwn.
Calles 2 & 4 Nte.
Tel.: 873 0202 Fax: 873 0204
posada@labnah.com
www.labnah.com

OTHERS

I-13 *Alux*
16
5a Av.
Calle 14 Norte
btwn. 10 & 15 Av.
Tel.: (998) 884 3046
hotelaluxplaya@aol.com
www.hotelalux.com

F-13 *Azul*
20
5a Av. btwn.
Calles 10 & 12
Tel.: 873 0562 Fax: 879 3957
info@hotelazul.com
www.hotelazul.com

F-13 *Deep Blue Azul Profundo*
16
Calle 14 Nte. & the beach
Tel.: 873 0415 Fax: 873 2015
www.hotelesplayacarmen.com

L-09 *Dorymar*
19
30 Av. Nte.
btwn. Calles 28 & 30
Tel./Fax: 873 0425
www.hoteldorymar.com

L-18 *Dos Hermanos*
14
30 Av. btwn. Calles
2 Bis & 4 Nte.
Tel.: 873 0490

G-14 ***Eclipse***
PE 12
1a Av. Nte. Bis
btwn. Calles 12 & 14
Tel./Fax: 873 0629
www.hoteleclipse.com

K-18 ***El Acuario***
PE 12
25 Av. btwn.
Calles 2 & 4 Nte.
Tel./Fax: 873 2133
elacuario@caribe.net.mx
www.elacuariohotel.com

I-14 ***El Elefante***
PE 40
10a Av. esq. Calle 12 Nte.
Tel.: 873 0262 Fax: 873 0037

G-19 ***El Palomar***
PE 4
DORMITORIES FOR 18 MEN AND 18 WOMEN, WITH KITCHEN AND HAMMOCKS.
5 Av. btwn. Av. Juárez &
Calle 2 Nte., first floor
Tel.: 803 2606 Fax: 873 2461
hostelpalomar@hotmail.com
www.elpalomarhostel.com

H-09 ***El Patio Condotel***
PE 10
Calle 26 btwn. 5a & 10a Av.
Tel./Fax: 873 3886
condotelpatio@tisalinet.it
www.condotelelpatio.it

I-10 ***Girasol***
PE 7
10a Av. esq. Calle 24
Tel./Fax: 873 3068
hotelgirasol@cs.com
www.hotelgirasol.com

H-16 ***Happy Gecko***
PE 6
KITCHENETTE. SCUBA DIVING AND SNORKELING TOURS.
10a Av. Nte. btwn.
Calles 6 & 8
Tel./Fax: 873 2144
happygeckohotel@yahoo.com

J-16 ***Jabines***
PE 21
Calle 8 btwn. 15a & 20a Av.
Tel.: 873 0861 Fax: 873 1141
chiquitijabines@hotmail.com

H-15 ***La Muralla***
PE 3
10a Av. esq. Calle 10

J-17 ***La Ziranda***
PE 16
Calle 4 No. 169
btwn. 15a & 20a Av.
Tel.: 873 3933 Fax: 873 3929
info@hotellaziranda.com
www.hotellaziranda.com

H-17 ***Marasol***
PE 11
Calle 6 Nte.
btwn. 5a & 10a Av.
Tel.: 873 0112 Fax: 873 0113

I-15 ***Maya Inn***
PE 15
WITH BEACH CLUB.
10 Av. Norte Lote 2,
btwn. Calles 10 & 10 Bis
Tels.: 873 2796, 803 0522
reservaciones@hotelmayainn.com
www.hotelmayainn.com

I-16 ***Maya Turquesa***
PE 20
Calle 8 btwn. 10a & 15a Av.
Across from Plaza Pelícanos
Tel./Fax: 873 2519
www.mayaturquesa.com

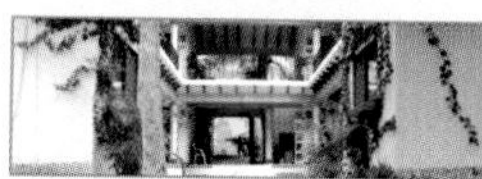

I-17 ***Nina***
PE 16
Calle 6 btwn. 10a & 15a Av.
Tel./Fax: 873 2214
www.eltukancondotel.com

G-13 ***Phantom Paradise***
PE 18
WITH KITCHENETTE.
1a Nte. btwn. Calles 12 & 14
Tel./Fax: 873 1974
phantomparadise@prodigy.net.mx

G-15 ***Posada D´Margo***
PE 19
Calle 10 Nte. L. 9-10
btwn. 5a Av. & the beach
Tel./Fax: 873 0492
hospedajedemargo@hotmail.com

H-20 ***Posada Fernández***
PE 10
10a Av. esq. Calle 1
Tel.: 873 0156

L-18 ***Posada La Doña***
PE 17
35 Av. esq. Calle 2 Nte. Bis
Tel.: 879 3055 Fax: 873 0834

G-11 ***Posada Las Iguanas***
PE 10
Av. Constituyentes
esq. 1a Nte.
Tel./Fax: 873 2170
posada_lasiguanas@hotmail.com
www.posada-las-iguanas.com

H-19 ***Posada Lily***
PE 25
Av. Juárez btwn.
5a & 10a Av.
Tel.: 873 0116

H-10 ***Posada Marina***
PE 20
5a Av. Nte. No. 380
Mz. 55 L. 1
Tel./Fax: 873 3240

L-20 ***Posada Marixchel***
PE 17
30 Av. btwn. Av. Juárez
& Calle 1a Sur
Tel.: 873 0628

H-15 ***Posada Mi Casa***
PE 17
5a Av. close to Calles 8 & 10
Tel./Fax: 873 1972
posada1@prodigy.net.mx

I-17 ***Posada Papagayo***
PE 19
15a Av. btwn.
Calles 4 & 6 Nte.
Tel.: 873 2497 Fax: 873 1196
nandofer@playa.com.mx

I-21 ***Posada Real de Mayab***
PE 13
Calle 3 Sur No. 153
btwn. 10a & 15a Av.
Tels.: 873 3155, 873 2092
Fax: 873 2092
realdelmayab@prodigy.net.com
www.realdelmayab.net.tf

H-09 ***Prisma Caribe***
PE 14
Calle 28 btwn. 10a & 5a Av.
Tel.: 873 2760 Fax: 873 2763
www.prisma.caribe.com

G-14 ***Rosa Mirador***
PE 20
1a Privada Nte.
btwn. Calles 12 & 14
Tel./Fax.: 873 0750
rosamirador@hotmail.com
www.rosamirador.com

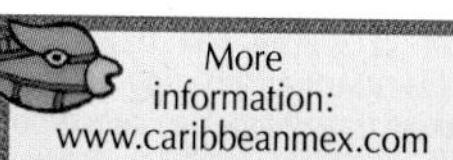

H-17 *Santa Lucía*
PE 11
5a Av. btwn. Calles 4 & 6
Tel.: 879 3321
stalucia@terra.com

H-15 *Siesta Fiesta*
PE 24
5a Av. btwn. Calles 8 & 10
Tel./Fax: 803 1166
info@siestafiestahotel.com
www.siestafiestahotel.com

H-13 *Suites Yovaelgi*
PE 7
WITH BEACH CLUB.
10a Av. Nte. No. 247 btwn. Calles 14 & 14 Bis Nte.
Tel./Fax: 873 0249
yovaelgi@prodigy.net.mx
www.xaac.com/playacar/yovaelgi.htm

G-14 *Tropical Casa Blanca*
PE 20
1a Calle Nte. No. 27
Tel./Fax: 873 0057
tropicalcasablanca@prodigy.net.mx
www.tropicalcasablanca.com.mx

I-17 *Urban Hostel Bed & Breakfast*
20
100 PESOS PER NIGHT.
10 Av. btwn. Calles 4 & 6
Tel.: 879 9342
urbanhostel@yahoo.com

H-18 *Villa del Mar*
PE 7
10a Av. No. 130 - A, btwn. Calles 2 & 4 Nte.
Tel.: 873 0863 Fax: 873 2376
www.hotelvilladelmar.com

L-16 *Valmar*
PE 20
30 Av. esq. Calle 8
Tel./Fax: 873 2335
valmarhotel@hotmail.com

G-13 *Villa Catarina*
PE 16
Calle Privada Nte. btwn. Calles 12 & 14 Nte.
Tel.: 873 2098 Fax: 873 2097
villacatarina@prodigy.net.mx
www.travelbymexico.com/qroo

G-14 *William Caribe*
PE 12
Calle 12 Norte btwn. 1a Av. & 1a Privada Norte.
Tels.: 804 8133, 877 8127

H-09 *Zanzíbar*
PE 17
Calle 26 Nte. L. 4 btwn. 5a & 10a Av. Nte.
Tel.: 873 0990
Fax: 873 3380
info@hotelzanzibar.com
www.hotelzanzibar.com

PLAYACAR

MOST HOTELS IN PLAYACAR OFFER GOLF AS ONE OF THEIR ACTIVITIES DUE TO THE PROXIMITY OF THE GOLF COURSE.

DELUXE ★★★★★★

D-34 *Occidental Royal Hideaway Resort & Spa*
208
Lote Hotelero 6 Mz. 6
Tel.: 873 4500 Fax: 873 4506
www.royalhideaway.com

FIVE STAR ★★★★★

D-39 *Gala Beach Resort Playacar*
460
Paseo Xaman-Ha L. 1 Mz. 1
Tels.: 877 4040
01 800 713 5504
USA 1 877 888 GALA
Fax: 873 1169
www.galaresorts.com.mx

J-31 *Hacienda Vista Real*
PE 78
KITCHENETTE. BEACH CLUB.
Paseo Xaman Ha Retorno 3, Playacar
Tel.: 803 1585
info@vistareal.com.mx
www.vistareal.com.mx

D-38 *Iberostar Tucán & Quetzal*
812
DRESSEL DIVERS MARINA.
Av. Xaman-Ha Lote Hotelero 2
Tels.: 877 2000
01 800 557 4879
USA 1 888 923 2722
Fax: 873 0424
www.iberostar.com

F-22 *Playacar Palace*
PA PE PC 247
Bahía del Espíritu Santo
Tel.: 877 4900 Fax: 877 4924
www.palaceresorts.com

I-33 *Riu Lupita*
300
Manzana 20, Lote Hotelero 1
Tel.: 873 0505 Fax: 873 1045
hotel.lupita@riu.com
www.riu.com

D-35 *Riu Playacar*
404
Av. Xaman-Ha L. 1 Mz. 6
Tels.: 877 2300, 877 2310
hotel.playacar@riu.es
www.riu.com

D-37 *Riu Palace México*
454
Av. Xaman-Ha Mz. 3 L. 4
Tel.: 877 4200 Fax: 877 4210
USA 01 800 225 5748
palace.mexico@riu.com
www.riu.com

G-35 *Riu Tequila Club Hotel*
664
RIGHT ON THE GOLF COURSE.
Paseo Xaman-Ha Mz. 25
Tel.: 873 4300 Fax: 873 2201
clubhotel.tequila@riu.com
www.riu.com

D-37 *Riu Yucatán*
543
Av. Xaman-Ha Mz. 3 L. 1
Tels.: 873 1300, 873 0320
Fax: 873 1266
reservations.cunriu.com
www.riu.com

E-26 *Sunset Fisherman*
PE 32
WITH MEAL PLAN OPTION.
Bahía del Espíritu Santo 9
Tel./Fax: 873 4950
www.sunsetworld.net

D-32 *Viva Wyndham Azteca*
234
Paseo Xaman-Ha Lote Hotelero 8
Tels.: 877 4100, 877 4107
01 800 716 3372
Fax: 877 4138
galia@vivaresorts.com
www.vivaresorts.com

XCARET

Xcaret is an experience for all your senses. The name of this paradise means "small inlet" in Maya; it was a sacred place and one of the ancient civilization's most important ports. Nowadays, this enchanting spot invites visitors to discover timeless traditions and a wealth of natural wonders. You'll be captivated by the beauty and magic of this singular paradise.

FOUR STAR ★★★★

K-34 *Caribbean Village Playacar Occidental*

300

RIGHT ON THE GOLF COURSE.
Lote Hotelero 1 Mz. 20
Tels.: 873 0506, 873 0508
USA 1 800 716 6470
Fax: 873 1047, 873 0437
www.occidentalhotels.com

F-22 *Condominos Playa Inn Xaman-Ha*

PE 20

WITH KITCHENETTE.
Plaza Antigua Suite 24
Tels.: 873 0558
01 800 711 4080
USA 1 800 888 5995
Fax: 873 2150
info@playainn.com
www.playainn.com

D-33 *Occidental Allegro Playacar*

286

Lote Hotelero 7
Tels.: 873 0339, 873 0340
Fax: 873 0378
USA 1 800 858 2258
www.occidentalhotels.com

F-22 *Playacar Vacation Rentals*

PE 42

HOLIDAY VILLAS AND CONDOS.
10 Av. Sur por privada 3 Sur
Tels.: 873 0148, 873 0418
USA 1 800 822 3274
Fax: 873 0539
info@playacarvacationrentals.com
wwww.playacarvationrentals.com

D-31 *The Reef Playacar*

202

Paseo Xaman-Ha
Retorno Sayil
Tel.: 873 4120
Fax: 873 2001
sales@thereefplayacar.com
www.thereefplayacar.com

E-35 *Viva Wyndham Maya*

400

Paseo Xaman-Ha
Lote Hotelero 5
Tels.: 873 4600, 877 4107
USA 305 266 6465
1 800 898 9968
Fax: 873 4624
galia@vivaresorts.com
www.vivaresorts.com

XCARET

Xcaret
ECO-ARCHEOLOGICAL PARK.
8:30 AM. - 9 PM.
ADMISSION: $49 US ADULT, $24.50 US CHILDREN UNDER 12 YEARS, WITH MEALS $69 US ADULT, $34.50 US CHILDREN UNDER 12 YEARS.
Hwy. Cancún-Tulum km 74
Tels.: 883 3143, 883 3144
Fax: 883 3324
OFFICES IN CANCÚN:
Tel.: 881 2400
Fax: 881 2424
grupos@xcaret.net
www.xcaret.net

HOTELS

FIVE STAR ★★★★★

 # 21 *Occidental Grand Flamenco Xcaret*

814

NEXT TO XCARET PARK.
Chetumal-Cancún km 282
Tel.: 871 5400 Fax: 871 5406
USA 1 800 858 2258
www.xcaretresort.com

PAAMUL

RESTAURANTS

Brasil en Paamul
8 AM. - 9 PM.
Cancún-Tulum km 85
www.paamul.com.mx

HOTELS

 # 22 *Cabañas Paamul*

PE PA 21

CAMPING AREA.
Cancun-Tulum km 85
Tels.: 875 1051, 875 1053
Fax: 875 1051
paamulmx@yahoo.com
www.cabanaspaamul.com

PUERTO AVENTURAS

ATTRACTIONS

CENOTES

THERE ARE SEVERAL NATURAL SINKHOLES TO VISIT IN THE AREA SUCH AS KANTUN CHI, CENOTE AZUL AND CRISTALINO.

Ecopark Kantun Chi
CAVE, NATURAL SINKHOLES & AREAS WITH REGIONAL WILDLIFE.
ADMISSION: $10 US ADULT
$6 US CHILDREN UNDER 12 YEARS.
Hwy. Cancún-Tulum km 100
Tel.: (984) 873 0021
www.kantunchi.com

DOLPHINS

D-12 *Dolphin Discovery*
ENGLISH, SPANISH.
9 AM. - 6 PM.
SWIMMING WITH DOLPHINS
Marina Loc. 11
Tels.: 873 5017
01 800 713 8862
reservaslangosta@hotmail.com
www.dolphindiscovery.com.mx

MARINAS

D-12 *Aquanauts Dive Shop*
8:30 AM. - 5 PM.
Marina Loc. 24
Tel.: 873 5041
Fax: 873 5280
www.aquanauts-online.com

Marina Puerto Aventuras

Tels.: 873 5108, 873 5000
Fax: 873 5008
www.puertoaventuras.com.mx

Captain Rick´s Sportfishing Center

Puerto Aventuras
Tels.: 873 5195, 873 5387
info@fishyucatan.com
www.fishyucatan.com

Mexican Adventure

Tel.: 0614 873
navegantey@hotmail.com

C-13 *Dive Aventuras*

8 AM. - 6 PM.
Hotel Omni
Tels.: 875 5031
01 800 237 8348
Fax: 873 5129
info@diveaventuras.com
www.diveaventuras.com

CATAMARAN TRIPS

Bleu Magic

TOUR THAT INCLUDES SNORKELING, DRINKS AND LUNCH.
Calle 1a Nte. esq. 14
Edif. Las Flores, Dpto. Jazmín
Tel.: 876 2402
Fax: 873 4774
reservas@bleumagic.com
www.bleumagic.com

Fat Cat

TOUR THAT INCLUDES TRANSPORTATION, FISHING, DRINKS, SNACKS AND SNORKELING.
Cel.: 044 984 876 3316
www.fatcatsail.com

GOLF COURSES

D-12 *Club de Golf Puerto Aventuras*

7:30 AM. - 3 PM.
COST: $49 US ALL DAY LONG.
Tel./Fax: 873 5109

RESTAURANTS

HOME-STYLE FOOD

C-12 *Caribana*

STUFFED CHILES, BARBECUE.
8 AM. - 8 PM.
Plaza Marina
Edificio A Loc. 8-A y B
Tel.: 873 5175

Palapa Manatí

SNACKS, SEAFOOD.
9 AM. - 6 PM.
Opposite the manatee pool
Tel.: 873 5017

INTERNATIONAL

D-12 *Mediterráneo*

VI MC
LOBSTER.
11:30 AM. - 11:30 PM.
Plaza Marina Loc. 4-A
across from the dolphins
Tel.: 873 5418
fabrius@hotmail.com

D-12 *Reiki Bakery*

BAKERY, PIZZAS.
7 AM. - 10 PM.
Plaza Marina
Edificio F Loc. 3-A
Tel./Fax: 873 5220
donna@reikibakery.com

D-12 *Richard's Steak House & Pizza*

AE VI MC
LOBSTER, STEAKS.
8 AM. - 10 PM.
Plaza Marina
Edificio E Loc. 3-B
Tel.: 873 5086

D-12 *The Pub*

LIVE FLAMENCO MUSIC AND DANCE OCCASIONALLY.
SEAFOOD, HAMBURGERS.
8 AM. - MIDNIGHT.
Plaza Marina Loc. 5 & 6-A
Tels.: 873 5316, 873 5130
thepubmx@hotmail.com

D-12 *Tiramisu*

AE VI MC
PASTA, SEAFOOD.
NOON - 11 PM.
Plaza Marina
Edificio E Loc. 5-A
Tel.: 873 5199
Fax: 873 5220
donna@reikibakery.com

MEXICAN

D-12 *Dos Chiles*

SEAFOOD.
8 AM. - MIDNIGHT.
Plaza Marina
Tel.: (998) 841 6778

SNACKS

D-12 *Jones Sports Bar*

VI MC
11 AM. - 11 PM.
Plaza Marina
Edificio C No. 104
Tel.: 873 5381

SUSHI BAR

C-12 *Arigato Sushi Bar*

FRESH FISH SUSHI.
1:30 PM. - 10 PM
Plaza Marina
Edificio C Loc. 3
Tel.: 801 0196 Fax: 804 6692

HOTELS

FIVE STAR ★★★★★

D-03 *Aventura Spa Palace*

1266
ADULTS ONLY.
Rancho El Trébol
Cancún-Tulum Hwy.
Tel.: 875 1100
Fax: 875 1101
reservations@palaceresorts.com
www.palaceresorts.com

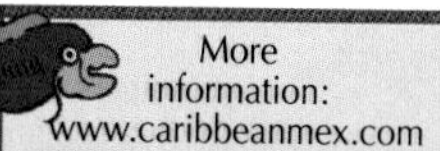

D-07 ***Catalonia Riviera Maya***
326
Av. Xcacel Mz. 18 L. 1
Tel.: 875 1020 Fax: 875 1037
vacaciones@hoteles-catalonia.es
www.cataloniarivieramaya.com

C-13 ***Omni Puerto Aventuras Beach Resort***
PC 30
Chetumal-Cancún km 269.5
Tels.: 875 1950
01 800 221 1150
USA 1 800 843 6664
Fax: 873 1958
omnipave@sybcom.com
www.omnihotels.com

FOUR STAR ★★★★

C-09 ***Condominios Marina San Carlos***
PE 70
MONTHLY RENTAL OPTION.
Caleta Xel-Há esq.
privada Xel-Há
Tels.: 873 5132, 873 5133
Fax: 873 5134
cmsc@pa.com.mx

B-12 ***Condominios Península de Chac Hal Al***
PE 35
Hotel Omni Loc. 5
Tels.: 873 5137, 873 5433
USA 888 509 9827
Fax: 873 5139
info@bluecaribbean.com
www.bluecaribbean.com

D-06 ***Club Lookea***
200
Av. Xcacel
Tels.: 875 1020
1 800 005 1005
Fax: 873 5363
vacaciones@hoteles-catalonia.es
www.cataloniarivieramaya.com

More information:
www.caribbeanmex.com

B-09 ***Sunscape Puerto Aventuras***
297
Chetumal-Cancún km 269.5
Tel./Fax: 875 3000
info@sunscaperesorts.com
www.sunscaperesorts.com

OTHERS

D-16 ***Casa del Agua***
PC 8
Punta Matzoma No. 21
Tel./Fax: 873 5184
relax@casadelagua.com
www.casadelagua.com

C-05 ***Jungle Beach***
24
Sección Fuentes L. 11
Tels.: 873 5426, 873 5396
junglebeach2002@yahoo.com.mx

D-17 ***La Misión***
PA PE PC 6
WEEKLY RENTAL.
FOR GROUPS OF UP TO 18 PEOPLE. WITH KITCHEN.
40 meters from the beach.
Tel.: 873 5179
Fax: 873 5109
la_mision@prodigy.net.mx
www.akumal-villas.com

C-11 ***Puerta del Mar II***
69
CONDOMINIUMS, MONTHLY RENTAL.
Chetumal-Cancún km 269.5
Tel./Fax: 873 5249

XPU-HÁ

RESTAURANTS

Café del Mar
GRILLED FISH,
ORIENTAL RICE.
TUE. - SUN 8 AM. - 9 PM.
Tels.: 873 2194, 876 9945
www.cafedelmarxpuha.com

HOTELS

DELUXE ★★★★★★

\# 25 ***Xpu-Há Palace***
464
Chetumal-Cancún km 265
Tel/Fax.: 875 1010
USA 1 877 327 1989
www.xpuhapalaceresort.com

FIVE STAR ★★★★★

\# 23 ***Barceló Maya Beach***
645
WITH SCUBA DIVING CENTER.
Chetumal-Cancún km 266.3
Tel.: 875 1500
USA 1 800 202 6192
Fax: 875 1509
reservas@barcelomaya.com
www.barcelo.com

\# 24 ***Barceló Maya Caribe***
410
Chetumal-Cancún km 266.3
Tel.: 875 1500 Fax: 875 1501
sales@barcelomaya.com
www.barcelo.com

\# 28 ***Copacabana Beach Resort - Riviera Maya***
288
Cancún-Chetumal km 264.5
Tels.: 875 1800
01 800 500 0101
USA 1 866 321 6880
Fax: 875 1818
riviera_maya@hotelcopacabana.com
www.hotelcopacabana.com

\# 29 ***Club Maeva***
300
Cancún-Tulum km 90
Tel.: 871 3000
Fax: 871 3005
info@maevatulum.com
www.clubmaeva.com

THREE STAR ★★★

\# 27 ***Villas del Caribe***
PE 18
YOGA.
Cancún-Tulum Hwy.
Tel.: 876 9945
Cel.: 044 984 876 9945
Fax: 873 2194
www.xpuhahotel.com

Hoteles CATALONIA Buenos Hoteles Riviera Maya

The all INCLUSIVE where everybody is INCLUDED. Located on the shores of the beautiful Mexican Caribbean, in the heart of the Mayan Riviera. The hotel features 524 comfortable rooms, 5 swimming pools, fitness center, 4 restaurants, snack bar, 5 bars, disco, tennis court, kid's club for children from 4 to 12 years old and Entertainment Program for all our guests of all ages.

Av. Xcacel, Puerto Aventuras, Quintana Roo, Mexico C.P. 77750, Tels.: 52 (984) 875 1020; Fax: +52 (984) 875 1037;
• *vacaciones@hoteles-catalonia.com* • *www.cataloniarivieramaya.com* •

★★★★★

Spectacular ALL INCLUSIVE resort located on one of the most beautiful beaches in Mexico, with over a mile of white sand. Enjoy its two pools with jacuzzi, large, fully equipped rooms, sport facilities including 5 tennis courts, 18-hole mini-golf, sailing, windsurfing, kayak and much more. Rooms for special events.

Our six restaurants will please the most demanding visitors. Day or night, take part in a variety of activities for all ages, organized by our entertainment team. Nightly shows with live music at Teatro Kukulkán.

Chetumal - Puerto Juárez Hwy.
km 266.3, Riviera Maya
Quintana Roo, Mexico
Tel.: (984) 875 1500
Fax: (984) 875 1501
Call Center: 01 800 227 2356
75 km from Cancún airport,
25 km south of Playa del Carmen

sales@barcelomaya.com
reservas@barcelomaya.com
www.barcelo.com

★★★★★

Club MAEVA®
All Inclusive Resort
TULUM, RIVIERA MAYA, MEXICO

Mexico´s favorite all inclusive.
Located on the Riviera Maya´s most beautiful bay, this resort offers a world of entertainment with our animation staff, the Maevamigos. Eight tennis courts, theater for shows and much more.

Cancún-Tulum Hwy. km. 90, Xpu-Há, Q. Roo, Mexico 77710, Tel.: +52 (984) 871 3000; Fax: +52 (984) 871 3005
• www.clubmaeva.com •

118
Há 15

KANTENAH

HOTELS

FIVE STAR ★★★★★

 # 31 *Colonial Palladium Grand Resort & Spa*
414
Chetumal-Cancún km 259.5
Tel.: 877 2100 Fax: 877 2101
riviera@fiesta-hotels.com
www.fiesta-hotels.com

 # 32 *Kantenah Palladium Grand Resort & Spa*
422
Chetumal-Cancún km 259.5
Tel.: 847 2100
USA 1 610 485 3791
Fax: 877 2101
www.fiesta-hotels.com

FOUR STAR ★★★★

 # 27 *El Dorado Seaside Suites*
175
ONLY ADULTS.
Cancún-Chetumal km 95
Tel.: 875 1910 Fax: 875 1911
USA 1 866 527 4762
sales@eldorado-resort.com
www.karismahotels.com

AKUMAL

AGENCIES & TOURS

G-03 *Akumal Excursiones*
PERSONALIZED TOURS FOR SMALL GROUPS.
Nin Ha Akumal
Condominios La Joya
Tel.: 875 9066
hilariohiler@yahoo.com

G-09 *Travel Services of Akumal*
LODGING IN THE RIVIERA MAYA IN VILLAS AND CONDOMINIUMS.
MON. - SAT. 9 AM. - 1 PM., 3 PM. - 5 PM.
Cancún-Tulum km 104
Fracc. Akumal L. 3-A
Tels.: 875 9030, 875 9031
tsa@akumaltravel.com
www.akumaltravel.com

 # 30 *Vea Excursiones*
8 AM. - 2 PM.
JEEP SAFARI TO SIAN KA'AN AND ATVS THROUGH THE JUNGLE. MEALS & BEVERAGES INCLUDED.
Hotel Bahía Príncipe
Tel./Fax: 875 5040
vea66@hotmail.com
www.jeep-safari.com

MARINAS

G-05 *Akumal Dive Adventures*
ENGLISH, GERMAN, SPANISH.
8 AM. - 5 PM.
L. 41 Sección G
Tels.: 875 9059
USA 1 505 992 3333
1 877 425 8625
Fax: 875 9058
www.akumaldiveadventures.com

F-20 *Aquatech Villas de Rosa*
ENGLISH, SPANISH, FRENCH, GERMAN.
8 AM. - 6 PM.
Aventuras Akumal
Tel./Fax: 875 9020
www.cenotes.com

G-09 *The Akumal Dive Shop*
8 AM. - 5 PM.
ENGLISH, GERMAN, ITALIAN, SPANISH, MAYA.
NITROX SCUBA DIVING, CAVERNS.
Bahía de Akumal
Tels.: 875 9032, 875 9030
Fax: 875 9033
gonzalo@akumal.com
www.akumal.com

RESTAURANTS

INTERNATIONAL

G-05 *La Buena Vida*
VI MC
8 AM. - 11 PM.
L. 3 Sección F
Tel.: 875 9061 Fax: 875 9058
labuenavida@yahoo.com

G-03 *La Lunita*
VI MC
COCONUT SHRIMP, SEAFOOD SHISH KEBAB.
5 PM. - 10 PM.
Hacienda de la Tortuga
Tel./Fax: 875 9068

G-10 *Lol Ha*
AE VI MC
SEAFOOD, LOBSTER.
7:30 AM. - 11 PM.
Club Akumal Caribe
Tel.: 875 9014
Fax: 875 9013

ITALIAN

G-02 *Qué Onda*
VI MC
SEAFOOD LASAGNA.
8 - 10:30 AM., NOON - 10 PM.
Caleta Yalkú
Tels.: 875 9102, 875 9101
www.queondaakumal.com

HOTELS

FIVE STAR ★★★★★

F-19 *Adventure Akumal Vacations*
PE 12 984
Aventuras Akumal L. 30
Tel.: 875 9099 Fax: 875 9098
bobbidluxe@aol.com
www.adventure-akumal.com

More information:
www.caribbeanmex.com

 # 33 *Bahía Príncipe Club Resorts*
1440
Chetumal-Cancún km 250
Tel.: 875 5000
Fax: 875 5001
info.akumal@bahia-principe.com
www.bahia-principe.com

FOUR STAR ★★★★

G-11 *Akumal Beach Resort*
241
Cancún-Tulum km 104
Tel.: 875 7500
Fax: 875 7501
www.akumalbeachresort.com

G-12 *Las Villas Akumal*
52
Cancún-Tulum km 104
Tel.: 875 7050
Fax: 875 7070
reservations@lasvillasakumal.com
www.lasvillasakumal.com

E-18 *Oasis Akumal*
187
Chetumal-Cancún km 251
Tels.: 875 7300, 848 9977
01 800 44 OASIS
USA 770 448 7700
Fax: 875 7300
www.oasishotels.com.mx

THREE STAR ★★★

H-10 *Club Akumal Caribe Villas Maya*
61
Cancún-Tulum km 104
Tels.: 875 9010, 875 9012
01 800 351 1622
Fax: 875 9011
www.hotelakumalcaribe.com

G-03 *Hacienda de la Tortuga*
16
EQUIPPED CONDOMINIUMS.
Bahía Media Luna
Akumal Nte. hacia Yalkú
Tel.: 875 9068
Fax: 875 9069
htortuga@prodigy.net.mx
www.haciendatortuga.com

F-09 *Las Casitas Akumal*
18
VILLAS WITH 2 BEDROOMS.
Cancún-Tulum km 104
Tels.: 875 9071
USA 1 800 5 AKUMAL
Fax: 875 9072
www.lascasitasakumal.com

G-02 *Posada Qué Onda*
7
Caleta Yalkú L. 98-99
Tels.: 875 9102, 875 9101
info@queondaakumal.com
www.queondaakumal.com

G-05 *Vista del Mar*
29
L. 41 Sección G
Tels.: 875 9059, 875 9060
USA 1 877 425 8625
www.mexicovacations.com

F-20 *Villas de Rosa Resort*
19
Cancún-Tulum km 104 L. 36
Tels.: 875 9020, 875 9021
01 800 509 4376
USA 1 866 619 9050
dive@cenotes.com
www.cenotes.com

OTHERS

G-03 *Condominios La Joya*
7
Fracc. Yalkú L. 47
Tels.: 875 9129
USA 1 800 523 6618
Fax: 875 9130
nanarmstrong@prodigy.net.mx

G-04 *Condominios Playa Caribe*
15
Cancún-Tulum km 104
Tel.: 875 9085
Fax: 875 9084
www.playacaribe.com

F-01 *Condominios Yalkucai*
6
Cancún-Tulum km 104
L. 26-H
Tel.: 875 9113
Fax: 875 9031
www.akumaltravel.com

F-03 *Condominios Yool Caanal*
5
Fracc. Akumal L. 43
Tel.: 875 9129
Fax: 875 9130
nanarmstrong@prodigy.net.mx

G-04 *Luna Azul*
12
Road to Yalkú
Tels.: 875 9169, 875 9137
Fax: 875 9185
www.playacaribe.com

G-05 *Playa Blanca*
5
CONDOS
Fracc. Akumal L. 41
Tel.: 875 9085 Fax: 875 9084
turquesa@mail.caribe.net.mx
www.playacaribe.com

G-06 *Villa Balam Ek*
4
PRIVATE VILLA (UP TO 12 GUESTS).
OPTIONAL SCUBA DIVING.
Cancún-Tulum km 104 L. 27
Tels.: 875 9030, 875 9031
www.villabalamek.com

G-04 *Villas On The Reef*
6
Fracc. Yalkú L. 46
Tel.: 875 9129
Fax: 875 9130
www.playacaribe.com

AKTUN CHÉN

CAVE, CENOTE, SERPENTARIUM AND REGIONAL WILDLIFE CORNER. ADMISSION $18 US ADULT $10 US CHILDREN UNDER 12 YEARS.
8:30 AM. - 5 PM. WINTER; 8:30 AM. - 4:30 PM. SUMMER.
Cancún-Tulum km 107
Tel.: 877 8550
www.aktunchen.com

CHEMUYIL

RESTAURANTS

Pizzería Leo
1:30 PM. - 10:30 PM.
LOBSTER PIZZA.
Mz. 29, Sur de Akumal

MARINAS

Speleotech
ENGLISH, SPANISH. BY APPOINTMENT.
Pizzería Leo; Tel.: 875 4100
bil@speleotech.com

★★★★

FREEDOM PARADISE
All Sizes and Ages

All inclusive. Freedom Paradise is the first and only size-friendly vacation club in the world. Its Mexican-Caribbean style is in perfect harmony with nature. Our hotels focus on satisfying the special needs of overweight guests by providing them with a friendly environment. The hotel features one story buildings, chairs without arms and comfortable deck chairs.

FREEDOM PARADISE®
RIVIERA MAYA

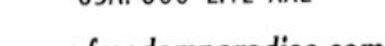

Cancún - Tulum Hwy km 237
Riviera Maya,
Quintana Roo, C.P. 77780
Tels.: (998) 887 1101, 887 3323
Fax: (998) 887 1102
01 800 624 7919
USA: 866-LIVE-XXL
www.freedomparadise.com

XEL-HÁ

ECOLOGICAL WATER PARK. RESTAURANTS, SNORKELING TOUR, SNUBA, SEA TREK, SWIMMING WITH DOLPHINS, BIKES, NURSERY, TURTLES.
9 AM. - 6 PM.
ADMISSION: SAT. & SUN. $19 US ADULT, $10 US CHILDREN.
Cancún-Tulum km 122
Tels.: 884 9422, 873 3588
ventas@xel-ha.com.mx
www.xelha.com.mx

DOS OJOS

Hidden Worlds Cenotes Park
SCUBA DIVING AND SNORKELING TO NATURAL SINKHOLES.
9 AM. - 5 PM. TOURS & DIVING 9, 11 AM. & 1 PM.
2 kilometers from Xel-Há
Hwy. 307
Tel.: 877 8535
www.hiddenworlds.com.mx

PUNTA SOLIMÁN

RESTAURANTS

Oscar y Lalo
WITH CAMPING AREA.
FISH & SEAFOOD.
Bahía de Punta Solimán
Cel.: 044 984 804 6973

TANKAH

RESTAURANTS

Caleta Tankah
9 AM. - 6 PM.
TIKIN XIK FISH.
Chetumal-Cancún km 235
Tel.: (988) 210 2198
www.tankah.com

FIVE STAR ★★★★★

 # 37 *Sunscape Tulum* 338
SPA WITH TRADITIONAL MEXICAN STEAM BATH AND NATURAL SINKHOLE.
Chetumal-Cancún km 234
Tel.: 871 3333 Fax: 871 3353
reservas@soleresorts.com
www.sunscaperesorts.com/tulum

FOUR STAR ★★★★

 # 36 *Freedom Paradise* 112
Cancún-Tulum km 237
Tel.: 887 1101
01 800 624 7919
EUA 866 LIVE XXL
info@freedomparadise.com
www.freedomparadise.com

THREE STAR ★★★

 # 34 *Casa Cenote* 7
CENOTE, SAILING, DIVE, FISHING.
Tankah Tres
Tels.: 806 6677
Cancún (998) 874 5170
01 800 769 9638
www.casacenote.com

TWO STAR ★★

 # 35 *Blue Sky Casitas* 6
Tel.: 801 4004
www.blueskymexico.com

JM

TOURS

 # 22 Cabañas Ana y José
TOURS TO THE SIAN KA'AN RESERVE IN KAYAK OR BOAT.
Cabañas Ana y José
Tel.: 887 5470
Fax: 897 5469
anayjose@cancun.com.mx
www.anayjose.com

 # 36 Ecocolors
BIKE TOURS; TOURS TO SIAN KA'AN, HOLBOX.
Calle 15 Mz. 12 L. 22-A
Villa Tulum
Tel.: (998) 884 3667
info@ecotravelmexico.com
www.ecotravelmexico.com

Sian Ka'an Info Tours
BOAT TOUR THROUGH THE SIAN KA'AN RESERVE.
Tulum-Boca Paila km 8.4
Tel.: 871 2499
www.cesiak.com

E-09 Sian Ka'an Tours
TOUR TO MUYIL, WATCHTOWER, SOAP TRIP THROUGH THE LAGOONS TO THE BEACH.
Av. Tulum btwn. Beta & Osiris
Tels.: 871 2363, 876 3257
siankaan_tours@hotmail.com

ASSOCIATIONS

Hotel & Restaurant Association
Av. Cobá Sur
www.hotelstulum.com

MARINAS

Aktun Dive Center
CENOTES & CAVERN DIVING.
8:30 AM. - 6 PM.
Av. Tulum, Crucero de Cobá
Tel.: 871 2311 Fax: 871 2312
gunnar.wagner@aktundive.com
www.aktundive.com

E-10 Cenote Dive Center
8 AM. - 7 PM.
Av. Tulum btwn. Alfa & Osiris opposite the HSBC bank.
Tel.: 871 2232
www.cenotedive.com

CAR RENTALS

E-10 Ana y José Car Rental
8 AM. - 4 PM., 6 PM. - 8 PM.
Av. Tulum Pte. esq. Alfa Nte.
Tel.: 871 2477 Fax: 887 5469
www.anayjose.com

BUS COMPANIES

D-12 Terminal de Autobuses
SERVICES: ADO, RIVIERA, MAYAB, TRP, SUPER EXPRESSO, ORIENTE, ALTOS, CRISTÓBAL COLÓN & MAYA DE ORO. REGULAR DEPARTURES TO PLAYA DEL CARMEN.
Av. Tulum; Tel.: 871 2122

RESTAURANTS

INTERNATIONAL

 # 6 El Paraíso
SEAFOOD.
8 AM. - 11 PM.
Cabañas Paraíso
Fax: 871 2007

D-09 París de Noche
SEAFOOD GRILL.
8 AM. - 2 AM.
Av. Tulum No. 33
btwn. Osiris & Beta Sur
www.intulum.com

ITALIAN

E-08 Il Basilico
FISH & SEAFOOD LASAGNA, PIZZA BASILICO.
12:30 PM. - 11 PM.
Av. Tulum esq. Beta Nte. L. 4
Tel.: 876 3352
ilbasilico@hotmail.com

F-03 Il Giardino di Toni e Simone
VI
PASTA & SEAFOOD.
1 PM. - 11 PM.
Av. Satélite; Tel.: 879 6664

D-07 La Nave
BRIE PIZZA, PROSCIUTTO.
8 AM. - 11 PM.
Av. Tulum No. 570
Tel.: 841 2592

L'Incontro
VI MC
PASTA & PIZZA.
1 PM. - 2 AM.
Tulum-Boca Paila Road, next to Villa Tulum
Tel.: 807 4640

E-08 Nero di Sole
PASTA AND PIZZA, TAGLIATELLE WITH LOBSTER, FRUTTI DI MARE TRENETTE
7 AM. - 11 PM.
Av. Tulum 378
Tels.: 100 4920, 108 3705

SEAFOOD

 # 9 Gringo Dave's
LOBSTER-FILLED GROUPER.
9 AM. - 9 PM.
Gringo Dave's Cabañas
Tel.: 804 0446
www.gringodaves.com

MEXICAN

E-12 Charlie's
VI MC
STUFFED CHILE.
11 AM. - 11 PM.
Av. Tulum
Tels.: 871 2573, 871 2136
zaptulum@yahoo.com.mx

D-06 *Don Cafeto*

MEXICAN PLATE.
7 AM. - 11 PM.
Av. Tulum No. 64 L. 12
Tel.: 871 2207
doncafeto@correoweb.com

HOTELS

FOUR STAR ★★★★

 # 26 *Los Lirios Hotel Cabañas Tulum*
PA 30
Tulum-Boca Paila km 7.5
Tels.: (998) 887 9602
(998) 887 3205
info@loslirios.com
www.loslirios.com

THREE STAR ★★★

 # 23 *Cabañas Tulum*
PE 32
Tulum-Boca Paila km 7
Tel./Fax: 871 2010
www.hotelstulum.com

 # 13 *La Perla*
PE 6
Tulum-Boca Paila km 4 L. 7
Tel./Fax: 871 2382
laperlatulum@hotmail.com
www.hotelstulum.com

 # 31 *Las Ranitas*
PC 18
Tulum-Boca Paila km 9
Tel./Fax: 877 8554
info@lasranitas.com
www.lasranitas.com

 # 7 *La Vita e Bella*
10
BED & BREAKFAST.
Tulum-Boca Paila km 1.5
Tel.: 879 5029
www.lavitaebella-tulum.com

 # 21 *Los Arrecifes*
PE 24
Tulum-Boca Paila km 7
Tel.: 879 7307
Fax: 871 2092
www.losarrecifestulum.com

B-07 *Suites Playa Kin Ha*
PE 8
WITH BEACH CLUB.
Calle Orion Sur btwn. Sol & Venus Ote.
Tel./Fax: 871 2321
info@hotelkinha.com
www.hotelkinha.com

 # 36 *Villa Tulum*
PE 22
Av. Cobá Sur, road to Boca Paila km 0.3
Tels.: 871 2418, 871 2419
(55) 8596 0249
reservations@villatulum.com
www.villatulum.com

TWO STAR ★★

 # 1 *Acuario*
PE 35
On the Tulum crossroad
Tels.: 871 2195, 871 2303
Fax: 871 2194
hotel_acuario@yahoo.com.mx

 # 6 *Cabañas Paraíso*
PE 14
BEACH CLUB.
Tulum-Boca Paila km 0.8
Tel.: 879 5069
elparaiso_tulum@hotmail.com
www.elparaisotulum.com

ONE STAR ★

E-14 *The Weary Traveler*
PE 17
TOURS TO SIAN KA'AN, PUNTA LAGUNA AND TO NATURAL SINKHOLES.
Av. Tulum No. 36
Tels.: 871 2389, 871 2386
www.intulum.com

OTHERS

 # 2 *Cabañas Andrea's Tulum*
PE 10
On the Tulum crossroad
Tel.: 871 2256
Fax: 871 2258
hotel_acuario@yahoo.com.mx

 # 16 *Cabañas Azulik*
15
Tulum-Boca Paila km 5
Tels.: 806 7819
USA & Canada
877 532 6737
info@azulik.com
www.eco-res.com

 # 17 *Cabañas Copal*
47
WITH TEMAZCAL; 28 CABINS.
Tulum Boca-Paila km 5
Tel./Fax: 879 5054
www.cabanascopal.com

 # 4 *Cabañas Don Armando*
PE 44
Tulum-Boca Paila km 0.47
Tel./Fax: 871 2743
cabanasarmando@yahoo.com.mx
www.hotelstulum.com

 # 5 *Cabañas El Mirador*
PE 31
Tulum-Boca Paila km 0.7
Tel.: 806 4552
Fax: 879 6019
savana@qroo1.telmex.net.mx

 # 24 *Cabañas La Ballena Jr.*
PE 8
Tulum-Boca Paila km 7
Tel.: 871 2062

 # 14 *Cabañas La Conchita*
PE 8
Tulum-Boca Paila km 4.5
Tel./Fax: 871 2092
www.differentworld.com

 # 35 *Cabañas La Zebra*
PE 10
Tulum-Boca Paila km 12
Tel. USA: 580 224 9320
la-zebra-tulum@hotmail.com
www.zebratulum.net

 # 3 *El Crucero*
PE 16
On the Tulum crossroad
Tel./Fax: 871 2610
info@el-crucero.com
www.el-crucero.com

 # 9 *Gringo Dave's*
PE 6
Tulum-Boca Paila km 2.8
Tel.: 804 0446
www.gringodaves.com

 # 11 *La Posada del Sol*
4
Tulum-Boca Paila km 4
Tel.: 804 8515
laposadadelsol@hotmail.com
www.intulum.com

E-07 *L'Hotelito*
9
Av. Tulum esq. Beta
Tel./Fax: 871 2081

 # 12 *Nohoch Tunich*
PE 17
Tulum-Boca Paila km 4
Tel./Fax: 871 2470
nohochtunich@secom.net

 # 19 *Papaya Playa Villas & Beach Paradise*
PE 28
Tulum-Boca Paila km 5.5
Tel./Fax: 804 6444
info@papayaplaya.com
www.papayaplaya.com

 # 10 *Piedra Escondida*
PE 8
Tulum-Boca Paila km 3.5
Tel.: 871 2217 Fax: 871 2092
piedraescondida@tulum.com
www.piedraescondida.com

 # 25 *Retiro Maya*
PE 14
Tulum-Boca Paila km 7
Tel./Fax: (998) 101 1154
reservations@retiromaya.com
www.retiromaya.com

 # 27 *Shambala Petit Hotel*
PE 13
Adults, nudists.
Tulum-Boca Paila km 7.5
Tel.: 807 3894
www.shambalapetithotel.com

 # 33 *Tierras del Sol*
4
Tulum-Boca Paila km 10.5
www.tierrasdelsol.com

Special Category

 # 34 *Amansala*
PE 6
Yoga classes, massages.
Tulum-Boca Paila km 12
Tel.: 806 4582
erica@amansala.com
www.amansala.com

 # 22 *Ana y José*
PE PA 21
Tours to Sian Ka'an.
Tulum-Boca Paila km 7
Tel.: (998) 887 5470
Fax: (998) 887 5469
anayjose@cancun.com.mx
www.anayjose.com

 # 8 *Diamante K*
PE 32
Tulum-Boca Paila km 2.5
Tel./Fax: 807 3894
info@diamantek.com
www.diamantek.com

 # 28 *Esmeralda K*
PE 13
Tulum-Boca Paila km 8
Tel.: (998) 883 4083
info@esmeraldak.com
www.esmeraldak.com

 # 20 *Maya Tulum*
PE 43
Yoga rooms and classes.
Tulum-Boca Paila km 7
Tels.: 877 8638 Fax: 8712094
USA 1 888 515 4580
reservations@mayatulum.com
www.mayatulum.com

 # 30 *Nueva Vida de Ramiro*
PC 7
Adults only.
Tulum-Boca Paila km 8.5
Tels.: 877 8512, 806 4418
USA 609 716 7777
Fax: 871 2092
gea@tulumnv.com
www.tulumnv.com

 # 32 *Posada Dos Ceibas*
PE 8
Meditation and yoga room.
Tulum-Boca Paila km 9
Tel.: 877 6024 Fax: 871 2335
info@dosceibas.com
www.dosceibas.com

 # 15 *Posada Margherita*
PA 6
Massage; scuba diving for disabled. Solar energy.
Tulum-Boca Paila Road
Tel.: 100 3780
info@posadamargherita.com
www.posadamargherita.com

 # 29 *Tita Tulum*
PE 8
Ecological cabins with solar energy.
Tulum-Boca Paila km 8
Tels.: 877 8513, 871 2033
titatulum5@yahoo.com
www.titatulum.com

 # 18 *Zamas*
PE 21
Tulum-Boca Paila km 5
Tel./Fax: 877 8523
USA 1 415 387 9806
zamas@tulumabc.com
www.zamas.com

BOCA PAILA

 # 38 *Boca Paila Fishing Lodge*
PE 9
Tulum-Punta Allen km 25
Tels.: (998) 892 1200
(998) 842 6039
www.bocapaila-lodge.com

SIAN KA'AN

Posada Sirena
PE 2
Equipped cabins.
Tulum-Punta Allen Hwy.
Tel.: (984) 892 1200
www.casasirena.com

COBÁ

 # 1 *Villas Arqueológicas*
PE 40 ★★★★
Tulum-Nuevo Xcan km 47
Tel.: 858 1527 Fax: 858 1526
USA 1 800 514 8244
www.clubmedvillas.com

Others

 # 2 *El Bocadito*
PE 14
Tulum-Nuevo Xcan km 47

CHETUMAL & THE SOUTH

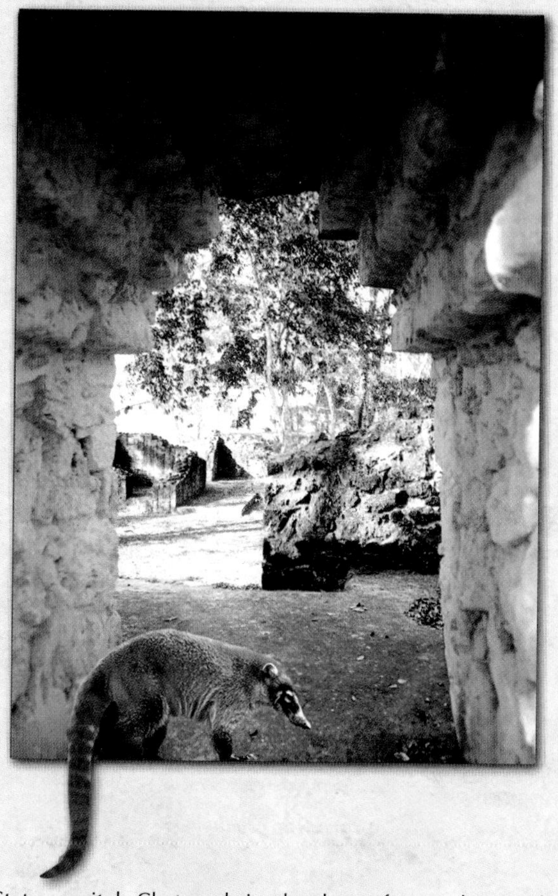

State capital Chetumal is the base for exploring the archaeological sites, lagoons, beaches and reserves of Southern Quintana Roo. Accommodation ranges from five-star city hotels to modest inns. Travel agencies offer excursions to sites of interest in the area, neighboring Campeche, northern Belize and Guatemala.

AIRLINES

G-01 ***Aerocaribe***
International Airport
Tels.: 832 6336, 832 6336
www.aerocaribe.com.mx

E-01 ***Aero Premier***
Av. Manuel Acuña No. 21
Tel./Fax: 837 4700
premierplus@prodigy.net.mx

I-08 ***Aviacsa***
• Lázaro Cárdenas esq. 5 de Mayo
Tels.: 832 7676, 832 7765
• Airport:
Tels.: 832 7787
01 800 006 2200
• Plaza Las Américas
Tels.: 837 6034 al 37
www.aviacsa.com.mx

G-01 ***Chetumal International Airport***
Prolongación Av. Revolución No. 660
Tel.: 832 0465 Fax: 832 3078
www.asa.gob.mx

TRAVEL AGENCIES

THE AGENCIES, EXCEPT FOR VIAJES SACBÉ TRAVEL & MAYAN WORLD ADVENTURES, HANDLE AIRLINE TICKETING.

J-08 ***Bacalar Tours***
Av. Álvaro Obregón 167-A
Tel.: 832 3875 Fax: 832 8587
www.geocities.com/bacalartours/

I-10 ***Intermar Caribe***
Calzada Veracruz No. 84-A
Tels.: 832 4729, 833 0162
Fax: 833 0162
www.travel2mexico.com

J-10 ***Jungle Eco-Adventures***
Ignacio Zaragoza No. 103
Tel.: 832 0340
www.jungle-ecoadventures.com

I-08 ***Mayan World Adventures***
Calzada Veracruz No. 84-A
Tel.: 833 2509, 833 0162
Fax: 833 0162
www.mayanworldadventures.com

H-05 ***Opciones Turísticas del Sur***
SPECIALIZING IN THE COSTA MAYA.
Av. Andrés Q. Roo No. 141
Tel.: 832 4882
otsurl@prodigy.net.mx

C-05 ***Sacbé Tours***
Av. Nápoles No. 399
Tels.: 833 2080
01 800 036 4892
www.sacbetours.com

J-10 ***Sijil Viajes***
Av. Álvaro Obregón 115-A
Tels.: 832 8792, 832 8793
Fax: 832 8794
sijilviajes@yahoo.com.mx

H-09 ***Tu Maya***
Av. Héroes No. 165-A
Tels.: 832 0555, 832 2058
Fax: 832 9711
www.casablancachetumal.com/tumaya

G-10 ***Turissste Chetumal***
Calzada Veracruz No. 235-B,
Tels.: 832 3157
01 800 705 0500
Fax: 832 2414
www.issste.gob.mx/turissste

I-08 ***Viajes Premier Plus***
• Av. Juárez No. 83, Dwntn.
• Av. Manuel Acuña No. 21
Tels.: 832 1247, 832 9033
01 800 716 5817
01 800 614 5212
Fax: 832 3096
www.explorapremier.com

Viajes Sacbé
Josefa Ortiz de Domínguez No. 90
Tel.: 832 3496
www.sacbetravel.com

H-03 ***VIP***
Av. Revolución No. 115
Tel.: 832 2860

BUS COMPANIES

B-09 ***ADO, Mundo Maya, Omni Tours del Caribe, Riviera***
DELUXE BUSES, 1ST AND 2ND CLASS, AND CHARTERS.
Salvador Novo No. 179
Tel.: 832 5110
www.ado.com.mx

B-10 ***Sociedad Cooperativa de Operadores del Caribe***
Salvador Novo No. 179
Tel.: 832 3964

BANKS

J-08 ***Banamex***
ATMS: IMSS CLINIC, GOVERNMENT OFFICES, CANTO PHARMACY.
Av. Juárez No. 51
Tel.: 832 1198

Banorte Bancrecer
ATM: IMSS CLINIC.
I-08 Av. Héroes No. 105-A
Tels.: 832 5819, 832 5849
E-02 Av. San Salvador
Tel.: 832 9703

BBVA Bancomer
J-07 Álvaro Obregón 222
Tel.: 832 5300
I-08 Av. Lázaro Cárdenas esq. Av. Héroes
Tel.: 833 0097

J-08 ***HSBC***
ATM machines in San Francisco supermarket, Bus Station, Customs and IMSS branch office.
Av. Othón P. Blanco 184
Tels.: 832 1574, 832 1552

I-08 ***Santander Serfín***
Av. Juárez esq. Lázaro Cárdenas
Tels.: 832 2422, 832 2602

I-08 ***Scotiabank Inverlat***
Av. 5 de Mayo No. 76
Tels.: 832 8050, 832 3718

CAR RENTALS

H-08 ***Aventura Maya***
Av. Independencia No. 168
Tel./Fax.: 285 5940
reservaciones@hotelloscocos.com.mx

J-08 ***Bacalar Tours***
Av. Álvaro Obregón
Tels.: 832 3875, 837 0122
Fax: 832 8587
www.geocites.com/bacalartours/

Continental Rent a Car
H-09• Av. Héroes No. 171-B
Hotel Holiday Inn
• Chetumal Airport
Tel.: 835 0400 ext. 191
Fax: 832 2411
www.continental.com.mx

G-01 ***Sol Maya Rent a Car***
Av. Revolución No. 549
Tel.: 832 3757 Fax: 832 4300
solmaya5@hotmail.com

H-03 ***Vipsaesa***
Av. Revolución No. 115
Tel.: 832 2860 Fax: 832 0092
vipsaesa@hotmail.com

Taxis

B-09 ***Radio Taxi***
Tels.: 832 0267, 832 8164

ATTRACTIONS

F-08 ***Chetubol***
Bowling, bar, spinning.
11 am. - 1 pm.
Venustiano Carranza No. 201
Tel.: 833 3922

La Casa Internacional del Escritor
Exhibits staged.
8 am. - 9 pm.
Av. 3, Col. Magisterial
Tel.: 834 2123

G-08 ***Instituto de la Cultura Quintanarroense***
Mon. - Fri. 8 am. - 4 pm.
Av. Héroes No. 68
Tel.: 832 2270
www.iqc.gob.mx

Shopping Center

Plaza las Américas
Av. Insurgentes km. 5
Tels.: 837 5662, 837 5664
Fax: 837 5663

Museums

H-08 ***Museum of Mayan Culture***
Tue. - Thu. & sun. 9 am. - 7 pm; fri. - sat. 9 am. - 8 pm.
Av. Héroes esq. M. Gandhi
Tel.: 832 6838 Fax: 832 2270
www.iqc.gob.mx

G-08 ***City Museum***
Tue. - sun. 9 am. - 7 pm.
Av. Héroes No. 65
Tels.: 832 3002
www.iqc.gob.mx

K-09 ***Maqueta de Payo Obispo*** *(Luis Rehinard M.)*
Tue. - sat. 9 am. - 8 pm., sun. 10 am - 3 pm.
Free entrance.
22 de Enero, northeast of the Legislative Building

Surrounding areas

I-02 ***Río Huach Adventure***
9 am. - 6 pm.
Majahual-Xcalak km 35
Offices and information:
Av. Álvaro Obregón No. 1
Tels.: 833 2121, 832 0359

Caste War Museum Tihosuco
Tue. - sun. 9 am. - 7 pm.

Museo del Fuerte de Bacalar
Plaza Central de Bacalar
Tue. - sun. 9 am. - 8 pm.
Tel.: 834 2098

Cenote Azul, Bacalar
Natural sinkhole, handicrafts, aviary, restaurant. Free entrance.
Blvd. Costero No. 610
Tel.: 834 2460

ASSOCIATIONS

D-11 ***Restaurant Asociation CANIRAC***
9 am. - 3 pm.
Marciano González 119-A
Tel.: 832 9145

K-09 ***Chamber of Commerce CANACO***
Av. 22 Enero esq. Reforma
Tels.: 832 1002, 832 0161
Fax: 832 0088
www.canacochetumal.com

K-09 ***Chetumal Tourist Promotion Fund***
Calle 22 de Enero Int.1
Tel.: 832 6647 Fax: 832 5130
fidctm@yahoo.com.mx

A-12 ***Fidecaribe***
9 am. - 6 pm.
Calzada del Centenario 622
Tel.: 832 0084
www.qroo.gob.mx/fidecaribe

Consulates

H-03 ***Belize***
Armada de México No. 91
Tels.: 832 1803, 833 1936
bzeconsulate@prodigy.net.mx

EMERGENCIES

Customs	834 5044
Fire Brigade	832 1578
Emergencies	066
Immigration	832 0221
Highway Patrol	832 0193
Police	832 1500

Medical Services

F-02 ***Clínica Campestre***
Av. Agustín Olachea 540
Tel.: 837 0102

F-05 ***Clínica Carranza***
Av. V. Carranza No. 366
Tel.: 832 8881

H-08 ***Cruz Roja***
Av. Héroes de Chapultepec No. 239 esq. Independencia
Tel.: 833 0223

C-06 ***Hospital General***
Av. Andrés Quintana Roo No. 399, Col. Taxistas
Tel.: 832 1932

G-04 *IMSS*
Calle Nápoles esq.
Adolfo López Mateos
Tel.: 832 2678

NIGHT CLUBS

C-11 *Caribbean Cats*
10 PM. - 5 AM.
Calzada Veracruz No. 451
Tel.: 832 9145

J-08 *Rock Shot's Café*
THU. - SUN. 10 PM. - 4 AM.
Av. Benito Juárez No. 25
Tel.: 833 4720

Snaks Las Américas
SNACKS & KARAOKE.
10 AM. - 3 AM.
Plaza Las Américas
Tel./Fax: 208 7196

Mambo Café
WED. - SAT. 9 PM. - 3 AM.
Plaza Las Américas
Tels.: 837 6039, 837 6040

I-12 *Tequila Rock*
10:30 PM. - 4 AM.
Blvd. Bahía No. 101
Tel./Fax: 833 0144

RESTAURANTS

CHINESE

K-09 *El Junco de Hong Kong*
NOON - 7 PM.
Av. 22 Enero No. 153 esq.
Av. Miguel Hidalgo
Tel.: 833 1700

F-05 *Koncholing*
KONCHOLING RICE.
NOON - 7 PM.
Av. Carranza No. 230
Tel.: 832 8076

INTERNATIONAL

I-08 *El Fenicio*
24 HRS.
Av. Héroes No. 74
Tel.: 832 0026 Fax: 832 8940

K-09 *Espresso Café*
8 AM. - MIDNIGHT.
Calle 22 de Enero No. 141
Tels.: 833 3013, 832 5752
Fax: 832 5052

K-10 *La Botana*
11 AM. - 2 PM. Blvd. Bahía
Tels.: 832 6632, 832 6503

K-10 *La Mansión*
THE SLEEPING WOMAN.
8 AM. - MIDNIGHT.
Blvd. Bahía No. 8
Tel.: 832 2654

C-11 *Los Cebollones*
FLAMBÉED SHRIMP.
11 AM. - 3 AM.
Calzada Veracruz No. 451
Tel.: 832 9145 ext. 104

I-12 *Mediterráneo*
LEBANESE AND MEXICAN FOOD.
8 PM. - 1 AM.
Blvd. Bahía No. 98

E-04 *Terenga*
SUN. - THU. 8 PM. - MIDNIGHT
Av. San Salvador No. 441
Tel.: 832 5540

ITALIAN

I-08 *La Terraza della Piccola Italia*
WOOD OVEN PIZZA, PASTA.
MON - SAT. 7:30 AM. - 12 PM., 4 PM. - MIDNIGHT.
Av. Héroes No. 83
Tel./Fax: 833 6277

J-08 *Sergio's Pizzas*
7 AM. - MIDNIGHT.
- Av. Álvaro Obregón 182
Tels.: 832 0882, 832 2355
- Av. López Mateos 424
Tels.: 832 2355, 832 0825
- Campestre, Tel.: 832 0491

SEAFOOD

K-09 *Cristy's Punta Maya*
11 AM. - 6 PM.
Blvd. Bahía No. 169

J-07 *La Casita de Madera*
MON. - SAT. 11 AM. - 8 PM.
Othón P. Blanco No. 248
Tel./Fax: 832 6582

G-08 *El Vaticano*
SAT. 9 AM. - 6 PM.,
SUN. 10 AM. - 3:30 PM.
Mahatma Ghandi 198
Tel.: 832 9174

F-09 *Mandinga*
1 PM. - MIDNIGHT.
Av. San Salvador No. 182
Tel./Fax: 837 3191

C-04 *Marisquería Alex*
8 AM. - 6 PM.
Isla Cancún No. 450
Tel.: 832 8877

MEXICAN

G-05 *Chicho's*
1 PM. - MIDNIGHT.
Calle Turín No. 411
Tel.: 837 1905

I-08 *El Taquito de Don Julio*
NOON - 5 PM., 7 PM. - 1 AM.
Plutarco E. Calles No. 8
Tel.: 833 1602

E-08 *Forasteros*
Bugambilias No. 261
Tel.: 832 3477

Las Arracheras de Don José
6 PM. 1 AM.
- **K-11** Othón P. Blanco No. 62
- Plaza las Américas

Tel./Fax: 832 8895

Taquería Díaz
- **J-08** Av. Obregón 261
  Tel.: 837 1043
  2 PM. - MIDNIGHT.
- **F-09** Av. Héroes No. 261
  Tel.: 832 7882
  NOON - 2 PM.

FAST FOOD

F-07 *Dominos Pizza*
6 AM. - MIDNIGHT.
Av. San Salvador No. 293
Tel.: 833 0303

BACALAR

Cenote Azul
11 AM. - 7 PM.
SEAFOOD.
Blvd. Costero No. 610
Tel.: 834 2460

HOTELS

FIVE STAR ★★★★★

H-09 *Holiday Inn Chetumal*
PE 85
Av. Héroes No. 171-A
Tels.: 835 0400 al 29
01 800 712 717
USA 1 800 712 1717
Fax: 832 1607
www.holiday-inn.com/chetumalmex

FOUR STAR ★★★★

H-08 *Los Cocos*
PE 140
Av. Héroes No. 134 Dwntn.
Tels.: 832 0544, 832 0542
01 800 719 5840
Fax: 832 0920
www.hotelloscocos.com.mx

THREE STAR ★★★

I-02 *Caribe Princess*
PE 36
Av. Álvaro Obregón 168
Tel.: 832 0520 Fax: 832 0900
01 800 282 0595

I-10 *El Marqués*
PE 67
Lázaro Cárdenas No. 121
Tel.: 832 2955, 832 2888
Fax: 832 2977
hotelelmarques@prodigy.net.mx

I-08 *Marlon*
50
Av. Juárez No. 87, Dwntn.
Tels.: 832 1065, 832 9411
Fax: 832 6555
hotel_marlon@hotmail.com

D-10 *Marlon Héroes*
PE 30
Av. Héroes No. 368
Tel.: 832 6589 Fax: 832 6233
marlon_heroes@hotmail.com

E-09 *Príncipe*
PE 54
Prol. Héroes No. 326
Tels.: 832 5191, 832 4799
01 800 714 6379
USA 1 866 313 6860
Fax: 832 5191, ext. 409
principearlequin@hotmail.com

I-08 *Suites Arges*
PE 40
Av. Lázaro Cárdenas 212
Tels.: 832 9525, 832 9414
hotelarges@eclipo.com

K-08 *Villanueva*
PE 83
Av. Carmen Ochoa No. 166
Tel.: 832 6900 Fax: 832 0128

TWO STAR ★★

J-08 *Big Ben*
17
Av. Héroes No. 48
Tel./Fax: 833 1710

H-08 *Brasilia*
PE 46
Av. Héroes No. 159-B
Tels.: 832 0964, 832 0950

J-06 *Casa Blanca*
PE 51
Av. Álvaro Obregón 312
Tel.: 832 1248 Fax: 832 1658
casablancachetumal@hotmail.com

G-08 *Cristal*
PE 41
Av. Cristóbal Colón 207
Tels.: 832 3878, 832 1949

I-08 *El Cedro*
PE 22
Av. Héroes No. 103 Altos
Tel.: 832 6360 Fax: 832 5399

J-08 *El Dorado*
PE 27
Av. 5 de Mayo No. 42 Altos
Tels.: 832 0316, 832 1118
Fax: 832 0315

Golden Suites
PE 12
Federal Hwy. to FCP km 6.5
Tel.: 831 0216

G-10 *Hospedaje Leyrana*
PE 20
Heriberto Jara No. 233,
Col. Adolfo López Mateos
Tel.: 832 7404 Fax: 833 1681

D-05 *El Rey*
PE 24
Leona Vicario No. 346,
Col. Benito Juárez
Tel./Fax: 832 9254

D-10 *Nachancán Ruta Maya*
PE 20
Calzada Veracruz No. 379
Tel./Fax: 832 3232

J-08 *Palma Real*
PE 10
Av. Álvaro Obregón 193
Tels./Fax: 833 0963, 833 0964
htidenegocios@yahoo.com

F-10 *Posada Pantoja*
PE 24
Lucio Blanco No. 95
Tel./Fax: 832 1781

G-08 *Real Azteca*
PE 34
Av. Belice No. 186, Dwntn.
Tel.: 832 0720 Fax: 832 0666
hotelrealazteca@prodigy.net.mx

ONE STAR ★

F-08 *Boston*
PE 19
Av. Belice 290; Tel.: 832 1164

I-07 *Guadalupe del Carmen*
PE 17
Av. Ignacio Zaragoza 226
Tel.: 832 8649

A-15 *Hostal Universitario*
10
Lote 3, Mza. 27, Cedros
& Ceiba, Col. del Bosque
Cel.: 105 0130

I-08 *María Dolores*
PE 41
Av. Álvaro Obregón 206
Tel./Fax: 832 0508

E-10 *Maya Bahía*
PE 19
Calzada Veracruz No. 362
Tel.: 832 5567

D-11 *Posada Rosas del Mar*
PE 20
Calzada Veracruz No. 407
Tel.: 832 3125

H-09 *Ucum*
68
Av. M. Gandhi No. 167
Tel.: 832 0711 Fax: 832 6186

CALDERITAS

THREE STAR ★★★

Cabañas Yax-Ha
7
Av. Yucatán No. 421
Tels.: 834 4000, 834 4127
Fax: 834 4076
yax_ha@hotmail.com

BACALAR

THREE STAR ★★★

 # 2 *Laguna*
31
Blvd. Costero Bacalar 479
Tels.: 834 2206, 832 3517
01 800 713 6947
Fax: 834 2205

Puerta del Cielo
18
Bacalar-Carrillo Puerto
km 40, Crucero Reforma
Tel./Fax: 837 0413

Rancho Encantado
13
Bacalar-Carrillo Puerto km 3
Tel.: 831 0037 Fax: 834 2035
EUA 1 800 505 MAYA
www.encantado.com

TWO STAR ★★

 # 3 *El Paraíso*
6
Calle 14 btwn. Blvd.
Costero & Laguna
Tel.: 837 1242
magcastillo@hotmail.com

OTHERS

 # 1 *Amigo's B & B*
3
Blvd. Costero Bacalar L. D
Mz. 4; Tel.: 834 2093
www.bacalar.net

Cabañas Ak'Al'Kí
5
ECO-TOURISM.
Chetumal- Carrillo Puerto
km 23.5
Cel.: 835 8795

Villas Ecotucán
5
ECO-TOURISM.
Bacalar- Carillo Puerto
km 27.3, 5 km to the
North of Bacalar
Tel.: 834 2516
Cel.: 752 4461
ecotucan@yahoo.com

KOHUNLICH

SPECIAL CATEGORY

The Explorean Kohunlich
40
Chetumal-Escarcega km 5.6
Tels.: (55) 5201 8350
01 800 366 6666
EUA 1 877 EXPLORA
Fax: (55) 5201 8450
contact@explorean.com
www.theexplorean.com

COSTA MAYA

In the southern part of the state, the area between Punta Herrero and Xcalak has been developed and is ideal for ecotourism.

HOTEL	ADDRESS	TEL.	WEBSITE / E-MAIL
# 14 *Maya Ha Resort & Spa* 4★	Majahual- Xcalak km 10	831 0065	*www.mayaharesort.com*
# 10 *Villa La Guacamaya* 4★	8.5 km North of Xcalak	831 0334	*www.villalaguacamaya.com*
# 17 *Balamkú* 3★	Majahual-Xcalak km. 5.7	831 0404	*www.balamku.com*
# 20 *Majahual Caribe* 2★	Majahual, Dwntn.	831 0478	*hotmahca@mpsnet.com.mx*
# 22 *Tirovino* 1★	Av. Mahahual km 1.4		*chiaramiguel@yahoo.com*
OTHERS			
# 18 *Cabañas Chac Che*	Costera Majahual km 2	884 1199	
# 19 *Cabañas del Doctor*	Av. Majahual No. 6	832 2102	
# 16 *Cabañas Garza Azul*	Majahual-Xcalak km 6	832 4214	*patuch6@hotmail.com*
# 23 *Cabañas Sol y Mar*	Majahual-Uvero km 4.5	833 0026	*solymar@prodigy.net.mx*
# 11 *Cabañas Xahuayxol*	Majahual-Xcalak km 24.6	837 0732	*www.xahuayxol.com.mx*
# 5 *Casa Carolina Beach Resort*	2.5 km North of Xcalak	831 0444	*www.casacarolina.net*
# 2 *Costa de Cocos*	1.4 km North of Xcalak	732 6333	*www.costadecocos.com*
# 25 *El Placer del Caribe*	Majahual-Uvero km 21.9	831 0056	*www.elplacerdelcaribe.com*
# 15 *Kabah Na*	Costera Majahual km 8.6	838 2195	*www.kabahna.com.mx*
# 24 *Kailuumcito*	Majahual-Uvero km 12	879 3456	*www.kailuum.com*
# 6 *Kimmel's Kabana*	2.7 km North of Xcalak		*www.majahual.com*
# 1 *Marina Mike's*	Xcalak	831 0063	*www.xcalak.com*
# 26 *Mayan Beach Garden*	Majahual-Uvero km 22		*www.mayanbeachgarden.com*
# 13 *Luna Floja*	Majahual-Xcalak Km 10.5		
# 12 *Paytocal Diving*	Majahual-Xcalak Km 11	831 5292	*www.majahual.org*
# 7 *Playa Sonrisa*	6.9 km North of Xcalak	838 1872	*www.playasonrisa.com*
# 21 *Posada Los 40 Cañones*	Av. Majahual, por Mojarra	834 5692	*www.los40canones.com*
# 4 *Reef House*	2.4 km North of Xcalak		*www.xcalak.tv*
# 8 *Sand Wood Villas*	7.9 km North of Xcalak	831 0034	*www.sandwood.com*
# 9 *Sin Duda Villas*	8 km North of Xcalak	831 0006	*www.sindudavillas.com*
# 3 *Tierra Maya*	2.1 km North of Xcalak	831 0404	*www.tierramaya.net*